Today's Hottest
DIE-CAST
Vehicles

EDITED BY ELIZABETH A. STEPHAN

What's on the Cover

(All values are for items in Mint condition or Mint in Pack.)

Front Cover:
Custom Continental Mark III, Hot Wheels, $40
1936 Unic Auto Transporter, Dinky Toys. Sold at auction for
    $2,088. Photo courtesy Christie's South Kennsington.
James Bond's Aston-Martin, Corgi, $90
Y-5 1905 Peugot, Matchbox, $35
Tootsietoy, 1947 Mack L-Line Dump Truck,
    1950s-60s, $75
Custom Turbine, Johnny Lightning/Topper, $500

Back Cover:
1968 Torero, Hot Wheels, $60
Penelope Pitstop's Compact Pussycat, Wacky Racers,
    Johnny Lightning/Playing Mantis, $4
No. 52 Maserati 4CLT, Matchbox, $25
310 Corvette Sting Ray, Corgi, $175
Y-7 1912 Rolls Royce, Matchbox, $50
No. 519 Scorchin Scooter, 1997 First Edition, Hot Wheels, $4
DAVO Albums Delivery truck, Lledo, $5

© 2000 by
Krause Publications

Published by

700 E. State Street • Iola, WI 54990-0001
Telephone: 715/445-2214

www.krause.com

Please call or write for our free catalog.
Our toll-free number to place an order or obtain a free catalog is 800-258-0929
or please use our regular business telephone 715-445-2214
for editorial comment and further information.

Library of Congress: 00-102683
ISBN: 0-87341-918-9

Printed in the United States of America

Dedication

Jon, Shawn and Kendra Brecka

In Memory of Jon K. Brecka (1964-2000)

Contents

Introduction

To say that die-cast is popular would be an understatement. Walk through any toy show, flea market or antique show, and you will see tables full of die-cast cars. Die-cast has enjoyed a double-digit growth over the past three years. Retail sales have reached an astounding $923 million, and that excludes what is bought and sold on the secondary market. What does this all mean? Die-cast is hot.

Today's Hottest Die-Cast covers just that—the largest areas of die-cast, new and old, expensive and inexpensive. You will find some models in these pages that are worth thousands of dollars, while some are worth only a dollar. But with any hobby, most collectors aren't in it for the money—they're in it for fun.

What's Hot?

Hot Wheels.

These 1:64-scale California-style cars are super hot. Mattel has sold more than two billion Hot Wheels in the past thirty-one years, and sales don't seem to be slowing. Cars from the redline era are bringing in huge sums at auction and at toy shows. In 1999, an ultra-rare pink prototype of the rear-boarded Volkswagen Beach Bomb sold for $72,000. The blue rear-boarded Beach Bomb is worth $7,000. Numbered Packs have created a collecting frenzy. There are entire clubs, newsletters, websites and conventions dedicated to these little metal cars.

But Hot Wheels aren't the only die-cast cars drawing high prices and leagues of collectors.

Johnny Lightnings, originally made by Topper Toys to compete with Hot Wheels, are seeing a resurgence on the secondary market. Some early—and rare—Johnny Lightnings can sell for $5,000. Playing Mantis has made a dent in the current Hot Wheels-dominated 1:64-scale market by reviving the Johnny Lightning name. The cars in the White Lightning sets are currently selling in the $25 range.

The rising popularity of NASCAR and auto racing in general has created a market for racing-themed die-cast. Fans of one driver will buy die-cast of every scale available from manufacturers like Racing Champions.

Corgi, Tootsietoy, Dinky and the Matchbox 1-75 Series are the evergreen properties of the die-cast market with some cars bringing prices over $4,000. Values in these areas are not as likely to change much. This is the area collectors will find the most investment potential.

Why Collect?

Some view collecting as a form of investment. A dealer can get a two hundred percent profit by selling a Hot Wheels car he bought for three dollars. Try to get that kind of return on the New York Stock Exchange. But just like the stock market, the return isn't guaranteed. A die-cast car that was worth twenty dollars today may only be worth five the next month. It's an unpredictable market.

Collecting is an ongoing game of hide and seek. Those that collect Hot Wheels First Editions want all variations of the 1996 FEs. They trade with other collectors, search the pegs at the local discount store and scout flea markets and toy shows. It's a challenge. It's fun. And that's why we collect.

Why Die-Cast?

Imagination and fantasy are the key components of die-cast collecting. Whether you collect die-cast because you always wanted a Ferrari or because you like the futuristic look of Hot Wheels Beatnik Bandit—it's all make believe.

I collect one kind of die-cast—Volkswagens. I come from a family of Volkswagen drivers. My Grandfather had two—one red and one green. My mom drives a bright orange 1974 Super Beetle. I have grown to love the little cars. So, on my computer I have a Volkswagen Concept 1 car by Matchbox. On my shelf I have a Baha Bug from Hot Wheels. There are even a few 1:43-scale models that grace my windowsill.

Why do I concentrate solely on Volkswagens? Because I think they're cool. And I want one—a real one.

Condition

As with all collectibles, condition is key. Below are definitions of grading categories used in this book.

MIB or MIP: Mint in Box, Mint in Pack. Looks like it did the day it hit toy shelves. Tape, ink, creases or dents in packaging can affect value. Equivalent to C10.

MNB or MNP: Mint no Box, Mint no Pack. Car is in pristine condition without packaging and looks as though it never has been played with. In some instances, the lack of packaging can greatly affect the value. A MIP Hot Wheels Custom Camaro with white enamel is listed at $2,500. The same car in MNP condition drops to $500. Equivalent to C9.

Mint: Much the same as MNB/MNP. Equivalent to C9.

Excellent: Car shows some minor wear but still suitable for display. Equivalent to C8.

Good: Car had noticeable wear. Item can still be displayed but best used as a "filler" piece until a better example can be found. Equivalent to C6.

Acknowledgements

There are many people who helped with *Today's Hottest Die-Cast.*

Doug Sadecky offered his pricing and photography skills to the chapter on Corgi.

Longtime friends, Tom Brown and Ray Falcoa are the Johnny Lightning guys. They supplied all the information on Topper Toys Johnny Lightnings.

Many thanks go to Playing Mantis, especially Angie Harmon, for supplying a complete list of new Johnny Lightnings.

Mark Rich, toy collector and all around good guy supplied the Tootsietoy information. John Gibson, corporate historian for Strombecker Corporation, was also of assistance.

Andrew Dudek, Jim Wilson, and Steve and Anna Cinnamon were able to provide pricing information for the Hot Wheels chapter. Tom Michael took time from his busy schedule to help me identify stack upon stack of Hot Wheels photos.

Trish Glore, editor of CB's Museum (*www.cbsmuseum.com*) provided advice, information and some much needed support.

Sharon Korbeck, editor of *Toy Shop*, and Merry Dudley, associate editor of *Toy Cars & Vehicles*, were able to answer many of my questions regarding the toy market and die-cast in general. They also lent their support when I needed it most.

One Final Thank You

Lastly, I would like to thank Jon Brecka. Without him, this book wouldn't have happened. A book editor in Krause Publications' book division, Jon also wrote the wildly popular "Hot Wheels: Collect by Numbers" column for *Toy Shop* and *Toy Cars & Vehicles* magazines.

Jon was the consummate collector. He collected everything from animal-shaped letter holders to coffeepots—that is until he tired of them. Jon's collecting passion was Hot Wheels Numbered Packs. His lunch hours were spent at local stores where he searched the pegs for new releases. He stopped at the local discount stores on his daily commute to work. He was always hoping to find that one Hot Wheels he didn't have.

Jon provided the Numbered Pack listing seen in this book. Unfortunately, he never saw it in print. Jon was critically injured in a car accident shortly before Christmas of 1999. Less than two months later, he died from complications related to his injuries.

Jon was my friend, and I had looked forward to working on this project with him. I wasn't able to do that. I have dedicated this book to his memory. I think he'd be proud.

Elizabeth A. Stephan, editor
700 East State St.
Iola, WI 54945
stephane@krause.com

Corgi

First introduced in 1956, Corgi Toys was a division of the Mettoy Company of Northampton, England. Since 1933 Mettoy had produced various tin-lithographed clockwork mechanical toys, doll houses and train sets. Castoys, larger scale mechanical die-cast vehicles, were Mettoy's first foray into the die-cast market. Produced from 1948 to 1958, Castoys are considered to be the precursors to Corgi Toys.

Competition from Meccano's Dinky Toys always forced Corgi to try to stay one step ahead in terms of sales gimmicks. Pioneering innovations included such things as spring suspensions, jeweled headlights, chrome plating, multiple working features, detailed engines, Trans-o-Lites, and Take-Off Wheels. Corgi Major Toys were introduced in 1957 to compete with Dinky's Super-toys and were a nice addition to the smaller cars and vans that were being produced.

Corgi kept its toy line current by producing models based on real-life vehicles. Several Corgi models were released at the same time as the actual cars. In 1965, Corgi produced the Saint's Volvo based on the car in the British TV series starring Roger Moore. This initiated a plethora of character- and television-based models that would lend Corgi notoriety, awards, and good revenue under Mettoy's reign.

Corgi expanded its category lines until the late 1960s when competition from other toy companies began to affect sales. Mattel introduced Hot Wheels, with the ever-popular redline tires, in 1968; Corgi answered back by producing WhizzWheels. Corgi produced the popular 1:64-scale Husky models from 1965 until 1969 to compete with Matchbox's 1-75 series. In 1970, the Husky name was changed to Corgi Juniors. Corgi also experimented with the short-lived Corgi Rockets series from 1970 to 1972. Collectors should note that a wide variety of track and accessories were created to accompany the Corgi Juniors and Corgi Rockets.

Corgi, trying to move one step ahead in terms of futuristic toys, combined their die-cast vehicles with technology. Called Corgitronics, these toys featured various electronic features such as working lights, sound effects and even a working radio.

The original Mettoy Company closed its doors in late 1983 due to bankruptcy, but another investor purchased the Corgi name. Over the last two decades, the Corgi Toy Company has been resold several times, most notably to the Mattel Corporation in 1991. Zindart, a Hong-Kong based collectibles company, bought Corgi in 1999.

Novice collectors should do their homework before diving head-first into the Corgi market. What may appear to be an original 1960s or 1970s Corgi model could easily be a recently issued model. Over the last decade, Corgi has reissued many of their popular character models such as the James Bond Aston-Martin, Chitty Chitty Bang Bang, Beatles' Yellow Submarine and Kojack's Buick. The new die-cast are clearly marked on the bottom as new, and the boxes, thus far, have been different from the original. However, an unscrupulous dealer could easily sell a reissued model to an unknowing collector. Reissues have not affected the price of original Mint in Box releases, but original loose models without their box have become increasingly difficult to sell.

Condition is crucial if one hopes to see a good return on their investment. The original box should be present and in good shape. This is extremely important for the Corgi gift sets as most of the models were regular stock issue, but were packaged in special presentation boxes. Sometimes figures and accessories were included in with the various gift sets and they must also be present to get the full market value of the set.

The current Corgi Company is still producing many new detailed vehicles, as well as reissuing some of the popular models from the past several decades. The marketplace should continue to be strong for Corgi in the new millennium. Corgi Toys will continue to excite collectors for many years to come.

Market Update

In today's die-cast market, Corgi is a name associated with quality and innovation. Chipperfields Circus, character-related, military and racing vehicles remain in favor with collectors. The current secondary market is still strong for the old Corgi models manufactured from the 1950s to the mid 1970s. This is particularly true for gift sets and rare model variations that can fetch outrageous sums of money at auction. The 1970s Corgi Rockets and character-related Corgi Juniors vehicles remain desirable and some can get very pricey. The market tends to be soft for the Corgi die-cast produced in the 1980s and 1990s. Oversaturation of the die-cast market by Corgi and many other companies from around the world has caused the stagnation of more recently released issues.

Contributor: Dr. Douglas Sadecky, Medical Arts Plaza, 1619 Union Ave., Natrona Heights, PA 15065

Clubs

Corgi Collector Club
14 Industrial Road
Pecquannock, NJ 07440

Corgi Collectors Club of the Corgi Heritage
Center
53 York St.
Heywood
Hochdale, Lancs OL10 4NR
United Kingdom

Name	Good	EX	Mint
Adams Drag-Star, orange body, red nose, gold engines, chrome pipes and hood panels, Whizz Wheels, No. 165, 1972-74, 4-3/8".....................20		30	45
Adams Probe 16, one-piece body, blue sliding canopy; metallic burgundy, or metallic lime/gold w/and without racing stripes, Whizz Wheels, No. 384, 1970-73, 3-5/8".....................15		25	40
Agricultural Set, 1962-64 issue: No. 55 Fordson Tractor, No. 51 Tipping Trailer, No. 438 Land Rover, No. 101 Flat Trailer w/No. 1487 Milk Churns; 1965-66 issue: No. 60 Fordson Tractor, No. 62 Tipping Trailer, No. 438 Land Rover, red No. 100 Dropside Trailer w/No. 1487 Milk Churns, No. 22-A, 1962-66 280		450	1000
Agricultural Set, No. 69 Massey Ferguson tractor, No. 62 trailer, No. 438 Land Rover, No. 484 Livestock Truck w/pigs, No. 71 harrow, No. 1490 skip and churns; w/accessories: four calves, farmland, dog and six sacks, No. 5, 1967-72 120		180	400
Agricultural Set, No. 55 Tractor, No. 56 Tipping Trailer, Silo and mustard yellow conveyor, No. 42, 1978-80 60		90	130
Alfa Romeo P33 Pininfarina, white body, gold or black spoiler, red seats, Whizz Wheels, No. 380, 1970-74, 3-5/8" 16		24	45
All Winners Set, first issue: No. 310 Corvette, No. 312 Jaguar XKE, No. 314 Ferrari 250LM, No. 324 Marcos, No. 325 Mustang; second issue: No. 312 Jaguar XKE, No. 314 Ferrari 250LM, No. 264 Toronado, No. 327 MGB, No. 337 Corvette, No. 46-A, 1966-69 100		240	450
Allis-Chalmers AFC 60 Fork Lift, yellow body, white engine hood, w/driver, tan pallets and red containers, No. 409-C, 1981, 4-3/8"...15		20	45

Name	Good	EX	Mint
AMC Pacer, metallic red body, white Pacer X decals, working hatch, clear windows, light yellow interior, chrome bumpers and wheels, No. 291-A, 1977-78, 4-3/4" 15		20	50
AMC Pacer Rescue Car, chrome roll bars and red roof lights, white w/black engine hood; w/or without Secours decal, No. 484-B, 1978-80, 4-7/8"....... 10		15	30
American LaFrance Ladder Truck, first issue: red cab, trailer, ladder rack and wheels; chrome decks and chassis, yellow plastic three-piece operable ladder, rubber tires, six firemen figures, issued 1968-70; second issue: same as first issue except for unpainted wheels, issued 1970-72; third issue: same as earlier issues except for white decks and chassis, silver wheels, plastic tires, issued 1973-81; later issues only had four firemen, No. 1143-A, 1968-81, 11-1/8"... 60		90	150
AMX 30D Recovery Tank, olive body w/black plastic turret and gun, accessories and three figures, No. 908-A, 1976-80, 6-7/8" 35		50	80
Army Heavy Equipment Transporter, olive cab and trailer w/white U.S. Army decals w/red interior and driver, No. 1135-A, 1964-65, 9-1/2"............... 70		105	325
Army Troop Transporter, olive w/white U.S. Army decals, No. 1133-A, 1964-65, 5-1/2" 70		105	175
Aston Martin DB4, white top w/aqua green sides, yellow plastic interior, racing Nos. 1, 3 or 7, No. 309-A, 1962-65, 3-3/4" 50		75	125
Aston Martin DB4, red or yellow body w/working hood, detailed engine, clear windows, plastic interior, silver lights, grille, license plate and bumpers, red taillights, rubber tires, smooth or cast spoked wheels; working scoop on early models, No. 218-A, 1960-65, 3-3/4" 45		65	110

Name	Good	EX	Mint
Austin A40, one-piece light blue or red body w/black roof and clear windows, smooth wheels, rubber tires, No. 216-A, 1959-62, 3-1/8"	35	50	100
Austin A40-Mechanical, friction motor, red body w/black roof, No. 216M-A, 1959-60, 3-1/8"	55	75	170
Austin A60 Driving School, medium blue body w/silver trim, left-hand drive steering wheel, steering control on left; came w/five language leaflet (US version of No. 236), No. 255-A, 1964-68, 3-3/4"	45	65	160
Austin A60 Motor School, light blue body w/silver trim, red interior, single body casting, right-hand drive steering wheel, two figures, steering control on roof; came w/Highway Patrol leaflet, No. 236-A, 1964-69, 3-3/4"	45	65	120
Austin Cambridge, available in gray, green/gray, silver/green, aqua, green/cream, two-tone green, smooth wheels, No. 201-A, 1956-61, 3-1/2"	40	60	120
Austin Cambridge-Mechanical, fly-wheel motor, available in orange, cream, light or dark gray, cream, or silver over metallic blue, smooth wheels, No. 201M-A, 1956-59, 3-1/2"	50	75	150
Austin Healey, blue body w/cream seats, shaped hubs, No. 300-A, 1956-63	75	125	250
Austin London Taxi, black body w/yellow plastic interior, w/or without driver, shaped hubs, smooth or rubber tires, No. 418-A, 1960-65, 3-7/8"	36	55	90
Austin London Taxi, black body w/two working doors, light brown interior, Whizz Wheels, No. 425-A, 1978, 4-5/8"	15	20	35
Austin London Taxi/Reissue, updated version w/Whizz Wheels, black or maroon body, No. 418-A, 1971-74, 3-7/8"	15	20	35
Austin Mini Countryman, turquoise body, jeweled headlights, opening rear doors, chrome roofrack w/two surfboards, shaped or cast wheels, w/surfer figure, No. 485-A, 1965-69, 3-1/8"	55	80	150
Austin Mini Van, w/two working rear doors, clear windows, metallic deep green body, No. 450-A, 1964-67, 3-1/8"	40	60	100
Austin Mini-Metro, blue or red body w/plastic interior, working rear hatch and doors, clear windows, folding seats, chrome headlights, orange taillights, black plastic base, grille, bumpers, Whizz Wheels, No. 275-B, 1981, 3-1/2"	18	27	45
Austin Mini-Metro Datapost, white body, blue roof, hood and trim, red plastic interior, hepolite and No. 77 decals, working hatch and doors, clear windows, folding seats, chrome headlights, orange taillights, Whizz Wheels, No. 281-B, 1982, 3-1/2"	15	18	30
Austin Police Mini Van, dark blue body w/policeman and dog figures, white police decals, opening rear doors, gray plastic antenna, No. 448-A, 1964-69, 3-1/8"	50	75	175
Austin Seven Mini, red or yellow body, yellow interior, silver bumpers, grille and headlights, orange taillights, No. 225-A, 1961-67, 2-3/4"	50	75	125
Austin Seven Mini, primrose yellow, red interior, rare, No. 225-A, second issue, 1961-67, 2-3/4"	100	200	325
Austin-Healey, cream body w/red seats or red body w/cream seats, No. 300-A, 1956-63, 3-1/4"	50	75	125
Avengers Set, white Lotus, red or green Bentley; Jonathan Steed and Emma Peel figures w/three umbrellas, No. 40-A, 1966-69	260	390	800

Name	Good	EX	Mint

Basil Brush's Car, red body, dark yellow chassis, gold lamps and dash, Basil Brush figure, red plastic wheels, plastic tires; w/"Laugh Tapes" and soundbox, No. 808-A, 1971-73, 3-5/8" 70 105 200

Batbike, black body, one-piece body, black and red plastic parts, gold engine and exhaust pipes, clear windshield, chrome stand, black plastic five-spoked wheels, Batman figure and decals, No. 268-B, 1978-83, 4-1/4" 40 60 125

Batboat, black plastic boat, red seats, fin and jet, blue windshield, Batman and Robin figures, gold cast trailer, tinplate fin cover, cast wheels, plastic tires, w/plastic towhook for Batmobile, No. 107-A, 1967-72, 5-1/8" 60 90 175

Batboat, black plastic boat w/Batman and Robin figures, small decals on fin and on side of boat, chain link Whizz Wheels on trailer, No. 107-A, 1976-80, 5-1/8" 30 45 100

Batcopter, black body w/yellow/red/black decals, red rotors, Batman figure, operable winch, No. 925-A, 1976-81, 5-1/2" 26 39 95

Batman Set, three vehicle set: No. 267 Batmobile, No. 107 Batboat w/trailer and No. 925 Batcopter, Whizz Wheels on trailer, No. 40-B, 1976-81 ....150 300 800

Batboat

Batmobile, chrome hubs w/black plastic tires, red bat logos on door, light red interior, regular wheels, gold tow hook, plastic rockets, gold headlights and rocket control, tinted canopy w/chrome support, No. 267-A, 1974-79, 5".. 80 120 200

Batmobile, matte black (rare) or gloss black body, gold hubs, bat logos on door, maroon interior, black body, plastic rockets, gold headlights and rocket control, tinted canopy, working front chain cutter, no tow hook, rubber tires, No. 267-A, 1966, 5"....... 200 300 550

Batmobile, same as first issue except for gloss black body, gold towhook, No. 267-A, 1967-72 .... 200 300 500

Batmobile, chrome hubs w/red bat logos on door, maroon interior, red plastic tires, gold tow hook, plastic rockets, gold headlight and rocket control, tinted canopy w/chrome support, chain cutter, No. 267-A, 1973, 5".. 140 200 400

Batmobile, Batboat and Trailer, first and second versions: red bat hubs on wheels, 1967-72; red tires and chrome wheels, No. 3-B, 1967-72 ... 240 360 650

Batmobile, No. 267-A. Photo Courtesy Mark Arruda.

Batmobile, Batboat and Trailer, No. 3-B.

Name	Good	EX	Mint
Batmobile, Batboat and Trailer, third and fourth versions: 1973; black tires, big decals on boat, 1974-76; chrome wheels, boat decals, Whizz Wheels on trailer, No. 3-B, 1973-81	120	175	350
Beach Buggy & Sailboat, purple No. 381 buggy, yellow trailer and red/white boat, No. 26-A, 1971-76	20	30	55
Beast Carrier Trailer, red chassis, yellow body and tailgate, four plastic calves, red plastic wheels, black rubber tires, No. 58-A, 1965-71, 4-1/2"	24	36	60
Beatles' Yellow Submarine, yellow and white body, working red hatches w/two Beatles in each, No. 803-A, 1969-70, second issue, 5"	180	270	700
Beatles' Yellow Submarine, yellow and white hatches, red pinstripes, No. 803-A, 1969, 5"	200	500	1000
Bedford AA Road Service Van, dark yellow body in two versions: divided windshield, 1957-59; single windshield, 1960-62, No. 408-A, 1957-62, 3-5/8"	50	75	125
Bedford Army Tanker, olive cab and tanker, w/white U.S. Army and "No Smoking" decals, No. 1134-A, 1964-65, 7-3/8"	140	210	375
Bedford Articulated Horse Box, cast cab, lower body and three working ramps, yellow interior, plastic upper body, w/horse and Newmarket Racing Stables decals, dark metallic			

Beatles' Yellow Submarine, No. 803-A.

Name	Good	EX	Mint
green or light green body w/orange or yellow upper, four horses, No. 1104-B, 1973-76, 10"	32	48	80
Bedford Car Transporter, black die-cast cab base w/blue "S" cab, yellow semi trailer, blue lettering decals, No. 1101-A, 1957, first issue, 10-1/4"	100	200	350
Bedford Car Transporter, red "TK" cab w/blue lower and light green upper trailer, working ramp, yellow interior, clear windows, white wording and Corgi dog decals, No. 1105-A, 1962-66, 10-5/8"	60	90	150
Bedford Car Transporter, red cab, pale green upper and blue lower semi-trailer, white decals, lower tailgate, clear windshield, No. 1101-A, 1957-62, second issue, 10-1/4" long	70	105	175
Bedford Carrimore Low Loader, red or yellow "S" cab, metallic blue semi trailer and tailgate; smooth and/or shaped wheels, No. 1100-A, 1958-62, 8-1/2"	60	90	150
Bedford Carrimore Low Loader, yellow "TK" cab and working tailgate, red trailer, clear windows, red interior, suspension, shaped wheels, rubber tires, No. 1132-A, 1963-65, 9-1/2"	90	190	325
Bedford Corgi Toys Van, yellow upper/blue lower body, No. 422-A, 1962, 3-1/4" long	100	225	400
Bedford Corgi Toys Van, Corgi Toys decals, w/either yellow body/blue roof, No. 422-A, 1960-62, 3-1/4"	60	90	175
Bedford Daily Express Van, dark blue body w/white Daily Express decals, divided windshield, smooth wheels, rubber tires, No. 403-A, 1956-59, 3-1/4"	60	90	150
Bedford Dormobile, two versions and several colors: divided windshield w/cream, green or metallic maroon body; or single windshield w/yellow body/blue roof w/shaped or smooth wheels, No. 404-A, 1956-62, 3-1/4"	50	75	125

Name	Good	EX	Mint
Bedford Dormobile-Mechanical, friction motor, dark metallic red or turquoise body, smooth wheels, No. 404M-A, 1956-59, 3-1/4"	60	90	175
Bedford Evening Standard Van, black body/silver roof or black lower body/silver upper body and roof, Evening Standard decals, smooth wheels, No. 421-A, 1960-62, 3-1/4"	55	80	130
Bedford Fire Tender, divided windshield, red or green body, each w/different decals, smooth or shaped hubs, No. 405-A, 1956-61, 3-1/4"	60	90	175
Bedford Fire Tender, single windshield version, red body w/either black ladders and smooth wheels or unpainted ladders and shaped wheels, No. 423-A, 1960-62, 3-1/4"	60	90	150
Bedford Fire Tender-Mechanical, friction motor, red body w/Fire Dept. decals, divided windshield. Silver or black ladder, smooth or shaped hubs, No. 405M-A, 1956-59, 3-1/4"	70	105	175
Bedford KLG Van-Mechanical, w/friction motor, in either red body w/KLG Spark Plugs decals, smooth hubs, No. 403M-A, 1956-59, 3-1/4"	70	125	285
Bedford Military Ambulance, clear front and white rear windows, olive body w/Red Cross decals, w/or without suspension, No. 414-A, 1961-64, 3-1/4"	56	84	140
Bedford Milk Tanker, light blue "S" cab and lower semi, white upper tank, w/blue/white milk decals, shaped wheels, rubber tires, No. 1129-A, 1962-65, 7-1/2"	100	150	275
Bedford Milk Tanker, light blue "TK" cab and lower semi, white upper tank w/blue/white milk decals, No. 1141-B, 1966-67, 7-3/4"	110	165	375

Name	Good	EX	Mint
Bedford Mobilgas Tanker, red "TK" cab and tanker w/red, white and blue Mobilgas decals, shaped wheels, rubber tires, No. 1140-A, 1965-66, 7-3/4"	100	175	350
Bedford Mobilgas Tanker, red "S" cab w/Mobilgas decals, shaped wheels, rubber tires, No. 1110-A, 1959-65, 7-5/8"	100	150	250
Bedford Tanker, red cab w/black chassis, plastic tank w/chrome catwalk, Corgi Chemco decals, No. 1130-B, 1983, 7-1/2"	15	20	35
Bedford TK Tipper Truck, red cab and chassis w/yellow tipper, side mirrors, No. 494-A, 1968-72, 4-1/8"	26	39	65
Bedford Utilecon Ambulance, divided windshield, cream body w/red/white/blue decals, smooth wheels, No. 412-A, 1957-60, 3-1/4"	50	75	125
Beep Beep London Bus, battery-operated working horn, red body, black windows, BTA decals, No. 1004-A, 1981, 4-3/4"	26	39	65
Belgian Police Range Rover, white body, working doors, red interior, Belgian Police decal; includes policeman, Evergency signs, No. 483-B, 1976-77, 4"	22	33	55
Bell Army Helicopter, two-piece olive/tan camouflage body, clear canopy, olive green rotors, U.S. Army decals, No. 920-A, 1975-80, 5-1/4"	24	36	60
Bell Rescue Helicopter, two-piece blue body w/working doors, red interior, yellow plastic floats, black rotors, white N428 decals, No. 924-A, 1976-80, 5-3/4"	20	30	50
Bentley Continental, two-tone green or black and silver bodies, w/red interior, clear windows, chrome grille and bumpers, jewel headlights, red jeweled taillights, suspension, shaped wheels, gray rubber tires, No. 224-A, 1961-66, 4-1/4"	45	65	110

Bentley Continental, No. 224-A. Photo Courtesy Mark Arruda.

Berliet Fruehauf Dumper, No. 1102-B.

Name	Good	EX	Mint
Bentley T Series, red body, cream interior, working hood, trunk and doors, clear windows, folding seats, chrome bumper/grille, jewel headlights, Whizz Wheels, No. 274-A, 1970-72, 4-1/2"	36	55	90
Berliet Articulated Horse Box, bronze cab and lower semi body, cream chassis, white upper body, black interior, three working ramps, National Racing Stables decals, horse figures, chrome wheels, No. 1105-B, 1976-80, 10-7/8"	30	45	75
Berliet Container Truck, blue cab and semi fenders; white cab chassis and semi flatbed; each w/United States Lines label, No. 1107-B, 1978	30	45	75
Berliet Dolphinarium Truck, yellow and blue cab and trailer, clear plastic tank; includes two dolphins and a girl trainer, No. 1164-A, 1980-83	56	84	175
Berliet Fruehauf Dumper, yellow cab, fenders and dumper; black cab and semi chassis; plastic orange dumper body; or dark orange, black interior, No. 1102-B, 1974-76, 11-1/4"	30	45	75

Name	Good	EX	Mint
Berliet Holmes Wrecker, red cab and bed, blue rear body, white chassis, black interior, two gold booms and hooks, yellow dome light, driver, amber lenses and red/white/blue stripes, No. 1144-B, 1975-78, 5"	30	45	75
Bertone Barchetta Runabout, yellow and black body, black interior, amber windows, die-cast air foil, suspension, red/yellow Runabout decals, Whizz Wheels, No. 386-A, 1971-73, 3-1/4"	15	22	45
Bertone Shake Buggy, clear windows, green interior, gold engine, four variations: yellow upper/white lower body or metallic mauve upper/white lower body w/spoked or solid chrome wheels, No. 392-A, 1972-74, 3-3/8"	15	22	45
BL Roadtrain and Trailers, white and orange cab, dark blue freighter semi body w/Yorkie Chocolate labels and tanker semi body w/Gulf label; includes playmat, No. 1002-A, 1981	16	24	40
Bloodhound Launching Ramp, military green ramp, No. 1116-A, 1959-62	34	51	85
Bloodhound Loading Trolley, white and yellow missile, red rubber nose cone, No. 1117-A, 1959-62	40	60	100
Bloodhound Missile, white and yellow missile, red rubber nose cone, No. 1115-A, 1959-62	70	105	175
Bloodhound Missile on Trolley, white and yellow missile, red rubber nose cone; military green trolley, rubber tires, No. 1109-A, 1959-62	120	180	300
Bloodhound Missle and Launching Platform, white and yellow missile, red rubber nose cone; military green ramp, No. 1108-A, 1958-61	110	165	275
BMC Mini-Cooper, white body, black working hood, trunk, two doors, red interior, clear windows, orange/black stripes and No. 177 decals, suspension, Whizz Wheels, No. 282-A, 1971-74, 3"	30	45	95

Name	Good	EX	Mint
BMC Mini-Cooper Magnifique, metallic blue or olive green body w/working doors, hood and trunk, clear windows and sunroof, cream interior w/folding seats, jewel headlights, cast detailed wheels, plastic tires, No. 334-A, 1966-70, 2-7/8"	34	65	115
BMC Mini-Cooper S, bright yellow body, red plastic interior, chrome plastic roof rack w/two spare wheels, clear windshield, one-piece body silver grille, bumpers, headlights, red taillights, suspension, Whizz Wheels, No. 308-A, 1972-76, 3"	45	65	110
BMC Mini-Cooper S "Sun/RAC" Rally Car, red body, white roof w/six jewel headlights, RAC Rally and No. 21 decals, No. 333-A, 1967, 2-7/8"	90	180	350
BMC Mini-Cooper S Rally, red body, white roof, chrome roof rack w/two spare tires, Monte Carlo Rally and No. 177 decals, w/shaped wheels/rubber tires or cast detailed wheels/plastic tires, No. 339-A, 1967-72, 2-7/8"	40	90	180
BMC Mini-Cooper S Rally Car, red body, white roof, five jewel headlights, Monte Carlo Rally decals w/either No. 52 (1965) or No. 2 (1966); rare w/drivers' autographs on roof, No. 321-A, 1965-66, 2-7/8"	100	275	500
BMW M1, yellow body, black plastic base, rear panel and interior, white seats, clear windshield, multicolored stripes, lettering and No. 25 decal, Goodyear label, No. 308-B, 1981, 5"	15	20	35
BMW M1 BASF, red body, white trim w/black/white BASF and No. 80 decals, No. 380-B, 1983, 4-7/8"	15	18	30
Breakdown Truck, red body, black plastic boom w/gold hook, yellow interior, amber windows, black/yellow decals, Whizz Wheels, No. 702-A, 1975-79, 3-7/8"	15	18	30

Name	Good	EX	Mint
British Leyland Mini 1000, red interior, chrome lights, grille and bumper, No. 8 decal; three variations: silver body w/decals, 1978-82; silver body, no decals; orange body w/extra hood stripes, 1983, No. 201-C, 1978, 3-1/4"	16	24	40
British Leyland Mini 1000, metallic blue body, working doors, black base, clear windows, white interior, silver lights, grille and bumper, Union Jack decal on roof, Whizz Wheels, No. 200-B, 1976-78, 3-3/8"	18	27	45
British Racing Cars, set of three cars, three versions: blue No. 152 Lotus, green No. 151 BRM, green No. 150 Vanwall, all w/smooth wheels, 1959; same cars w/shaped wheels, 1960-61; red Vanwall, green BRM and blue Lotus, 1963, each set, No. 5-A, 1967-72	140	210	475
BRM Racing Car, silver seat, dash and pipes, smooth wheels, rubber tires, in three versions: dark green body, 1958-60; light green body w/driver and various number decals 1961-65; light green body, no driver, No. 152-A, 1958-65, 3-1/2"	50	75	145
Buck Rogers Starfighter, white body w/yellow plastic wings, amber windows, blue jets, color decal, Buck and Wilma figures, No. 647-A, 1980, 6-1/2"	32	48	90
Buick and Cabin Cruiser, three versions: light blue, dark metallic blue or gold metallic No. 245 Buick, red boat trailer, dolphin cabin cruiser w/two figures, No. 31-A, 1965-68	80	120	280
Buick Police Car, metallic blue body w/white stripes and Police decals, chrome light bar w/red lights, orange taillights, chrome spoke wheels, w/two policemen, No. 416-B, 1977-78, 4-1/8"	18	27	45

Name	Good	EX	Mint
Buick Riviera, metallic gold, dark blue, pale blue or gold body, red interior, gray steering wheel, and tow hook, clear windshield, chrome grille and bumpers, suspension, Tan-o-lite tail and headlights, spoked wheels and rubber tires, No. 245-A, 1964-68, 4-1/4"	30	45	75
Cadillac Superior Ambulance, battery-operated warning lights, red lower/cream upper body, No. 437-A, 1962-68, 4-1/2"	60	90	150
Cadillac Superior Ambulance, battery-operated warning lights, white lower body/blue upper body, No. 437-A, 1962-68, 4-1/2" long	60	90	150
Cafe Racer Motorcycle, No. 173-A, 1983	15	18	30
Campbell Bluebird, blue body, red exhaust, clear windshield, driver, in two versions: black plastic wheels, 1960; metal wheels and rubber tires, No. 153-A, 1960-65, 5-1/8"	56	84	175
Canadian Mounted Police Set, blue No. 421 Land Rover w/Police sign on roof and RCMP decals, No. 102 trailer; includes mounted Policeman, No. 45-B, 1978-80	30	50	100
Captain America Jetmobile, 6" white body, metallic blue chassis, black nose cone, red shield and jet, red-white-blue Captain America decals, light blue seats and driver, chrome wheels, red tires, No. 263-B, 1979-80	24	36	60

Cadillac Superior Ambulance, No. 437-A. Photo Courtesy Mark Arruda.

Name	Good	EX	Mint
Captain Marvel Porsche, white body, gold parts, red seat, driver, red/yellow/blue Captain Marvel decals, black plastic base, gold wheels, No. 262-B, 1979-80, 4-3/4"	20	30	60
Car Transporter & Cars, Scammell tri-deck transporter w/six cars: Ford Capri, the Saint's Volvo, Pontiac Firebird, Lancia Fulvia, MGC GT, Marcos 3 Litre, each w/Whizz Wheels; value is for complete set, No. 20-B, 1970-73	200	400	900
Car Transporter and Four Cars, two versions: No. 1105 Bedford TK Transporter w/Fiat 1800, Renault Floride, Mercedes 230SE and Ford Consul, 1963-65; No. 1105 Bedford TK Transporter w/Chevy Corvair, VW Ghia, Volvo P-1800 and Rover 2000, 1966 only; value is for individual complete set, No. 28-A, 1963-66	200	300	700
Carrimore and Cars, Ford "H" series Transporter and six cars; there are several car variations; sold by mail order only, No. 41-A, 1966	240	360	700
Carrimore Car Transporter, three versions: No. 1101 Bedford Carrimore Transporter w/Riley, Jaguar, Austin Healey and Triumph, 1957-60; No. 1101 Bedford Carrimore Transporter w/four American cars, 1959; No. 1101 Bedford Carrimore Transporter w/Triumph, Mini, Citroen and Plymouth, 1961-62; value is for individual complete sets, No. 1-A, 1957-62	300	450	800
Caterpillar Tractor, lime green body w/black or gray rubber treads, gray plastic seat, driver figure, controls, stacks, No. 1103-A, 1960-64, 4-1/4"	70	105	250
Centurion Mark III Tank, tan and brown camouflage or olive drab body, rubber tracks; includes twelve shells, No. 901-A, 1974-78	30	45	75

Carrimore Car Transporter, No. 1-A.

Chevrolet Astro I, No. 347-A. Photo Courtesy Mark Arruda.

Name	Good	EX	Mint
Centurion Tank and Transporter, No. 901 olive tank and No. 1100 transporter, No. 10-B, 1973-78	55	80	130
Chevrolet Astro I, dark metallic green/blue body w/working rear door, cream interior w/two passengers, in two versions: gold wheels w/red plastic hubs or Whizz wheels, No. 347-A, 1969-74, 4-1/8"	18	40	85
Chevrolet Camaro SS, metallic gold body w/two working doors, black roof and stripes, red interior, take-off wheels, No. 338-A, 1968-70, 4"	30	45	75

Name	Good	EX	Mint
Chevrolet Camaro SS, blue or turquoise body w/white stripe, cream interior, working doors, white plastic top, clear windshield, folding seats, silver air intakes, red taillights, black grille and headlights, suspension, Whizz Wheels, No. 304-B, 1972-73, 4"	30	45	95
Chevrolet Caprice Classic, working doors and trunk, whitewall tires, two versions: light metallic green body w/green interior or silver on blue body w/brown interior, No. 325-B, 1981-82, 5-7/8"	24	36	60
Chevrolet Caprice Classic, white upper body, red sides w/red/white/blue stripes and No. 43 decals, tan interior, STP labels, No. 341-B, 1981, 6"	24	36	60
Chevrolet Caprice Fire Chief Car, red body, red-white-orange decals, chrome roof bar, opaque black windows, red dome light, chrome bumpers, grille and headlights, orange taillights, Fire Dept. and Fire Chief decals, chrome wheels; includes working siren and dome light, No. 1008-A, 1982, 5-3/4"	28	42	70
Chevrolet Caprice Police Car, black body w/white roof, doors and trunk, red interior, silver light bar, Police decals, No. 326-A, 1980-81, 5-7/8"	20	30	50
Chevrolet Caprice Taxi, orange body w/red interior, white roof sign, Taxi and TWA decals, No. 327-B, 1979-81, 5-7/8"	20	30	50
Chevrolet Charlie's Angels Van, light rose-mauve body w/Charlie's Angels decals, in two versions: either solid or spoked chrome wheels, No. 434-B, 1977-80, 4-5/8"	15	30	55
Chevrolet Coca-Cola Van, red body, white trim, w/Coca Cola logos, No. 437-B, 1978-80, 4-5/8"	15	20	35

Name	Good	EX	Mint
Chevrolet Corvair, either blue or pale-blue body w/yellow interior and working hood, detailed engine, clear windows, silver bumpers, headlights and trim, red taillights, rear window blind, shaped wheels, rubber tires, No. 229-A, 1961-66, 3-3/4"	36	55	90
Chevrolet Impala, pink body, yellow plastic interior, clear windows, silver headlights, bumpers, grille and trim, suspension, die-cast base w/rubber tires; a second version has a blue body w/red or yellow interior and smooth or shaped hubs, No. 220-A, 1960-62, 4-1/4"	50	75	125
Chevrolet Impala, tan body, cream interior, gray steering wheel, clear windshields, chrome bumpers, grille, headlights, suspension, red taillights, shaped wheels and rubber tires, No. 248-A, 1965-67, 4-1/4"	50	75	125
Chevrolet Impala Fire Chief, w/Fire Chief decal on hood, yellow interior w/driver, red on white body w/either round or rectangular "Fire Chief" decals on doors, spun or cast wheels, No. 482-A, 1965-69, 4"	55	80	130
Chevrolet Impala Fire Chief, red body, yellow interior, w/four white doors, w/round either shield or			

Chevrolet Charlie's Angels Van, No. 434-B.

Name	Good	EX	Mint
rectangular decals on two doors; includes two fireman, No. 439-A, 1963-65, 4-1/8"	55	80	130
Chevrolet Impala Police Car, black lower body and roof, white upper body, yellow interior w/two policemen, Police and Police Patrol decals on doors and hood, No. 481-A, 1965-69, 4"	55	80	130
Chevrolet Impala Taxi, light orange body, base w/hexagonal panel under rear axle and smooth wheels, or two raised lines and shaped wheels, one-piece body, clear windows, plastic interior, silver grille, headlights and bumpers; smooth or shaped spun wheels w/rubber tires, No. 221-A, 1960-65, 4-1/4"	50	75	125
Chevrolet Impala Yellow Cab, red lower body, yellow upper, red interior w/driver, white roof sign, red decals, No. 480-A, 1965-67, 4"	80	120	200
Chevrolet Kennel Club Van, white upper, red lower body, working tailgate and rear windows, green interior, four dog figures, kennel club decals; shaped spun or detailed cast wheels, rubber tires, No. 486-A, 1967-69, 4"	56	84	140
Chevrolet Rough Rider Van, yellow body w/working rear doors, cream interior, amber windows, Rough Rider decals, No. 423-B, 1977-78, 4-5/8"	15	18	30
Chevrolet Spider-Van, dark blue body w/Spider-Man decals, in two versions: w/either spoke or solid wheels, No. 436-B, 1978-80, 4-5/8"	26	39	65
Chevrolet State Patrol Car, black body, State Patrol decals, smooth wheels w/hexagonal panel or raised lines and shaped wheels, yellow plastic interior, gray antenna, clear windows, silver bumpers, grille, headlights and trim, rubber tires, No. 223-A, 1959-61, 4"	50	75	125

Name	Good	EX	Mint
Chevrolet Superior Ambulance, white body, orange roof and stripes, two working doors, clear windows, red interior w/patient on stretcher and attendant, Red Cross decals, No. 405-B, 1978-80, 4-3/4"	30	45	75
Chevrolet Vanatic Van, off white body w/Vantastic decals, No. 431-B, 1977-80, 4-5/8"	10	15	25
Chevrolet Vantastic Van, black body w/Vantastic decals, No. 432-A, 1977-80, 4-5/8"	10	15	25
Chieftain Medium Tank, olive drab body, black tracks, Union Jack labels; includes twelve shells, No. 903-A, 1974-80	30	45	75
Chipperfield Bedford Giraffe Transporter, red "TK" Bedford truck w/blue giraffe box w/Chipperfield decal, two giraffes, shaped or detailed wheels, No. 503-A, 1964-71	60	90	175
Chipperfield Circus Cage Wagon, red body, yellow chassis, smooth or spun hubs; includes lions, tigers or polar bears, No. 1123-A, 1961-68	56	84	140
Chipperfield Circus Chevrolet Performing Poodles Van, blue upper body and tailgate, red lower body and base, clear windshield, pale blue interior w/poodles in back and ring of poodles and trainer, plastic tires, No. 511-A, 1970-72, 4"	160	240	550
Chipperfield Circus Crane and Cage, No. 114 crane truck, cage w/rhinoceros, red and blue trailer w/three animal cages and animals; very rare gift set, No. 21-B, 1970-72	400	700	2000
Chipperfield Circus Crane and Cage Wagon, No. 1121 crane truck, No. 1123 cage wagon and accessories, No. 12-A, 1961-65	150	225	375

Name	Good	EX	Mint
Chipperfield Circus Horse Transporter, red Bedford "TK" cab, red cover, blue upper horse trailer, three wheel variations; includes six horses, No. 1130-A, 1962-72	80	120	235
Chipperfield Circus Karrier Booking Office, red body, light blue roof, clear windows, tin lithographed interior, circus decals, smooth or shaped wheels, rubber tires, No. 426, 1962-64, 3-5/8"	105	165	325
Chipperfield Circus Land Rover and Elephant Cage, red No. 438 Range Rover w/blue canopy, Chipperfields Circus decal on canopy, burnt orange No. 607 elephant cage on red bed trailer, No. 19-A, 1962-68	90	135	275
Chipperfield Circus Menagerie Transporter, Scammell Handyman MKIII red/blue cab, blue trailer w/three animal cages, two lions, two tigers and two bears, No. 1139-A, 1968-72	120	180	350
Chipperfield Circus Scammell Crane Truck, red upper cab and rear body, light blue lower cab, crane base and winch crank housing, red interior, tow hook, jewel headlights, No. 1144-A, 1969-72, 8"	175	275	450
Chipperfield Circus Set, vehicle and accessory set in two versions: w/No. 426 Booking Office, No. 23-A, 1963-65	380	600	1300
Chipperfield Circus Set, vehicle and accessory set w/No. 503 Giraffe Truck, No. 23-A, 1966	340	500	1000

Chipperfield Circus Horse Transporter, No. 1130-A.

Chipperfield Circus Set, No. 23-A.

Chitty Chitty Bang Bang, No. 266-A. Photo Courtesy Mark Arruda.

Name	Good	EX	Mint
Chipperfield Land Rover Circus Vehicle, red body, yellow interior, blue rear and speakers, revolving clown, chimp figures, Chipperfield decals, No. 487, 1967-69, 3-1/2"	60	90	175
Chitty Chitty Bang Bang, metallic copper body, dark red interior and spoked wheels, four figures, black chassis w/silver running boards, silver hood, horn, brake, dash, tail and headlights, gold radiator, red and orange wings, handbrake operates side wings, No. 266-A, 1968-72, 6-1/4"	180	270	425
Chopper Squad Helicopter, blue and white body, Sure Rescue decals, No. 927-A, 1978-79	20	30	50
Chopper Squad Rescue Set, blue No. 919 Jeep w/Chopper Squad decal and red/white boat w/Surf Rescue decal, No. 927 Helicopter, No. 35-B, 1978-79	40	60	100
Chrysler Imperial Convertible, red body w/gray base, working hood, trunk and doors, golf bag in trunk, detailed engine, clear windshield, aqua interior, driver, chrome bumpers, No. 246-A, 1967-68, 4-1/4"	50	90	160
Chrysler Imperial Convertible, red body w/gray base, working hood, trunk and doors, golf bag in trunk, detailed engine, clear windshield, aqua interior, driver, chrome bumpers, No. 246-A, 1965-66, 4-1/4"	45	65	110

Name	Good	EX	Mint
Chubb Pathfinder Crash Tender, red body, Emergency Unit decals, working water pump, No. 1118-B, 1981-83	45	65	110
Chubb Pathfinder Crash Truck, red body w/either "Airport Fire Brigade" or "New York Airport" decals, upper and lower body, gold water cannon unpainted and sirens, clear windshield, yellow interior, black steering wheel, chrome plastic deck, silver lights; w/working pump and siren, No. 1103-B, 1974-80, 9-1/2"	60	90	150
Circus Crane Truck, red body, embossed blue logo, tinplate boom, blue wheels, No. 1121-A, 1960-68	80	120	225
Circus Human Cannonball Truck, red and blue body; w/Marvo figure, No. 1163-A, 1978-81	30	45	75
Circus Land Rover and Trailer, yellow/red No. 421 Land Rover w/Pinder-Jean Richard decals; accessories include blue loudspeakers and figures, No. 30-B, 1978-81	30	50	90
Citroen 2CV Charleston, yellow/black or maroon/black body versions w/opening hood, No. 346-A, 1981, 4-1/8"	15	18	30

Name	Good	EX	Mint
Citroen Alpine Rescue Safari, white body, light blue interior, red roof and rear hatch, yellow roof rack and skis, clear windshield, man and dog, gold die-cast bobsled, Alpine Rescue decals, No. 513-A, 1970-72, 4"	80	150	375
Citroen DS 19 Rally, light blue body, white roof, yellow interior, four jewel headlights, Monte Carlo Rally and No. 75 decals, w/antenna, No. 323-A, 1965-66, 4"	70	105	175
Citroen DS19, one-piece body in several colors, clear windows, silver lights, grille and bumpers, smooth wheels, rubber tires; colors: red, metallic green w/black roof, yellow w/red roof, No. 210-A, 1957-65, 4"	56	84	140
Citroen Dyane, metallic yellow or green body, black roof and interior, working rear hatch, clear windows, black base and tow bar, silver bumpers, grille and headlights, red taillights, marching duck and French flag decals, suspension, chrome wheels, No. 287-A, 1974-78, 4-1/2"	15	18	30
Citroen ID-19 Safari, orange body w/red/brown or red/green luggage on roof rack, green/brown interior, working hatch, two passengers, Wildlife Preservation decals, No. 436-A, 1963-65, 4"	40	60	100
Citroen Le Dandy Coupe, metallic maroon body and base, yellow interior, working trunk and two doors, clear windows, plastic interior, folding seats, chrome grille and bumpers, jewel headlights, red taillights, suspension, spoked wheels, rubber tires, No. 259-A, 1966, 4"	50	75	125
Citroen Le Dandy Coupe, metallic dark blue hood, sides and base, plastic aqua interior, white roof and trunk lid, clear windows, folding seats, chrome grille and bumpers, jewel headlights, red taillights, suspension, spoked wheels, rubber tires, No. 259-A2, 1967-69, 4"	70	105	175
Citroen SM, metallic lime gold w/chrome wheels or mauve body w/spoked wheels, pale blue interior and lifting hatch cover, working rear hatch and two doors, chrome inner drs., window frames, bumpers, grille, amber headlights, red taillights, Whizz Wheels, No. 284-A, 1971-75, 4-3/16"	16	24	40
Citroen Tour de France Car, red body, yellow interior and rear bed, clear windshield and headlights, driver, black plastic rack w/four bicycle wheels, swiveling team manager figure w/megaphone in back of car, Paramount and Tour de France decals, Whizz Wheels, No. 510-A, 1970-72, 4-1/4"	40	60	100
Citroen Winter Olympics Car, white body, blue roof and hatch, blue interior, red roof rack w/yellow skis, gold sled w/rider, skier, gold Grenoble Olympiade decals on car roof, No. 499-A, 1967-69, 4-1/8"	70	105	200
Citroen Winter Sports Safari, white body in three versions: two w/Corgi Ski Club decals and either w/or without roof ski rack, or one w/1964 Winter Olympics decals, No. 475-A, 1964-67, 4"	56	84	140
Coast Guard Jaguar XJ12C, blue and white body, Coast Guard labels, No. 414-B, 1975-77, 3-1/4"	18	27	45
Combine, Tractor and Trailer, set of three: No. 1111 combine, No. 50 Massey Ferguson tractor, and No. 51 trailer, No. 8-A, 1959-62	110	185	350
Commer 3/4 Ton Police Bus, battery operated working dome light, in several color combinations of dark or light metallic blue or green bodies, various foreign issues, No. 464-A, 1963-68, 3-1/2"	45	65	110

Commer 3/4-Ton Van, No. 462-A. Photo Courtesy Dr. Doug Sadecky.

Name	Good	EX	Mint
Commer 3/4-Ton Ambulance, in either white or cream body, red interior, blue dome light, red Ambulance decals, shaped wheels, No. 463-A, 1964-66, 3-1/2"	36	55	90
Commer 3/4-Ton Milk Float, white cab w/either light or dark blue body, w/CO-OP decals, No. 466-A, 1970, 3-1/2"	40	80	160
Commer 3/4-Ton Milk Float, white cab w/either light or dark blue body, No. 466-A, 1964-65, 3-1/2"	32	48	80
Commer 3/4-Ton Pickup, either red cab w/orange canopy, yellow interior, Trans-o-Lites, No. 465-A, 1963-66, 3-1/2"	30	45	75
Commer 3/4-Ton Van, either dark blue body w/Hammonds decals (1971) or white body w/CO-OP decals (1970), both w/cast spoked wheels w/plastic tires, No. 462-A, 1970-71, 3-1/2"	45	90	180
Commer 5-Ton Dropside Truck, either blue or red cab, both w/cream rear body, sheet metal tow hook, smooth or shaped wheels, rubber tires, No. 452-A, 1956-62, 4-5/8"	40	60	110
Commer 5-Ton Platform Truck, either yellow or metallic blue cab w/silver body, smooth or shaped wheels, No. 454-A, 1957-62, 4-5/8"	40	60	120

Name	Good	EX	Mint
Commer Holiday Mini Bus, white upper body w/orange lower body, white interior, clear windshield, silver bumpers, grille and headlights, Holiday Camp Special decal, roof rack, two working rear doors, No. 508-A, 1968-69, 3-1/2"	30	60	110
Commer Military Ambulance, olive drab body, blue rear windows and dome light, driver, Red Cross decals, No. 354-A, 1964-66, 3-5/8"	50	75	125
Commer Military Police Van, olive drab body, barred rear windows, white MP decals, driver, No. 355-A, 1964-65, 3-5/8"	55	80	130
Commer Mobile Camera Van, metallic blue lower body and roof rack, white upper body, two working rear doors, black camera on gold tripod, cameraman, No. 479-A, 1967-72, 3-1/2"	60	90	175
Commer Refrigerator Van, either light or dark blue cab, both w/cream bodies and red/white/blue Wall's Ice Cream decals, smooth wheels, No. 453-A, 1956-60, 4-5/8"	80	120	225
Commuter Dragster, maroon body w/Ford Commuter, Union Jack and No. 2 decals, cast silver engine, chrome plastic suspension and pipes, clear windshield, driver, spoke wheels, No. 161-A, 1971-73, 4-7/8"	30	45	75
Concorde-First Issues, BOAC decals, No. 650, 1969-72	20	30	50
Concorde-First Issues, Air France decals, No. 651, 1969-72	20	45	85
Concorde-First Issues, Air Canada decals, No. 652, 1969-72	80	120	200
Concorde-First Issues, Japan Airlines decals, No. 653, 1969-72	280	420	700
Concorde-Second Issues, BOAC and Air France models on display stands, No. 650-651, 1976-82	15	20	35

Name	Good	EX	Mint
Constructor Set, one red and one white cab bodies, w/four different interchangeable rear units; van, pickup, milk truck, and ambulance; various accessories include a milkman figure, No. 24-A, 1963-68	48	72	140
Cooper-Maserati Racing Car, yellow/white body w/yellow/black stripe and No. 3 decals, driver tilts to steer car, No. 159-A, 1969-72, 3-3/8"	18	27	45
Cooper-Maserati Racing Car, blue body w/red/white/blue Maserati and No. 7 decals, unpainted engine and suspension, chrome plastic steering wheel, roll bar, mirrors and pipes, driver, cast eight-spoke wheels, plastic tires, No. 156-A, 1967-69, 3-3/8"	26	39	65
Corgi Flying Club Set, blue/orange No. 438 Land Rover w/red dome light, blue trailer w/either orange/yellow or orange/white plastic airplane, No. 19-B, 1972-77	24	45	90
Corgi Junior James Bond SPECTRE Bobsled, orange body w/wild boar decals, No. 1012, 1970-72, 2-7/8"	75	140	295
Corgi Juniors James Bond Bobsled, yellow body, silver base, Bond figure, 007 decals, Whizz Wheels, No. 1011, 1970-72, 2-7/8"	75	140	295
Corgie Junior Popeye's Paddle Wagon Jr., smaller version of No. 802 w/Whizz Wheels, No. 1008	70	105	200
Corporal Missile & Erector Vehicle, white missile, red rubber-nose cone, olive green body on erector body, No. 1113-A, 1959-62	240	360	600
Corporal Missile Launching Ramp, sold in temporary pack, No. 1124-A, 1960-61	36	55	90
Corporal Missile on Launching Ramp, white missile, red rubber-nose cone, No. 1112-A, 1959-62	80	120	200
Corporal Missile Set, No. 1112 missile and No. 1113 ramp, erector vehicle and No. 1118 army truck, No. 9-A, 1959-62	340	510	850
Corvette Sting Ray, metallic green or red body, yellow interior, black working hood, working headlights, clear windshield, amber roof panel, gold dash, chrome grille and bumpers, decals, gray die-cast base, Golden jacks, cast wheels, plastic tires, No. 300-B, 1970-72, 4"	40	90	185
Corvette Sting Ray, metallic silver or red body, two working headlights, clear windshield, yellow interior, silver hood panels, four jewel headlights, suspension, chrome bumpers, w/spoked or shaped wheels, rubber tires, No. 310-A, 1963-68, 3-3/4"	60	90	175
Corvette Sting Ray, yellow body, red interior, suspension, No. 13 decals, No. 337-A, 1967-69, 3-3/4"	30	55	95
Corvette Sting Ray, metallic gray body w/black hood, Go-Go-Go labels, Whizz Wheels, No. 376-A, 1970-73, 3-5/8"	40	65	100
Corvette Sting Ray, either dark metallic blue or metallic mauve-rose body, chrome dash, Whizz Wheels, No. 387-A, 1972, 3-7/8"	40	65	100
Country Farm Set, No. 50 Massey Ferguson tractor, red No. 62 hay trailer w/load, fences, figures, No. 4-B, 1974-75	30	45	75
Country Farm Set, same as 4-B but without hay load on trailer, No. 5-C, 1976	30	45	75
Daily Planet Helicopter, red and white body, rocket launcher w/ten spare missiles, No. 929-A, 1979-81	24	36	60
Daimler 38 1910, orange-red body, gray and yellow chassis, yellow spoked wheels; w/four figures, No. 9021-A, 1964-69	20	30	50

Name	Good	EX	Mint
Daktari Set, two versions: No. 438 Land Rover, green w/black stripes, cast wheels, 1968-73; Whizz Wheels, 1974-75, each set, No. 7-B, 1967-75 50		75	150
Datsun 240Z, red body w/No. 11 and other decals, two working doors, white interior, orange roll bar and tire rack; one version also has East Africa Rally decals, No. 394-A, 1973-76, 3-5/8" 15		20	35
Datsun 240Z, white body w/red hood and roof, No. 46 and John Morton labels, Whizz Wheels, No. 396-A, 1973-76, 3-5/8" 15		20	35
David Brown Combine, No. 55 Tractor, red and yellow combines, white JF labels, No. 1112-B, 1978-79 30		45	75
David Brown Tractor, white body w/black/white David Brown No. 1412 decals, red chassis and plastic engine, No. 55-B, 1977-82, 4-1/8" 15		25	45
David Brown Tractor & Trailer, two-piece set; No. 55 tractor and No. 56 trailer, No. 34-A, 1976-79 30		45	75
De Tomaso Mangusta, metallic dark green body w/gold stripes and logo on hood, silver lower body, clear front windows, cream interior, amber rear windows and headlights, gray antenna, spare wheel, Whizz Wheels, No. 203-B, 1970-73, 3-7/8"..................26		39	65
De Tomaso Mangusta, white upper/light blue lower body/base, black interior, clear windows, silver engine, black grille, amber headlights, red taillights, gray antenna, spare wheel, gold stripes and black logo decal on hood, suspension, removable gray chassis, No. 271-A, 1969, 5"............................32		48	80
Decca Airfield Radar Van, cream body w/four or five vertical bands, working rotating scanner and aerial, No. 1106-A, 1959-60........................120		180	350
Decca Radar Scanner, w/either orange or custard colored scanner frame, silver scanner face, w/gear on base for turning scanner, No. 353-A, 1959-60, 3-1/4" 34		51	85
Dick Dastardly's Racing Car, dark blue body, yellow chassis, chrome engine, red wings, Dick and Muttley figures, No. 809-A, 1973-76, 5"......... 40		60	150
Dodge Kew Fargo Tipper, white cab and working hood, blue tipper, red interior, clear windows, black hydraulic cylinders, cast wheels, plastic tires, No. 483-A, 1967-72, 5-1/4"... 34		51	85
Dodge Livestock Truck, tan cab and hood, green body, working tailgate and ramps, five pigs, No. 484-A, 1967-72, 5-3/8" 34		51	85
Dolphin Cabin Cruiser, white hull, blue deck plastic boat w/red/white stripe decals, driver, blue motor w/white cover, gray prop, cast trailer w/smooth wheels, rubber tires, No. 104-A, 1965-68, 5-1/4" 24		36	70
Dougal's Magic Roundabout Car, yellow body, red interior, clear windows, dog and snail, red wheels w/gold trim, Magic Roundabout decals, No. 807-A, 1971-74, 4-1/2" ... 70		105	175
Drax Jet Helicopter, white body, yellow rotors and fins, yellow/black Drax decals, No. 930-A, 1979-81, 5-7/8".. 24		36	75
Dropside Trailer, cream body, red chassis in five versions: smooth wheels 1957-61; shaped wheels, 1962-1965; white body, cream or blue chassis; or silver gray body, blue chassis, each, No. 100-A, 1957-65, 4-3/8" 10		21	45
Ecurie Ecosse Racing Set, metallic dark or light blue No. 1126 transporter w/three cars in two versions: BRM, Vanwall and Lotus XI, 1961-64; BRM, Vanwall and			

Name	Good	EX	Mint
Ferrari, 1964-66, value is for individual complete set, No. 16-A, 1961-66 140		210	450
Ecurie Ecosse Transporter, in dark blue body w/either blue or yellow lettering, or light blue body w/red or yellow lettering, working tailgate and sliding door, yellow interior, shaped wheels, rubber tires, No. 1126-A, 1961-65, 7-3/4".....................70		105	200
Emergency Set, three-vehicle set w/figures and accessories, No. 402 Ford Cortina Police car, No. 921 Police Helicopter, No. 481 Range Rover Ambulance, No. 18-B, 1976-77 40		60	100
Emergency Set, No. 339 Land Rover Police Car and No. 921 Police Helicopter w/figures and accessories, No. 19-C, 1979-81 30		50	80
ERF 44G Dropside Truck, yellow cab and chassis, metallic blue bed, smooth or shaped wheels, No. 456-A, 1961-64 36		55	110
ERF 44G Moorhouse Van, yellow cab, red body, Moorhouse Lemon Cheese decals, smooth wheels, rubber tires, No. 459-A, 1958-60, 4-5/8" 100		150	295

ERF 64G Earth Dumper, No. 458-A.

Name	Good	EX	Mint
ERF 44G Platform Truck, light blue cab w/either dark blue or white flatbed body or yellow cab and blue flatbed, smooth hubs, No. 457-A, 1958-64, 4-5/8" 36		55	110
ERF Dropside Truck and Trailer, No. 456 truck and No. 101 trailer w/No. 1488 cement sack load and No. 1485 plank load, No. 11-A, 1960-64 60		90	200
ERF Neville Cement Tipper, yellow cab, gray tipper, cement decal, plastic or metal filler caps, w/either smooth or shaped wheels, No. 460-A, 1959-66, 3-3/4" 32		48	80
ERF 64G Earth Dumper, red cab, yellow tipper, clear windows, unpainted hydraulic cylinder, spare tire, smooth wheels, rubber tires, No. 458-A, 1958-67, 4".....................30		45	85
Euclid Caterpillar Tractor, TC-12 lime green body w/black or pale gray rubber treads, gray plastic seat, driver figure, controls, stacks, silver grille, painted blue engine sides and Euclid decals, No. 1103-A, 1960-63, 4-1/4"..50		100	190
Euclid TC-12 Bulldozer, lime green body w/black or pale gray treads, silver blade surface, gray plastic seat controls and stacks, silver grille and lights, painted blue engine sides, sheet metal base, rubber treads and Euclid decals, No. 1102-A, 1958-62, 5" 80		120	225
Euclid TC-12 Bulldozer, yellow or pale lime-green body, metal control rod, driver, black rubber treads, No. 1107-A, 1963-66, 6-1/8" 80		120	200
Ferrari 206 Dino, black interior and fins, in either red body w/No. 30 and gold hubs or Whizz Wheels, or yellow body w/No. 23 and gold hubs or Whizz Wheels, No. 344-A, 1969-73, 4-1/8" 24		36	60

Name	Good	EX	Mint
Ferrari 308GTS, red or black body w/working rear hood, black interior w/tan seats, movable chrome headlights, detailed engine, No. 378-B, 1982, 4-5/8" 15		20	35
Ferrari 308GTS Magnum, red body w/solid chrome wheels, No. 298-A, 1982, 4-5/8" 24		36	60
Ferrari 312 B2 Racing Car, red body, white fin, gold engine, chrome suspension, mirrors and wheels, Ferrari and No. 5 decals, No. 152-B, 1973-75, 4" 16		24	40
Ferrari Berlinetta 250LM, red body w/yellow stripe, blue windshields, chrome interior, grille and exhaust pipes, detailed engine, No. 4 Ferrari logo and yellow stripe decals, spoked wheels and spare, rubber tires, No. 314-A, 1965-72, 3-3/4" 30		45	75
Ferrari Daytona, apple green body, black tow hook, red-yellow-silver-black Daytona No. 5 and other racing decals, amber windows, headlights, black plastic interior, base, four spoke chrome wheels, No. 300-C, 1979, 5" 15		20	35
Ferrari Daytona, white body w/red roof and trunk, black interior, two working doors, amber windows and headlights, No. 81 and other decals, No. 323-B, 1973-78, 4-3/4" 15		30	55
Ferrari Daytona and Racing Car, blue/yellow No. 323 Ferrari and No. 150 Surtees on yellow trailer, No. 29-B, 1975-77 25		40	85
Ferrari Daytona JCB, orange body w/No. 33, Corgi and other decals, chrome spoked wheels, No. 324-B, 1973-74, 4-3/4" 15		25	50
Ferrari Racing Car, red body, chrome plastic engine, roll bar and dash, driver, silver cast base and exhaust, Ferrari and No. 36 decals, shaped or spoked wheels, No. 154-A, 1963-72, 3-5/8" 24		36	75
Fiat 1800, one-piece body in several colors, clear windows, plastic interior, silver lights, grille and bumpers, red taillights, smooth wheels, rubber tires, colors: blue body w/light or bright yellow interior, light tan, mustard, light blue or two-tone blue body, No. 217-A, 1960-63, 3-3/4" 24		40	80
Fiat 2100, light two-tone mauve body, yellow interior, purple roof, clear windows w/rear blind, silver grille, license plates and bumpers, red taillights, shaped wheels, rubber tires, No. 232-A, 1961-64, 3-3/4" 22		33	75
Fiat X 1/9 & Powerboat, green and white automobile, w/white and gold boat, Carlsberg decals, No. 37-B, 1979-82 30		45	75
Fiat X1/9, metallic blue body and base, white Fiat No. 3, multicolored lettering and stripe decals, black roof, trim, interior, rear panel, grille, bumpers and tow hook, chrome wheels and detailed engine, No. 306-B, 1980-81, 4-3/4" 15		20	35
Fiat X1/9, metallic light green or silver body w/black roof, trim and interior, two working doors, rear panel, grille, tow hook and bumpers, detailed engine, suspension, chrome wheels, No. 314-B, 1975-79, 4-1/2" ..15		20	35
Fire Bug, orange body, Whizz Wheels, No. 395-A, 1972-73 20		30	50
Flying Club Set, green and white No. 419 Jeep w/Corgi Flying Club decals, green trailer, blue/white airplane, No. 49-A, 1978-80 36		55	90
Ford 5000 Super Major Tractor, blue body/chassis w/Ford Super Major 5000 decals, gray cast fenders and rear wheels, gray plastic front wheels, black plastic tires, driver, No. 67-A, 1967-73, 3-3/4" 30		45	75

Name	Good	EX	Mint
Ford 5000 Tractor with Scoop, blue body/chassis, gray fenders, yellow scoop arm and controls, chrome scoop, black control lines, No. 74-A, 1969-72, 3-1/8"	55	80	130
Ford Aral Tank Truck, light blue cab and chassis, white tanker body, Aral labels, No. 1161-A, 1977-80	20	30	50
Ford Capri, orange-red or dark red body, gold wheels w/red hubs, Whizz Wheels, two working doors, clear windshield and headlights, black interior, folding seats, black grille, silver bumpers, No. 311-A, 1970-72, 4"	40	80	145
Ford Capri 3 Litre GT, white and black body, racing number 5, No. 331-A, 1973-76	15	20	35
Ford Capri 30 S, Silver or yellow body, black markings, opening doors and hatchback, No. 343-B, 1980-81	15	20	35
Ford Capri S, white body, red lower body and base, red interior, clear windshield, black bumpers, grille and tow hook, chrome headlights and wheels, red taillights, No. 6 and other racing decals, No. 312-C, 1982, 4-3/4"	15	20	35
Ford Capri Santa Pod Gloworm, white and blue body w/red, white and blue lettering and flag decals, red chassis, amber windows, gold-based black engine, gold scoop, pipes and front suspension, w/driver, plastic wheels, No. 163-A, 1971-76, 4-3/8"	18	27	45
Ford Car Transporter, metallic lime green or metallic cab and semi, cream cab chassis, deck and ramp, No. 1159-A, 1976-79	20	30	60
Ford Car Transporter, white cab, red chassis and trailer, white decals and ramps, No. 1170-A, 1982	20	30	50

Name	Good	EX	Mint
Ford Cobra Mustang, white, black, red and blue body and chassis, Mustang decal, No. 370-A, 1982	15	18	30
Ford Consul, one-piece body in several colors, clear windows, silver grille, lights and bumpers, smooth wheels, rubber tires, No. 200, 1956-61, 3-5/8"	45	65	120
Ford Consul Classic, cream or gold body and base, yellow interior, pink roof, clear windows, gray steering wheel, silver bumpers, grille, opening hood, No. 234, 1961-65, 3-3/4"	35	55	90
Ford Consul-Mechanical, same as model 200-A but w/friction motor and blue or green body, No. 200-M, 1956-59	55	85	160
Ford Cortina Estate Car, red body and base or metallic charcoal gray body and base, cream interior, chrome bumpers and grille, jewel headlights, No. 491, 1966-69, 3-3/4"	35	55	90
Ford Cortina Estate Car, 3-1/2" metallic dark blue body and base, brown and cream simulated wood panels, cream interior, chrome bumpers and grille, jewel headlights, No. 440-A, 1966-68	35	55	90
Ford Cortina GXL, tan or metallic silver blue body, black roof and stripes, red plastic interior, working doors, clear windshield, No. 313, 1970-73, 4"	30	45	75
Ford Cortina Police Car, white body, red or pink and black stripe labels, red interior, folding seats, blue dome light, clear windows, chrome bumpers, Police labels, opening doors, No. 402, 1972-76, 4"	15	25	45
Ford Covered Semi-Trailer, blue cab and trailer, black cab chassis and trailer fenders, yellow covers, No. 1109, 1979-80	15	25	50

Name	Good	EX	Mint
Ford Escort 13 GL, red, blue or yellow body, opening doors, No. 334, 1980	8	15	25
Ford Escort Police Car, blue body and base, tan interior, white doors, blue dome lights, red Police labels, black grille and bumpers, No. 297, 1982, 4-3/16"	8	15	30
Ford Esso Tank Truck, white cab and tank, red tanker chassis and fenders, chrome wheels, Esso labels, No. 1157, 1976-81	15	30	60
Ford Express Semi-Trailer, metallic blue cab and trailer, silver roof on trailer, chrome doors marked "Express Service," shaped or detailed cast wheels, No. 1137, 1965-70	60	110	225
Ford Exxon Tank Truck, white cab and tank, red tanker chassis and fenders, chrome wheels, Exxon labels, No. 1158, 1976-81	15	30	60
Ford GT 70, green and black body, white interior, No. 32 label, No. 316-B, 1972-73	10	25	45
Ford Guinness Tanker, orange, tan, black cab, tan tankers body, Guinness labels, No. 1169, 1982	20	30	50
Ford Gulf Tank Truck, white cab w/orange chassis, blue tanker body, Gulf labels, chrome wheels, No. 1160, 1976-78	15	25	40
Ford Holmes Wrecker, white upper cab, black roof, red rear body and lower cab, mirrors, unpainted or gold booms, No. 1142, 1967-74	60	90	200
Ford Michelin Container Truck, blue cab and trailer, white cab chassis and trailer fenders, yellow containers; includes Michelin Man figure, No. 1108, 1981	15	25	50
Ford Mustang Fastback, metallic lilac, metallic dark blue, silver or light green body, spoked or detailed cast wheels, No. 320-A, 1965-66	30	45	95
Ford Mustang Fastback, white body w/double red stripe, blue interior, spun, detailed cast, wire or cast alloy wheels, No. 325, 1965-69	25	45	85
Ford Mustang Mach 1, green upper body, white lower body and base, cream interior, folding seat backs, chrome headlights and rear bumper, No. 329, 1973-76, 4-1/4"	25	35	60
Ford Sierra, many body color versions w/plastic interior, working hatch and two doors, clear windows, folding seat back, lifting hatch cover, No. 299, 1982, 5"	8	15	25
Ford Sierra and Caravan Trailer, blue No. 299 Sierra, two-tone blue/white No. 490 Caravan, No. 1-C, 1983	15	20	35
Ford Sierra Taxi, cream body, No. 451, 1983	8	15	20
Ford Thames Airborne Caravan, various color versions of body and plastic interior w/table, white blinds, silver bumpers, grille and headlights, two doors, No. 420, 1962-67, 3-3/4"	35	55	95
Ford Thames Wall's Ice Cream Van, light blue body, cream pillar, chimes, chrome bumpers and grille, crank at rear to operate chimes, no figures, No. 474, 1965-68, 4"	55	110	225
Ford Thunderbird 1957, cream body, dark brown, black or orange plastic hardtop, black interior, open hood and trunk, chrome bumpers, No. 801-B, 1982, 5-3/16"	10	20	35
Ford Thunderbird 1957, white body, black interior and plastic top, amber windows, white seats, chrome bumpers, headlights and spare wheel cover, No. 810, 1983, 5-1/4"	10	20	35
Ford Thunderbird Hardtop, light green body, cream roof, clear windows, silver lights, grille and bumpers, red taillights, rubber tires, No. 214, 1959-65, 4-1/8"	50	80	130

Name	Good	EX	Mint
Ford Thunderbird Hardtop-Mechanical, same as 214-A but w/friction motor and pink or light green body and cream or black roof, No. 214-M, 1959, 4-1/8"	70	105	195
Ford Thunderbird Roadster, clear windshield, silver seats, lights, grille and bumpers, red taillights, rubber tires, white body, No. 215, 1959-65, 4-1/8"	50	75	125
Ford Torino Road Hog, orange-red body, yellow and gray chassis, gold lamps, chrome radiator shell, windows and bumpers, one-piece body, working horn, No. 1003, 1981, 5-3/4"	15	20	35
Ford Tractor and Beast Carrier, No. 67 Ford 5000 tractor and No. 58 Beast Carrier, No. 1-B, 1966-72	60	90	150
Ford Tractor and Conveyor, No. 67 tractor, conveyor w/trailer, figures and accessories, No. 47-A, 1966-69	60	90	175
Ford Tractor with Trencher, blue body/chassis, gray fenders, cast yellow trencher arm and controls, chrome trencher, black control lines, No. 72, 1970-74, 5-5/8"	50	75	125
Ford Transit Milk Float, white one-piece body, blue hood and roof, tan interior, chrome and red roof lights, open compartment door and milk cases, No. 405, 1982, 5-1/2"	15	25	40
Ford Transit Tipper, orange cab and chassis, tan tipper, chrome wheels, No. 1121, 1983	10	15	25
Ford Transit Wrecker, white cab and rear body, red roof, silver bed, "24-hour Service" labels, No. 1140, 1981	25	35	60
Ford Wall's Ice Cream Van, light blue body, dark cream pillars, plastic striped rear canopy, white interior, silver bumpers, grille and headlights; includes salesman and boy figures, No. 447-A, 1965-67, 3-1/4"	80	160	325
Ford Zephyr Estate Car, light blue one-piece body, dark blue hood and stripes, red interior, silver bumpers, grille and headlights, red taillights, No. 424-A, 1960-65, 3-7/8"	30	45	75
Ford Zephyr Patrol Car, white or cream body, blue and white Politie/ Rijkspolitie decals, red interior, blue dome light, silver bumpers; import, No. 419-A, 1960-65	60	125	225
Ford Zephyr Patrol Car, white or cream body, blue and white Police red interior, blue dome light, silver bumpers, No. 419-A, 1960-65, 3-3/4"	35	50	85
Fordson Power Major Halftrack Tractor, blue body/chassis, silver steering wheel, seat and grille, three versions: orange cast wheels, gray treads, lights in radiator or on sides of radiator, No. 54-A, 1962-64, 3-1/2"	90	135	225
Fordson Power Major Tractor, blue body/chassis w/Fordson Power Major decals, silver steering wheel, seat, exhaust, grille and lights, No. 55, 1961-63, 3-1/4"	45	65	110
Fordson Power Major Tractor, blue body w/Fordson Power Major decals, driver, blue chassis and steering wheel, silver seat, hitch, exhaust, No. 60, 1964-66, 3-3/8"	50	75	125
Fordson Tractor and Plow, No. 60 tractor and No. 61 four-furrow plow, No. 13-A, 1964-66	55	85	140
Fordson Tractor and Plow, No. 55 Fordson Tractor and No. 56 Four Furrow plow, No. 18, 1961-64	55	85	140
Four Furrow Plow, red frame, yellow plastic parts, No. 56-A, 1961-63, 3-5/8"	15	20	35
Four Furrow Plow, blue frame w/chrome plastic parts, No. 61-A, 1964-70, 3-3/4"	15	20	35

Ghia L64 Chrysler V8, No. 241. Photo Courtesy Mark Arruda.

Name	Good	EX	Mint
German Life Saving Set, red/white No. 421 Land Rover and lifeboat, white trailer, German decals, No. 33-B, 1980-82	30	45	75
Ghia L64 Chrysler V8, metallic light blue, green, copper or yellow, plastic interior, hood, trunk and two doors working, detailed engine, clear windshield, shaped or detailed cast wheels, No. 241, 1963-69, 4-1/4"	25	40	75
Ghia-Fiat 600 Jolly, light or dark blue body, red and silver canopy, red seats, two figures, windshield, chrome dash, floor, steering wheels, No. 240, 1963-65, 3-1/4"	45	75	130
Ghia-Fiat 600 Jolly, dark yellow body, red seats, two figures and a dog, clear windshield, silver bumpers and headlights, red taillights, No. 242, 1965-66, 3-1/4"	80	175	325
Giant Daktari Set, black and green No. 438 Land Rover, tan No. 503 Giraffe truck, blue and brown No. 484 Dodge Livestock truck, figures, No. 14-B, 1969-73	225	350	650
Giant Tower Crane, white body, orange cab and chassis, No. 1154-B, 1981-82	35	50	85
Glider Set, two versions: white No. 345 Honda, 1981-82; yellow Honda, 1983, value is for individual complete sets, No. 12-C, 1981-83	30	45	75

Name	Good	EX	Mint
Golden Eagle Jeep, tan and brown or white and gold body, tan plastic top, chrome plastic base, bumpers and steps, chrome wheels, No. 441-B, 1979-82, 3-3/4"	8	15	25
Golden Guinea Set, three vehicle set, gold plated No. 224 Bentley Continental, No. 229 Chevy Corvair and No. 234 Ford Consul, No. 20, 1961-63	90	150	325
GP Beach Buggy, metallic blue or orange-red body, two surfboards, flower label, Whizz Wheels, No. 381-A, 1970-76	15	20	35
Grand Prix Racing Set, four vehicle set includes: No. 490 Volkswagen Breakdown Truck w/No. 330 Porsche (1969), Porsche No. 371(1970-72), No. 155 Lotus, No. 156 Cooper-Maserati, red trailer, No. 12-B, 1968-72	135	210	425
Grand Prix Set, sold by mail order only; kit version of No. 151 Yardley, No. 154 JPS, No. 152 Surtees and No. 153 Surtees, No. 30-A, 1973	60	125	275
Green Hornet's Black Beauty, black body, green window/interior, two figures, working chrome grille and panels w/weapons, green headlights, red taillights, No. 268, 1967-72, 5"	175	275	550
Green Line Bus, green body, white interior and stripe, TDK labels, six spoked wheels, No. 470-C, 1983, 4-7/8"	10	15	25
Half Track Rocket Launcher & Trailer, two rocket launchers and single trailer castings, gray plastic roll cage, man w/machine gun, front wheels and hubs, No. 907-A, 1975-80, 6-1/2"	20	35	55
Hardy Boys' Rolls-Royce, red body w/yellow hood, roof and window frames, band figures on roof on removable green base, No. 805-A, 1970, 4-5/8"	70	105	200

Hardy Boys' Rolls-Royce, No. 805-A. Photo Courtesy Mark Arruda.

Hillman Hunter, No. 302-B. Photo Courtesy Mark Arruda.

Name	Good	EX	Mint
HDL Hovercraft SR-N1, blue superstructure, gray base and deck, clear canopy, red seats, yellow SR-N1 decals, No. 1119, 1960-62	60	90	150
Hesketh-Ford Racing Car, white body w/red/white/blue Hesketh, stripe and No. 24 decals, chrome suspension, roll bar, mirrors and pipes, No. 160, 1975-78, 5-5/8"	15	18	30
HGB-Angus Firestreak, chrome plastic spotlight and ladders, black hose reel, red dome light, white water cannon, in two interior versions, electronic siren and lights, No. 1001, 1980, 6-1/4"	35	50	85
Hi-Speed Fire Engine, red body, yellow plastic ladder, No. 703-A, 1975-78	16	24	40
Hillman Hunter, blue body, gray interior, black hood, white roof, unpainted spotlights, clear windshield, red radiator screen, black equipment, Golden Jacks wheels; came w/Kangaroo figure, No. 302-B, 1969-72, 4-1/4"	45	65	125

Name	Good	EX	Mint
Hillman Husky, one-piece tan or metallic blue/silver body, clear windows, silver lights, grille and bumpers, smooth wheels, No. 206, 1956-60, 3-1/2"	40	70	125
Hillman Husky-Mechanical, same as 206-A but w/friction motor, black base and dark blue, gray or cream body, No. 206-M, 1956-59, 3-1/2"	50	90	125
Hillman Imp, metallic copper, blue, dark blue or gold one-piece bodies, w/white/yellow interior, silver bumpers, headlights, No. 251, 1963-67, 3-1/4"	30	45	85
Hillman Imp Rally, in various metallic body colors, w/cream interior, Monte Carlo Rally and No. 107 decals, No. 328, 1966, 3-1/4"	30	65	110
Honda Ballade Driving School, red body/base, tan interior, clear windows, tow hook, mirrors, bumpers, No. 273-B, 1982-83, 4-3/4"	10	15	25
Honda Prelude, dark metallic blue body, tan interior, clear windows, folding seats, sunroof, chrome wheels, No. 345-B, 1981-82, 4-3/4"	8	15	20
Hughes Police Helicopter, red interior, dark blue rotors, in several international imprints, Netherlands, German, Swiss, in white or yellow, No. 921, 1975-80, 5-1/2"	20	30	50
Hyster 800 Stacatruck, clear windows, black interior w/driver, No. 1113, 1977, 8-1/2"	35	50	85

Name	Good	EX	Mint
Incredible Hulk Mazda Pickup, metallic light brown body, gray or red plastic cage, black interior, Hulk decal on hood, chrome wheels; includes green and red Hulk figure, No. 264-B, 1979-80, 5"	20	30	75
Inter-City Mini Bus, orange body w/brown interior, clear windows, green/yellow/black decals, Whizz Wheels, No. 701, 1973-79, 4-3/16"	8	15	25
International 6x6 Army Truck, olive drab body w/clear windows, red/blue decals, six cast olive wheels w/rubber tires, No. 1118, 1959-63, 5-1/2"	70	105	225
Iso Grifo 7 Litre, metallic blue body, light blue interior, black hood and stripe, clear windshield, black dash, folding seats, chrome bumpers, Whizz Wheels, No. 301-B, 1970-73, 4"	15	18	30
Jaguar 1952 XK120 Rally, cream body w/black top and trim, red interior, Rally des Alps and No. 414 decals, No. 803-A, 1983, 4-3/4"	8	15	25
Jaguar 2.4 Litre, one-piece white body w/no interior 1957-59, or yellow body w/red interior 1960-63, clear windows, smooth hubs, No. 208, 1957-63, 3-7/8"	50	80	130

Jaguar 2.4 Litre-Mechanical, No. 208-M.

Name	Good	EX	Mint
Jaguar 2.4 Litre Fire Chief's Car, red body w/unpainted roof signal/siren, red/white fire and shield decals on doors, in two versions, smooth or spun hubs, No. 213, 1959-61, 3-3/4"	60	90	150
Jaguar 2.4 Litre-Mechanical, same as 208-A but w/friction motor and metallic blue body, No. 208-M, 1957-59, 3-7/8"	60	90	180
Jaguar E Type, maroon or metallic dark gray body, tan interior, red and clear plastic removable hardtop, clear windshield, folded top, spun hubs, No. 307-A, 1962-64, 3-3/4"	45	65	110
Jaguar E Type 2+2, red or blue body and chassis, working hood, doors and hatch, black interior w/folding seats, copper engine, pipes and suspension, spoked wheels, No. 335, 1968-69, 4-3/16"	40	60	120
Jaguar E Type 2+2, in five versions: red or yellow w/nonworking doors; or w/V-12 engine in yellow body or metallic yellow body, Whizz Wheels, No. 374, 1970-76, 4-1/8"	35	55	90
Jaguar E Type Competition, gold or chrome plated body, black interior, blue and white stripes and black No. 2 decals, no top, clear windshield, headlights, w/driver, No. 312-A, 1964-68, 3-3/4"	45	65	110
Jaguar Mark X Saloon, several different color versions w/working front and rear hood castings, clear windshields, plastic interior, gray steering wheel; includes suitcase in trunk, No. 238, 1962-67, 4-1/4"	35	55	110
Jaguar XJ12C, five different metallic versions, working hood and two doors, clear windows, tow hook, chrome bumpers, grille and headlights, No. 286, 1974-79, 5-1/4"	10	15	35

Name	Good	EX	Mint
Jaguar XJ12C Police Car, white body w/blue and pink stripes, light bar w/blue dome light, tan interior, police decals, No. 429, 1978-80, 5-1/8"	15	18	45
Jaguar XJS, metallic burgundy body, tan interior, clear windows, working doors, spoked chrome wheels, No. 319-C, 1978-81, 5-3/4"	10	15	25
Jaguar XJS Motul, black body w/red/white Motul and No. 4, chrome wheels, No. 318-B, 1983, 5-3/4"	8	15	25
Jaguar XJS-HE Supercat, black body w/silver stripes and trim, red interior, dark red taillights, light gray antenna, no tow hook, clear windshield, No. 314, 1982-83, 5-1/4"	8	15	25
Jaguar XK120 Hardtop, red body, black hardtop, working hood and trunk, detailed engine, cream interior, clear windows, chrome wheels, No. 803, 1983, 4-3/4"	8	15	25
James Bond Aston Martin, metallic silver body, red interior, two figures, working roof hatch, ejector seat, bullet shield and guns, chrome bumpers, spoked wheels, No. 270, 1968-77, 4"	100	150	325

Name	Good	EX	Mint
James Bond Aston Martin, metallic silver body and die-cast base, red interior, two figures, clear windows, passenger seat raises to eject, No. 271, 1978, 5"	30	45	90
James Bond Aston Martin DB5, metallic gold body, red interior, working roof hatch, clear windows, two figures, left seat ejects, spoked wheels, accessory pack, No. 261-A, 1965-68, 3-3/4"	70	105	275
James Bond Citroen 2CV6, dark yellow body and hood, red interior, clear windows, chrome headlights, red taillights, black plastic grille, No. 272, 1981-86, 4-1/4"	15	35	70
James Bond Lotus Esprit, white body and base, black windshield, grille and hood panel, white plastic roof device that triggers fins and tail, rockets, No. 269-B, 1977, 4-3/4"	30	45	95
James Bond Moon Buggy, white body w/blue chassis, amber canopy, yellow tanks, red radar dish, arms and jaws, yellow wheels, No. 811-A, 1972-73, 4-3/8"	175	275	525
James Bond Mustang Mach 1, red and white body w/black hood and opening doors, No. 391, 1972-73, 4-3/8"	100	150	300

James Bond Aston Martin, No. 270.

James Bond Citroen 2CV6, No. 272. Photo Courtesy Mark Arruda.

James Bond Lotus Esprit, No. 269-B. Photo Courtesy Mark Arruda.

James Bond Toyota 2000GT, No. 336.

Jeep FC-150 Pickup, No. 409-A.

Name	Good	EX	Mint
James Bond Set, set of three: No. 271 Lotus Esprit, No. 649 Space Shuttle and No. 269 Aston Martin, No. 22, 1979-81	80	135	295
James Bond Space Shuttle, white body w/yellow/black Moonraker decals, No. 649, 1979-81, 5-7/8"	30	45	75
James Bond Toyota 2000GT, white body, black interior w/Bond and passenger, working trunk and gun rack, spoked wheels, plastic tires, accessory pack, No. 336, 1967-69, 4"	115	180	375
JCB 110B Crawler Loader, white cab, yellow body, working red shovel, red interior w/driver, clear windows, black treads, JCB decals, No. 1110, 1976-80, 6-1/2"	20	30	50
Jean Richard Circus Set, yellow and red Land Rover and cage trailer w/Pinder-Jean Richard decals, No. 426 office van and trailer, No. 1163 Human Cannonball truck, ring and cut-out "Big Top" circus tent, No. 48-C, 1978-81	90	135	275

Name	Good	EX	Mint
Jeep & Horse Box, metallic painted No. 441 Jeep and No. 112 trailer; accessories include girl on pony, three jumps and three hay bales, No. 29-C, 1981-83	15	30	50
Jeep and Motorcycle Trailer, red working No. 441 Jeep w/two blue/yellow bikes on trailer, No. 10-C, 1982-83	15	20	40
Jeep CJ-5, dark metallic green body, removable white top, white plastic wheels, spare tire, No. 419-B, 1977-79, 4"	8	15	30
Jeep FC-150 Covered Truck, four versions: blue body, rubber tires (1965-67); yellow/brown body; rubber tires w/spun hubs (1965-67); blue body, plastic tires w/cast spoked hubs, No. 470-A, 1965-72	30	45	75
Jeep FC-150 Pickup, blue body, clear windows, sheet metal tow hook, in two wheel versions: smooth or shaped wheels, No. 409-A, 1959-65, 3-1/2"	35	55	90
Jeep FC-150 Pickup with Conveyor Belt, red body, yellow interior, orange grille, two black rubber belts, shaped wheels, black rubber tires; accessories farmland figure and sacks, No. 64, 1965-69, 7-1/2"	45	65	130

Karrier Field Kitchen, No. 359. Photo Courtesy Mark Arruda.

Name	Good	EX	Mint
Jeep FC-150 Tower Wagon, metallic green body, yellow interior and basket w/workman figure, clear windows, w/either rubber or plastic wheels, No. 478, 1965-69, 4-5/8"	40	60	100
Jet Ranger Police Helicopter, white body w/chrome interior, red floats and rotors, amber windows, Police decals, No. 931, 1980, 5-7/8"	25	40	65
JPS Lotus Racing Car, black body, scoop and wings w/gold John Player Special, Texaco and No. 1 decals, gold suspension, pipes and wheels, No. 190, 1974-77, 10-1/2"	30	45	75
Karrier Bantam Two Ton Van, blue body, red chassis and bed, clear windows, smooth wheels, rubber tires, No. 455, 1957-60, 4"	35	55	95
Karrier Butcher Shop, white body, blue roof, butcher shop interior, Home Service decals, in two versions: w/or without suspension, smooth hubs, No. 413-A, 1960-64, 3-5/8"	65	100	165
Karrier Dairy Van, light blue body w/Drive Safely on Milk decals, white roof, w/either smooth or shaped wheels, No. 435-B, 1962-64, 4-1/8"	50	75	145

Name	Good	EX	Mint
Karrier Field Kitchen, olive body, white decals, w/figure, No. 359, 1964-66, 3-5/8"	60	90	175
Karrier Ice Cream Truck, cream upper, blue lower body and interior, clear windows, sliding side windows, Mister Softee decals, figure inside, No. 428-A, 1963-66, 3-5/8"	90	150	275
Karrier Lucozade Van, yellow body w/gray rear door, Lucozade decals, rubber tires, w/either smooth or shaped wheels, No. 411-A, 1958-62, 4-1/8"	70	120	225
Karrier Mobile Canteen, blue body, white interior, amber windows, roof knob rotates figure, working side panel counter, Patates Frites label, Belgium issue, No. 471-A, 1965-66	90	150	325
Karrier Mobile Canteen, blue body, white interior, amber windows, roof knob rotates figure, working side panel counter, Joe's Diner label, No. 471-A, 1965-66, 3-5/8"	60	90	150
Karrier Mobile Grocery, light green body, grocery store interior, red/white Home Service decals, smooth hubs, rubber tires, No. 407-A, 1957-61, 3-5/8"	70	110	185
King Tiger Heavy Tank, tan and rust body, working turret and barrel, tan rollers and treads, German decals, No. 904, 1974-78, 6-1/8"	30	45	75
Kojak's Buick Regal, metallic bronze brown body, off-white interior, two opening doors, clear windows, chrome bumpers, grille and headlights, red taillights; accessories include Kojak and Crocker figures, No. 290, 1976-81, 5-3/4"	25	55	95
Lamborghini Miura, silver body, black interior, yellow/purple stripes and No. 7 decal, Whizz Wheels, No. 319-B, 1973-74, 3-3/4"	30	45	75

Name	Good	EX	Mint
Lamborghini Miura P400, w/red or yellow body, working hood, detailed engine, clear windows, jewel headlights, bull, Whizz Wheels, No. 342-A, 1970-72, 3-3/4"..............	40	60	100
Lancia Fulvia Zagato, metallic blue body, metallic green or yellow and black body, light blue interior, working hood and doors, folding seats, amber lights, cast wheels, No. 332-A, 1967-69, 3-5/8"................	25	35	70
Lancia Fulvia Zagato, orange body, black working hood and interior, Whizz Wheels, No. 372, 1970-72, 3-5/8"	15	25	40
Land Rover & Horse Box, blue/white Land Rover w/horse trailer in two versions: cast wheels (1968-74) and Whizz Wheels (1975-77); accessories include a mare and a foal; value is for an individual and complete set, No. 15-B, 1968-77	50	75	125
Land Rover 109WB, working rear doors, tan interior, spare on hood, plastic tow hook, No. 421, 1977-79, 5-1/4"	15	18	30
Land Rover and Ferrari Racer, red and tan No. 438 Land Rover and red No. 154 Ferrari F1 on yellow trailer, No. 17-A, 1963-67	60	90	150
Land Rover and Pony Trailer, two versions: green No. 438 Land Rover and a red and black No. 102 Pony trailer (1958-62); tan/cream No. 438 Land Rover and a pony trailer (1963-68); value given is for an individual and complete set, No. 2-A, 1958-62	50	90	175
Land Rover Breakdown Truck, red body, yellow canopy, chrome revolving spotlight, Breakdown Service decals, shaped hubs or Whizz Wheels, No. 477, 1965-77, 4-3/8"	25	35	60

Name	Good	EX	Mint
Land Rover Breakdown Truck, red body w/silver boom and yellow canopy, revolving spotlight, Breakdown Service decals, No. 417, 1960-65, 4-3/8"	35	55	90
Land Rover Pickup, yellow, green or metallic blue body, spare on hood, clear windows, sheet metal tow hook, smooth hubs, rubber tires, No. 406-A, 1957-62, 3-3/4"	45	70	100
Land Rover with Canopy, long, one-piece body w/clear windows, plastic interior, spare on hood, issued in numerous colors, No. 438, 1963-77, 3-3/4".................................	35	55	90
Lincoln Continental, metallic gold or light blue body, black roof, maroon plastic interior, working hood, trunk and doors, clear windows; accessories include TV w/picture strips for TV, No. 262, 1967-69, 5-3/4"	60	90	150
Lions of Longleat, black/white No. 438 Land Rover pickup w/lion cages and accessories, two versions: cast wheels, 1969-73; Whizz Wheels, 1974, each, No. 8-B, 1968-74	60	90	200
London Set, orange No. 226 Mini, Policeman, No. 418 London Taxi and No. 468 Outspan Routemaster bus, Whizz Wheels, No. 11-B, 1971-75	50	75	125
London Set, No. 425 London Taxi and No. 469 Routemaster B.T.A. bus in two versions: w/mounted Policeman (1980-81); without Policeman, (1982-on); value is for an individual and complete set, No. 11-C, 1980-82	25	35	60
London Set, No. 418 taxi and No. 468 bus w/policeman, in two versions: "Corgi Toys" on bus (1964-66); "Outspan Oranges" on bus (1967-68); values for an individual and complete set, No. 35, 1964-68	55	85	150

Name	Good	EX	Mint
London Transport Routemaster Bus, clear windows w/driver and conductor, released w/numerous advertiser logos, shaped or cast spoked wheels, No. 468, 1964-75, 4-1/2"	35	50	85
London Transport Routemaster Bus, long, clear windows, interior, some models have driver and conductor, released w/numerous advertiser logos, Whizz Wheels, No. 469-A, 1975, 4-7/8"	25	35	60
Lotus Elan S2 Hardtop, cream interior w/folding seats and tan dash, working hood, separate chrome chassis, issued in blue body w/white top or red body w/white top, No. 319-A, 1967-68, 2-1/4"	30	45	75
Lotus Elan S2 Roadster, working hood, plastic interior w/folding seats, shaped wheels and rubber tires, issued in metallic blue, "I've got a Tigger on my Back" decal on trunk, No. 318-A, 1965-67, 3-3/8"	30	50	110
Lotus Eleven, red, green or light green body, clear windshield and plastic headlights, smooth wheels, rubber tires, racing decals, No. 151-A, 1958-64, 2-1/4"	60	95	160
Lotus Elite, red body, white interior, two working doors, clear windshield, black dash, hood panel, grille, bumpers, base and tow hook, No. 315-C, 1976-78, 5-1/8"	15	18	35
Lotus Elite 22, dark blue body w/silver trim, Whizz Wheels, No. 382-B, 1970-75, 4-3/4"	15	18	35
Lotus Racing Car, black body and base, gold cast engine, roll bar, pipes, dash and mirrors, driver, gold cast wheels, in two versions, No. 154, 1973-82, 5-5/8"	25	35	60
Lotus Racing Set, three versions: "3" on No. 301 Elite and "JPS" on No. 154 Lotus racer; "7" on No. 301 Elite and "JPS" on racer; "7" on			

Name	Good	EX	Mint
No. 301 Elite and "Texaco" on No. 154 Lotus racer; value is for an individual and complete set, No. 32-B, 1976-79	30	45	95
Lotus Racing Team Set, 490 VW Breakdown Truck, red trailer w/No. 318 Lotus Elan Open Top, No. 319 Lotus Elan Hard Top, No. 155 Lotus Climax; includes pack of cones, sheet of racing number labels, No. 37-A, 1966-69	125	200	375
Lotus-Climax Racing Car, green body and base w/black/white No. 1 and yellow racing stripe decals, unpainted engine and suspension, w/driver, No. 155-A, 1964-69, 3-5/8"	25	35	65
Lotus-Climax Racing Car, orange/white body w/black/white stripe and No. 8 decals, unpainted cast rear wing, cast eight-spoke wheels, w/driver, No. 158-A, 1969-72, 3-5/8"	15	25	50
Lunar Bug, white body w/red roof, blue interior and wings, clear and amber windows, red working ramp, Lunar Bug decals, No. 806-A, 1970-72, 5"	25	40	95
M60 A1 Medium Tank, green/tan camouflage body, working turret and barrel, green rollers, white decals, No. 902, 1974-80, 4-3/4"	30	45	75
Mack Container Truck, yellow cab, red interior, white engine, red suspension, white ACL decals, No. 1106, 1972-78, 11-3/8"	30	50	80
Mack Esso Tank Truck, white cab and tank w/Esso labels, red tank chassis and fenders, No. 1152-A, 1971-75, 10-3/4"	20	40	80
Mack Exxon Tank Truck, white cab and tank, red tank chassis and fenders, red interior, chrome catwalk, Exxon labels, No. 1151-B, 1974-75, 10-3/4"	15	35	75

Name	Good	EX	Mint
Mack Trans Continental Semi, orange cab body and semi chassis and fenders, metallic light blue semi body, unpainted trailer rests, No. 1100, 1971-73, 10"	35	55	90
Mack-Priestman Crane Truck, red truck, yellow crane cab, red interior, black engine, Hi Lift and Long Vehicle or Hi-Grab labels, No. 1154-A, 1972-76, 9"	50	75	125
Magic Roundabout Musical Carousel, plastic roundabout w/Swiss musical movement, w/Dylan, Rosalie, Paul, Florence and Basil figures, rare, No. 852, 1973	275	425	750
Magic Roundabout Playground, contains No. 851 Train, No. 852 Carousel, six figures, seesaw, park bench, shrubs and fowers, rare, No. 853, 1973	295	500	900
Magic Roundabout Train, red and blue plastic three-piece train; accessories include figures of Mr. Rusty, Basil, Rosaile, Paul and Dougal, No. 851, 1973	70	195	350
Man From U.N.C.L.E. THRUSH-Buster, plastic interior, blue windows, two figures, two spotlights, dark metallic blue body, w/3-D Waverly ring, No. 497, 1966-68, 4-1/8"	80	120	250
Man From U.N.C.L.E. THRUSH-Buster, plastic interior, blue windows, two figures, two spotlights, cream body, w/3-D Waverly ring, No. 497, 1968-69, 4-1/8"	100	350	550

Man From U.N.C.L.E. THRUSH-Buster, No. 497.

Name	Good	EX	Mint
Marcos 3 Litre, working hood, detailed engine, black interior, Marcos decal, Whizz Wheels, issued in orange or metallic blue-green, No. 377, 1970-73, 3-3/8"	20	30	55
Marcos Mantis, metallic red body, opening doors, cream interior and headlights, silver gray lower body base, bumpers, hood panel, spoked wheels, No. 312-B, 1971-73, 4-1/4"	20	35	55
Marcos Volvo 1800 GT, issued w/either white body w/two green stripes or blue body w/two white stripes, plastic interior w/driver, spoked wheels, rubber tires, No. 324, 1966-69, 3-5/8"	25	40	70
Massey Ferguson 165 Tractor, gray engine and chassis, red hood and fenders w/black/white Massey Ferguson 165 decals, white grille, red cast wheels; makes engine sound, No. 66, 1966-72, 3"	35	55	90
Massey Ferguson 165 Tractor with Saw, red hood and fenders, gray engine and seat, cast yellow arm and control, chrome circular saw, No. 73, 1969-73, 3-1/2"	55	85	140
Massey Ferguson 165 Tractor with Shovel, gray chassis, red hood, fenders and shovel arms, unpainted shovel and cylinder, red cast wheels, black plastic tires, w/figure, No. 69, 1967-73, 5-1/8"	45	65	120
Massey Ferguson 50B Tractor, yellow body, black interior and roof, red plastic wheels w/black plastic tires, widows, No. 50-B, 1973-77, 4"	15	18	75
Massey Ferguson 65 Tractor, silver metal or plastic steering wheel, seat and grille, red engine hood, red metal or plastic wheels w/black rubber tires, No. 50-A, 1959-66, 3"	40	60	100

Name	Good	EX	Mint
Massey Ferguson 65 Tractor And Shovel, two versions: red bonnet w/either cream or gray chassis, red metal or orange plastic wheels; value is for each, No. 53, 1960-66, 4-3/4"	55	85	140
Massey Ferguson Combine, red body w/yellow metal blades, metal tines, black/white decals, yellow metal wheels, No. 1111-A, 1959-63, 6-1/2"	70	105	175
Massey Ferguson Combine, red body, plastic yellow blades, red wheels, No. 1111-B, 1968-73, 6-1/2"	60	90	150
Massey Ferguson Tipping Trailer, two versions: red chassis w/either yellow or gray tipper and tailgate, red metal or plastic wheels, value is for each, No. 51, 1959-65, 3-5/8"	10	18	35
Massey Ferguson Tractor and Tipping Trailer, No. 50 tractor and No. 51 trailer, no driver, No. 7, 1959-63	50	75	125
Massey Ferguson Tractor and Tipping Trailer, No. 50 MF tractor w/driver, No. 51 trailer, No. 29-A, 1965	50	75	125
Massey Ferguson Tractor with Fork, red cast body and shovel, arms, cream chassis, red plastic wheels, black rubber tires, Massey Ferguson 65 decals, w/driver, No. 57, 1963-67, 4-7/8"	60	90	150
Massey Ferguson Tractor with Shovel, two versions: either yellow and red or red and white body colors; value is for each, No. 54-B, 1974-81, 6"	20	30	50
Massey Ferguson Tractor with Shovel & Trailer, No. 54 MF tractor w/driver and shovel, No. 62 trailer, No. 32-A, 1965-66	30	75	150
Matra & Motorcycle Trailer, red No. 57 Talbot Matra Rancho w/two yellow and blue bikes on trailer, No. 25-C, 1980-81	15	20	35
Matra and Racing Car, black/yellow No. 457 Talbot Matra Rancho and No. 160 Hesketh yellow car w/Team Corgi trailer and decals, No. 26, 1983	15	35	65

Name	Good	EX	Mint
Mazda 4X4 Open Truck, blue body, white roof, black windows, no interior, white plastic wheels, No. 495, 1983, 4-7/8"	15	20	35
Mazda B-1600 Pickup Truck, issued in either blue and white or blue and silver bodies w/working tailgate, black interior, chrome wheels, No. 493, 1975-78, 4-7/8"	15	20	35
Mazda Camper Pickup, red truck and white camper w/red interior and folding supports, No. 415, 1976-78, 5-3/8"	15	25	451
Mazda Custom Pickup, orange body w/red roof, United States flag label, No. 440-B, 1979-80, 4-7/8"	15	18	30
Mazda Motorway Maintenance Truck, deep yellow body w/red base, black interior and hydraulic cylinder, yellow basket w/workman figure, No. 413-B, 1976-78, 6-1/8"	18	25	45
Mazda Pickup and Dinghy, two versions: red No. 493 Mazda w/"Ford" decals; or w/"Sea Spray" decals, dinghy and trailer, No. 28, 1975-78	25	35	60
McLaren M19A Racing Car, white body, orange stripes, chrome engine, exhaust and suspension, black mirrors, driver, Yardley McLaren No. 55 decals, Whizz Wheels, No. 151-B, 1972-77, 4-5/8"	15	25	40
McLaren M23 Racing Car, large 1:18-scale red and white body and wings w/red, white and black Texaco-Marlboro No. 5 decals, chrome pipes, suspension and mirrors, removable wheels, No. 191, 1974-77, 10-1/4"	30	60	110
Mercedes-Benz 220SE Coupe, metallic maroon or blue body, cream plastic interior, medium gray base, clear windows, silver bumpers, headlights, grille and license; accessories include plastic luggage and spare wheel in boot, No. 253-A, 1967-68, 4"	40	60	100

Name	Good	EX	Mint
Mercedes-Benz 220SE Coupe, cream, black or dark red body, red plastic interior, clear windows, working trunk, silver bumpers, grille and plate, spare wheel in boot, No. 230, 1962-64, 3-3/4"	40	60	100
Mercedes-Benz 240D, silver, blue or copper/beige body, working trunk, two doors, clear windows, plastic interior, two hook, chrome bumpers, grille and headlights, Whizz Wheels, No. 285, 1975-81, 5-1/4"	10	15	25
Mercedes-Benz 240D Rally, cream or tan body, black, red and blue lettering and dirt, red plastic interior, clear windows, black radiator guard and roof rack, opening doors, racing No. 5, No. 291, 1982, 5-1/8"	10	15	25
Mercedes-Benz 240D Taxi, orange body, orange interior, black roof sign w/red and white Taxi labels, black on door, No. 411-B, 1975-80, 5"	15	18	30
Mercedes-Benz 300SC Convertible, black body, black folded top, white interior, folding seat backs, detailed engine, chrome grille and wheels, lights, bumpers, No. 806-B, 1983, 5"	8	12	25
Mercedes-Benz 300SC Hardtop, maroon body, tan top and interior, open hood and trunk, clear windows, folding seat backs, top w/chrome side irons, No. 805-B, 1983, 5"	8	15	25
Mercedes-Benz 300SL, red body and base, tan interior, open hood and two gullwing doors, black dash, detailed engine, clear windows, chrome bumpers, No. 802-B, 1982, 5"	8	15	25
Mercedes-Benz 300SL, silver body, tan interior, black dash, clear windows, open hood and two gullwing doors, detailed engine, chrome bumpers, No. 811-B, 1983, 4-3/4"	8	15	25

Name	Good	EX	Mint
Mercedes-Benz 300SL Coupe, chrome body, red hardtop, red stripe, clear windows, '59-60 smooth wheels no suspension, '61-65 racing stripes, No. 304, 1959-65, 3-3/4"	45	65	130
Mercedes-Benz 300SL Roadster, blue or white body, yellow interior, plastic interior, smooth, shaped or cast wheels, racing stripes and number, driver, No. 303-A, 1958-66, 3-3/4"	45	75	140
Mercedes-Benz 350SL, white body, spoke wheels or metallic dark blue body solid wheels, pale blue interior, folding seats, detailed engine, No. 393, 1972-79, 3-3/4"	15	30	60
Mercedes-Benz 600 Pullman, metallic maroon body, cream interior and steering wheel, clear windshields, chrome grille, trim and bumpers, working windshield operators; includes instruction sheet, No. 247, 1964-69, 4-1/4"	40	60	100
Mercedes-Benz Ambulance, white body and base, red stripes and taillights, Red Cross and black and white ambulance labels, open rear door, white interior, no figures, No. 407-B, 1981, 5-3/4"	15	20	35
Mercedes-Benz Ambulance, four different foreign versions, white interior, open rear and two doors, blue windows and dome lights, chrome bumpers, grille and headlights, various labels; accessories include two attendant figures, No. 406-C, 1980-81, 5-3/4"	15	20	35
Mercedes-Benz and Caravan, truck and trailer in two versions: w/blue No. 285 Mercedes truck and No. 490 Caravan (1975-79); w/brown No. 285 Mercedes and No. 490 Caravan (1980-81); value is for each set, No. 24, 1975-81	15	30	50

Name	Good	EX	Mint
Mercedes-Benz C-111, orange main body w/black lower and base, black interior, vents, front and rear grilles, silver headlights, red taillights, Whizz Wheels, No. 388, 1971-74, 4"	15	20	45
Mercedes-Benz Fire Chief, light red body, black base, tan plastic interior, blue dome light, white Notruf 112 decals, red taillights, no tow hook, German export model, No. 284, 1982-83, 5"	15	25	40
Mercedes-Benz Police Car, white body w/two different hood versions, brown interior, polizei or police lettering, blue dome light, No. 412, 1975-80, 5"	15	18	30
Mercedes-Benz Refrigerator, yellow cab and tailgate, red semi-trailer, two-piece lowering tailgate and yellow spare wheel base, red interior, clear window, No. 1131, 1983, 8"	15	18	30
Mercedes-Benz Semi-Trailer, red cab and trailer, black chassis, No. 1144-C, 1983	15	18	30
Mercedes-Benz Semi-Trailer Van, black cab and plastic semi trailer, white chassis and airscreen, red doors, red-blue and yellow stripes, white Corgi lettering, No. 1129, 1983, 8-1/4"	15	18	30
Mercedes-Benz Tanker, tan cab, plastic tank body, black chassis, black and red Guinness labels, w/chrome or black plastic catwalk, clear windows, No. 1166, 1983, 7-1/4"	15	18	30
Mercedes-Benz Tanker, two different versions, white cab and tank, green chassis, chrome or black plastic catwalk, red/white/green 7-Up labels or Corgi Chemo labels, No. 1167, 1983, 7-1/4"	15	18	30
Mercedes-Benz Unimog & Dumper, yellow cab and tipper, red fenders and tipper chassis, charcoal gray cab chassis, black plastic mirrors or without, No. 1145-A, 1969-76, 6-3/4"	25	35	60
Mercedes-Benz Unimog 406, yellow body, red and green front fenders and bumpers, metallic charcoal gray chassis w/olive or tan rear plastic covers, red interior, No. 406-B, 1970-76, 3-3/4"	18	25	45
Mercedes-Faun Street Sweeper, orange body w/light orange or brown figure, red interior, black chassis and unpainted brushing housing and arm castings, No. 1117, 1980, 5"	15	25	40
Metropolis Police Car, metallic blue body, off white interior, white roof/stripes, two working doors, clear windows, chrome bumpers, grille and headlights, two roof light bars, City of Metropolis labels, No. 260-B, 1979-81, 6"	20	30	50
MG Maestro, yellow body, black trim, opaque black windows, black plastic grille, bumpers, spoiler, trim and battery hatch, clear headlights, AA Service label, No. 1009, 1983, 4-1/2"	15	20	35
MGA, red or metallic green body, cream seats, black dash, clear windshield, silver bumpers, grille and headlights, smooth or shaped wheels, No. 302-A, 1957-65, 3-3/4"	60	90	150
MGB GT, dark red body, pale blue interior, open hatch and two doors, jewel headlights, chrome grille and bumpers, orange taillights, spoked wheels, w/suitcase, No. 327, 1967-69, 3-1/2"	50	75	110
MGC GT, red body, black hood and base, black interior, open hatch and two doors, folding seat backs, luggage, orange taillights, Whizz Wheels, No. 378, 1970-73, 3-1/2"	50	75	125

Name	Good	EX	Mint
MGC GT, bright yellow body and base, black interior, hood and hatch, folding seats, luggage, jewel headlights, red taillights, No. 345-A, 1969, 3-1/2"	50	75	125
Midland Red Express Coach, red one-piece body, black roof w/shaped or smooth wheels, yellow interior, clear windows, silver grille and headlights, No. 1120, 1961-62, 5-1/2"	70	105	225
Military Set, set of three, No. 904 Tiger tank, No. 920 Bell Helicopter, No. 906 Saladin Armored Car, No. 17-B, 1975-80	60	90	150
Milk Truck and Trailer, blue and white No. 456 milk truck w/No. 101 trailer and milk churns, No. 21-A, 1962-66	60	130	250
Mini Camping Set, cream Mini, w/red/blue tent, grille and two figures, No. 38-B, 1977-78	25	40	65
Mini-Marcos GT850, white body, red-white-blue racing stripe and No. 7 labels, clear headlights, Whizz Wheels, opening doors and hood, No. 305-B, 1972-73, 2-1/8"	20	30	50
Mini-Marcos GT850, metallic maroon body, white name and trim decals, cream interior, open hood and doors, clear windows and headlights, Golden Jacks wheels, No. 341, 1966-70, 3-1/4"	30	45	75
Minissima, cream upper body, metallic lime green lower body w/black stripe centered, black interior, clear windows, headlights, No. 288, 1975-79, 2-1/4"	15	20	35
Monkeemobile, red body/base, white roof, yellow interior, clear windows, four figures, chrome grille, headlights, engine, orange taillights, No. 277-A, 1968-70, 4-3/4"	145	225	450
Monte Carlo Rally Set, three vehicle set, No. 326 Citroen, No. 318 Mini and No. 322 Land Rover rally cars, No. 38-A, 1965-67	295	450	900

Name	Good	EX	Mint
Morris Cowley, long, one-piece body in several colors, clear windows, silver lights, grille and bumper, smooth wheels, rubber tires, No. 202-A, 1959-60, 3-1/8"	45	75	140
Morris Cowley-Mechanical, long, same as 202-A but w/friction motor, available in off-white or green body, No. 202-M, 1956-59, 3-1/8"	55	95	170
Morris Marina 1.8 Coupe, metallic dark red or lime green body, cream interior, working hood and two doors, clear windshield, chrome grille and bumpers, Whizz Wheels, No. 306, 1971-73, 3-3/4"	15	30	60
Morris Mini-Cooper, yellow or blue body and base and/or hood, white roof and/or hood, two versions, red plastic interior, jewel headlights, flag, No. 1 and No. 7 decals, No. 227, 1962-65, 2-3/4"	80	150	300
Morris Mini-Cooper, red body and base, white roof, yellow interior, chrome spotlight, No. 37 and Monte Carlo Rally decals, No. 317, 1964-65, 2-7/8"	60	125	250
Morris Mini-Cooper Deluxe, black body/base, red roof, yellow and black wicker work decals on sides and rear, yellow interior, gray steering wheel, jewel headlights, No. 249, 1965-68, 2-3/4"	45	65	120
Morris Mini-Minor, one-piece body in dark or metallic blue or orange body, plastic interior, silver lights, grille and bumpers, red taillights, Whizz Wheels, No. 204-B, 1972-73, 2-7/8"	30	45	75

Monkeemobile, No. 277-A.

Name	Good	EX	Mint
Morris Mini-Minor, light blue or red body w/shaped and/or smooth wheels, plastic interior, silver bumpers, grille and headlights, No. 226, 1960-71, 2-3/4"	40	60	100
Morris Mini-Minor, sky blue body w/shaped and/or smooth wheels, plastic interior, silver bumpers, grille and headlights, No. 226, 1960-71	100	175	350
Motorway Ambulance, white body, dark blue interior, red-white-black Accident and Red Cross labels, dark blue windows, clear headlights, red die-cast base and bumpers, No. 700, 1973-79, 4"	10	15	30
Mr. McHenry's Trike, red and yellow trike and trailer; accessories include Mr. McHenry and Zebedee figures, No. 859, 1972-74	70	105	175
Muppet Vehicles, Kermit's Car, No. 2030	15	35	60
Muppet Vehicles, Miss Piggy's Sports Coupe, No. 2032	15	30	50
Muppet Vehicles, Fozzie Bear's Truck, No. 2031	15	30	50
Muppet Vehicles, Animal's Percussionmobile, No. 2033	15	30	50
Mustang Organ Grinder Dragster, yellow body w/green/yellow name, No. 39 and racing stripe decals, black base, green windshield, red interior, roll bar, w/driver, No. 166, 1971-74, 4"	20	30	50
NASA Space Shuttle, white body, two open hatches, black plastic interior, jets and base, unpainted retracting gear castings, black plastic wheels, w/satalite, No. 648, 1980, 6"	30	45	75
National Express Bus, variety of colors and label variations, No. 1168, 1983	8	15	25

Noddy's Car, No. 801-A.

Name	Good	EX	Mint
Noddy's Car, second issue: same as first issue except Master Tubby is substituted for Golliwog, No. 801-A, 1972-73, 3-3/4"	100	200	350
Noddy's Car, first issue: yellow body, red chassis and fenders, figures of Noddy, Big-Ears, and black, gray, or light tan face Golliwog, No. 801-A, 1969-71, 3-3/4"	200	400	600
Noddy's Car, yellow body, red chassis, Noddy alone, closed trunk w/spa	60	90	175
NSU Sport Prinz, metallic burgundy or maroon body, yellow interior, one-piece body, silver bumpers, headlights and trim, shaped wheels, No. 316-A, 1963-66, 3-1/4"	30	45	75
Off Road Set, No. 5 decal on No. 447 Jeep, blue boat, trailer, No. 36-C, 1983	15	20	45

Noddy's Car.

Open Top Disneyland Bus, No. 470-B.

Penguinmobile, No. 259. Photo Courtesy Mark Arruda.

Name	Good	EX	Mint
Olds Toronado and Speedboat, blue No. 276 Toronado, blue and yellow boat and chrome trailer, w/swordfish decals and three figures, No. 36-A, 1967-70	60	90	165
Oldsmobile 88 Staff Car, olive drab body, four figures, white decals, No. 357, 1964-66, 4-1/4"	50	75	125
Oldsmobile Sheriff's Car, black upper body w/white sides, red interior w/red dome light and County Sheriff decals on doors, single body casting, No. 237, 1962-66, 4-1/4"	50	75	125
Oldsmobile Super 88, three versions: light blue, light or dark metallic blue body w/white stripes, red interior, single body casting, No. 235, 1962-68, 4-1/4"	40	60	100
Oldsmobile Toronado, metallic copper, metallic blue or red one-piece body, cream interior, Golden jacks, gray tow hook, clear windows, bumpers, grille, headlights, No. 276-A, 1968-70, 4-3/16"	35	55	90
Oldsmobile Toronado, metallic medium or dark blue body, cream interior, one-piece body, clear windshield, chrome bumpers, grille, headlight covers, shaped or cast spoked wheels, No. 264-A, 1967-68, 4-1/8"	35	55	90
Opel Senator Doctor's Car, No. 332-B, 1980-81	10	15	25

Name	Good	EX	Mint
Open Top Disneyland Bus, yellow body, red interior and stripe, Disneyland labels, eight-spoked wheels or orange body, white interior and stripe, No. 470-B, 1977-78, 4-3/4"	30	50	95
OSI DAF City Car, orange/red body, light cream interior, textured black roof, sliding left door, working hood, hatch and two right doors, Whizz Wheels, No. 283, 1971-74, 2-3/4"	18	25	45
Penguinmobile, white body, black and white lettering on orange-yellow-blue decals, gold body panels, seats, air scoop, chrome engine, w/penguin figure, No. 259, 1979-80, 3-3/4"	20	30	65
Pennyburn Workmen's Trailer, blue body w/working lids, red plastic interior, three plastic tools, shaped wheels, plastic tires, No. 109, 1968-69, 3-1/8"	15	35	50

Name	Good	EX	Mint
Peugeot 505 STI, red body and base, red interior, blue-red-white Taxi labels, black grille, bmpers, tow hook, chrome headlights and wheels, opening doors, No. 373-B, 1981-82, 4-7/8".....................................8		15	25
Peugeot 505 Taxi, cream body, red interior, red, white and blue taxi decals, No. 450, 1983, 4-7/8" 8		15	25
Platform Trailer, in five versions: silver body, blue chassis; silver body, yellow chassis; blue body, red chassis; blue body, yellow chassis, No. 101, 1958-64, 4-3/8" 10		20	45
Plymouth Sports Suburban, dark cream body, tan roof, red interior, die-cast base, red axle, silver bumpers, trim and grille and rubber tires, No. 219, 1959-63, 4-1/4" 40		60	100
Plymouth Sports Suburban, pale blue body w/silver trim, red roof, yellow interior, gray die-cast base without rear axle bulge, shaped wheels, No. 445, 1963-65, 4-1/4" 40		60	100
Plymouth Suburban Mail Car, white upper, blue lower body w/red stripes, gray die-cast base without rear axle bulge, silver bumpers and grille, U.S. Mail decals, No. 443, 1963-66, 4-1/4" 55		85	140
Police Land Rover, white body, red and blue police stripes, black lettering, open rear door, opaque black windows, blue dome light, working roof light and siren, No. 1005, 1981, 5".....................................15		25	50

Name	Good	EX	Mint
Police Land Rover and Horse Box, white No. 421 Land Rover w/police decals and mounted policeman, No. 112 Horse Box, No. 44, 1978-80 30	45	75	
Police Vigilant Range Rover, white body, red interior, black shutters, blue dome light, two chrome and amber spotlights, black grille, silver headlights, Police decals, w/police figure, No. 461, 1972-79, 4" 25	35	60	
Pontiac Firebird, metallic silver body and base, red interior, black hood, stripes and convertible top, doors open, clear windows, folding seats, Golden Jacks wheels, No. 343, 1969-72, 4"..50	75	125	

Police Vigilant Range Rover, No. 461.

Popeye's Paddle Wagon, No. 802-A.

Plymouth Sports Suburban, No. 445.

Name	Good	EX	Mint
Pony Club Set, brown/white No. 421 Land Rover w/Corgi Pony Club decals, horse box, horse and rider, No. 47-B, 1978-80	30	45	75
Pop Art Mini-Motest, light red body and base, yellow interior, jewel headlights, orange taillights, yellow-blue-purple pop art and "Motest" decals; very rare, No. 349, 1969, 2-3/4"	1000	1500	2700
Popeye's Paddle Wagon, yellow and white body, red chassis, blue rear fenders, bronze and yellow stacks, white plastic deck, blue lifeboat w/Swee' Pea; includes figures of Popeye, Olive Oyl, Bluto and Wimpey, No. 802-A, 1969-72, 4-7/8"	195	300	525
Porsche 917, red or metallic blue body, black or gray base, blue or amber tinted windows and headlights, open rear hood, headlights, Whizz Wheels, No. 385, 1970-76, 4-1/4"	15	20	45
Porsche 92 Turbo, black body w/gold trim, yellow interior, four chrome headlights, clear windshield, taillight-license plate decal, opening doors and hatchback, No. 310, 1982, 4-1/2"	15	20	35
Porsche 924, bright orange body, dark red interior, black plastic grille, multicolored stripes, swivel roof spotlight, No. 303-C, 1980-81, 4-1/2"	10	15	25
Porsche 924, red or metallic light brown or green body, dark red interior, two doors open and rear window, chrome headlights, black plastic grille, racing No. 2, No. 321, 1978-81, 4-7/8"	10	25	50
Porsche 924 Police Car, white body w/different hood and doors versions, blue and chrome light, Polizei white on green panels or Police labels, "1" or "20" decals, No. 430-B, 1978-80, 4-1/4"	15	25	40

Name	Good	EX	Mint
Porsche Carrera 6, white upper body, red front hood, doors, upper fins and base, black interior, purple rear window, tinted engine cover, racing No. 60 decals, No. 371, 1970-73, 3-3/4"	25	35	60
Porsche Carrera 6, white body, red or blue trim, blue or amber tinted engine covers, black interior, clear windshield and canopy, red jewel taillights, No. 1 or No. 20 decals, No. 330, 1967-69, 3-7/8"	30	45	75
Porsche Targa 911S, metallic blue, silver-blue or green body, black roof w/or without stripe, orange interior, open hood and two doors, chrome engine and bumpers, Whizz Wheels, No. 382-A, 1970-75, 3-1/2"	25	35	60
Porsche Targa Police Car, white body and base, red doors and hood, black roof and plastic interior also comes w/an orange interior, unpainted siren, Polizei labels, No. 509, 1970-75, 3-1/2"	25	35	60
Porsche-Audi 917, white body, red and black No. 6, L and M, Porsche Audi and stripe labels or orange body, orange, two-tone green, white No. 6, racing driver, No. 397, 1973-78, 4-3/4"	15	20	35
Powerboat Team, white/red No. 319 Jaguar w/red/white boat on silver trailer, Team Corgi Carlsberg, Union Jack and No. 1 decals on boat, No. 38-C, 1980-81	25	35	60
Priestman Cub Crane, orange body, red chassis and two-piece bucket, unpainted bucket arms, lower boom, knobs, gears and drum castings, clear window, Hi-Grab labels, No. 1153-A, 1972-74, 9"	50	75	125
Priestman Cub Power Shovel, orange upper body and panel, yellow lower body, lock rod and chassis, rubber or plastic treads, pulley panel, gray boom, w/figure of driver, No. 1128, 1963-76, 6"	40	60	100

Name	Good	EX	Mint

Priestman Shovel and Carrier, No. 1128 cub shove and No. 1131 low loader machinery carrier, No. 27-A, 1963-72 ....90 135 225

Professionals Ford Capri, metallic silver body and base, red interior, black spoiler, grille, bumpers, tow hook and trim, blue windows, chrome wheels; includes figures of Cowley, Bodie and Doyle, No. 342-B, 1980-82, 5" 30 45 85

Psychedelic Ford Mustang, light blue body and base, aqua interior, red-orange-yellow No. 20 and flower decals, cast eight spoke wheels, plastic tire, No. 348-A, 1968, 3-3/4".....30 45 95

Public Address Land Rover, green No. 438 Land Rover body, yellow plastic rear body and loudspeakers, red interior, clear windows, silver bumper, grille and headlights; includes figure w/microphone and girl figure w/pamphlets, No. 472, 1964-66, 4" 50 75 145

Quartermaster Dragster, long, dark metallic green upper body w/green/yellow/black No. 5 and Quartermaster decals, light green lower body, w/driver, No. 162-A, 1971-73, 5-3/4" 30 45 75

RAC Land Rover, light or dark blue body, plastic interior and rear cover, gray antenna, RAC and Radio Rescue decals, No. 416, 1959-64, 3-3/4"..........60 90 150

Radio Luxembourg Dragster, long, blue body w/yellow, white and blue John Wolfe Racing, Radio Luxembourg and No. 5 decals, silver engine, w/driver, No. 170, 1972-76, 5-3/4" 30 45 85

Radio Roadshow Van, white body, red plastic roof and rear interior, opaque black windows, red-white-black Radio Tele Luxembourg labels, gray plastic loudspeakers and working radio in van, No. 1006, 1982, 4-3/4" 25 35 60

Name	Good	EX	Mint

RAF Land Rover, blue body and cover, one-piece body, sheet metal rear cover, RAF rondel decal, w/or without suspension, silver bumper, No. 351, 1958-62, 3-3/4" 60 90 150

RAF Land Rover & Bloodhound, set of three standard colored, No, 351 RAF Land Rover, No. 1115 Bloodhound Missile, No. 1116 Ramp and No. 1117 Trolley, No. 4, 1958-61 ....150 300 600

RAF Land Rover and Thunderbird, Standard colors, No. 350 Thunderbird Missile on Trolley and 351 RAF Land Rover, No. 3, 1958-63 ....100 150 300

Rambler Marlin Fastback, red body, black roof and trim, cream interior, clear windshield, folding seats, chrome bumpers, grille and headlights, opening doors, No. 263, 1966-69, 4-1/8" 35 55 90

Rambler Marlin with Kayak and Trailer, blue No. 263 Marlin w/roof rack, blue/white trailer, w/two kayaks, No. 10-A, 1968-69 ....100 150 250

Range Rover Ambulance, two different versions of body sides, red interior, raised roof, open upper and lower doors, black shutters, blue dome light, Ambulance label; includes stretcher and two ambulance attendants, No. 482, 1975-77, 4" 20 30 50

Raygo Rascal Roller, No. 459.

Name	Good	EX	Mint
Raygo Rascal Roller, dark yellow body, base and mounting, green interior and engine, orange and silver roller mounting and castings, clear windshield, No. 459, 1973-78, 4-7/8" 15		25	45
Red Wheelie Motorcycle, red plastic body and fender w/black/white/ yellow decals, black handlebars, kickstand and seat, chrome engine, pipes, flywheel-powered rear wheel, No. 171, 1982, 4" 10		15	25
Reliant Bond Rug 700 E.S., bright orange or lime green body, off white seats, black trim, silver headlights, red taillights, Bug label, No. 389, 1971-74, 2-1/2" 15		25	50
Renault 11 GTL, light tan or maroon body and base, red interior, opening doors and rear hatch, lifting hatch cover, folding seats, grille, No. 384-C, 1983, 4-1/4" 15		25	40
Renault 16, metallic maroon body, dark yellow interior, chrome base, grille and bumpers, clear windows, opening bonnet and hatch cover, Renault decal, No. 260-A, 1969, 3-3/4" 25		35	60
Renault 16TS, metallic blue body w/Renault decal on working hatch, clear windows, detailed engine, yellow interior, No. 202-B, 1970-72, 3-7/8" 20		25	50
Renault 5 Police Car, white body, red interior, blue dome light, black hood, hatch and doors w/white Police labels, orange taillights, aerial, No. 428-B, 1978-79, 3-7/8" 15		20	35
Renault 5 Turbo, bright yellow body, red plastic interior, black roof and hood, working hatch and two doors, black dash, chrome rear engine, racing No. 8 Cibie and other sponsor decals, No. 307-B, 1981, 3-3/4" 15		18	25

Name	Good	EX	Mint
Renault 5 Turbo, white body, red roof, red and blue trim painted on, No. 5 lettering, blue and white label on windshield, facom decal, No. 381-B, 1983, 4" 15		18	25
Renault 5TS, light blue body, red plastic interior, dark blue roof, dome light, S.O.S. Medicine lettering, working hatch and two doors, French issue, No. 293-A, 1980-81, 3-3/4" 20		35	70
Renault 5TS, metallic golden orange body, black trim, tan plastic interior, working hatch and two doors, clear windows and headlights, No. 293-A, 1977-80, 3-3/4" 15		18	30
Renault 5TS Fire Chief, red body, tan interior, amber headlights, gray antenna, black/white Sapeurs Pompiers decals, blue dome light, French export issue, No. 295, 1982, 3-3/4" 15		25	40
Renault Alpine 5TS, dark blue body, off white interior, red and chrome trim, clear windows and headlights, gray base and bumpers, black grille, opening doors and hatchback, No. 294, 1980, 3-3/4" 15		25	40
Renault Floride, one-piece dark red, maroon or lime green body, clear windows, silver bumper, grille, lights and plates, red taillights, smooth or shaped hubs, rubber tires, No. 222, 1959-65, 3-5/8" 35		55	95
Renegade Jeep, dark blue body w/no top, white interior, base and bumper, white plastic wheels and rear mounted spare, No. 447-B, 1983, 4" 8		15	25
Renegade Jeep with Hood, yellow body w/removable hood, red interior, base, bumper, white plastic wheels, side mounted spare, No. 8, No. 448, 1983, 4" 8		15	25

Name	Good	EX	Mint
Rice Beaufort Double Horse Box, long, blue body and working gates, white roof, brown plastic interior, two horses, cast wheels, plastic tires, No. 112, 1969-72, 3-3/8"	15	30	50
Rice Pony Trailer, cast body and chassis w/working tailgate, horse, in six color variations, smooth or shaped hubs, cast or wire drawbar, No. 102, 1958-65, 3-3/8"	20	30	50
Riley Pathfinder, red or dark blue one-piece body, clear windows, silver lights, grille and bumpers, smooth wheels, rubber tires, No. 205, 1956-61, 4"	45	65	125
Riley Pathfinder Police Car, black body w/blue/white Police lettering, unpainted roof sign, gray antenna, No. 209, 1958-61, 4"	50	75	135
Riley Pathfinder-Mechanical, w/friction motor and either red or blue body, No. 205-M, 1956-59, 4"	60	95	170
Riot Police Quad Tractor, white body and chassis, brown interior, red roof w/white panel, gold water cannons, gold spotlight w/amber lens, Riot Police and No. 6 labels, No. 422, 1977-80, 3-3/4"	15	20	35
Road Repair Unit, dark yellow Land Rover w/battery hatch and trailer w/red plastic interior w/sign and open panels, stripe and Roadwork labels, No. 1007, 1982, 10"	15	25	40
Rocket Age Set, set of eight standard models including: No. 350 Thunderbird Missile on Trolley, No. 351 RAF Land Rover, No. 352 RAF Staff Car, No. 353 Radar Scanner, No. 1106 Decca Radar Van and No. 1108 Bloodhound missile w/ramp, No. 6-A, 1959-60	325	650	1400
Rocket Launcher and Trailer, steel blue and red launcher, fires rocket, No. 907-A, 1975-80	25	35	60

Name	Good	EX	Mint
Roger Clark's Capri, white body, black hood, grille and interior, open doors, folding seats, chrome bumpers, clear headlights, red taillights, Racing No. 73, decal sheet, Whizz Wheels, No. 303-B, 1970-72, 4"	15	25	55
Rolls-Royce Corniche, different color versions w/light brown interior, working hood, trunk and two doors, clear windows, folding seats, chrome bumpers, No. 279, 1979, 5-1/2"	10	20	40
Rolls-Royce Silver Ghost, silver body/hood, charcoal and silver chassis, bronze interior, gold lights, box and tank, clear windows, dash lights, radiator, No. 9041-A, 1966-69, 4-1/2"	15	30	60
Rolls-Royce Silver Shadow, metallic blue or gold body, bright blue interior, working hood, trunk and two doors, clear windows, folding seats, spare wheel, No. 280-A3, 1974-78, 4-3/4"	25	40	65
Rolls-Royce Silver Shadow, metallic white upper/dusty blue lower body, working hood, trunk and two doors, clear windows, folding seats, chrome bumpers, Golden Jacks wheels, No. 273-A, 1970, 4-3/4"	30	50	95
Rolls-Royce Silver Shadow, metallic silver upper and metallic blue lower body, light brown interior, no hole in trunk for spare tire, Whizz Wheels, No. 280-A2, 1971-73, 4-3/4"	25	40	65
Rolls-Royce Silver Shadow, metallic silver upper and metallic blue lower body, light brown interior, hole in trunk for spare tire mounting, Whizz Wheels, No. 280, 1970, 4-3/4"	25	40	65
Routemaster Bus-Promotionals, different body and interior versions and labels promotional, No. 467, 1977, 4-7/8"	15	25	40

Name	Good	EX	Mint
Rover 2000, metallic blue w/red interior or maroon body w/yellow interior, gray steering wheel, clear windshields, No. 252, 1963-66, 3-3/4"	30	45	75
Rover 2000 Rally, two different versions, metallic dark red body, white roof, shaped wheels, No. 136 and Monte Carlo Rally decal, No. 322, 1965-66, 3-3/4"	50	95	175
Rover 2000 Rally, white body, red interior, black bonnet, No. 21 decal, spoked wheels, No. 322, 1965-66, 3-3/4"	55	100	200
Rover 2000TC, metallic olive green or maroon one-piece body, light brown interior, chrome bumpers/grille, jewel headlights, red taillights, Golden Jacks wheels, No. 275, 1968-70, 3-3/4"	30	45	75
Rover 2000TC, metallic purple body, light orange interior, black grille, one-piece body, amber windows, chrome bumpers and headlights, Whizz Wheels, No. 281, 1971-73, 3-3/4"	25	35	60
Rover 3500, three different body and interior versions, plastic interior, open hood, hatch and two doors, lifting hatch cover, No. 338, 1979, 5-1/4"	8	15	25
Rover 3500 Police Car, white body, light red interior, red stripes, white plastic roof sign, blue dome light, red and blue Police and badge label, No. 339, 1980, 5-1/4"	8	15	25

Name	Good	EX	Mint
Rover 3500 Triplex, white sides and hatch, blue roof and hood, red plastic interior and trim, detailed engine, red-white-lack No. 1, No. 340-B, 1981, 5-1/4"	8	15	20
Rover 90, one-piece body in several colors, silver headlights, grille and bumpers, smooth wheels, rubber tires; multiple colors available, No. 204, 1956-60, 3-7/8"	50	75	145
Rover 90-Mechanical, w/friction motor and red, green, gray or metallic green body, No. 204-M, 1956-59, 3-7/8"	60	90	170
Safari Land Rover and Trailer, black and white No. 341 Land Rover in two versions: w/chrome wheels, 1976; w/red wheels, 1977-80; came w/Waren and Lion figures, No. 31, 1976-80	20	30	60
Saint's Jaguar XJS, white body, red interior, black trim, Saint figure hood label, opening doors, black grille, bumpers and tow hook, chrome headlights, No. 320-B, 1978-81, 5-1/4"	30	45	85

Rover 3500, No. 338.

Saint's Jaguar XJS, No. 320-B.

Saint's Volvo P-1800, No. 258. Photo Courtesy Mark Arruda.

Name	Good	EX	Mint
Saint's Volvo P-1800, one-piece white body w/red Saint decals on hood, gray base, clear windows, black interior w/driver, Whizz Wheels, No. 201, 1970-72, 3-5/8"	55	95	200
Saint's Volvo P-1800, three versions of white body w/silver trim and different colored Saint decals on hood, driver, one-piece body, No. 258, 1965-69, 3-3/4"	55	85	175
Saladin Armored Car, olive drab body, swiveling turret and raising barrel castings, black plastic barrel end and tires, olive cast wheels, w/twelve shells, fires shells, No. 906, 1974-77, 3-1/4"	30	45	75
Scammell Carrimore Tri-deck Car Transporter, orange lower cab, chassis and lower deck, white upper cab and middle deck, blue top deck, red interior, black hydraulic cylinders, detachable rear ramp, No. 1146-A, 1970-73, 11"	35	60	130
Scammell Coop Semi-Trailer Truck, white cab and trailer fenders, light blue semi-trailer, red interior, gray bumper base, jewel headlights, black hitch lever, spare wheel, No. 1151-A, 1970, 9"	135	210	350
Scammell Ferrymasters Semi-Trailer Truck, white cab, red interior, yellow chassis, black fenders, clear windows, jewel headlights, cast wheels, plastic tires, No. 1147-A, 1969-72, 9-1/4"	60	90	150

Name	Good	EX	Mint
Scania Bulk Carrier, white cab, orange and white silos, clear windows, orange screen, black/orange Spillers Flour decals, Whizz Wheels, No. 1151-C, 1983, 5-5/8"	7	15	30
Scania Bulk Carrier, white cab, blue and white silos, ladders and catwalk, amber windows, blue British Sugar decals, Whizz Wheels, No. 1150-B, 1983, 5-5/8"	7	15	30
Scania Container Truck, yellow truck and box w/red Ryder Truck rental decals, clear windows, black exhaust stack, red rear doors, six-spoke Whizz Wheels, No. 1147-B, 1983, 5-1/2"	7	15	30
Scania Container Truck, blue cab w/blue and white box and rear doors, white deck, Securicor Parcels decals, in red or white rear door colors, No. 1148, 1983, 5-1/2"	7	15	30
Scania Container Truck, white cab and box w/BRS Truck Rental decals, blue windows, red screen, roof and rear doors, No. 1149, 1983, 5-1/2"	7	15	30
Scania Dump Truck, yellow truck and tipper w/black Wimpey decals, in two versions: either clear or green windows; six-spoked Whizz Wheels, No. 1153-B, 1983, 5-3/4"	7	15	30
Scania Dump Truck, white cab w/green tipper, black/green Barratt decals, black exhaust and hydraulic cylinders, six-spoked Whizz Wheels, No. 1152-B, 1983, 5-3/4"	7	15	30
Security Van, black body, blue mesh windows and dome light, yellow/black Security decals, Whizz Wheels, No. 424-B, 1976-79, 4"	7	15	25
Service Ramp, metallic blue and silver operable ramp, No. 1401, 1958-60	30	45	95

Name	Good	EX	Mint
Shadow-Ford Racing Car, black body and base w/white/black No. 17, UOP and American flag decals, cast chrome suspension and pipes, Embassy Racing label, No. 155-B, 1974-76, 5-5/8"	10	20	50
Shadow-Ford Racing Car, white body, red stripes, driver, chrome plastic pipes, mirrors and steering wheel, in two versions, Jackie Collins driver figure, No. 156, 1974-77, 5-5/8"	10	20	45
Shell or BP Garage, gas station/garage w/pumps and other accessories including five different cars; in two versions: Shell or B.P., rare; value is for each set, No. 25-A, 1963-65	295	550	1200
Shelvoke and Drewry Garbage Truck, long, orange or red cab, silver body w/City Sanitation decals, black interior, grille and bumpers, clear windows, No. 1116, 1979, 5-7/8"	15	25	40
Sikorsky Skycrane Army Helicopter, olive drab and yellow body w/Red Cross and Army decals, No. 923, 1975-78, 5-1/2"	15	20	40
Sikorsky Skycrane Casualty Helicopter, red and white body, black rotors and wheels, orange pipes, working rear hatch, Red Cross decals, No. 922, 1975-78, 6-1/8"	15	20	40
Silo & Conveyor Belt, w/yellow conveyor and Corgi Harvesting Co. decal on silo, No. 43, 1978-80	35	50	85
Silver Jubilee Landau, Landua w/four horses, two footmen, two riders, Queen and Prince figures, and Corgi dog, in two versions, No. 41, 1977-80	15	25	40
Silver Jubilee London Transport Bus, silver body w/red interior, no passengers, decals read "Woolworth Welcomes the World" and "The Queen's Silver, No. 471-B, 1977, 4-7/8"	15	18	30

Name	Good	EX	Mint
Silver Streak Jet Dragster, metallic blue body w/Firestone and flag decals on tank, silver engine, orange plastic jet and nose cone, No. 169, 1973-76, 6-1/4"	15	25	45
Silverstone Racing Layout, seven-vehicle set w/accessories; Vanwall, Lotus XI, Aston Martin, Mercedes 300SL, BRM, Ford Thunderbird, Land Rover Truck; another version has a No. 154 Ferrari substituted for Lotus XI, No. 15-A, 1963-66	400	700	1500
Simca 1000, chrome plated body, No. 8 and red-white-blue stripe decals, one-piece body, clear windshield, red interior, No. 315-A, 1964-66, 3-1/2"	30	45	75
Simon Snorkel Fire Engine, red body w/yellow interior, blue windows and dome lights, chrome deck, black hose reels and hydraulic cylinders, No. 1126, 1977-81, 10-1/2"	30	45	75
Simon Snorkel Fire Engine, red body w/yellow interior, two snorkel arms, rotating base, five firemen in cab and one in basket, various styles of wheels, No. 1127, 1964-76, 9-7/8"	35	55	90
Skyscraper Tower Crane, red body w/yellow chassis and booms, gold hook, gray loads of block, black/white Skyscraper decals, black tracks, No. 1155, 1975-79, 9-1/8" tall	30	45	75
Spider-Bike, medium blue body, one-piece body, dark blue plastic front body and seat, blue and red Spider-Man figure, amber windshield, black or white wheels, No. 266, 1979-83, 4-1/2"	40	60	85
Spider-Buggy, red body, blue hood, clear windows, dark blue dash, seat and crane, chrome base w/bumper and steps, silver headlights; includes Spider-Man and Green Goblin figures, No. 261-B, 1979-81, 5-1/8"	50	75	150

Spider-Buggy, No. 261-B. Photo Courtesy Mark Arruda.

Name	Good	EX	Mint
Spider-Copter, blue body w/Spider-Man decals, red plastic legs, tongue and tail rotor, black windows and main rotor, No. 928, 1979-81, 5-5/8"	30	45	85
Spider-Man Set, set of three: No. 266 Spider-Bike, No. 928 Spider-Copter and No. 261 Spider-Buggy, No. 23, 1980-81	80	160	350
Standard Vanguard, one-piece red and pale green body, clear windows, silver lights, grille and bumpers, smooth wheels, rubber tires, No. 207, 1957-61, 3-5/8"	50	75	125
Standard Vanguard RAF Staff Car, blue body, RAF decals, No. 352, 1958-62, 3-3/4"	55	85	140
Standard Vanguard-Mechanical, w/friction motor and yellow or off-white body w/black or gray base, or cream body w/red roof, No. 207-M, 1957-59, 3-5/8"	55	90	170
Starsky and Hutch Ford Torino, red one-piece body, white trim, light yellow interior, clear windows, chrome bumpers, grille and headlights, orange taillights; includes Starsky, Hutch and Bandit figures, No. 292, 1977-81, 5-3/4"	35	55	100
STP Patrick Eagle Racing Car, red body w/red, white and black STP and No. 20 decals, chrome lower engine and suspension, black plastic upper engine; includes Patrick Eagle driver figure, No. 159, 1974-77, 5-5/8"	20	30	50

Name	Good	EX	Mint
Stromberg Jet Ranger Helicopter, black body w/yellow trim and interior, clear windows, black plastic rotors, white/blue decals, No. 926, 1978-79, 5-5/8"	30	45	85
Studebaker Golden Hawk, second issue: gold painted body, shaped hubs, No. 211S, 1960-65	60	180	180
Studebaker Golden Hawk, first issue: gold plated body, white flashing, shaped hubs, No. 211S, 1960-65	55	85	140
Studebaker Golden Hawk, one-piece body in blue and gold or white and gold, clear windows, silver lights, grille and bumpers, smooth wheels, rubber tires, No. 211, 1958-60, 4-1/8"	55	85	140
Studebaker Golden Hawk-Mechanical, w/friction motor and white body w/gold trim, No. 211-M, 1958-59, 4-1/8"	70	105	175
Stunt Motorcycle, made for Corgi Rockets race track, gold cycle, blue rider w/yellow helmet, clear windshield, plastic tires, No. 681, 1971-72, 3"	70	105	175
SU-100 Medium Tank, olive and cream camouflage upper body, gray lower, working hatch and barrel, black treads, red star and No. 103 decals; twelve shells included, fires shells, No. 905, 1974-77, 5-5/8"	30	50	80
Sunbeam Imp Police Car, three versions, white or light blue body, tan interior, driver, black or white hood and lower doors, dome light, Police decals, cast wheels, No. 506, 1968-72, 3-1/4"	25	45	85
Sunbeam Imp Rally, metallic blue body w/white stripes, Monte Carlo Rally and No. 77 decals, cast wheels, No. 340-A, 1967-68, 3-3/8"	20	45	85
Super Karts, two carts, orange and blue, Whizz Wheels in front, slicks on rear, silver and gold drivers, No. 46, 1982	15	18	30

Name	Good	EX	Mint
Superman Set, set of three: No. 265 Supermobile, No. 925 Daily Planet Helicopter and No. 260 Metropolis Police Car, No. 21-C, 1979-81	70	120	225
Supermobile, blue body, red, chrome or gray fists, red interior, clear canopy, driver, chrome arms w/removable "striking fists", No. 265, 1979-81, 5-1/2"	30	45	75
Supervan, silver van w/Superman decals, working rear doors, chrome spoked wheels, No. 435-A, 1978-81, 4-5/8"	15	25	50
Surtees TS9 Racing Car, black upper engine, chrome lower engine, pipes and exhaust, driver, Brook Bond Oxo-Rob Walker decals, eight-spoke Whizz Wheels, No. 150-B, 1972-74, 4-5/8"	15	20	40
Surtees TS9B Racing Car, red body w/white stripes and wing, black plastic lower engine, driver, chrome upper engine, pipes, suspension, eight-spoke wheels, No. 153, 1972-74, 4-3/8"	15	20	40
Talbot-Matra Rancho, red and black, green and black or white and blue body, working tailgate and hatch, clear windows, plastic interior, black bumpers, grille and tow hook, No. 457, 1981-84, 4-3/4"	10	15	25

Tarzan Set, No. 36-B.

Name	Good	EX	Mint
Tandem Disc Harrow, yellow main frame, red upper frame, working wheels linkage, unpainted linkage and cast discs, black plastic tires, No. 71, 1967-72, 3-5/8"	15	20	45
Tarzan Set, metallic green No. 421 Land Rover w/trailer and Dinghy; cage, five figures and other accessories, No. 36-B, 1976-78	100	150	275
Thunderbird Bermuda Taxi, white body w/blue, yellow or green plastic canopy w/red fringe, yellow interior, driver, yellow and black labels, No. 430-A, 1962-65, 4"	50	75	125
Thunderbird Missile and Trolley, ice blue or silver missile, RAF blue trolley, red rubber nose cone, plastic tow bar, steering front and rear axles, No. 350, 1958-62, 5-1/2"	55	85	165
Thwaites Tusker Skip Dumper, yellow body, chassis and tipper, driver and seat, hydraulic cylinder, red wheels, black tires two sizes, name labels, Whizz Wheels, No. 403, 1974-79, 3-1/8"	10	20	40
Tiger Mark I Tank, tan and green camouflage finish, German emblem, swiveling turret and raising barrel castings, black plastic barrel end, antenna; includes twelve shells, fires shells, No. 900, 1973-78, 6"	30	45	75
Tipping Farm Trailer, cast chassis and tailgate, red plastic tipper and wheels, black tires, in two versions, No. 56-B, 1977-80, 5-1/8"	10	15	25
Tipping Farm Trailer, red working tipper and tailgates, yellow chassis, red plastic wheels, black tires, w/detachable raves, No. 62, 1965-72, 4-1/4"	10	15	30
Tour de France Set, white and black body Renault w/Paramount Film roof sign, rear platform w/cameraman and black camera on tripod, plus bicycle and rider, No. 13-B, 1968-72	60	90	200

Name	Good	EX	Mint
Tour de France Set, w/white No. 373 Peugeot, red and yellow Raleigh and Total logos, Racing cycles, includes manager figures, No. 13-C, 1961-82	25	45	90
Touring Caravan, white body w/blue trim, white plastic open roof and door, pale blue interior, red plastic hitch and awning, No. 490-B, 1975-79, 4-3/4"	15	25	40
Tower Wagon and Lamp Standard, red No. 409 Jeep Tower wagon w/yellow basket, workman figure and lamp post, No. 14-A, 1961-65	40	60	120
Toyota 2000 GT, metallic dark blue or purple body, cream interior, one-piece body, red gear shift and antenna, two red and two amber taillights, Whizz Wheels, No. 375, 1970-72, 4"	15	30	55
Tractor and Beast Carrier, No. 55 Fordson tractor, figures and No. 58 beast carrier, No. 33-A, 1965-66	65	100	165
Tractor with Shovel and Trailer, standard colors, No. 69 Massey Ferguson Tractor and No. 62 Tipping Trailer, No. 9, 1968-73	65	100	165
Tractor, Trailer and Field Gun, tan tractor body and chassis, trailer body, base and opening doors, gun chassis and raising barrel castings, brown plastic interior; twelve shells included, fires shells, No. 909, 1976-80, 10-3/4"	30	50	80
Transporter & Six Cars, Scammell transporter w/six cars: No. 180 Mini DeLuxe, No. 204 Mini, No. 339 Mini Rally, No. 201 The Saint's Volvo, No. 340 Sunbeam Imp, No. 378 MGC GT; includes bag of cones and leaflet, No. 48-B, 1970-73	250	450	900
Transporter and Six Cars, first issue: No. 1138 Ford 'H' Series Transporter w/six cars, No. 252 Rover 2000, blue No. 251 Hillman Imp, No. 440			

Name	Good	EX	Mint
Ford Cortina Estate, No. 180 Mini w/'wickerwork', metallic maroon No. 204 Mini, and No. 321 Mini Rally ('1966 Monte Carlo Rally') racing No. 2; second issue: same as first issue except No. 251 Hillman is metallic gold, No. 204 Mini is blue, No. 321 Mini is substituted for No. 333 SUN/RAC Rally Mini w/autographs on roof, No. 48-A, 1966-69	225	365	700
Triumph Acclaim Driving School, yellow or red body/base, Corgi Motor School decals, black roof mounted steering wheel steers front wheels, clear windows, No. 278, 1982-83, 4-3/4"	15	25	50
Triumph Acclaim Driving School, dark yellow body w/black trim, black roof mounted steering wheel steers front wheels, clear windows, mirrors, bumpers, No. 277-B, 1982, 4-3/4"	15	25	40
Triumph Acclaim HLS, metallic peacock blue body/base, black trim, light brown interior, clear windows, mirrors, bumpers, vents, tow hook, No. 276-B, 1981-83, 4-3/4"	15	18	30
Triumph Herald Coupe, blue or gold top and lower body, white upper body, red interior, clear windows, silver bumpers, grille, headlights, shaped hubs, No. 231, 1961-66, 3-1/2"	35	65	110
Triumph TR2, cream body w/red seats, light green body w/white or cream seats, one-piece body, clear windshield, silver grille, No. 301-A, 1956-59, 3-1/4"	70	105	175
Triumph TR3, metallic olive or cream body, red seats, one-piece body, clear windshield, silver grille, bumpers and headlights, smooth or shaped hubs, No. 305-A, 1960-62, 2-1/4"	60	90	150

Name	Good	EX	Mint
Trojan Heinkel, issued in mauve, red, orange or lilac body, plastic interior, silver bumpers and headlights, red taillights, suspension, smooth spun or detailed cast wheels, No. 233-A, 1962-72, 2-1/2"	35	55	95
Tyrrell P34 Racing Car, without yellow decals, First National Bank labels, w/driver in red or orange helmet, No. 162-B, 1978-79	20	30	55
Tyrrell P34 Racing Car, dark blue body and wings w/yellow stripes, No. 4 and white Elf and Union Jack decals, chrome plastic engine, w/driver in red or blue helmet, No. 161, 1977, 4-3/8"	20	30	55
Tyrrell-Ford Racing Car, dark blue body w/blue/black/white Elf and No. 1 decals, chrome suspension, pipes, mirrors, Jackie Stewart driver figure, No. 158-B, 1974-78, 4-5/8"	18	25	50
U.S. Racing Buggy, white body w/red/white/blue stars, stripes and USA No. 7 decals, red base, gold engine, red plastic panels, driver, No. 167, 1972-74, 3-3/4"	18	25	50
Unimog Dump Truck, yellow cab, chassis, rear frame and blue tipper, fenders and bumpers, red interior, no mirrors, gray tow hook, hydraulic cylinders, No. 409-B 2, 1976-77, 4"	20	30	50
Unimog Dump Truck, blue cab, yellow tipper, fenders and bumpers, metallic charcoal gray chassis, red interior, black mirrors, gray tow hook, No. 409-B 1, 1971-73, 3-3/4"	20	30	50

Name	Good	EX	Mint
Unimog Dumper & Priestman Cub Shovel, standard colors, No. 1145 Mercedes-Benz unimog w/Dumper and 1128 Priestman Cub Shovel, No. 2-B, 1971-73	70	105	175
Unimog with Snowplow (Mercedes-Benz), 6" four different body versions, red interior, cab, rear body, fender-plow mounting, lower and charcoal upper chassis, rear fenders, No. 1150-A, 1971-76	30	45	75
Vanwall Racing Car, clear windshield, unpainted dash, silver pipes and decals, smooth wheels, rubber tires, in three versions: green body or red body w/silver or yellow seats, No. 150-A, 1957-65, 3-3/4"	35	55	120
Vauxhall Velox, one-piece body in red, cream, yellow or yellow and red body, clear windows, silver lights, grille and bumpers, smooth wheels, rubber tires, No. 203, 1956-60, 3-3/4"	50	75	150
Vauxhall Velox-Mechanical, w/friction motor; orange, red, yellow or cream body, No. 203-M, 1956-59, 3-3/4"	60	90	170
Vegas Ford Thunderbird, orange/red body and base, black interior and grille, open hood and trunk, amber windshield, white seats, driver, chrome bumper, No. 348-B, 1980-81, 5-1/4"	25	40	75

Vauxhall Velox, No. 203.

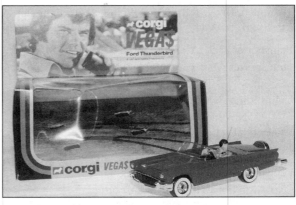

Vegas Ford Thunderbird, No. 348-B. Photo Courtesy Mark Arruda.

Name	Good	EX	Mint
VM Polo Mail Car, bright yellow body, black DBP and Posthorn labels, German issue, No. 289-B, 1976-80	25	35	60
Volkswagen 1200, dark yellow body, white roof, red interior and dome light, unpainted base and bumpers, black and white ADAC Strassenwacht, Whizz Wheels, No. 383-A, 1970-76, 3-1/2"	60	90	150
Volkswagen 1200, seven different color and label versions, plastic interior, one-piece body, silver headlights, red taillights, die-cast base and bumpers, No. 383-A, 1970-76, 3-1/2"	20	45	85
Volkswagen 1200 Driving School, metallic red or blue body, yellow interior, gold roof mounted steering wheel that steers, silver headlights, red taillights, No. 400, 1974-75, 3-1/2"	25	35	60
Volkswagen 1200 Police Car, two different body versions made for Germany, Netherlands and Switzerland, blue dome light in chrome collar, Polizei or Politie decals, No. 492, 1966-69, 3-1/2"	40	60	100
Volkswagen 1200 Rally, light blue body, off-white plastic interior, silver headlights, red taillights, suspension, Whizz Wheels, No. 384-B, 1976-77, 3-1/2"	20	30	50
Volkswagen Breakdown Van, tan or white body, red interior and equipment boxes, clear windshield, chrome tools, spare wheels, red VW emblem, no lettering, No. 490-A, 1966-72, 4"	50	75	125
Volkswagen Delivery Van, white upper and red lower body, plastic red or yellow interior, silver bumpers and headlights, red VW emblem, shaped wheels, No. 433, 1962-64, 3-1/4"	55	85	140
Volkswagen Driving School, metallic blue body, yellow interior, gold roof mounted steering wheel that steers, silver headlights, red taillights, No. 401, 1975-77, 3-1/2"	25	40	70
Volkswagen East African Safari, light red body, brown interior, working front and rear hood, clear windows, spare wheel on roof steers front wheels, jewel headlights, w/rhinoceros figure, No. 256, 1965-69, 3-1/2"	60	130	285
Volkswagen Kombi Bus, off-green upper and olive green lower body, red interior, silver bumpers and headlights, red VW emblem, shaped wheels, No. 434, 1962-66, 3-3/4"	50	75	125
Volkswagen Military Personnel Carrier, olive drab body, white decals, driver, No. 356, 1964-66, 3-1/2"	55	95	180
Volkswagen Pickup, dark yellow body, red interior and rear plastic cover, silver bumpers and headlights, red VW emblem, shaped wheels, No. 431, 1964-66, 3-1/2"	45	65	110
Volkswagen Police Car/Foreign Issues, five different versions, one-piece body, red interior, dome light, silver headlights, red taillights, clear windows, Whizz Wheels, No. 373-A, 1970-76, 3-1/2"	60	90	150
Volkswagen Tobler Van, light blue body, plastic interior, silver bumpers, Trans-o-lite headlights and roof panel, shaped wheels, rubber tires, No. 441-A, 1963-67, 3-1/2"	55	85	140
Volvo Concrete Mixer, yellow or orange cab, red or white mixer w/yellow and black stripes, rear chassis, chrome chute and unpainted hitch casings, No. 1156, 1977-81, 8-1/4"	30	45	75

Name	Good	EX	Mint
Volvo P-1800, one-piece body light brown, dark red, pink or dark red body, clear windows, plastic interior, shaped wheels, rubber tires, No. 228, 1962-65, 3-1/2" 40		60	100
VW 1500 Karmann-Ghia, cream, red or gold body, plastic interior and taillights, front and rear working hoods, clear windshields, silver bumpers; includes spare wheel and plastic suitcase in trunk, No. 239, 1963-68, 3-1/2" 35		55	90
VW Polo, apple green or bright yellow body, black DBP and posthorn (German Post Office) decals, off white interior, black dash, No. 289-A, 1976-79, 3-3/4" 25		40	65
VW Polo, metallic light brown body, off-white interior, black dash, clear windows, silver bumpers, grille and headlights, No. 302-C, 1979-81, 3-3/4" 15		18	30
VW Polo Auto Club Car, yellow body, white roof, yellow dome light, ADAC Strassenwacht labels, No. 489-B, 1977-79 15		25	40
VW Polo German Auto Club Car, yellow body, off-white interior, black dash, silver bumpers, grille and headlights, white roof, yellow dome light, No. 489-A, 1977-79, 3-1/2" 25		35	60

Name	Good	EX	Mint
VW Polo Police Car, white body, green hood and doors, black dash, silver bumpers, grille and headlights, white roof, blue dome light, No. 489, 1976-80, 3-1/2" 15		25	40
VW Polo Turbo, cream body, red interior w/red and orange trim, working hatch and two door castings, clear windshield, black plastic dash, No. 309, 1982, 3-3/4" 15		18	30
VW Racing Tender and Cooper, white No. 490 VW breakdown truck w/racing decals, blue No. 156 Cooper on trailer, No. 6-B, 1967-69 50		75	150
VW Racing Tender and Cooper Maserati, two versions: tan or white No. 490 VW breakdown truck, and No. 159 Cooper-Maserati on trailer; value is for each set, No. 25-B, 1970-71 50		75	150
Warner & Swasey Crane, yellow cab and body, blue chassis, blue/yellow stripe decals, red interior, black steering wheel, silver knob, gold hook, No. 1101, 1975-81, 8-1/2" 30		45	75
White Wheelie Motorcycle, white body w/black/white police decals, No. 172, 1982, 4" 15		20	35
Wild Honey Dragster, yellow body w/red/yellow Wild Honey and Jaguar Powered decals, green windows and roof, black grille, driver, Whizz Wheels, No. 164, 1971-73, 3"...............25		40	65

Dinky

Meccano, founded in 1900 by Frank Hornby, began production of Model Miniatures in December 1933. Originally designed to accompany Hornby model trains, Model Miniatures, later known as Dinky Toys, went on to become one of the best selling British toys of the 1930s-50s. In the United States, Dinky Toys were a competitor to Tootsietoys.

Over time, the Dinky line expanded to include over 1,000 cars, buses, ships, airplanes, military vehicles and farm machinery. Because they were intended as accessories on a train platform, models of pedestrians, street signs and animals were also made.

As with many toy manufacturers, Dinky halted production during World War II. The Dinky toys that were available in 1945 were prewar left-overs. Postwar Dinky models were not introduced until 1946. (Collectors should note that prewar models were used in conjunction with postwar items and it is difficult to date items made during this period.) Any hopes for a quick return to the prewar production went unfulfilled. The metal alloys used in toy production were needed for domestic products and export projects on which the British economy depended for its survival. By 1947, Dinky had introduced Supertoys—the postwar boom was in full swing.

The 1950s were a big decade for Dinky Toys. Because the original numbering system had become cumbersome for the growing line, a new, easier to follow system was developed. The new system was made up of a three-digit numbers as opposed to a one-, two- or three-digit number followed by a letter. The next big change for Dinky was the introduction of Corgi, the first British die-cast manufacturer to pose a real threat to Dinky's dominance.

The introduction of Hot Wheels in 1968 rocked the entire die-cast world. Dinky countered this with the introduction of Speedwheels. These chrome wheels became the standard Dinky wheel. Fantasy cars began to replace the realistic look of vehicles in the Dinky Line. By the 1970s, Mecanno was in financial trouble.

After being bought and sold several times, the original factory on Binns Road in Liverpool, England was closed on November 30, 1979.

Market Update

There is an active market for Dinky die-cast, but finding a Dinky Toys in pristine condition can be difficult. Replacement parts for Dinky toys are readily available to collectors. While collectors can restore their beloved Dinkys, others may replace absent parts and sell the model at a Mint condition price. Collectors new to the hobby should educate themselves by attending toy shows, visit antique malls and shops and correspond with other collectors.

Clubs

Dinky Toy Club of America
P.O. Box
Highland, Maryland 20777

AIRCRAFT

Name	Good	EX	Mint
A.W. Ensign, forty-seat airliner, olive/dark green, G-AZCA, No. 62x, 1945-49	95	275	350
A.W. Ensign, camouflaged, dark variation, No. 68a, 1940	150	300	450
A.W. Ensign, A.W. Airliner, silver, G-ADSV, No. 62P, 1945-49	65	145	175
Airspeed Envoy, King's Aeroplane, red, blue, and silver, G-AEXX, No. 62k, 1938-40	70	200	300
Airspeed Envoy, silver, G-ACVI, No. 62m, 1938-41	55	175	250
Airspeed Envoy, light transport, red, G-ATMH, No. 62m, 1945-49	40	125	200
Amiot 370, No. 64a, 1939-48	70	130	200
Arc-en-Ciel, No. 60a, 1935-40	200	375	450
Armstrong Whitworth Ensign, silver, G-ADSR, No. 62p, 1938-41	90	175	250
Atalanta, camouflaged, dark variation, No. 66a, 1940	200	450	650
Atalanta (Imperial Airways Liner), gold, G-ABTI, No. 60a, 1934-41	150	375	500
Autogyro, gold, blue rotor, w/pilot, No. 60f, 1934-41	90	180	250
Autogyro, Army cooperation, silver, RAF roundels, No. 66f, 1940	125	250	350
Avro Vulcan Delta Wing Bomber, No. 749/992, 1955-56	800	1500	4500
Avro York, silver, G-AGJC, No. 70a/704, 1946-59	45	155	200
Beechcraft Baron, No. 715, 1968-76	25	60	90
Beechcraft Bonanza, No. 710, 1965-76	20	55	80
Beechcraft T42A, No. 712, 1972-77	30	75	110
Bell 47 Police Helicopter, No. 732, 1974-80	10	30	55
Bloch 220, No. 64b, 1939-48	75	150	250
Boeing 737, No. 717, 1970-75	20	45	90
Boeing Flying Fortress, "Long Range Bomber" under wings, No. 62g, 1945-48	50	125	225
Boeing Flying Fortress, silver, USAAC stars on wings, No. 62g, 1939-41	100	200	300

Name	Good	EX	Mint
Breguet Corsair, No. 60d, 1935-40	100	200	300
Bristol 173 Helicopter, turquoise, red rotors, G-AUXR, No. 715, 1956-63	20	60	95
Bristol Blenheim, No. 62B	60	85	130
Bristol Blenheim, medium bomber; silver, red, and blue roundels, No. 62B, 1945-48	35	95	120
Bristol Blenheim, silver, roundels w/outer yellow ring, No. 62b/62d, 1940-41	60	140	175
Bristol Brittania, silver, blue line, CF-CZA, No. 998, 1959-65	50	250	500
Cierva Autogyro, No. 60f, 1935-40	100	250	250
Clipper III Flying Boat, silver, NC16736, No. 60w, 1938-41	150	250	400
Clipper III Flying Boat, silver, no registration, No. 60w, 1945-49	75	175	250
D.H. Albatross, camouflaged, dark variation, No. 68b, 1940	150	300	450
D.H. Albatross, silver, G-AEVV, No. 62r, 1939-41	75	275	400
D.H. Albatross, Frobisher Class Liner, silver, G-AFDI, No. 62w, 1939-41	75	275	400
D.H. Albatross, four-engine liner; gray, G-ATPV, No. 62R, 1945-49	75	170	250
D.H. Comet Jetliner, silver wings, G-ALYX, No. 702/999, 1954-65	35	100	200
D.H. Comet Racer, yellow, G-RACE, No. 60g, 1946-49	50	110	155
D.H. Comet Racer, silver, G-ACSR, No. 60g, 1935-40	60	125	225
D.H. Sea Vixen, gray, white undersides, No. 738, 1960-65	30	65	110
Dewoitine 500, No. 60e, 1935-40	100	200	300
Dewoitine D338, No. 61a/64, 1937-46	225	350	500
Douglas DC3, silver, PH-ALI, No. 60t, 1938-41	125	300	650
Empire Flying Boat, silver, G-ADUV, solid front to hull, No. 60r, 1937-41	150	325	450
Empire Flying Boat, MAIA, silver, G-AVKW, No. 700, 1937-41	150	275	350
Empire Flying Boat, Atlantic Flying Boat, blue, cream wings, G-AZBP, No. 60x, 1938-40	350	600	1000

Name	Good	EX	Mint
Empire Flying Boat, silver, G-ADUV, hollowed out front to hull, No. 60r, 1945-49	90	175	250
Fairy Battle, camouflaged, one roundel, light variation, No. 60s, 1937-41	50	125	200
Fairy Battle, silver, "Fairy Battle Bomber" under wing, No. 60n, 1937-41	40	100	140
General Monospar, camouflaged, dark, No. 66e, 1940	90	300	350
General Monospar, silver, blue wing tips, No. 60e, 1934-41	75	225	300
Gloster Gladiator, silver, RAF roundels, no words under wing, No. 60p, 1937-40	90	175	225
Gloster Javelin, green/gray camouflage, No. 735, 1956-65	15	50	90
Gloster Meteor, silver, RAF roundels, No. 70e/732, 1946-62	10	25	35
Hanriot 180M, No. 61e, 1937-40	90	150	225
Hawker Harrier, No. 722, 1970-80	25	65	95
Hawker Hunter, green/gray camouflage, No. 736, 1955-63	15	45	85
Hawker Hurricane, three-blade prop; red, white, and blue roundels, No. 62S, 1945-49	40	95	130
Hawker Hurricane, silver, no undercarriage, No. 62h, 1939-41	30	70	115
Hawkr Hurricane IIc, No. 718, 1972-75	50	95	155
Hawker Siddeley HS 125, No. 723/728, 1970-75	20	50	75
Hawker Tempest II, silver, RAF roundels, flat spinner, No. 70b/730, 1946-55	15	45	75
Henriot 180T, No. 60c, 1935-40	110	170	225
Junkers JU87B Stuka, No. 721, 1969-80	40	75	145
Junkers JU89, high speed monoplane, green/dark green, D-AZBK, No. 62y, 1938-41	100	275	350
Junkers JU89, high speed monoplane, silver, G-ATBK, No. 62Y, 1945-49	70	160	225
Junkers JU89 Heavy Bomber, black, German cross, No. 67a, 1941	100	400	600
Junkers JU90 Airliner, silver, D-AIVI, No. 62n, 1938-40	90	250	325
Leopard Moth, light green, G-ACPT, No. 60b, 1934-41	50	140	180
Leopard Moth, camouflaged, dark, No. 66b, 1940	70	225	300
Lockheed Constellation, No. 60c/892, 1956-63	90	200	350
Lockheed P-80 Shooting Star, silver, USAF stars, No. 701/733, 1947-62	10	20	30
M.D. F-4 Phantom, No. 725/727/73, 1972-77	70	125	175
Mayo Composite, No. 63, 1939-41	200	450	750
ME BI 109, motorized, No. 726, 1972-76	50	100	175
Mercury Seaplane, silver, G-AVKW, No. 700, 1949-57	35	75	110
Mercury Seaplane, silver, G-ADHJ, No. 63b, 1939-41	50	100	175
Mitsubishi A65M Zero, motorized, No. 739, 1975-78	75	150	225
MRCA Tornado, No. 729, 1974-76	35	90	155
Mystere IV, No. 60a/800, 1957-63	30	75	110
Nord Noratlas, No. 804, 1960-64	125	250	400
P1B Lightning, silver, RAF roundels, No. 737, 1959-69	20	55	100
Percival Gull, white, blue wing tips, No. 60c, 1934-41	70	150	225
Percival Gull, Light Tourer, light green, No. 66c, 1945-48	65	125	150
Percival Gull, camouflaged, dark, No. 66c, 1940	100	225	275
Potez 56, No. 61b, 1937-40	125	200	270
Potez 58, No. 60b/61d, 1935-40	100	260	350
Potez 58 Sanitaire, No. 61d, 1937-40	110	175	250
Potez 63, No. 64c, 1939-48	150	250	400
Potez 662, No. 64d, 1939-40	125	250	400
Republic P47 Thunderbolt, motorized, No. 734, 1975-78	75	175	250
S.E. Caravelle Airliner, Air France, F-BGNY, starboard wing, No. 997, 1962-69	70	150	250
Sea King Helicopter, motorized, No. 724/736, 1971-79	15	35	85
SEPCAT Jaguar, No. 731, 1973-76	25	70	115

Name	Good	EX	Mint
Short Shetland Flying Boat, silver, G-AGVD, No. 701, 1947-49	200	550	750
Sikorsky S58 Helicopter, No. 60d/802, 1957-61	45	135	190
Singapore Flying Boat, four-engine, silver, G-EUTG, No. 60m, 1936-41	125	400	550
Singapore Flying Boat, silver, RAF roundels, No. 60h, 1936-41	100	300	400
Spitfire, silver, large canopy, roundels red, white, and blue, No. 62A, 1945-49	30	75	125
Spitfire, silver, small canopy, roundels red, white, and blue, No. 62e/62a, 1940-41	35	150	200
Spitfire II, chrome, No. 700, 1979	65	165	250
Spitfire II, non-motorized, No. 741, 1978-80	40	80	135
Sud Est Caravelle, No. 60f/891, 1959-62	40	165	225
Supermarine Spitfire II, motorized, No. 719, 1969-78	60	95	175
Supermarine Swift, green/gray camouflage, No. 734, 1955-63	10	45	85
Twin Engined Fighter, silver, no registration, No. 70d/731, 1946-55	10	25	35
Vautour, No. 60b/801, 1957-63	30	80	125
Vickers Jockey, camouflaged, dark, No. 66d, 1940	75	175	225
Vickers Jockey, red, cream wing tips, No. 60d, 1934-41	75	110	150
Vickers Viking, silver, G-AGOL, flat spinners, No. 70c/705, 1947-63	15	40	65
Vickers Viscount, BEA, G-AOJA, No. 706, 1956-65	40	125	200
Vickers Viscount, Air France, F-BGNL, No. 708, 1956-65	40	125	200
Viscount, No. 60e/803, 1957-60	75	125	195
Vulcan Bomber, silver, RAF roundels, No. 749/707/99, 1955-56	500	1500	4000
Westland Sikorsky Helicopter, red/cream, G-ATWX, No. 716, 1957-63	30	75	125
Whitley Bomber, silver, RAF roundels, No. 60v, 1937-41	95	150	225
Whitley Bomber, camouflaged, light variation, No. 62t, 1937-41	95	300	350

BUSES AND TAXIS

Name	Good	EX	Mint
Austin Taxi, No. 40H/254, 1951-62	60	95	135
Austin/London Taxi, No. 284, 1972-79	25	35	75
Autobus Parisien, No. F29D, 1948-51	80	135	200
Autocar Chausson, No. F29F/571, 1956-60	70	120	200
B.O.A.C. Coach, No. 283, 1956-63	55	80	115
Continental Touring Coach, No. 953, 1963-66	135	200	350
Ford Vedette Taxi, No. F24XT, 1956-59	60	95	150
Observation Coach, No. 29F/280, 1954-60	50	75	100
Peugeot 404 Taxi, No. F1400, 1967-71	50	75	100
Plymouth Plaza Taxi, No. 266, 1960-67	60	95	150
Routemaster Bus, Tern Shirts, No. 289, 1964-80	75	100	150
Silver Jubilee Bus, No. 297, 1977	25	35	70

CARS

Name	Good	EX	Mint
Armstrong Siddeley, blue or brown, No. 36A, 1937-40	85	130	225
Austin Atlantic Convertible, blue, No. 106/140A, 1954-58	60	95	150
Austin Mini-Moke, No. 342, 1967-75	20	30	55
Cadillac Eldorado, No. 131, 1956-62	60	95	135
Chrysler Airflow, No. 32/30A, 1935-40	130	250	450
Chrysler Saratoga, No. F550, 1961-66	70	100	190
Citroen 2 CV, No. F535/24T, 1959-63	50	70	90

B.O.A.C. Coach, No. 283.

Name	Good	EX	Mint
Citroen DS-19, No. F522/24C, 1959-68 60		90	135
DeSoto Diplomat, green, No. F545, 1960-63 70		100	190
DeSoto Diplomat, orange, No. F545, 1960-63 60		85	125
Dodge Royal, No. 191, 1959-64 75		115	150
Estate Car, No. 27D/344, 1954-61 45		70	115
Ford Cortina Rally Car, No. 212, 1967-69 35		55	75
Ford Fairlane, South African Issue, bright blue, No. 148, 1962-66...........150		300	700
Ford Fairlane, pale green, No. 148, 1962-66 30		55	80
Ford Thunderbird, South African Issue, blue, No. F565 120		250	600
Ford Thunderbird, (Hong Kong), No. 57/005, 1965-67 50		70	100
Jaguar D-Type, No. 238, 1957-65 60		86	125
Jaguar XK 120, white, No. 157, 1954-62 120		200	400
Jaguar XK 120, green, yellow, red, No. 157, 1954-62 50		95	135
Jaguar XK 120, turquoise, cerise, No. 157, 1954-62 80		125	250
Jaguar XK 120, yellow/gray, No. 157, 1954-62 80		125	250
Lotus Racing Car, No. 241, 1963-70 20		30	50
Maserati Race Car, No. 231, 1954-64...45		75	110
Mustang Fastback, No. 161, 1965-73 ...35		55	75
Panhard PL17, No. F547, 1960-68 45		80	120
Peugeot 403 Sedan, No. F521/24B, 1959-61 50		90	135
Plymouth Fury Sports, No. 115, 1965-69 35		55	80
Renault Dauphine, No. F524/24E, 1959-62 50		80	125

Rolls-Royce, No. 30B.

Name	Good	EX	Mint
Rolls-Royce, No. 30B, 1946-50 65		100	125
Rolls-Royce Phantom V, No. 198, 1962-69 50		75	100
Singer Vogue, No. 145, 1962-67 50		75	100
Standard Vanguard, No. 153, 1954-60.60		85	120
Studebaker Commander, No. F24Y/540, 1959-61 65		90	150
Town Sedan, No. 24C, 1934-40 85		130	200
Triumph TR-2, gray, No. 105, 1957-60...........60		85	135
Triumph TR-2, yellow, No. 105, 1957-60 75		120	200
Volkswagen 1300 Sedan, No. 129, 1965-76 20		35	75
VW Karmann-Ghia, No. 187, 1959-64...........45		80	125

EMERGENCY VEHICLES

Name	Good	EX	Mint
Ambulance, No. 30F...........100		160	275
Bedford Fire Escape, No. 956, 1969-74 75		110	175
Citroen DS19 Police Car, No. F501, 1967-70 75		95	175
Citroen Fire Van, No. F25D/562, 1959-63 80		110	250
Commer Fire Engine, No. 955, 1955-69 60		85	135
Delahaye Fire Truck, No. F32D/899, 1955-70 120		190	375
Fire Chief Land Rover...........35		50	85
Ford Police Car, No. F551, 1960s 50		100	150
Mersey Tunnel Police Land Rover, No. 255, 1955-61 60		85	135
Plymouth Police Car, No. 244, 1977-80 25		35	50
Range Rover Ambulance, No. 268, 1974-78 25		35	50
Streamlined Fire Engine, No. 25H/25, 1946-53 75		100	175
Superior Criterion Ambulance, No. 263, 5075100USA Police Car (Pontiac), No. 251 35		50	85
Vauxhall Victor Ambulance, No. 278, 1964-70 55		85	115

FARM AND CONSTRUCTION

Name	Good	EX	Mint
Atlas Digger, No. 984	30	45	70
Blaw Knox Bulldozer, No. 561	45	75	115
David Brown Tractor, No. 305, 1966-75	35	50	75
Euclid Dump Truck	45	75	115
Field Marshall Tractor, No. 37N/301, 1954-65	60	85	150
Garden Roller, No. 105A	15	25	35
Hayrake, No. 324, 1954-71	30	40	60
Massey-Harris Tractor, No. 27A/300	50	75	120
Moto-Cart, No. 27G/342, 1954-60	35	50	75
Muir Hill Two-Wheel Loader, No. 437, 1962-78	30	40	60
Richier Road Roller, No. F830, 1959-69	75	100	150
Road Grader, No. 963, 1973-75	30	45	70
Salev Crane, No. F595, 1959-61	65	100	175

MILITARY

Name	Good	EX	Mint
10 Ton Army Truck, No. 622, 1954-63	30	50	75
5.5 Medium Gun, No. 692	15	30	50
AEC with Helicopter, No. 618	50	85	125

Name	Good	EX	Mint
AMX Bridge Layer, No. F883	75	110	200
AMX Tank, No. F80C/817	50	75	100
Armoured Command Vehicle, No. 677	50	85	125
Austin Covered Truck, No. 30SM/625	85	135	275
Austin Paramoke, No. 601	25	35	50
Bedford Military Truck, No. 25WM/60	80	125	250
Berliet Missile Launcher, No. 620	75	100	175
Berliet Wrecker, No. F806	60	90	140
Centurian Tank, No. 651	30	50	75
Commando Jeep, No. 612	25	35	50
Daimler Ambulance, No. 30HM/624	80	125	250
Dodge Command Car, No. F810	40	60	85
Ferret Armoured Car, No. 630	25	35	50
GMC Tanker, No. F823	125	250	500
Jeep, No. F816	50	75	115
Military Ambulance, No. F80F/820	50	75	100
Military Ambulance, No. 626	25	45	75
Missile Servicing Platform, No. 667	80	115	225
Reconnaisance Car, No. 152B	40	60	100
Recovery Tractor, No. 661	60	90	140
Searchlight, prewar, No. 161A	125	250	500
Tank Transporter, No. 660	75	100	175
Three Ton Army Wagon, No. 621, 1954-63	50	85	125

Commer Fire Engine, No. 955.

Range Rover Ambulance, No. 268.

Blaw Knox Bulldozer, No. 561.

Road Grader, No. 963.

MOTORCYCLES AND CARAVANS

Name	Good	EX	Mint
A.A. Motorcycle Patrol, No. 270/44B, 1946-64	30	45	70
Caravan, No. 190, 1956-64	30	45	60
Caravan, postwar, No. 30G	40	60	85
Caravan, prewar, No. 30G	55	85	150
Caravane Caravelair	75	150	250
Police Motorcycle Patrol, No. 42B, 1946-53	30	45	70
Police Motorcycle Patrol, No. 42B, 1936-40	50	75	125
Police Motorcyclist, No. 37B, 1946-48	30	45	70
Police Motorcyclist, No. 37B, 1938-40	50	75	125
Touring Secours Motorcycle Patrol, Swiss version, No. 271, 1960s	70	110	200

10 Ton Army Truck, No. 622.

Berliet Missile Launcher, No. 620.

SPACE VEHICLES

Name	Good	EX	Mint
Galactic War Chariot, No. 361, 1979-80	30	45	70
Joe's Car, No. 102, 1969-75	60	90	140
Klingon Battle Cruiser, No. 357, 1976-79	30	45	70
Lady Penelope's Fab 1, shocking pink version, No. 100, 1966-76	115	200	340
Lady Penelope's Fab 1, pink version, No. 100, 1966-76	80	135	220

Missile Servicing Platform, No. 667.

Reconnaisance Car, No. 152B.

Tank Transporter, No. 660.

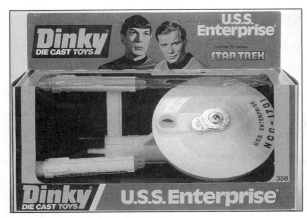

U.S.S. Enterprise, No. 371/803.

Name	Good	EX	Mint
Pathe News Camera Car	65	100	175
Prisoner Mini-Moke	115	200	340
Renault Sinpar, No. F1406, 1968-71	80	135	220
Santa Special Model T Ford, No. 485, 1964-68	65	100	150
Tiny's Mini-Moke, No. 350, 1970-73	60	85	120
U.S.S. Enterprise, No. 371/803, 1980	30	45	70

TRUCKS

Name	Good	EX	Mint
A.E.C. Hoynor Transporter, No. 974, 1969-75	60	90	130
Atco Delivery Van, type 3, No. 28N, 1935-40	135	200	350
Atco Delivery Van, type 2, No. 28N, 1935-40	200	375	850
Austin Van, Shell/BP, No. 470, 1954-56	60	110	175
Austin Van, Nestle's, No. 471, 1955-63	60	110	175
Austin Van, Raleigh, No. 472, 1957-60	60	110	175
B.E.V. Truck, No. 14A/400, 1954-60	15	30	70
Bedford Van, Dinky Toys, No. 482, 1956-58	60	115	200
Bedford Van, Heinz, No. 923, 1955-59	100	165	300
Berliet Transformer Carrier, No. F898, 1961-65	100	200	450
Big Bedford, maroon, fawn, No. 408/922	80	120	185
Big Bedford, blue, yellow, No. 408/922	90	135	210

B.E.V. Truck, No. 14A/400.

Bedford Van, No. 482.

Name	Good	EX	Mint
Chevrolet El Camino, No. 449, 1961-68.	35	65	100
Citroen Cibie Delivery Van, No. F561, 1960-63.	90	150	350
Citroen Milk Truck, No. F586, 1961-65.	145	275	600
Citroen Wrecker, No. F35A/582, 1959-71.	75	120	250
Coles Mobile Crane, No. 971, 1955-66.	40	70	110
Covered Wagon, Carter Paterson, No. 25B.	150	300	750
Covered Wagon, green, gray, No. 25B.	65	115	160
Electric Articulated Vehicle, No. 30W/421.	60	85	120
Ensign Delivery Van, type 1, No. 28E, 1934.	300	500	1000
Foden Flat Truck w/ Tailboard 1, red/black, No. 503/903.	140	210	450
Foden Flat Truck w/ Tailboard 2, blue/yellow, orange or blue, No. 503/903.	90	150	275
Foden Flat Truck w/Tailboard 1, gray/blue, No. 503/903.	140	210	450

Guy Van, No. 514.

Leland Comet Cement Truck, No. 419/933.

Name	Good	EX	Mint
Foden Mobilgas Tanker, No. 941, 1954-57	145	350	750
Foden Regent Tanker, No. 942	135	300	550
Ford Transit Van, No. 417, 1978-80	15	20	30
Forward Control Wagon, No. 25R, 1948-53	45	65	90
Guy Van, Slumberland, No. 514	135	300	575
Guy Van, Lyons, No. 514	275	550	1600
Guy Van, Spratts, No. 514	135	300	575
Guy Warrior 4 Ton, No. 431, 1958-64	150	270	450
Johnston Road Sweeper, No. 449/451, 1970s	25	50	75
Leland Comet Cement Truck, No. 419/933, 1956-59	85	150	250
Leland Tanker, Corn Products	700	1200	3000
Leland Tanker, Shell/BP, No. 944, 1963-69	125	215	450
Market Gardeners Wagon, yellow, No. 25F	65	115	160

Name	Good	EX	Mint
Midland Bank, No. 280, 1966-68	60	85	120
Mighty Antar with Propeller, No. 986, 1956-64	125	215	400
Mini Minor Van, R.A.C., No. 273, 1960s	65	115	150
Mini Minor Van, Joseph Mason Paints, No. 274	150	300	500
Motor Truck, red, blue, No. 22C	150	350	650
Motor Truck, red, green, blue, No. 22C	80	120	200
Panhard Esso Tanker, No. F32C, 1954-59	75	120	170
Panhard Kodak Semi Trailer, No. F32AJ, 1952-54	140	250	450
Panhard SNCF Semi Trailer, No. F32AB, 1954-59	100	165	280
Petrol Wagon, Power, No. 25D	150	300	500
Pickfords Delivery Van, type 1, No. 28B, 1934-35	300	500	1000
Pickfords Delivery Van, type 2, No. 28B, 1934-35	200	375	600
Pullmore Car Transporter, No. 982, 1954-63	75	125	175
Renault Estafette, No. F561	50	85	150
Royal Mail Van, No. 260, 1955-61	65	115	150
Saviem Race Horse Van, No. F571, 1969-71	125	225	400
Simca Glass Truck, gray, green, No. F33C/579	75	120	170
Simca Glass Truck, yellow, green, No. F33C/579	100	150	250
Studebaker Mobilgas Tanker, No. 440, 1954-61	70	100	175
Thames Flat Truck, No. 422/30R, 1951-60	45	75	110
Trojan Dunlop Van, No. 31B/451, 1952-57	70	110	185
Unic Bucket Truck, No. F38A/895, 1957-65	75	120	225
Willeme Log Truck, No. F36A/897, 1956-71	75	120	200
Willeme Semi Trailer Truck, No. F36B/896, 1959-71	85	130	225

Hot Wheels

When Mattel began making Hot Wheels in 1968—"The Fastest Metal Cars in the World"—they quickly became the most popular die-cast cars ever made. They succeeded Matchbox as the toy cars that little boys and girls played with and traded.

It all started when Ruth Handler, co-founder of Mattel, saw her grandkids playing with Matchbox cars. She began to wonder why her company couldn't make cars that were faster, funkier and cooler. Jack Ryan, head of Research and Development, was put in charge of this new project. Ryan's original team consisted of Harvey LaBranch, Howard Newman and Harry Bradley (Bradley left in 1967 and was replaced by Ira Gilford). Together they designed sixteen cars that would change the world of toy cars forever.

Based on California-style cars, Hot Wheels offered a radical departure in styles and colors from other die-cast cars, and they were fast on their loop-de-loops. Underestimating the market desire for Hot Wheels, Mattel was backlogged with orders for months. Since then, more than two billion Hot Wheels have been produced. There have been more than a thousand different regular-issue models and thousands more, if one considers variations in paint, wheels, interiors, windshields and so forth.

Hot Wheels could easily be divided up into three eras: the redline era (1968-1977), the blackwall era (1977-late 1980s) and the numbered packs era (late 1980s-present).

Hot Wheels from the redline era features cars with a red stripe around "mag" tires, and are the most valuable on the market. The original cars, painted in "Spectraflame" colors, are the most valuable on the secondary market. By 1973, Mattel began using enamel paint to lower costs. This was the beginning of the gas crisis and considered by some to be the low point in Hot Wheels history. In an interview in *Toy Cars & Vehicles*, legendary Hot Wheels designer, Larry Wood "figured it [the gas crisis] was the end of the hobby. Marketing wanted Pintos and Gremlins."

The blackwall era includes the cars made from the end of the redline era to the beginning of the numbered packs in the late 1980s. During this time, old-style Hot Wheels were phased out and there was a move toward the modern age and more colorful packaging.

By the late 1980s, Mattel realized people were collecting Hot Wheels. Wanting to make this easier, Mattel began numbering packs. Collectors have embraced the idea, and it has become the most active area in Hot Wheels collecting. Beginning with No 1, the numbered pack line has grown to over 1,000. Many of these are variation cars, either in paint, color, tampo or wheel type.

Hot Wheels enthusiasts can collect regular number pack cars, or they can concentrate on the series cars. Mattel introduced the Treasure Hunt series in 1995, and it was an overnight success.

Since then, over sixty series including First Editions, Artistic License Series, Dark Rider Series, Mega Graphics Series, Race Team Series and Tattoo Machines, have been introduced.

Limited edition Hot Wheels were introduced in the early '90s, when Hot Wheels clubs, individuals and other businesses contracted with Mattel to make special cars for promotions or giveaways. The easiest way to get a limited edition is to join the club, attend the convention or subscribe to the magazine that is offering the car. If that isn't possible, many Hot Wheels dealers sell them at shows, through mail-order and via the Internet.

Market Update

Hot Wheels are one of the most sought after items in the toy market. There are several different reasons for their collectibility. Redline Hot Wheels are desirable because of nostalgia. These cars were played with and destroyed, and people want to recapture a bit of their childhood.

The original sixteen Hot Wheels are the most desirable and finding them Mint in Pack is a rarity. Another factor in value is color. Cars were issued in a variety of colors, pink and white were generally the least popular and least produced car color. As a result, these colors can be worth one-and-a-half to two times the value of the same model.

Cars from the blackwall era used to be inexpensive, but have recently seen a spike in value. The cars that dealers had in stock were sold long ago and have become more difficult to find as a result. As with redlines, finding blackwall cars Mint in Pack can be a challenge.

Numbered pack cars are almost exclusively bought, sold and traded Mint in Pack—even a tiny crease in the package can alter the value of a car. This area of Hot Wheels is still active. Some cars are so valuable that they never hit the store shelves. Or, as some collectors believe, the cars become valuable **because** they never hit store shelves.

There is a lot of bitterness between Hot Wheels collectors and retail outlets. Many collectors believe that retail stores allow stock boys, so-called scalpers and hoarders to pick through boxes of newly-arrived Hot Wheels. This is what collectors feel is driving up the value of some cars. On the other hand, stores have reported fights breaking out in the toy aisles after new Hot Wheels are on the shelves. This feeling led one retail chain—Target—to deface the packs before placing them on the shelves.

Contributors: Andrew Dudek, adudak@aol.com; Jim Wilson, jw1962pw@aol.com; and Steve and Anna Cinnamon, cinman@provide.net; They can all be reached at: P.O. Box 55, Belleville, MI 48112-0055.

Clubs

There are numerous Hot Wheels clubs across the nation; unfortunately, space permits listing them all here. The official hot Wheels club, sponsored by Mattel is listed below.

Hot Wheels Collectors Club
800-852-1075

Name	MNP	MIP
#43-STP, petty blue, gray rollbars, blackwalls, 1992	10	30
'31 Doozie, orange, redline, No. 9649, 1977	15	60
'31 Doozie, orange, blackwall, No. 9649, 1977	8	15
'32 Ford Delivery, white/pink, Early Times logo, blackwalls, 1993	25	35
'40 Ford Two-Door, black w/white hubs, Real Rider, No. 4367, 1983	30	50
'55 Chevy, blue No. 92, Real Rider, 1992	10	30
'55 Chevy, black No. 92, Real Rider, 1992	10	30
'55 Nomad, purple, Real Rider, 1993	10	30
'55 Nomad, purple, blackwalls, 1992	10	30
'56 Hi Tail Hauler, orange, redline, No. 9647, 1977	15	60
'56 Hi Tail Hauler, orange, blackwall, No. 9647, 1977	10	35
'57 Chevy, red, blackwall, No. 9638, 1977	10	30
'57 Chevy, white No. 22, Real Rider, 1992	15	30

Name	MNP	MIP
'57 Chevy, red, redline, No. 9638, 1977	20	85
'57 T-Bird, black w/white hubs, Real Rider, No. 9522, 1986	30	150
'59 Caddy, pink, Canadian, cal custom w/w, 1990	35	65
'59 Caddy, gold, blackwalls, 1993	10	30
3 Window '34, black, Real Rider, No. 4352, 1984	300	750
A-OK, red, Real Rider, 1981	75	275
Alien, blue, 1988	10	20
Alive '55, chrome, redline, No. 9210, 1977	15	55
Alive '55, green, No. 6968, 1974	50	110
Alive '55, assorted, No. 6968, 1973	125	600
Alive '55, blue, No. 6968, 1974	90	350
Alive '55, chrome, blackwall, No. 9210, 1977	15	30

American Hauler, No. 9118.

Alive '55, No. 6968.

American Tipper, No. 9089.

AMX/2, No. 6460; Mighty Maverick, No. 6414; Mercedes Benz 280SL, No 6275.

Beatnik Bandit, No. 6217.

Boss Hoss, chrome, Club Kit, No. 6499.

Name	MNP	MIP
Ambulance, assorted, No. 6451, 1970	30	50
American Hauler, blue, No. 9118, 1976	25	65
American Tipper, red, No. 9089, 1976	25	65
American Victory, light blue, No. 7662, 1975	20	60
AMX/2, assorted, No. 6460, 1971	40	150
Aw Shoot, olive, No. 9243, 1976	15	25
Backwoods Bomb, light blue, No. 7670, 1975	40	125
Backwoods Bomb, green, redline or blackwall, No. 7670, 1977	30	120
Baja Bruiser, orange, No. 8258, 1974	30	75

Name	MNP	MIP
Baja Bruiser, light green, No. 8258, 1976	400	1300
Baja Bruiser, blue, redline or blackwall, No. 8258, 1977	25	85
Baja Bruiser, yellow, blue in tampo, No. 8258, 1974	300	1200
Baja Bruiser, yellow, magenta in tampo, No. 8258, 1974	300	1200
Beatnik Bandit, assorted, No. 6217, 1968	15	45
Black Passion, black, 1990	15	45
Boss Hoss, assorted, No. 6406, 1971	125	300
Boss Hoss, chrome, Club Kit, No. 6499, 1970	50	160

Boss Hoss, No. 6406.

Carabo, No. 6420.

Chaparral 2G, No. 6256.

Circus Cats, No. 3303.

Name	MNP	MIP
Brabham-Repco F1, assorted, No. 6264, 1969	20	65
Bronco 4-Wheeler, Toys R Us, No. 1690, 1981	75	150
Bugeye, assorted, No. 6178, 1971	30	75
Buzz Off, assorted, No. 6976, 1973	110	500
Buzz Off, blue, No. 6976, 1974	30	90
Buzz Off, gold plated, redline or blackwall, No. 6976, 1977	15	30
Bye Focal, assorted, No. 6187, 1971	125	400
Bywayman, Toys R Us, No. 2509, 1979	75	150
Bywayman, blue, red interior, No. 2196, 1989	60	120
Cadillac Seville, gold, Mexican, Real Rider, 1987	80	140
Cadillac Seville, gray, French, Real Rider, 1983	80	140
Captain America, white, Heroes, No. 2879, 1979	90	175
Carabo, yellow, No. 7617, 1974	500	1400
Carabo, light green, No. 7617, 1974	35	100
Carabo, assorted, No. 6420, 1970	35	80
Cement Mixer, assorted, No. 6452, 1970	30	60
Chaparral 2G, assorted, No. 6256, 1969	20	45

Name	MNP	MIP
Chevy Monza 2+2, orange, No. 7671, 1975	40	110
Chevy Monza 2+2, light green, No. 9202, 1975	200	800
Chief's Special Cruiser, red, No. 7665, 1975	30	75
Chief's Special Cruiser, red, redline, No. 7665, 1977	25	65
Chief's Special Cruiser, red, blackwall, No. 7665, 1977	10	20
Circus Cats, white, No. 3303, 1981	75	150
Classic '31 Ford Woody, assorted, No. 6251, 1969	30	90

Name	MNP	MIP
Classic '32 Ford Vicky, assorted, No. 6250, 1969	30	95
Classic '36 Ford Coupe, blue, No. 6253, 1969	20	60
Classic '36 Ford Coupe, assorted, No. 6253, 1969	35	100
Classic '57 T-Bird, assorted, No. 6252, 1969	30	100
Classic Caddy, red/white/blue, Museum Exhibit car, No. 2529, 1992	15	35
Classic Cobra, blue w/white hubs, Real Rider, 1985	40	80
Classic Nomad, assorted, No. 6404, 1970	55	150
Cockney Cab, assorted, No. 6466, 1971	50	160
Cool One, plum, blackwall, No. 9120, 1977	20	40
Corvette Stingray, chrome, blackwall set only, No. 9506, 1977	55	—

Name	MNP	MIP
Corvette Stingray, red, No. 9241, 1976	30	80
Corvette Stingray, chrome, No. 9506, 1976	20	50
Custom AMX, assorted, No. 6267, 1969	100	225
Custom Barracuda, assorted, No. 6211, 1968	80	400
Custom Camaro, white enamel, No. 6208, 1968	500	2500
Custom Camaro, assorted, No. 6208, 1968	100	450
Custom Charger, assorted, No. 6268, 1969	100	250
Custom Continental Mark III, assorted, No. 6266, 1969	20	60
Custom Corvette, assorted, No. 6215, 1968	90	300
Custom Cougar, assorted, No. 6205, 1968	80	275

Classic '36 Ford Coupe, No. 6253.

Custom Barracuda, No. 6211.

Cockney Cab, No. 6466.

Custom Charger, No. 6268.

Custom El Dorado, No. 6218.

Custom Mustang with open hood scoops or ribbed windows, No. 6206.

Name	MNP	MIP
Custom El Dorado, assorted, No. 6218, 1968	40	140
Custom Firebird, assorted, No. 6212, 1968	50	250
Custom Fleetside, assorted, No. 6213, 1968	60	250
Custom Mustang, assorted, No. 6206, 1968	80	425
Custom Mustang, assorted w/open hood scoops or ribbed windows, No. 6206, 1968	400	1200
Custom Police Cruiser, assorted, No. 6269, 1969	55	200
Custom T-Bird, assorted, No. 6207, 1968	50	165
Custom VW Bug, assorted, No. 6220, 1968	30	125

Custom T-Bird, No. 6207.

Custom VW Bug, No. 6220.

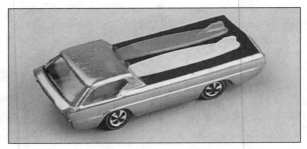

Deora, No. 6210.

Double Header, No. 5880.

Name	MNP	MIP
Datsun 200SX, maroon, Canada, No. 3255, 1982	75	175
Demon, assorted, No. 6401, 1970	25	50
Deora, assorted, No. 6210, 1968	60	375
Double Header, assorted, No. 5880, 1973	120	450
Double Vision, assorted, No. 6975, 1973	110	400
Dune Daddy, assorted, No. 6967, 1973	110	400
Dune Daddy, light green, No. 6967, 1975	25	75
Dune Daddy, orange, No. 6967, 1975	225	600
El Rey Special, dark blue, No. 8273, 1974	225	900
El Rey Special, green, No. 8273, 1974	40	75
El Rey Special, light blue, No. 8273, 1974	300	1200
El Rey Special, light green, No. 8273, 1974	75	175
Emergency Squad, red, No. 7650, 1975	15	65
Evil Weevil, assorted, No. 6471, 1971	75	150
Ferrari 312P, red, No. 6973, 1974	40	80

Fire Chief Cruiser, No. 6469.

Name	MNP	MIP
Ferrari 312P, assorted, No. 6417, 1970	30	60
Ferrari 312P, assorted, No. 6973, 1973	300	1100
Ferrari 512-S, assorted, No. 6021, 1972	75	250
Fire Chief Cruiser, red, No. 6469, 1970	15	45
Fire Engine, red, No. 6454, 1970	25	100
Flat Out 442, orange, No. 2506, 1979	8	10
Flat Out 442, green, Canada, 1984	75	150
Ford J-Car, assorted, No. 6214, 1968	20	70
Ford MK IV, assorted, No. 6257, 1969	15	60
Formula 5000, white, No. 9119, 1976	20	50
Formula 5000, chrome, No. 9511, 1976	30	65
Fuel Tanker, assorted, No. 6018, 1971	75	200
Funny Money, magenta, No. 7621, 1974	60	150
Funny Money, gray, blackwall, No. 7621, 1977	20	65
Funny Money, gray, redline, No. 7621, 1977	60	150
Funny Money, gray, No. 6005, 1972	60	325
GMC Motorhome, orange, redline, No. 9645, 1977	400	1200
GMC Motorhome, orange, blackwall, No. 9645, 1977	10	25
Gold Passion, gold, Toy Fair promo, 1992	40	100
Good Humor Truck, white, 1986	55	125
Goodyear Blimp, chrome, Mattel promo, 1992	65	—
Grass Hopper, assorted, No. 6461, 1971	45	100
Grass Hopper, light green, no engine, No. 7622, 1975	90	350
Grass Hopper, light green, No. 7621, 1974	40	100
Greased Gremlin, red, Mexican, Real Rider, 1987	350	1000

Name	MNP	MIP
Gremlin Grinder, chrome, blackwall, No. 9201, 1977	20	40
Gremlin Grinder, green, No. 7652, 1975	35	75
GT Racer, blue, No. 1789, 1989	50	100
Gun Bucket, olive, No. 9090, 1976	25	60
Gun Bucket, olive, blackwall, No. 9090, 1977	25	60
Gun Slinger, olive, blackwall, No. 7664, 1976	30	75
Gun Slinger, olive, No. 7664, 1975	25	50
Hairy Hauler, assorted, No. 6458, 1971	20	65
Hammer Down, red set only, 1980	125	—
Heavy Chevy, light green, No. 7619, 1974	200	750
Heavy Chevy, chrome, Club Kit, No. 6189, 1970	75	300
Heavy Chevy, yellow, No. 7619, 1974	90	200
Heavy Chevy, chrome, redline or blackwall, No. 9212, 1977	40	120
Heavy Chevy, assorted, No. 6408, 1970	65	200
Hiway Robber, assorted, No. 6979, 1973	75	250
Hood, assorted, No. 6175, 1971	25	110
Hot Bird, blue, 1980	60	125
Hot Bird, brown, 1980	90	200
Hot Heap, assorted, No. 6219, 1968	20	65
Human Torch, black, No. 2881, 1979	20	40
Ice T, light green, No. 6980, 1974	25	75
Ice T, yellow w/hood tampo, No. 6980, 1974	200	525
Ice T, assorted, No. 6980, 1973	200	650
Ice T, light green, blackwall, No. 6980, 1977	20	35
Ice T, yellow, No. 6184, 1971	40	200
Incredible Hulk Van, white, Scene Machine, No. 2850, 1979	75	125
Indy Eagle, gold, No. 6263, 1969	75	240
Indy Eagle, assorted, No. 6263, 1969	15	40

Jack Rabbit Special, No. 6421.

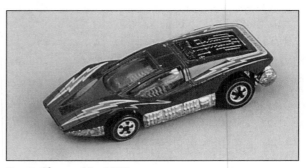

Large Charge, No. 8272.

Name	MNP	MIP
Inferno, yellow, No. 9186, 1976	30	60
Jack Rabbit Special, white, No. 6421, 1970	15	55
Jack-in-the-Box Promotion, white, Jack Rabbit w/decals, No. 6421, 1970	300	—
Jet Threat, assorted, No. 6179, 1971	45	160
Jet Threat II, magenta, No. 8235, 1976	35	80
Khaki Kooler, olive, No. 9183, 1976	15	30
King Kuda, assorted, No. 6411, 1970	25	100
King Kuda, chrome, Club Kit, No. 6411, 1970	75	300
Large Charge, green, No. 8272, 1975	25	60
Letter Getter, white, redline, No. 9643, 1977	175	550
Letter Getter, white, blackwall, No. 9643, 1977	8	15
Light My Firebird, assorted, No. 6412, 1970	35	75
Lola GT 70, assorted, No. 6254, 1969	20	60

Lola GT 70, No. 6254.

Mantis, No. 6423.

McClaren M6A, No. 6255.

Mod-Quad, No. 6456.

Mongoose, No. 6970.

Name	MNP	MIP
Lotus Turbine, assorted, No. 6262, 1969	20	60
Lowdown, gold plated, redline or blackwall, No. 9185, 1977	15	30
Lowdown, light blue, No. 9185, 1976	30	75
Mantis, assorted, No. 6423, 1970	20	60
Masterati Mistral, assorted, No. 6277, 1969	50	125
Maxi Taxi, yellow, blackwall, No. 9184, 1977	20	60
Maxi Taxi, yellow, No. 9184, 1976	25	60
McClaren M6A, assorted, No. 6255, 1969	20	65
Mercedes 280SL, assorted, No. 6962, 1973	100	450
Mercedes 280SL, assorted, No. 6275, 1969	25	70

Name	MNP	MIP
Mercedes C-111, assorted, No. 6978, 1973	300	1200
Mercedes C-111, red, No. 6978, 1974	40	90
Mercedes C-111, assorted, No. 6169, 1972	80	250
Mighty Maverick, assorted, No. 6414, 1970	45	130
Mighty Maverick, blue, No. 7653, 1975	50	100
Mighty Maverick, light green, No. 9209, 1975	300	750
Mighty Maverick, chrome, blackwall, No. 9209, 1977	25	50
Mod-Quad, assorted, No. 6456, 1970	20	60
Mongoose, red/blue, No. 6970, 1973	400	1400

Name	MNP	MIP
Mongoose Funny Car, red, No. 6410, 1970	50	160
Mongoose II, metallic blue, No. 5954, 1971	75	350
Mongoose Rail Dragster, blue, two pack, No. 5952, 1971	75	—
Monte Carlo Stocker, dark blue and green, No. 7660,	55	70
Monte Carlo Stocker, yellow, No. 7660, 1975	45	90
Monte Carlo Stocker, yellow, blackwall, No. 7660, 1977	20	50
Motocross I, red, No. 7668, 1975	100	200
Motorcross Team Van, red, Scene Machine, No. 2853, 1979	50	125
Movin' On, white set only, 1980	125	—
Moving Van, assorted, No. 6455, 1970	50	125
Mustang Stocker, yellow w/red in tampo, No. 9203, 1975	300	900
Mustang Stocker, yellow w/magenta tampo, No. 7664, 1975	90	300
Mustang Stocker, chrome, redline or blackwall, No. 9203, 1977	40	90
Mustang Stocker, white, No. 7664, 1975	400	1200
Mustang Stocker, chrome, No. 9203, 1976	40	90
Mutt Mobile, assorted, No. 5185, 1971	75	175

Name	MNP	MIP
NASCAR Stocker, white, NASCAR/Mountain Dew base, No. 3927, 1983	90	165
Neet Streeter, blue, No. 9244, 1976	30	75
Neet Streeter, chrome, blackwall set only, No. 9510, 1977	40	—
Neet Streeter, chrome, No. 9510, 1976	20	40
Neet Streeter, blue, blackwall, No. 9244, 1977	15	30
Nitty Gritty Kitty, assorted, No. 6405, 1970	25	65
Noodle Head, assorted, No. 6000, 1971	40	150
Odd Job, assorted, No. 6981, 1973	100	600
Odd Rod, yellow, redline, No. 9642, 1977	30	50
Odd Rod, yellow, blackwall, No. 9642, 1977	20	40
Odd Rod, plum, blackwall or redline, No. 9642, 1977	200	400
Old Number 5, red, no louvers, No. 1695, 1982	10	20
Olds 442, assorted, No. 6467, 1971	400	800
Open Fire, , No. 5881, 1972	100	400
Paddy Wagon, blue, No. 6966, 1973	30	120
Paddy Wagon, blue, blackwall, No. 6966, 1977	10	20
Paddy Wagon, blue, No. 6402, 1970	15	30
Paramedic, yellow, No. 7661, 1976	30	50
Paramedic, yellow, blackwall or redline, No. 7661, 1977	25	45

Mutt Mobile, No. 5185.

Paddy Wagon, No. 6402.

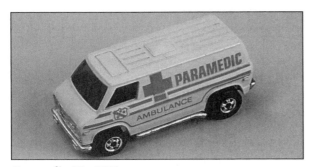

Paramedic, No. 7661.

Name	MNP	MIP
Paramedic, white, No. 7661, 1975	25	55
Peepin' Bomb, assorted, No. 6419, 1970	20	50
Pepsi Challenger, yellow funny car, No. 2023, 1982	20	25
Pit Crew Car, white, No. 6183, 1971	30	350
Poison Pinto, green, blackwall, No. 9240, 1977	15	30
Poison Pinto, chrome, blackwall set only, No. 9508, 1977	50	—
Poison Pinto, light green, No. 9240, 1976	25	65
Poison Pinto, chrome, No. 9508, 1976...........	20	40
Police Cruiser, white, No. 6963, 1973	200	550
Police Cruiser, white, blackwall, No. 6963, 1977	25	45
Police Cruiser, white, No. 6963, 1974	45	125
Police Cruiser, white w/blue light, No. 6963, 1977	30	65
Porsche 911, black, six pack blackwall, No. 7648, 1977	175	350
Porsche 911, chrome, redline or blackwall, No. 9206, 1977	20	40
Porsche 911, orange, No. 6972, 1975	25	65
Porsche 911, yellow, No. 7648, 1975	40	75
Porsche 917, assorted, No. 6416, 1970...........	25	65
Porsche 917, red, No. 6972, 1974	175	500
Porsche 917, orange, No. 6972, 1974	40	75
Porsche 917, orange, blackwall, No. 6972, 1977	15	25
Porsche 917, assorted, No. 6972, 1973..........	300	950
Power Pad, assorted, No. 6459, 1970	30	125

Power Pad, No. 6459.

Racing Team Van.

Name	MNP	MIP
Prowler, chrome, blackwall, No. 9207, 1977	35	70
Prowler, orange, No. 6965, 1974	35	75
Prowler, assorted, No. 6965, 1973	200	1000
Prowler, light green, No. 6965, 1974	500	1000
Python, assorted, No. 6216, 1968	20	75
Race Ace, white, No. 2620, 1986	15	30
Racer Rig, red/white, No. 6194, 1971	100	375
Racing Team Van, yellow, Scene Machine, 1981	60	125
Ramblin' Cruiser, white without phone number, No. 7659, 1977	15	25
Ramblin' Wrecker, yellow, No. 7659, 1975	15	20
Ramblin' Wrecker, white, blackwall, No. 7659, 1977	10	20
Ranger Rig, green, No. 7666, 1975	20	65
Rash I, blue, No. 7616, 1974	300	800
Rash I, green, No. 7616, 1974	50	75
Rear Engine Mongoose, red, No. 5699, 1972	200	600

Ramblin' Wrecker, No. 7659.

Ranger Rig, No. 7666.

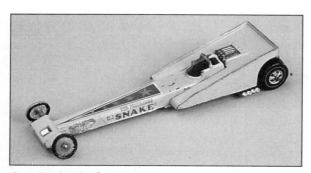

Rear Engine Snake, No. 5856.

Red Baron, No. 6400.

Rescue Squad, No. 3304.

Name	MNP	MIP
Rear Engine Snake, yellow, No. 5856, 1972	200	600
Red Baron, red, blackwall, No. 6964, 1977	15	25
Red Baron, red, No. 6964, 1973	30	200
Red Baron, red, No. 6400, 1970	15	40
Red Passion, red, 1994	10	20
Rescue Squad, red, Scene Machine, No. 3304, 1982	70	125
Road King Truck, yellow set only, No. 7615, 1974	600	1200

Name	MNP	MIP
Rock Buster, yellow, No. 9088, 1976	20	35
Rock Buster, chrome, No. 9507, 1976	15	30
Rock Buster, yellow, blackwall, No. 9088, 1977	10	15
Rock Buster, chrome, blackwall set only, No. 9507, 1977	45	—
Rocket Bye Baby, assorted, No. 6186, 1971	60	200
Rodger Dodger, magenta, No. 8259, 1974	40	90
Rodger Dodger, blue, No. 8259, 1974	200	550
Rodger Dodger, gold plated, blackwall or redline, No. 8259, 1977	30	80
Rolls-Royce Silver Shadow, assorted, No. 6276, 1969	30	125
Ruby Red Passion, red, 1992	25	45
S'Cool Bus, yellow, No. 6468, 1971	175	750
S.W.A.T. Van, blue, Scene Machine, No. 2854, 1979	70	125
Sand Crab, assorted, No. 6403, 1970	20	60
Sand Drifter, green, No. 7651, 1975	150	375
Sand Drifter, yellow, No. 7651, 1975	35	75

Name	MNP	MIP
Sand Witch, assorted, No. 6974, 1973	125	400
Scooper, assorted, No. 6193, 1971	100	325
Screamin', red w/light blue and yellow, No. 9521,	10	15
Seasider, assorted, No. 6413, 1970	60	135
Second Wind, white, blackwall or redline, No. 9644, 1977	35	75

Sand Crab, No. 6403.

Screamin', No. 9521.

Seasider, No. 6413.

Name	MNP	MIP
Shelby Turbine, assorted, No. 6265, 1969	20	55
Short Order, assorted, No. 6176, 1971	50	125
Show Hoss II, yellow, redline, No. 9646, 1977	300	600
Show Hoss II, yellow, blackwall, No. 9646, 1977	40	75
Show-Off, assorted, No. 6982, 1973	140	400
Sidekick, assorted, No. 6022, 1972	80	200
Silhouette, assorted, No. 6209, 1968	20	90
Simpsons Camper, blue, Scene Machine, 1990	10	20

Shelby Turbine, No. 6265.

Short Order, No. 6176.

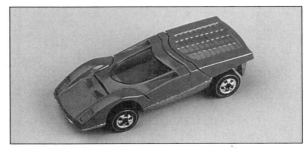

Sidekick, No. 6022.

Name	MNP	MIP
Simpsons Van, yellow, Scene Machine, 1990	10	20
Sir Rodney Roadster, yellow, blackwall, No. 8261, 1977	40	70
Sir Sidney Roadster, light green, No. 8261, 1974	325	650
Sir Sidney Roadster, orange/brown, No. 8261, 1974	375	700
Sir Sidney Roadster, yellow, No. 8261, 1974	50	90
Six Shooter, assorted, No. 6003, 1971	75	225
Sky Show Fleetside (Aero Launcher), assorted, No. 6436, 1970	400	850
Snake, white/yellow, No. 6969, 1973	600	1500
Snake Dragster, white, two-pack, No. 5951, 1971	75	—
Snake Funny Car, assorted, No. 6409, 1970	60	300
Snake II, white, No. 5953, 1971	60	275
Snorkel, assorted, No. 6020, 1971	90	200
Space Van, gray, Scene Machine, No. 2855, 1979	70	125
Special Delivery, blue, No. 6006, 1971	45	150
Spider-Man, black, No. 2852, 1979	15	35
Spider-Man Van, white, Scene Machine, No. 2852, 1979	50	125
Splittin' Image, assorted, No. 6261, 1969	15	50

Name	MNP	MIP
Spoiler Sport, light green, blackwall, No. 9641, 1977	10	20
Spoiler Sport, light green, redline, No. 9641, 1977	25	50
Staff Car, olive, blackwall, No. 9521, 1977	500	750
Staff Car, olive, six-pack only, No. 9521, 1977	600	850
Steam Roller, white w/seven stars, No. 8260, 1974	100	300
Steam Roller, white, No. 8260, 1974	25	70
Steam Roller, chrome w/seven stars, No. 9208, 1977	100	300
Steam Roller, chrome, redline or blackwall, No. 9208, 1977	25	55
Street Eater, black, No. 7669, 1975	40	60
Street Rodder, black, blackwall, No. 9242, 1977	30	50
Street Rodder, black, No. 9242, 1976	40	85
Street Snorter, assorted, No. 6971, 1973	110	400
Strip Teaser, assorted, No. 6188, 1971	65	200
Sugar Caddy, assorted, No. 6418, 1971	45	120

Staff Car, No. 9521.

Super Van, No. 7649.

Sky Show Fleetside (Aero Launcher), No. 6436.

Team Trailer, No. 6019.

Torino Stocker, No. 7647.

Tri-Baby, No. 6424.

Twinmill, No. 6258.

Name	MNP	MIP
Super Chromes, chrome, blackwall, six-pack, No. 9505, 1977	375	—
Super Van, black, blackwall, No. 7649, 1977	15	25
Super Van, blue, No. 7649, 1975	650	—
Super Van, Toys-R-Us, No. 7649, 1975	100	350
Super Van, plum, No. 7649, 1975	90	250
Super Van, chrome, No. 9205, 1976	20	40
Superfine Turbine, assorted, No. 6004, 1973	400	1100
Sweet 16, assorted, No. 6007, 1973	125	650
Swingin' Wing, assorted, No. 6422, 1970	25	75
T-4-2, assorted, No. 6177, 1971	50	175
T-Totaller, brown, blackwall, No. 9648, 1977	15	40
T-Totaller, black, Red Line, six-pack only, No. 9648, 1977	500	1000
T-Totaller, black, blackwall, No. 9648, 1977	15	40
Team Trailer, white/red, No. 6019, 1971	95	225
Thing, The, dark blue, No. 2882, 1979	20	50
Thor, yellow, No. 2880, 1979	15	30

Name	MNP	MIP
Thrill Driver Torino, red/white, blackwall, set of two, No. 9793, 1977	275	—
TNT-Bird, assorted, No. 6407, 1970	60	125
Top Eliminator, blue, No. 7630, 1974	50	165
Top Eliminator, gold plated, redline or blackwall, No. 7630, 1977	30	50
Torero, assorted, No. 6260, 1969	15	60
Torino Stocker, gold plated, redline or blackwall, No. 7647, 1977	30	70
Torino Stocker, red, No. 7647, 1975	35	70
Tough Customer, olive, No. 7655, 1975	25	55

WHEEL ABBREVIATIONS

3sp: 3-spoke
5d: chrome 5-dot or Lamborghini wheel
5sp: 5-spoke
6sp: 6-spoke
7sp: 7-spoke
b7sp: black 7-spoke
g7sp: gold 7-spoke
8d: 8-dot
bbs/2: new wire wheel (found on #669 First Edition and #28 Chaparral 2)
bbs: chrome wire wheel
bbw: black basic wheel
bk or b: black
bl: blue
bw: blackwall (basic wheel)
cct: construction tire (8-dot)
ccts: chrome construction tire spoke
crr: chrome Real Rider
ct/b: chrome tri-blade/sawblade
ct: construction (8-dot)
cw: construction wheels
gbbs: gold wire wheel
gd: gold
gn: green
ho: Hot Ones
hoc: chrome Hot Ones
lw: lace wheels
o: orange
t/b: tri-blades (sawblades/directional)
uh: Ultra Hots
w: white
w5d: white 5-dot
ww: whitewalls
yrr: yellow Real Rider
yt/b: yellow tri-blade/sawblade

WHEEL IDENTIFICATION

Here are examples of the most common current wheel styles.
Many of these styles are available in silver, gold, black and sometimes other colors.

Sawblade

Hot Ones

5-Dot

5-Spoke

3-Spoke

Lace

Fat Lace

Real Riders

7-Spoke

Ultra Hots

Whitewalls

Blackwall

6-Spoke (Pro Circuit)

8-Dot Construction

8-Spoke Construction

Sawblade Construction

Name	MNP	MIP
Tow Truck, assorted, No. 6450, 1970	30	80
Tri-Baby, assorted, No. 6424, 1970	20	55
Turbo Mustang, blue, 1984	35	65
Turbofire, assorted, No. 6259, 1969	15	50
Twinmill, assorted, No. 6258, 1969	15	50
Twinmill II, chrome, blackwall set only, No. 9502, 1977	45	—
Twinmill II, orange, blackwall, No. 8240, 1977	10	25
Twinmill II, chrome, No. 9509, 1976	20	45
Twinmill II, orange, No. 8240, 1976	10	35
Vega Bomb, green, No. 7658, 1975	250	800
Vega Bomb, orange, blackwall, No. 7654, 1977	40	75
Vega Bomb, orange, No. 7658, 1975	40	85
Volkswagen, orange w/bug on roof, No. 7620, 1974	30	60
Volkswagen, orange w/stripes on roof, No. 7620, 1974	100	400
Volkswagen Beach Bomb, surf boards on side raised panels, No. 6274, 1969	115	310
Volkswagen Beach Bomb, surf boards in rear window, No. 6274, 1969	7000	—
VW Bug, pink, Real Rider, 1993	40	75
Warpath, white, No. 7654, 1975	50	110
Waste Wagon, assorted, No. 6192, 1971	90	325
What-4, assorted, No. 6001, 1971	50	150
Whip Creamer, assorted, No. 6457, 1970	25	60

Warpath, No. 7654.

No.	Name	MIP
	White Passion, white, in box, 1990	15 30
	Winnipeg, yellow, No. 7618, 1974	90 300
	Xploder, assorted, No. 6977, 1973	100 500
	Z Whiz, blue, No. 9639, 1982	20 55
	Z Whiz, white, redline, No. 9639, 1977	1500 —
	Z Whiz, gray, blackwall, No. 9639, 1977	15 25
	Z Whiz, gray, redline, No. 9639, 1977	35 70

NUMBERED PACKS

No.	Name	MIP
1	Old No. 5	110
2	Sol-Aire CX4, black, no side tampo, yellow interior, uh	120
2	Sol-Aire CX4, black, side tampo 33, yellow interior, uh	10
2	Sol-Aire CX4, black, ho	25
3	Wheel Loader, yellow, yellow interior, yct	5
4	XT3, purple, chrome bw	6
5	Good Humor Truck, white, w/new larger tampos, blue interior, 5sp	3
5	Good Humor Truck, white, small window, blue interior, 7sp	4
5	Good Humor Truck, white, small window, blue interior, 5sp	3
5	Good Humor Truck, white, small window, blue interior, t/b	4
5	Good Humor Truck, white, small window, blue interior, bw	10
5	Good Humor Truck, white, large window, blue, interior bw	12
6	Blazer 4X4, black, ct	90
6	Blazer 4X4, blue, ct-bs	25
6	Blazer 4X4, black, ct-8s	80

No.	Name	MIP
6	Blazer 4X4, blue, ct-8d	25
7	Troop Convoy	175
8	Vampyra, dark Purple, tampo on wing, chrome interior, bw	10
8	Vampyra, light Purple, tampo on wing, chrome interior, uh	15
9	unreleased	
10	Baja Breaker, white, ct	60
11	'31 Doozie, maroon, w/tan top, maroon interior, ww	60
12	Jeep	275
13	Delivery van, red rrgyc	25
14	'58 Vette, red pc	30
15	Peterbilt Tank Truck, yellow, bw	45
16	Earth Mover, yellow, black seat, yct-8d	40
17	Suzuki Quadracer, yellow, blue seat, yct-8d	30
18	Mercedes 540K, black, w/tan top, tan interior, bw	20
19	Shadow Jet, yellow, w/red interior, blue in tampo, smoked window, bw	35
19	Shadow Jet, yellow, w/red interior, maroon in tampo, smoked window, bw	50
20	Rocket Tank, olive	8
21	Nissan Hardbody, white, black interior, clear window, ct	35
21	Nissan Hardbody, white, black interior, clear window, cts	45
22	Talbot Lago, white, chrome interior, smoked window, ww	12
23	'80's Firebird, yellow, red interior, bw	15
23	'80's Firebird, black, red interior, bw	10
24	Hiway Hauler Ocean Pacific, turquoise, tan interior, blue window, bw	12

No.	Name	MIP
24	Hiway Hauler Pepsi, (long) red cab, smoked window, bw	18
25	unreleased	
26	'65 Mustang Convertible, metallic blue, tan interior, ww	20
26	'65 Mustang Convertible, light blue, tan interior, ww	30
26	'65 Mustang Convertible, white, tan interior, ww	150
27	Command Tank, green camouflage	22
28	'37 Bugatti, yellow and red, w/yellow fenders, chrome interior, ww	30
28	'37 Bugatti, blue and gray, w/yellow fenders, chrome interior, ww	15
28	'37 Bugatti, blue/gray, chrome interior, ww	15
28	'37 Bugatti, blue/gray, chrome interior, bw	35
28	'37 Bugatti, blue/gray, chrome interior, 7sp	10
29	Tail Gunner, green camouflage, black window, bct	85
30	'80s Corvette, blue, gho	150
31	Classic Cobra, red, w/metal base, black interior, 7sp	4
31	Classic Cobra, red, w/metal base, black interior, bw	4
31	Classic Cobra, red, w/black metal base, black interior, 3sp	3
31	Classic Cobra, red, w/black plastic base, black interior, 7sp	2
31	Classic Cobra, red, w/black metal base, black interior, 7sp	5
32	Sharkruiser, lavender, uh	6
32	Sharkruiser, lavender, ho	12

No.	Name	MIP
33	Camaro Z28, red, w/metal base, black window, uh	6
33	Camaro Z28, red, w/black plastic base, black window, uh	15
33	Camaro Z28, red, w/black plastic base w/skids, black window, bw	15
33	Camaro Z28, orange, w/black plastic base, black window, bw	8
33	Camaro Z28, orange, w/black plastic base, black window, uh	75
33	Camaro Z28, purple, w/black plastic base, black window, bw	8
34	Bulldozer, yellow, yellow rubber treads	30
35	Ferrari Testarossa, red, tan and red interior, uh	3
35	Ferrari Testarossa, black, black interior, gbbs	2
35	Ferrari Testarossa, black, tan interior, guh	2
35	Ferrari Testarossa, black, tan interior, g3sp	3
35	Ferrari Testarossa, black, tan interior, all small/gbbs	2
35	Ferrari Testarossa, red, black interior, uh	3
35	Ferrari Testarossa, black, tan interior, gbbs	2
36	Baja Bug, white w/flames, red interior, bw	22
37	Hot Bird, black, red interior, gho	20
37	Hot Bird, black, tan interior, gho	80
37	Hot Bird, white, red interior, uh	10
37	Hotbird, blue, tan interior, gho	35
37	Hotbird, white, tan interior, ho	17

No.	Name	MIP
37	Hotbird, white, red interior, guh	150
37	Hotbird, white, tan interior, gho	28
37	Hotbird, white, tan interior, uh	30
37	Hotbird, blue, tan interior, uh	20
38	Dump Truck, yellow w/plastic box, yct	5
38	Dump Truck, yellow w/metal box, yct-8d	10
39	Monster Vette, yellow, ct-8s	75
39	Monster Vette, yellow, ct-8d	75
39	Monster Vette, purple w/red flames, black window, ct-8d	20
39	Monster Vette, purple, ct-8d	25
40	Power Plower, black, ct-bd	12
41	unreleased	
42	Oshkosh Snow Plow, green, ct-8s	17
42	Oshkosh Snow Plow, orange, oct-8d	18
42	Oshkosh Snow Plow, orange, 0ct-8s	18
42	Oshkosh Snow Plow, green, plastic cab, green interior, ct	12
43	Tall Ryder, gray, ct-8d	20
43	Tall Ryder, gray, cts	40
44	Classic Caddy, blue w/black fenders, tan interior, ww	8
44	Classic Caddy, blue, w/black fenders, tan interior, t/b	3
44	Classic Caddy, blue w/black fenders, tan interior, 5sp	6
45	Rescue Ranger, red, bw	12
46	Rig Wrecker	45
47	'57 Chevy, turquoise, gho	175
47	57 Chevy, turquoise, uh	100
48	Passion, white, 5sp	28
49	Gulch Stepper, red, black window, ct	12
50	Rolls Royce Phantom II, blue, ww	250

82   •   Hot Wheels

No.	Name	MIP
51	40s Woodie, yellow, ww	700
52	Delivery Truck, Larry's Mobile Tune-up, white, red interior, bw	25
53	Zombot, gold, chrome pink gun, uh	8
53	Zombot, gold, chrome pink gun, hoc	8
54	Nissan 300ZX, metallic red, tan interior, uh	20
54	Nissan 300ZX, white, uh	15
54	Nissan 300ZX, white, gw	100
55	Road Roller, yellow, black seat	8
56	Bronco 4-Wheeler, light blue, red interior, ct	20
56	Bronco 4-Wheeler, white, red interior, ct	75
57	3-Window '34, purple, chrome interior, bw	30
58	Blown Camaro Z28, turquoise, bw	65
58	Blown Camaro Z28, turquoise, gray interior, uh	55
58	Blown Camaro Z28, turquoise, gho	90
59	Sheriff Patrol, blue and white, black interior, bw	10
59	Sheriff Patrol, black and white, tan interior, bw	4
59	Sheriff Patrol, black and white, tan interior, 7sp	8
60	Lamborghini Countach, white w/tampo, smoked window, uh	10
61	unreleased	
62	Alien, light red, smoked window, silver interior 7sp	2
62	Alien, dark red, silver interior, uh	3
62	Alien, light red, silver interior, 5sp	2
62	Alien, light red, silver interior, uh	3
63	Radar Ranger, chrome dish, metallic silver, black interior, t/b	2
63	Radar Ranger, gray dish, metallic silver, black interior, t/b	2
63	Radar Ranger, chrome dish, metallic silver, black interior ct	7
63	Radar Ranger, chrome dish, metallic silver, black interior, cts	15
63	Radar Ranger, chrome dish, metallic silver, black interior, ctb	30
64	unreleased	
65	VW Bug, turquoise, bw	25
65	VW Bug, red, blue flame outline, bw	22
65	VW Bug, red, green flame outline, bw	27
66	Custom Corvette, metallic red, black base, tan interior, uh	30
67	'32 Delivery, yellow w/Delivery in blue, yellow interior, bw	20
68	T-Bucket, yellow, red interior, bw	10
68	T-Bucket, yellow, red interior, 5sp	8
69	Ferrari F40, red, tan interior, guh	4
69	Ferrari F40, red, tan interior, g3sp	3
69	Ferrari F40, red, tan interior, g5sp	4
69	Ferrari F40, red, tan interior, gbbs	2
69	Ferrari F40, red, tan interior, cuh	4
70	Chevy Stocker, black, five tam, bw	30

No.	Name	MIP
70	Chevy Stocker, black, three tam, bw	15
71	Ambulance, white, white interior, bw	5
71	Ambulance, white, white interior, 7sp	4
71	Ambulance, white, white interior, t/b	4
71	Ambulance/Rescue, yellow, yellow interior, 7sp	4
71	Ambulance/Rescue, yellow, yellow interior, 5sp	3
71	Ambulance/Rescue, yellow, yellow interior, 5dot	2
72	Bus Prisoner Transport, black w/gray plastic base, blue interior, w/o bar windows, 5dot	35
72	Bus Prisoner Transport, black w/gray plastic base, blue interior, w/bared windows, 5dot	2
72	School Bus, yellow, black interior, bw	4
73	Street Roader, white, black interior, ct	15
73	Street Rodder, white, cts	50
74	GT Racer, purple w/o "V" decal and metal base, smoked window, bw	15
74	GT Racer, purple w/"V" decal and metal base, smoked window, uh	10
75	Pontiac Banshee, red, black window, uh	3
75	Pontiac Banshee, red, guh	200
75	Pontiac Banshee, red, black window, 5sp	3
75	Pontiac Banshee, red, black window, 7sp	3
76	Kenworth Big Rig, black, w/red, orange and blue tampo, gray window, bw	5
76	Kenworth Big Rig, black, w/red, orange and blue tampo, gray window, t/b	3
76	Kenworth Big Rig, black, w/red, orange and blue tampo, gray window, 7sp	3
77	Bywayman, black, red interior, ct	10
77	Bywayman, maroon, ct-8d	15
77	Bywayman, blue, ct-8d	75
77	Bywayman, maroon, wct-8d	150
78	Peterbilt Cement Truck, red, bw	25
79	Big Bertha, olive	17
80	Porsche 959, metallic red, tan interior, clear window, uh	12
80	Porsche 959, red w/No. 59, gray interior, uh	10
80	Porsche 959, red w/No. 7, gray interior, uh	12
81	Ratmobile, white, chrome motor, uh	3
81	Ratmobile, white w/metal base, chrome motor, hoc	7
82	Fire-Eater, red, blue interior, 7sp	3
82	Fire-Eater, yellow w/red insert, black interior, 5sp	2
82	Fire-Eater, yellow w/red insert, black interior, smoked window, t/b	2
82	Fire-Eater, red, blue interior, 5sp	2
82	Fire-Eater, red, blue interior, bw	7
83	Tank Gunner, olive, bbw	60
84	Probe Funny Car Motorcraft, red, metal interior, bw	35
85	unreleased	
86	Propper Chopper, white, News Chopper 2, blue interior, blue window	10

No.	Name	MIP
86	Proper Chopper, white, News Chopper 2, w/triangle, blue interior, blue window	25
87	Purple Passion, purple w/scallops, red interior, ww	15
87	Purple Passion, purple w/flames, tan interior, ww	12
88	Thunderbird Stocker, black and white, uh	20
88	Thunderbird Stocker, black and white, bw	250
88	Thunderbird Stocker, red w/Motorcraft, black interior, bw	25
88	Thunderbird Stocker, black and white w/Valvoline, black interior, bw	8
89	Mini Truck, turquoise w/light tampo, blue interior, uh	8
89	Mini Truck, turquoise w/dark tampo, blue interior, hoc	250
90	unreleased	
91	unreleased	
92	Mercedes 380SEL, black, tan interior/clear window, hoc	12
92	Mercedes 380SEL, black, tan interior, clear window, uh	8
93	unreleased	
94	Auburn 852, red, red interior, ww	10
94	Auburn 852, red, bw	140

No.	Name	MIP
95	'55 Chevy, yellow, purple window, bw	15
95	'55 Chevy, white, purple window, bw	20
96	unreleased	
97	unreleased	
98	Nissan Custom Z, red, uh	8
98	Nissan Custom Z, red, guh	200
98	Nissan Custom Z, red, tan interior, uh	6
99	Ford Stake Truck, blue, chrome interior, bw	8
100	Peterbuilt Dump Truck, red, metal interior, bw	7
100	Peterbuilt Dump Truck, red, metal interior, 7sp	3
100	Peterbuilt Dump Truck, red, metal interior, wbw	70
100	Peterbuilt Dump Truck, red, metal interior, 3sp	3
101	unreleased	
102	Surf Patrol, yellow, red interior, ct	3
102	Surf Patrol, yellow, red/smoked window, ct/b	2
103	Range Rover, white, tan interior, ct	6
104	Turbostreak, fl. Red, metal interior, bw	12
104	Turbostreak, fl. red, w/pink in tampo, metal interior, bw	75
105	Peugot 205, white, bw	75
106	VW Golf, white w/pink base, pink interior, clear window, bw	65
106	VW Golf, red, tan interior, bw	10
107	unreleased	
108	Ramp Truck, white, clear window, bw	20
108	Ramp Truck, white, black window, bw	15
109	unreleased	

No. 108 Ramp Truck, white, clear window, bw.

No.	Name	MIP
110	Trailbuster, turquoise, pink interior, w/blue in tampo, ct	10
110	Trailbuster, turquoise, pink interior, black in tampo, ct	20
111	Street Beast, teal and white, teal interior, ww	5
112	Limozeen, white, white interior, ww	8
113	Speed Shark, purple, pink interior, bw	4
113	Speed Shark, black, red interior, bw	3
113	Speed Shark, black, 5sp	3
114	Pontiac Fiero, black, red interior, sho	20
114	Pontiac Fiero, black, red interior, uh	8
114	Pontiac Fiero, black, red interior, bw	15
115	Roll Patrol Army, green w/camouflage on hood, black interior, bct	15
116	Mazda MX-5 Miata, red, no tampo on hood, tan interior, bw	10
116	Mazda MX-5 Miata, red, no tampo, tan interior, bw	15
117	Ferrari 250, yellow w/chrome base and pipes, black interior, bw	12

No.	Name	MIP
117	Ferrari 250, yellow w/yellow base and chrome pipes, black interior, bw	8
117	Ferrari 250, yellow w/yellow base and black pipes, black interior, bw	4
117	Ferrari 250, yellow w/yellow base and black pipes, black interior, 7sp	4
118	Ferrari 348, yellow, black and yellow interior, hoc	13
118	Ferrari 348, yellow, black and yellow interior, uh	6
119	unreleased	
120	unreleased	
121	unreleased	
122	Toyota MR2 Rallye, white w/chrome lights, red interior, uh	10
122	Toyota MR2 Rallye, white w/chrome lights, red interior, sho	15
122	Toyota MR2 Rallye, white w/black lights, red interior, uh	25
123	Lamborghini Diablo, red tan interior, uh	5
124	unreleased	
125	Zender Fact 4, metallic silver, black interior, sho	15
125	Zender Fact 4, metallic silver, black interior, uh	6

No. 115 Roll Patrol Army, green with cammo on hood, black interior, bct.

No. 125 Zender Fact 4, metallic silver, black interior, uh.

No.	Name	MIP
126	Lumina Minivan, red, tan interior, small bw	6
126	Lumina Minivan, red, tan interior, large bw	20
127	Power Plower, metallic purple, yellow interior, ct	15
127	Power Plower, purple enamel, yellow interior, ct	10
128	Baja Breaker, metallic purple and yellow, w/blue tint base, red interior, bw	5
129	Suzuki Quadracer, white, blue seat, yct	10
129	Suzuki Quadracer, white, blue seat, ct	6
130	unreleased	
131	Nissan Hardbody, black, yellow interior, ct	5
131	Nissan Hardbody, red w/checkered flag, black interior, ct/b	3
131	Nissan Hardbody, black, dark tampo, yellow interior, bct	5
131	Nissan Hardbody, white w/black base, pink interior, ct	50
131	Nissan Hardbody, black, pink interior, ct	10
131	Nissan Hardbody, black, yellow interior, ct/b	5
132	unreleased	
133	Shadow Jet, purple, purple interior bw	6
133	Shadow Jet, purple, yellow interior, bw	20
134	Mercedes 540K, white, w/tan top, red interior, bw	10
135	'32 Ford Delivery, white w/turquoise, pink and blue tampo, turquoise interior, bw	10
135	'32 Ford Delivery, white w/turquoise, pink and blue tampo, 7sp	7

No.	Name	MIP
136	'56 Flashider, turquoise, chrome window, c5dot	18
136	'56 Flashsider, turquoise, black window, sho	20
136	'56 Flashsider, turquoise, black window, uh	8
136	'56 Flashsider, turquoise, black window, 5sp	4
136	'56 Flashsider, turquoise, black window, c5dot	3
137	Goodyear Blimp, gray w/rev it up, white gondola	5
138	unreleased	
139	unreleased	
140	Flashfire, black, red interior, w5dot	4
140	Flashfire, black, red interior, hoc	15
140	Flashfire, black, red interior, uh	4
140	Flashfire, black, red interior, t/b	3
140	Flashfire, black, red interior, 5sp	3
140	Flashfire, black, red interior, c5dot	6
141	Shock Factor, black and bright pink, pink interior, ct	4
141	Shock Factor, black and med. pink, pink interior, ct	4
141	Shock Factor, black and red, red interior, ct	45
141	Shock Factor, black and dark pink, pink interior, ct	4
142	Hyway Hauler, red w/Kool-Aid, thick ribbon (B), black window, bw	10
142	Hyway Hauler, red w/Kool-Aid, thin ribbon (A), black window, bw	10
143	Recycling Truck, lime green, black window, 7sp	3
143	Recycling Truck, lime green, black window, 5sp	2

No.	Name	MIP
143	Recycling Truck, lime green, black window, t/b	2
143	Recycling Truck, orange, black window, bw	4
143	Recycling Truck, orange, black window, 7sp	4
144	Oshkosh Cement Mixer, red, white and blue, blue seat, bw	4
145	Tractor, yellow, yellow seat, ytt	8
145	Tractor, red, red seat, ctt	4
145	Tractor, red, red seat, t/b front/ctt rear	4
145	Tractor, red w/black cab and hydraulics. red seat, t/b front/ctt rear	25
145	Tractor, green w/yellow cab and hydraulics. green seat, yt/b front/ytt rear	2
145	Tractor, short exhaust pipe, green w/yellow cab and hydraulics. green seat, yt/b front/ytt rear	4
146	Bulldozer, yellow, black seat	5
147	Tank Truck, red, chrome window, 7sp	5
147	Tank Truck, red w/matching red base, chrome window, bw	7
147	Tank Truck, orange, chrome window, 7sp	3
147	Tank Truck, Dust Control, white, w/orange base, black tank, 3sp	3
147	Tank Truck, Dust Control, white w/orange base, black tank, 5sp	3
147	Tank Truck, orange, chrome window, t/b	3
147	Tank Truck, red w/dark red base, chrome window, bw	7
148	Porsche 930, purple, black interior, bw	60

No.	Name	MIP
148	Porsche 930, red, black interior, bw	10
148	Porsche 930, fluorescent green, bw	80
148	Porsche 930, red, black interior, 5sp	3
149	BMW 850i, light blue, tan interior, gr	8
149	BMW 850i, light blue, tan interior, uh	3
149	BMW 850i, light blue, tan interior, hoc	15
150	BMW 323, black w/black base, tan interior, hoc	15
150	BMW 323, black, tan interior, uh	5
150	BMW 323, w/BMW, rear plate black, tan interior, bw	5
151	Ford Aerostar, purple, chrome window, bw	8
152	unreleased	
153	Thunderstreak, blue and green, green interior, bw	5
153	Thunderstreak, blue and green w/No. 1, green interior, bw	7
153	Thunderstreak, yellow w/Pennzoil, yellow interior, bw	10
154	'59 Caddy, white, red interior, ww	7
155	Turboa, yellow, chrome interior, uh	5
155	Turboa, yellow w/metal base, chrome interior, hoc	10
156	Rodzilla, light purple w/light purple plastic base, uh	5
156	Rodzilla, reddish purple w/reddish purple metal base, uh	10
157	'57 Chevy, yellow w/flames, blue interior, uh	15
157	'57 Chevy, yellow w/flames, blue interior, hoc	25

No.	Name	MIP
158	Mercedes Unimog, white and red, red interior, ct	7
159	Big Bertha, gray camouflage, n/a	6
160	Cammand Tank, white camouflage	6
161	Roll Patrol, gray camouflage, black interior, bct	10
162	'65 Mustang Convertible, light red, tan interior, 7sp	5
162	'65 Mustang Convertible, light red, tan interior, 5sp	4
162	'65 Mustang Convertible, dark red, tan interior, ww	15
162	'65 Mustang Convertible, light red, tan interior, ww	6
163	Talbot Lago, metalflake red, orange window, chrome interior, ww	10
164	Mercedes 540K, metalflake blue, red interior, 5dot	3
164	Mercedes 540K, metalflake blue, red interior, t/b	3
164	Mercedes 540K, metalflake blue, red interior, 5sp	3
164	Mercedes 540K, metalflake blue, red interior, 3sp	3
164	Mercedes 540K, metalflake blue, red interior, bw	4
165	Suzuki Quadracer, dull pink w/dark gray painted base, blue seat, ct	10
165	Suzuki Quadracer, bright pink w/dark gray painted base, blue seat, ct	10
166	Vampyra, black, no tampo on wing, uh	10
166	Vampyra, black, yellow, green and purple on wing, bw	8
166	Vampyra, black, yellow, green and purple on the wing reversed	25
167	'80's Firebird, orange, purple interior, bw	15

No.	Name	MIP
167	'80's Firebird, orange, purple interior, extra tampo, bw	20
168	GT Racer, black, silver window, bw	5
169	Sol-Aire CX-4, blue, w/metal base, chrome interior, uh	15
169	Sol-Aire CX4, blue, w/black plastic base, black interior, sho	15
170	Chevy Stocker, metalflake pink, yellow interior, bw	10
171	VW Bug, purple, red interior, 3sp	4
171	VW Bug, purple, red interior, bw	10
172	Mazda MX-5 Miata, metallic burgundy w/yellow and red side stripe, tan interior, 3sp	3

No. 171 VW Bug, purple, red interior, 3sp.

No.	Name	MIP
172	Mazda MX-5 Miata, yellow, pink interior, gr	10
172	Mazda MX-5 Miata, metallic burgundy, tan interior, 7sp	4
172	Mazda MX-5 Miata, metallic burgundy w/yellow and red side stripe, tan interior, 5sp	3
172	Mazda MX-5 Miata, yellow, pink, bw	4
172	Mazda MX-5 Miata, yellow, pink, 7sp	45
173	unreleased	
174	Limozeen, metalflake light blue, yellow interior, ww	5
175	Ferrari 348, white, red and white interior, sho	15
175	Ferrari 348, pearl white w/pink strips, red letters, red and white interior, uh	45
176	Lamborghini Diablo, metalflake blue, red interior, uh	6
177	Zender Fact 4, metalflake purple, orange interior, sho	15
177	Zender Fact 4, metalflake Purple, orange interior, uh	6
178	Hot Bird, metalflake black, pink interior, uh	8
179	Porsche 959, metallic purple, chrome window, sho	15
179	Porsche 959, metallic purple, chrome window, uh	7
180	unreleased	
181	Pontiac Fiero 2M4, light green flake, yellow interior, sho	15
181	Pontiac Fiero 2M4, light green flake, yellow interior, uh	7
182	Shadow Jet, green w/blue in tampo and blue metal base, smoked canopy, green interior, bw	5
182	Shadow Jet, green w/yellow in tampo and metal base, smoked canopy, green interior, bw	5
182	Shadow Jet, green w/yellow in tampo and metal base, smoked canopy, green, interior 5sp	3
183	VW Golf, metalflake green w/chrome base, yellow interior, bw	20
183	VW Golf, metalflake pink w/chrome base, yellow interior, bw	15
183	VW Golf, metalflake pink w/black base, yellow interior, bw	6
184	Mercedes 380SEL, metalflake blue, yellow interior, sho	15
184	Mercedes 380SEL, metalflake blue, yellow interior, uh	6
185	Propper Chopper, white and black, black interior, blue window, none	5
185	Propper Chopper Search & Rescue, yellow w/black base, black window, none	6
185	Propper Chopper Search & Rescue, yellow w/red base, black window, none	10
186	Ford Aerostar Speedie Pizza, w/phone number, white, chrome window, bw	10
186	Ford Aerostar Speedie Pizza, w/o phone number, white, chrome window, bw	6
187	Ramp Truck, yellow, black window, bw	5
187	Ramp Truck, yellow, black window, t/b	8
187	Ramp Truck, yellow, black window, 7sp	3

No.	Name	MIP
188	Hummer, plastic body, tan camouflage, no hood, tampo, black window, cct	4
188	Hummer, white w/metal base, small antenna, black window, t/b	4
188	Hummer, white w/silver base, small antenna, black window, t/b	3
188	Hummer, white w/silver base, big antenna, black window, t/b	3
188	Hummer, plastic body, tan camouflage, no gun, black window, t/b	4
188	Hummer, plastic body, pink camouflage, black window, cct	4
188	Hummer, metal body, tan camouflage, black window, cct	8
189	Gleamer Patrol, dark silver/chrome texture, tan interior, bw	6
189	Gleamer Patrol, medium silver/chrome texture, tan interior, bw	6
190	'57 T-Bird, med. gold chrome texture, black interior, bw	5
190	'57 T-Bird, dark gold chrome texture, black interior, bw	5
190	'57 T-Bird, light gold chrome texture, black interior, bw	5
191	Aeroflash, dark pink chrome texture, black window, guh	15
191	Aeroflash, dark pink chrome texture, black window, uh	6
192	Corvette Stingray, silver chrome texture, black interior, bw	6
192	Corvette Stingray, green chrome texture, black interior, bw	20

No.	Name	MIP
192	Corvette Stingray, silver chrome texture, black interior, uh	5
193	Porsche 959, pink chrome texture, dark smoked window, uh	5
193	Porsche 959, silver chrome texture, dark smoked window, uh	10
194	Goodyear Blimp, gray, silver gondola	2
194	Goodyear Blimp, gray, white gondola	3
195	Troop Convoy, tan, tan bbw	5
196	3-Window '34, white w/pink fenders, black interior, bw	25
196	3-Window '34, white w/purple fenders, black interior, bw	10
196	3-Window '34, light metallic Green, black interior, bw	150
197	Corvette Split Window, light blue w/gray base, red interior, 5sp	3
197	Corvette Split Window, light blue w/chrome base, red interior, ww	5
197	Corvette Split Window, light blue w/chrome base, red interior, bw	4
197	Corvette Split Window, light blue w/gray base, one rivet, red interior, ww	5

No. 197 Corvette Split Window, light blue with chrome base, red interior, ww.

No.	Name	MIP
198	Path Beater, fluorescent yellow, gray interior, bct	15
198	Path Beater, fluorescent yellow, gray interior, cct	6
198	Path Beater, fluorescent yellow, gray interior, t/b	2
199	Double Deamon, yellow and green, chrome interior, uh	4
199	Double Deamon, yellow and black, black interior, uh	5
200	Custom Corvette, dark metallic purple, light gray interior, 7sp	5
200	Custom Corvette, dark metallic purple, light gray interior, cbbs	3
200	Custom Corvette, dark metallic purple, light gray interior, 5sp	3
200	Custom Corvette, dark metallic purple, light gray interior, uh	3
200	Custom Corvette, white, red interior, uh	5
201	Oshkosh Snowplow, orange, orange interior, oct	4
201	Oshkosh Snowplow, orange, orange interior, ot/b	10
201	Oshkosh Snowplow/Grain & Feed, burgundy and gray, burgundy interior, t/b	3
202	'93 Camaro, (long pipe) purple, smoked window, gray interior, uh	4
202	'93 Camaro, (short pipe) purple, clear window, white interior, uh	4
202	'93 Camaro, (short pipe) purple, smoked window, white interior, uh	4
203	Jaguar XJ220, silver, metallic black interior, uh	8
203	Jaguar XJ220, light /dark blue, metallic black interior, clear window, gbbs	3

No. 203 Jaguar XJ220, dark blue, metallic gray interior, clear window, gbbs.

No.	Name	MIP
203	Jaguar XJ220, light /dark blue, metallic gray interior, clear window, gbbs	3
203	Jaguar XJ220, dark blue, metallic gray interior, clear window, gbbs	3
203	Jaguar XJ220, light /dark blue, metallic gray interior, clear window, four small gbbs	3
203	Jaguar XJ220, dark blue w/metallic black base, black interior, clear window, guh	15
203	Jaguar XJ220, dark blue w/metallic black base, black interior, clear window, uh	3
203	Jaguar XJ220, silver, metallic black interior, guh	20

No.	Name	MIP
204	Oscar Mayer Wienermobile, tan and light red, smoked window, 5dot	3
204	Oscar Mayer Wienermobile, tan and light red, smoked window, 7sp	3
204	Oscar Mayer Wienermoble, tan and light red, smoked window, 5sp	3
204	Oscar Meyer Wienermobile, tan and dark red, smoked window, bbw	3
204	Oscar Meyer Wienermobile, tan and light red, smoked window, bw	3
205	Treadator, neon green and purple, logo on front wing	2
205	Treadator, red and chrome	2
205	Treadator, green enamel, purple logo on front wing	2
205	Treadator, neon green and purple, no logo	2
206	Pipe Jammer, yellow, chrome interior, uh	3
207	Vector Avtech WX-3, lavender w/black base, white interior, smoked window, 5sp	4
207	Vector Avtech WX-3, lavender w/black base, white interior, smoked window, uh	4

No.	Name	MIP
207	Vector Avtech WX-3, dark lavender w/black base, white interior, smoked window, uh	4
208	Avus Quatro, metallic silver, red interior, 5sp	3
208	Avus Quatro, metallic silver, red interior, uh	3
209	Lexus SC 400, metallic black, white interior, uh	4
210	Viper R/T 10, red, black interior, bbs	8
210	Viper R/T 10, red, black interior, 5sp	65
210	Viper R/T 10, yellow w/logo on windshield, black interior, guh	7
210	Viper R/T 10, green, gray interior, guh	4
210	Viper R/T 10, green, gray interior, g3sp	4
210	Viper R/T 10, green, gray interior, g5sp	4
210	Viper R/T 10, green, gray interior, gbbs	4
210	Viper R/T 10, red, black interior, guh	4
210	Viper R/T 10, yellow, black interior, guh	7
210	Viper R/T 10, red, black interior, uh	4
211	Twin Mill II, neon yellow w/black base, black window, uh	30
211	Twin Mill II, neon yellow w/chrome base, black window, uh	10
211	Twin Mill II, neon yellow w/gray base, black window, uh	4
212	Silhoutte II, metallic purple w/chrome base, white interior, uh	3
212	Silhoutte II, metallic purple w/gray base, white interior, 5dot	3

No. 204 Oscar Mayer Wienermoble, tan and light red, smoked window, 5sp.

No.	Name	MIP
212	Silhoutte II, metallic purple w/gray base, white interior, uh	3
213	'57 Chevy, (no '57 on base) turquoise, smoked window, black interior, 5sp	4
213	'57 Chevy, turquoise, blue interior, uh	4
213	'57 Chevy, turquoise w/tampo on door, blue interior, uh	7
213	'57 Chevy, turquoise, blue window, blue interior, guh	12
213	'57 Chevy, (large '57 on base) turquoise, blue window, blue interior, 5sp	4
213	'57 Chevy, (small '57 on base) turquoise, blue window, blue interior, 5sp	4
213	'57 Chevy, (no '57 on base) turquoise, blue window, blue interior, 5sp	4
214	Swingfire, blue and white, white interior, 5sp	3
214	Swingfire, blue and white, white interior, ww	6
214	Swingfire, blue and white, white interior, 7sp	3
215	Auburn 852, red w/black fenders, black interior, clear window, 5sp	3
215	Auburn 852, red w/black fenders, black interior, ww	8
215	Auburn 852, red w/black fenders and 30th logo, black interior, clear window, 5sp	3
216	Fat Fendered '40, purple, black interior, bw	15
217	'40's Woodie, turquoise and black, clear window, yellow interior, 5sp	3
217	'40's Woodie, turquoise and black, clear window, yellow interior, bw	3
217	'40's Woodie, turquoise and black, clear window, yellow interior, 5dot	3
217	'40's Woodie, turquoise and black, clear window, yellow interior, 7sp	3
218	Street Roader, green, silver interior, ct	4
219	Gulch Stepper, fl. yellow, black window, ct	4
220	Bywayman, white, blue interior, t/b	3
220	Bywayman, white w/blue metal base, blue interior, clear window, ct	3
220	Bywayman, white, w/metal base, black interior, clear window, ct	3
220	Bywayman, white w/metal base blue, interior/clear window, ct	3
221	Range Rover, black, tan interior, ct	4
221	Range Rover, black, tan interior, t/b	4
222	Blazer 4X4, metalflake blue, yellow interior, ct	4
222	Blazer 4X4, metalflake blue, yellow interior, bct	15
223	Baja Bug, metalflake red, black interior, bw	18
224	Zombot, blue, chrome, pink gun uh	2
224	Zombot, dark gray, chrome, orange gun, uh	2
224	Zombot, chrome, orange gun, 7sp	2
224	Zombot, dark gray, chrome, pink gun, uh	2
225	Limozeen, metalflake Black, red interior, ww	5
226	Ferrari 348, fluorescent pink, black and red, interior, 5sp	3

No.	Name	MIP
226	Ferrari 348, fluorescent pink, black and red, interior, uh	3
226	Ferrari 348, fluorescent pink, smoked window, black and red interior, uh	3
226	Ferrari 348, black, black and red interior, 5sp	3
226	Ferrari 348, black, black and red interior, 7sp	7
227	Lamborghini Diablo, metallic purple, purple interior, 5sp	5
227	Lamborghini Diablo, yellow, silver interior, uh	5
227	Lamborghini Diablo, yellow, silver interior, 5sp	5
227	Lamborghini Diablo, pearl purple, purple interior, 5sp	5
227	Lamborghini Diablo, pearl purple, purple interior, t/b	5
228	Zender Fact 4, lime green, w/orange tampo, black interior, uh	20
228	Zender Fact 4, metallic blue, black window, black interior, uh	2
228	Zender Fact 4, maroon w/black and gold tampo, tan interior, clear window, 5sp	2
228	Zender Fact 4, metallic dark blue, smoked window, black interior, uh	3
228	Zender Fact 4, lime green w/orange tamp, black window, uh	10
228	Zender Fact 4, metallic blue, clear window, gray interior, uh	15
228	Zender Fact 4, lime green, w/yellow tampo, black interior, uh	5
228	Zender Fact 4, metallic blue, smoked window, black interior, uh	5

No.	Name	MIP
229	Mercedes 380SEL, metalflake pink, black interior, uh	4
230	XT-3, metalflake blue, blue window, 5sp	3
230	XT-3, metalflake blue, blue window, bw	5
230	XT-3, white, red window, bw	3
230	XT-3, white, blue window, bw	40
231	Mini Truck, orange, blue interior, clear window, uh	3
231	Mini Truck, orange, blue interior, clear window, 5sp	3
231	Mini Truck, orange, blue interior, clear window, t/b	3
231	Mini Truck, orange, blue interior, clear window, c5dot	3
231	Mini Truck, orange, blue interior, clear window, w5dot	10
232	Lamborghini Countach, red w/separate wing, tan interior, dark smoked window, uh	3
232	Lamborghini Countach, red w/molded wing, tan interior, smoked window, guh	3
232	Lamborghini Countach, white w/flush wing support, red interior, smoked window, 5dot	3
232	Lamborghini Countach, white w/inset wing support, red interior, smoked window, 5dot	3
232	Lamborghini Countach, white w/inset wing support, red interior, clear window, 5dot	6
232	Lamgoghini Countach, red w/molded wing, tan interior, dark smoke window, uh	3
233	Toyota MR2 Rallye, white, red interior, clear window, t/b	5
233	Toyota MR2 Rallye, black, red interior, clear window, 3sp	40

No.	Name	MIP
233	Toyota MR2 Rallye, white w/purple, green, blue enamel graphics, purple interior, cbbs	2
233	Toyota MR2 Rallye, white w/purple, green, metallic blue, graphics, purple interior, cbbs	2
233	Toyota MR2 Rallye, black, red interior, clear window, 5sp	90
233	Toyota MR2 Rallye, black, red interior, clear window, uh	100
233	Toyota MR2 Rallye, white, red interior, clear window, 5dot rear, 5sp front	4
233	Toyota MR2 Rallye, white, red interior, clear window, uh	4
233	Toyota MR2 Rallye, white, red interior, clear window, 3sp	4
233	Toyota MR2 Rallye, white, red interior, clear window, 5dot	4
234	Nissan Custom Z, metallic purple, black interior, gbbs	3
234	Nissan Custom Z, metallic purple, black interior, g5sp	3
234	Nissan Custom Z, metallic purple, black interior, g3sp	3
234	Nissan Custom Z, metallic purple, black interior, guh	3
234	Nissan Custom Z, metallic purple, black interior, uh	3
235	Turbo Streak, neon yellow, metal interior, bw	3
236	Ford Aerostar, black, chrome window, bw	8
237	Ford Stake Rack Truck, red w/chrome base, smoked window, chrome interior, 7sp	3
237	Ford Stake Rack Truck, red w/chrome base, clear window, chrome interior, 7sp	3
237	Ford Stake Rack Truck, red w/chrome base, clear window, chrome interior, bw	3
237	Ford Stake Rack Truck, red w/chrome base, smoked window, chrome interior, 3sp	3
237	Ford Stake Rack Truck, red w/chrome base, smoked window, chrome interior, 5sp	3
237	Ford Stake Rack Truck, red w/bright yellow tampo, chrome base, clear window, chrome interior, bw	3
237	Ford Stake Rack Truck, red, gray base, smoked window, chrome interior 7sp	3
238	Hyway Hauler, purple, black window, bw	8
239	Mercedes Unimog, tan/camouflage, tan interior, bct	3
239	Mercedes Unimog, tan/camouflage, tan interior, wt/b	3
239	Mercedes Unimog, tan/camouflage, tan interior, wct	3
239	Mercedes Unimog, tan/camouflage, tan interior, ct	10
240	unreleased	
241	unreleased	
242	'93 Camaro, blue, white interior, bw	3
242	'93 Camaro, blue, white interior, t/b	3
242	'93 Camaro, blue enamel, white interior, bw	25
242	'93 Camaro, blue, white interior, 5sp	3
242	'93 Camaro, blue enamel, white interior, uh	125

No.	Name	MIP
242	'93 Camaro, blue, white interior, uh	160
243	unreleased	
244	Hot Wheels 500, w/o No Fear or Racer, black w/black metal base, black driver, 5dot	3
244	Hot Wheels 500, No Fear, black w/black metal base, black driver, 5dot	3
244	Hot Wheels 500, w/o No Fear black, w/black metal base, black driver, 5dot	3
244	No Fear Race Car, black, black interior, bw	5
244	No Fear Race Car, black, black interior, 7sp	3

No.	Name	MIP
245	Driven To The Max, neon yellow, yellow interior, large 5sp	2
245	Driven To The Max, orange, gray interior, bw	8
246	Shadow Jet II, dark chrome, chrome interior, uh	3
246	Shadow Jet II, dark chrome, chrome interior, 5sp	3
247	Rigor Motor, maroon, chrome interior, bw	4
248	Splittn' Image II, dark blue w/white logo, chrome window, puh	4
248	Splittn' Image II, dark purple, chrome window, 7sp	4
248	Splittn' Image II, dark purple, pink window, 7sp	4

No. 242 '93 Camaro, blue, white interior, t/b.

No. 244 Hot Wheels 500, No Fear, black with black metal base, black driver, 5dot.

No.	Name	MIP
248	Splittn' Image II, dark blue, pink window, o7sp	4
248	Splittn' Image II, dark blue, pink window, puh	6
248	Splittn' Image II, dark blue w/pink logo, chrome window, puh	6
248	Splittn' Image II, dark blue, chrome window, uh	6
249	Fuji Blimp, white and green	3
250	Talbot Lago, black chrome interior, 7sp	3
250	Talbot Lago, black chrome interior, ww	5
251	Gulch Stepper, red, black window, ct	5
251	Gulch Stepper, black, black window, ct	3

No.	Name	MIP
251	Gulch Stepper, black, black window, w/reverse tampo, ct/b	40
252	Street Roader, Suzuki in grill white w/blue and pink, blue interior, ct	4
252	Street Roader, white w/blue and pink, blue interior, ct	3
252	Street Roader, white w/blue and pink, blue interior, ct/b	3
253	Mercedes 380SEL, maroon w/metal base, tan interior, clear window, uh	2
253	Mercedes 380SEL, maroon w/metal base, tan interior, clear window, t/b	2
253	Mercedes 380SEL, maroon w/metal base, tan interior, clear window, 5sp	2
253	Mercedes 380SEL, maroon w/metal base, tan interior, clear window, 7sp	2
254	Sol-Aire CX-4, metallic blue, white interior, guh	5
254	Sol-Aire-CX-4, metallic blue, white interior, 7sp	2
254	Sol-Aire-CX-4, metallic blue, white interior, gbbs	2
255	BMW 850i, dark blue w/black base and red logo, red interior, smoked window uh	2
255	BMW 850i, dark blue w/black base and red logo, red interior, smoked window guh	2
255	BMW 850i, dark blue w/black base and red logo, red interior, clear window guh	2
255	BMW 850i, dark blue w/black base and black logo, red interior, clear window guh	2
255	BMW 850i, dark blue w/black base and black logo, red interior, clear window g3sp	2

No. 253 Mercedes 380SEL, maroon with metal base, tan interior, clear window, t/b.

No.	Name	MIP
255	BMW 850i, dark blue w/black base and black logo, red interior, clear window gbbs	2
256	'80's Firebird, fl. Red, yellow interior, bw	10
257	3 Window '34, silver w/flames, silver interior, 3sp	5
257	3 Window '34, silver w/flames, silver interior, small rear bw	10
257	3 Window '34, silver w/flames, silver interior, large rear bw	10
257	3 Window '34, silver w/flames, silver interior, 7sp	5
258	Blazer 4x4, light blue, w/logo on front fender, silver interior, ct	3
258	Blazer 4x4, light blue, silver interior, bct	15
258	Blazer 4x4, light blue w/logo on window, silver interior, ct	3
259	Lumina Minivan/taxi, yellow, black interior, bw	5
259	Lumina Minivan/taxi, yellow, black interior, 5sp	5
260	Twinmill II, dark blue, red window, 5dot	3
260	Twinmill II, dark blue, red window, 5sp	3
260	Twinmill II, dark blue, red window, w5dot	3
260	Twinmill II, dark blue, red window, uh	3
261	Cybercruiser, purple w/black base, purple chrome, uh	12
261	Cybercruiser, purple w/metal base, purple chrome, uh	3
262	'93 Camaro, red, tan interior, 5sp	3
262	'93 Camaro, red, tan interior, uh	3
262	'93 Camaro, red white, interior, uh	3
262	'93 Camaro, dark blue and white, white interior, guh	3
262	'93 Camaro, metallic blue and white, white interior, guh	4
263	Mean Green Passion, green, tan interior, ww	12
264	Lexus SC400, maroon metallic w/black base, tan interior, clear window, 5sp	2
264	Lexus SC400, maroon metallic w/black base, tan interior, clear window, w5dot	6
264	Lexus SC400, maroon metallic w/black base, tan interior, clear window, c5dot	2
264	Lexus SC400, maroon metallic w/black base, tan interior, clear window, t/b	2
264	Lexus SC400, maroon metallic w/black base, tan interior, clear window, 3sp	2
264	Lexus SC400, maroon metallic w/black base, tan interior, clear window, 7sp	2
264	Lexus SC400, dark maroon metallic w/black base, cream interior, clear window, uh	2
264	Lexus SC400, dark maroon metallic w/black base, tan interior, clear window, uh	2
264	Lexus SC400, maroon metallic w/black base, tan interior, clear window, uh	2
265	Oldsmobile Aurora, police tampo, gray interior, b7sp	3
265	Oldsmobile Aurora, turquoise w/smoked window, gray interior, bw	20
265	Oldsmobile Aurora, turquoise, gray interior, bw	15
266	'59 Caddy Convertible, pearl lavender, white interior ww	3
266	'59 Caddy Convertible, pearl lavender, white interior 7sp	3

No.	Name	MIP
266	'59 Caddy Convertible, light pearl lavender, white interior 7sp	4
266	'59 Caddy Convertible, blue black interior, smoked window, gbbs	3
267	Olds 442 W-30, yellow, chrome base, black interior, 5dot	4
267	Olds 442 W-30, yellow, black interior, bw	8
267	Olds 442 W-30, yellow, black interior, 7sp	4
267	Olds 442 W-30, yellow, new casting, black interior, 7sp	4
267	Olds 442 W-30, yellow w/chrome, base black interior, 5sp	4

No. 266 '59 Caddy conv., blue black interior, smoked window, gbbs.

No.	Name	MIP
267	Olds 442 W-30, yellow w/gray base, black interior, 7sp	4
267	Olds 442 W-30, yellow w/gray base, black interior, 5sp	4
268	GM Lean Machine, neon yellow and black, black window 7sp	2
268	GM Lean Machine, neon yellow and black, smoked window, 5sp	2
268	GM Lean Machine, neon yellow and black, smoked window, t/b	2
268	GM Lean Machine, neon yellow and black, smoked window, 3sp	2
268	GM Lean Machine, neon yellow and black, smoked window, 5dot	2
268	GM Lean Machine, neon yellow and black, smoked window, uh	2
269	Oshkosh Cement Mixer, yellow/black yellow interior, bw	2
269	Oshkosh Cement Mixer, yellow/black yellow interior, 7sp	2
269	Oshkosh Cement Mixer, yellow/black yellow interior, t/b	2
269	Oshkosh Cement Mixer, yellow/black yellow interior, 5sp	2
270	Chevy Stocker, metalflake pink, yellow interior, guh	3
270	Chevy Stocker, metallic gold, red interior, guh	40
270	Chevy Stocker, metalflake pink, red interior, guh	50
271	Side Splitter	250
273	Tail Gunner, white camouflage, black window, wct	7

No. 269 Oshkosh Cement Mixer, yellow and black with yellow interior, t/b.

No.	Name	MIP
274	Super Cannon, green camouflage, black window, w5sp	5
274	Super Cannon, green camouflage, black window, wbw	5
440	Monte Carlo Stocker, race team blue, white interior, no letter, b7sp	4
440	Monte Carlo Stocker, race team blue, white interior, b7sp	4
441	Chevy Stocker, black, red interior, 7sp	2
442	Ferrari F40, white, smoked window, w5dot	2
442	Ferrari F40, white, smoked window, 7sp	2

No.	Name	MIP
442	Ferrari F40, white, smoked window, 5sp	2
443	Ferrari 348, black, red interior, clear window, 5dot	2
443	Ferrari 348, black, red interior, clear window, 7sp	2
443	Ferrari 348, black, red interior, clear window, 5sp	2
444	Aeroflash, white w/green and yellow tampo, orange base and window, gsp	2
445	Jaguar, green, gray interior, 5sp	4
445	Jaguar, green, gray interior, 7sp	6
446	'32 Ford Delivery, dark blue, black interior, 7sp	10
446	'32 Ford Delvery, dark blue, black interior, 3sp	15
447	'63 Split Window, green, tan interior, 7sp	2
447	'63 Split Window, green, w/gray base, tan interior, 3sp	2
447	'63 Split Window, green, tan interior, 5sp	2
447	'63 Split Window, green, tan interior, 3sp	2
447	'63 Split Window, green w/gray base, tan interior, 7sp	2
448	'67 Camaro, (no origin) yellow w/black stripes smoked window, black interior, 5sp	7
448	'67 Camaro, (Malaysia) yellow w/black stripes smoked window, black interior, 5sp	5
448	'67 Camaro, yellow w/black stripes, smoked window, black interior, 3sp	150
448	'67 Camaro, (Malaysia) yellow w/black stripes, smoked window, black interior, 5dot	3
449	Camaro Z-28, orange, black interior, 5sp	3
449	Camaro Z-28, orange, black interior, 3sp	3

No.	Name	MIP
450	Corvette Stingray, pearl white, chrome interior, 3sp	2
450	Corvette Stingray, pearl white, chrome interior, 7sp	2
450	Corvette Stingray, pearl white, chrome interior, all small 3sp	2
450	Corvette Stingray, pearl white, chrome interior, 5sp	2
451	3 Window '34, pink, pink interior, 7sp	5
451	3 Window '34, pink, pink interior, 3sp	5
452	Ferrari 250, green, tan interior, 7sp	3
452	Ferrari 250, green, tan interior, 5dot	2
452	Ferrari 250, green, tan interior, 5sp	2
453	Audi Avus, red, ta interior, smoked window, 7sp	2
453	Audi Avus, red, tan interior, smoked window, 5sp	2
453	Avus Quattro, red, tan interior, smoked window, 5sp	2
453	Avus Quattro, red, tan interior, smoked window, 7sp	2
453	Avus Quattro, red, tan interior, smoked window, t/b	2
454	Zender Fact 4, white, silver interior, blue window, 5sp	2
454	Zender Fact 4, white, silver interior, blue window, 7sp	2
455	'65 Mustang Convertible, gold, white interior, 5sp	5
455	'65 Mustang Convertible, dark metallic blue, metal China base, white interior, clear window, 5sp	3
455	'65 Mustang Convertible, gold, white interior, 7sp	3
455	'65 Mustang Convertible, gold, white interior, 3sp	7
457	Pontiac Banshee, black, neon yellow interior, 5sp	1

No.	Name	MIP
457	Pontiac Banshee, black, neon yellow interior, bbs	2
457	Pontiac Banshee, purple w/metal China base black interior, clear window, 5sp	1
458	Speed Shark, lavender, purple interior, 5sp	2
460	Zombot, black over silver, orange base and gun, 5sp	2
461	Enforcer, deep purple, silver-painted window 5sp	2
462	'80's Firebird, blue, tan interior, 5sp	2
462	'80's Firebird, blue, tan interior, bbs	2
463	Fiero 2M4, neon yellow, black interior, bbs	3
463	Fiero 2M4, neon yellow, black interior, 5sp	3

No. 452 Ferrari 250, green, tan interior, 5dot.

No.	Name	MIP
464	Blazer 4X4, metallic blue w/blue tint, China base, yellow interior, blue tint window, cts	3
464	Blazer 4X4, metallic blue w/blue tint, China base, yellow interior, blue tint window, ct	3
467	Peugeot 405, green, tan interior, 5sp	2
467	Peugeot 405, silver w/checks and orange stripe, black interior, 5sp	2
467	Peugeot 405, silver w/checks and orange stripe, black interior, bbs	2
467	Peugeot 405, silver w/orange stripe only, black interior, bbs	2
468	GT Racer, neon orange w/tampo, black window, 5sp	2
468	GT Racer, neon orange w/tampo, black window, bbs	2
468	GT Racer, neon orange, black window, 5sp	2
469	Hot Bird, gold, tan interior, 5sp	2
469	Hot Bird, gold, w/hood bird, black interior, 5sp	2
469	Hot Bird, gold w/hood bird, black interior, bbs	2
470	Turbo Streak, blue and white, white driver, 5sp	2
470	Turbo Streak, blue and white w/purple tampo, white driver, 5sp	2
471	Velocitor, blue and white, orange interior, 5sp	2
471	Velocitor, black w/Hot Wheels logo, red interior, 5sp	2
471	Velocitor, black w/Hot Wheels logo, red interior, bbs	2
472	Buick Stocker, neon yellow, red tampos, black interior, 5sp	2

No.	Name	MIP
472	Buick Stocker, neon yellow, red tampos, black interior, bbs	2
472	Buick Stocker, neon yellow, black interior, 5sp	2
473	BMW M1, silver and gray two-tone, black interior, 5sp	2
473	Street Beast, silver and gray two-tone, black interior, 5sp	2
473	Street Beast, green, gray interior, 5sp	2
474	VW Golf, black, red interior, 5sp	3
474	VW Golf, black w/fahrvergnugen, red interior, 5sp	3
474	VW Golf, black w/fahrvergnugen, red interior, bbs	3
475	Fork lift, yellow, black seat, bw front/5sp rear	2
477	Double Demon, green, purple chrome, 5sp	2
478	Dragon Wagon, neon yellow w/green base, 5sp	2
479	Computer Warrior, black over blue w/orange base, 5sp	2
481	Tall Ryder, pearl yellow w/silver China base, black window, cts	2
481	Tall Ryder, pearl gold w/silver China base, black window, cts	2

No. 479 Computer Warrior, black over blue with orange base, 5sp.

No.	Name	MIP
481	Tall Ryder, green w/chrome China base, chrome window, cts	2
482	Earth Mover, yellow, black seat, cts	3
483	Thunder Roller, maroon, tan interior, bw rear/5sp front	4
484	Grizzlor, white, metal base, orange engine, 5sp	2
484	Grizzlor, white, black spots, red base, metal engine, 5sp	2
485	Evil Weevil, light orange, neon orange base, 5sp	2
486	Command Tank, black, purple Nite Force	2
487	Troop Convoy, green, transparent canopy, 5sp	4
487	Troop Convoy, metallic gray, neon orange w/black canopy, 5sp	4
488	Sting Rod, metallic gray, neon orange base, ct	2
489	Big Bertha, metallic gray, orange turret	3
489	Big Bertha, Nite Force, black, purple black turret	2
489	Tough Customer, Nite Force, black, purple black turret	2
491	Rocket Shot, metallic gray orange top, gray rocket	4
491	Rocket Shot, candy purple, black camouflage and top purple rocket	2
492	Swingfire, neon orange, gray interior, 5sp	2
492	Swingfire, white w/blue snow patrol tampo, blue interior 5sp	2
493	Porsche 911 Targa, neon yellow, black China base, black interior, clear window, all large 5sp	2
493	Porsche 911 Targa, neon yellow, black China base, black interior, clear window, all small 5sp	2

No.	Name	MIP
494	Mercedes 500SL, metallic gray, red interior, 5sp	2
496	Ferrari 308GT, red w/black base, black interior, tinted window, 5sp	2
496	Ferrari 308GT, red w/black base, black interior, tinted window, bbs	2
497	Ferrari Testarossa, pearl white, black interior, bbs	2
497	Ferrari Testarossa, pearl white, black interior, 5sp	2
498	BMW 850i, metallic silver, red interior, 5sp	2
498	BMW 850i, metallic silver, red interior, bbs	2
499	Corvette Coupe, metallic green, red interior, bbs	2
499	Corvette Coupe, metallic green, red interior, 5sp	2
502	Chevy Nomad, red, tan interior, closed wheel, g7sp	2
502	Chevy Nomad, red, tan interior, open wheel, g7sp	2
503	'80's Corvette, red, gray interior, 3sp	2
503	'80's Corvette, red, gray interior, t/b	2
503	'80's Corvette, red, gray interior, 5sp	2
503	'80's Corvette, red, gray interior, bbs	2
504	Camaro Z28, pearl white, blue window, 3sp	2
504	Camaro Z28, pearl white, blue window, 5sp	2
505	1993 Camaro, black, tan interior, 5sp	2
505	1993 Camaro, black, tan interior, t/b	2
505	1993 Camaro, black, tan interior, bbs	2
505	1993 Camaro, black, tan interior, yellow letter, b7sp	2

No.	Name	MIP
506	Nissan 300ZX, purple w/gold tampo, purple interior, 5sp	2
507	Peugot 205, black, blue, purple w/gray interior, red painted base, 5sp	10
523	Barracuda, sublime w/chrome base, black interior and tinted windows, 5sp	10
524	GMC Motor Home, metallic blue w/gray India base, white interior, bw	15
525	Trail Buster Jeep, black and red stripes, India base, red interior, large bw	2
526	Neet Streater, yellow w/metal India base, black interior, bw	2
527	Second Wind, white w/No. 6, India base, blue interior, bw	2
528	Beach Blaster, white w/gray India base, red interior, bw	2
577	Police Cruiser, white w/Fire Chief tampo, black interior, 3sp	5
577	Police Cruiser, white w/Fire Chief tampo, black interior, 5sp	5
577	Police Cruiser, black and white, tan interior, b7sp	5
590	Porsche 911, red, smoked window, black interior, large rear t/b	2
590	Porsche 911, red, smoked window, black interior, t/b	2
590	Porsche 911, red, smoked window, black interior, large rear 5sp	2
590	Porsche 911, red, smoked window, black interior, 5sp	2
590	Porsche 911, red, smoked window, black interior, large rear 5dot	2
591	Porsche 959, silver, blue, smoked window, t/b	2
591	Porsche 959, silver, blue w/metal Malaysia base, smoked window, 5sp	2
591	Porsche 959, silver, blue w/metal China base, smoked window, 5sp	2
592	Porsche 930, blue, smoked window, black interior, t/b	2
592	Porsche 930, blue, smoked window, black interior, 5sp	2
593	Skullrider, light pink tint chrome, metal base, black interior, 5sp	3
593	Skullrider, dark pink chrome, metal base, black interior, 5sp	3
594	GM Ultralite, Police white and black, black window, 7sp	4
594	GM Ultralite, no tampo, white and black, black window, 3sp	2
594	GM Ultralite, no tampo, white and black, black window, 7sp	2
594	Police Car, white and black, black window, 3sp	2
595	Corvette Sting Ray III, metallic blue, white interior, smoked window, 3sp	2
595	Corvette Sting Ray III, metallic purple, gray interior, clear window, 5sp	2
595	Corvette Sting Ray III, metallic purple, gray interior, clear window, 7sp	2
596	Pontiac Salsa, orange, metallic silver window, gray interior 7sp	2
596	Pontiac Salsa, orange, metallic silver window, gray interior t/b	2
596	Pontiac Salsa, orange, metallic silver window, gray interior 3sp	2

No.	Name	MIP
597	Buick Wildcat, red enamel, black motor, black window, 7sp	2
597	Buick Wildcat, red enamel, black motor, black window, 3sp	2
597	Buick Wildcat, candy red, black motor, black window, 7sp	5
597	Buick Wildcat, dark metallic green, chrome motor, black window, 3sp	2
597	Buick Wildcat, light metallic green, gray motor, black window, 3sp	2
597	Buick Wildcat, dark metallic green, gray motor, black window, 3sp	2
598	Turboa, butterscotch w/metal China base, gold motor and seat, 5sp	2
599	Camaro Wind, white w/flames, pink chrome window, bbs	3
600	Nissan Custom Z, metallic dark blue, metal China base, black interior, clear window, 5sp	2
600	Nissan Custom Z, metallic dark blue, metal China base, black interior, clear window, bbs	2
600	Nissan Custom Z, light blue enamel, metal China base black interior, clear window, bbs	2
601	Commando, bronze w/metal base, black interior, clear window, ccts	3
602	Sharkruiser, black w/gray base and red chrome, bbs	2
603	BMW 325i, yellow and red w/silver painted China base, black interior, clear window, bbs	2
604	Ferrari 308 GTS, yellow and black, black interior, 5sp	2

No.	Name	MIP
605	Mercedes 2.6, gold w/black plastic base, black interior, bbs	2
606	Mercedes 300TD, green w/gray plastic base, gray interior, 5sp	2
607	Fat Fendered '40, aqua w/yellow, orange and purple tampo, black interior, 5sp	8
608	Porsche 911, metalflake silver w/black plastic base, black interior, 5sp	2
609	Jaguar XJ40, dark metallic blue, white interior, blue tint window, bbs	2
610	Land Rover MkII, orange w/blue and white tampo, black interior, 5sp	2

No. 604 Ferrari 308 GTS, yellow and black, black interior, 5sp.

No.	Name	MIP
611	Fire Eater II, red, blue tint window, 5sp	2
612	T-Bird, turquoise, white interior, bw	9
613	London Bus, red, black window, 5sp	5
615	Ford XR4Ti, metalflake silver w/butterscotch and purple stripe, red interior, 5sp	2
616	'80's Corvette, white w/yellow and blue tampo, blue interior, black dash, bbs	2
617	Flame Stopper II, red w/gray boom, black interior, 5sp	2
618	Chevy Stocker, white and silver, red No. 1, purple interior, 5sp	5
619	London Taxi, yellow, black interior, 5sp	2

No. 612 T-Bird, turquoise, white interior, bw.

No.	Name	MIP
620	Ford Transit Wrecker, light blue enamel w/white and red tampos, black window, 5sp	2
622	City Police, black and white Pontiac, gray interior, and bumpers, b5sp	2
623	Mustang Cobra, pearl pink and black, black interior, bbs	2
624	Assault Crawler, green camouflage, green interior, treads	2
625	Classic Packard, black, black interior, 5sp	3
641	Wheel Loader, orange w/China metal base, black cage, gray scoop, ct	2
642	Forklift, white w/metal China base, blue cage, black forks, rear 5sp/front bw	2
643	Digger, yellow w/yellow China base, w/o HW logo, gray boom and scoop, 5sp	2
643	Digger, yellow w/yellow China base, w/HW logo, gray boom and scoop, 5sp	2
700	Shock Factor, yellow and blue w/metal China base, blue interior, all large bw	2
702	Lumina Van, dark metallic green w/black China base, tan interior, smoked window, bbs	2
702	Lumina Van, dark metallic green w/black China base, tan interior, smoked window, 5sp	2
712	Tipper, dark blue w/black China base, white tip box, black window, 5sp	2
714	Talbot Lago, blue w/black fender, black metal base	350
715	1996 Mustang GT, white w/metal China base, red interior, clear window, 5sp	2
761	Flame Stopper, red w/gray boom, black window, t/b	2

No.	Name	MIP
765	Oshkosh P-Series, blue and white body w/metal base and gray plow, blue seats, t/b	2
767	Mercedes 380SEL, white w/gold base, tan interior, clear window, t/b	2
768	Lamborghini Countach, black w/black base, red interior, clear window, 5dot	2
770	Lexus SC400, metallic blue w/black base, white interior, clear window, bbs	2
770	Lexus SC400, metallic blue w/black base, white interior, smoked window, bbs	2
770	Lexus SC400, metallic purple w/black base, white interior, smoked window, bbs	2

No.	Name	MIP
771	'56 Flashsider, yellow pearl w/pink and blue tampo, black window, 5dot	2
771	'56 Flashsider, yellow pearl w/pink and blue tampo, black window, all small 5dot	2
773	Hot Wheels 500, neon yellow w/metal base, black driver, b/7sp	1
774	Ramp Truck, metallic green w/metallic gray ramp and metal China base, smoked window, 5sp	1
778	Speed Blaster, metallic maroon w/orange tampo, black base, chrome window, 3sp	1

No. 712 Tipper, dark blue with black China base, white tip box, black window, 5sp.

No. 765 Oshkosh P-Series, blue and white body with metal base and gray plow, blue seats, t/b.

No. 770 Lexus SC400, metallic purple with black base, white interior, smoked window, bbs.

No. 781 Lamborghini Diablo, dark red with black-painted base, tan interior, tinted window, 5dot.

No.	Name	MIP
778	Speed Blaster, metallic blue w/orange tampo, black base, chrome window, 3sp	1
778	Speed Blaster, metallic purple w/red tampo black base, chrome window, 3sp	1
779	Big Chill, blue w/white flames and white Thailand base, chrome driver, black front wheel, white skis	2
779	Big Chill, blue w/white flames and white China base, chrome driver, white front wheel, white skis	2
780	'58 Corvette, powder blue enamel w/motor chrome interior, smoked window, 5dot	2

No.	Name	MIP
780	'58 Corvette, powder blue enamel w/motor chrome interior, smoked window, all small 5dot	2
780	'58 Corvette, powder blue enamel w/hood chrome interior, smoked window, 5dot	2
780	'58 Corvette, powder blue w/hood and small rear plate chrome interior, smoked window, 5dot	2
781	Lamborghini Diablo, dark red w/black-painted base, tan interior, tinted window, 5dot	1
782	Radar Ranger, gold w/metal base black seat, clear canopy, large ct/b	1

No.	Name	MIP
783	Twinn Mill II, metallic silver w/black base, black window, all large bbs	1
784	Ferrari F512M, metallic silver w/black painted base, black interior, clear window, 5dot	1
784	Ferrari F512M, metallic silver w/black painted base, black interior, clear window, 5sp	1
784	Ferrari Testarossa, metallic silver w/black painted base, black interior, clear window, 5dot	1
784	Ferrari Testarossa, metallic silver w/black painted base, black interior, clear window, 5sp	1
787	'57 Chevy, (metal) purple w/chrome base black interior, smoked window, t/b	1
788	Mercedes 540K, metallic purple w/blue top and tampo, black interior, clear window, large bbs	2
788	Mercedes 540K, metallic purple w/blue top and tampo, black interior, clear window, small bbs	2
788	Mercedes 540K, metallic purple w/blue top and tampo, black interior, clear window, 3sp	2
791	Treadator, metallic blue w/black base, no white side tampo, chrome canopy, black treads	1
792	Camaro Race Car, white w/orange tampo and black base, black interior, clear window, 5sp	1
793	Auburn 852, black w/gold fenders and metal base, gold interior, tinted window, gbbs	1

No.	Name	MIP
795	Tractor, silver w/black base black cab and hydraulics, cct rear/ct/b front	1
796	'96 Camaro Convertible, white w/orange stripes and gray base orange interior, smoked window, w5sp	1
797	Dodge Ram 1500, red w/white China base, yellow interior, tinted window, 5sp	1
797	Dodge Ram 1500, red w/white Malaysia base, yellow interior, smoked window, 5dot	1
798	Propper Chopper POLICE, blue w/black base, black interior, blue tint window, n/a	1

No. 797 Dodge Ram 1500, red with white Maylasia base, yellow interior, smoked window, 5dot.

No.	Name	MIP
802	Flashfire, metallic gold w/green logo and gold base black spoiler and interior, smoked window, four large 5dot	1
802	Flashfire, metallic gold w/no logo and gold base, black spoiler and interior, smoked window, 5dot	1
802	Flashfire, metallic gold w/green logo and gold base, black spoiler and interior, smoked window, 5dot	1
803	'40 Woodie, white, black interior, 5sp	4
808	Driven To The Max, pearl white w/metal base, hot pink driver and spoiler, 5sp	2

No.	Name	MIP
812	GM Lean Machine, green and gold w/metal base gold seat, smoked window, t/b	1
813	Ferrari 355, black w/metal base, yellow interior, yellow window, 3sp	1
813	Ferrari 355, black w/metal base, yellow interior, yellow window, 5sp	1
814	Speed-A-Saurus, teal w/orange base, large rear 5sp	2
814	Speed-A-Saurus, teal w/orange base, medium rear 5sp	2
815	Mercedes 500SL, dark metallic green w/black base tan interior, smoked window, 3sp	1

No. 802 Flashfire, metallic gold with no logo and gold base, black spoiler and interior, smoked window, 5dot.

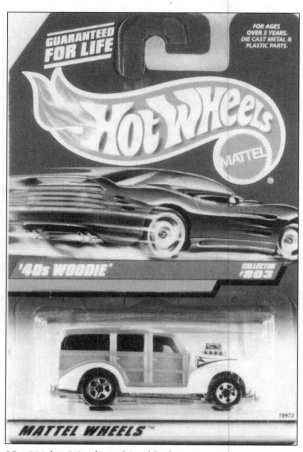

No. 803 '40 Woodie, white, black interior, 5s.

No. 815 Mercedes 500SL, dark metallic green with black base tan interior, smoked window, 3sp.

No.	Name	MIP
816	Ferrari 308, metallic brown w/black metal base, tan interior, smoked window, 5dot	2
816	Ferrari 308, metallic brown w/black base, tan interior, smoked window, gray rear, 5sp/5dot front	1
816	Ferrari 308, metallic brown w/black metal base, tan interior, smoked window, 5sp	2
817	Porsche 928, pearl white w/metal base, black window, bbs	1
818	Porsche Carrera, dark metallic red w/o flames, g5sp	2

No.	Name	MIP
818	Porsche Carrera, dark metallic red w/flames, g5sp	30
820	Zender Fact 4, metallic green w/black China base, black interior, clear window, bbs	1
821	'96 Mustang Convertible, white w/metal China base, red interior, clear window, 5sp	2
822	Camaro Z-28, teal w/metal base gray interior, clear window, 3sp	2
823	Sol-Aire CX4, race team blue, white base, white interior, clear window, gbbs	1
827	Radio Flyer Wagon, red w/metal Malaysia base, chrome motor, black seat, 5sp	2
829	Porsche Carrera, metallic silver w/metal base red interior, clear window, t/b	1
834	Ferrari Testarossa, black w/black painted India base, tan and black interior, clear window, bw	1
835	Baja Bug, red w/black and mustard tampo and metal India base, tan interior, large rear bw	2
835	Baja Bug, dark blue race team colors w/metal India base, white interior, all small bw	3
835	Baja Bug, light blue race team colors w/metal India base, white interior, all small bw	3
837	Radio Flyer, blue, white interior, 5s	2
850	Rail Rodder, gray w/gold chrome and metal Malaysia base, b5sp	2
851	Treadator, light pearl purple w/neon green Thailand base, chrome window, white scoops	2

No.	Name	MIP
851	Treadator, light pearl blue w/neon green Thailand base, chrome window, white scoops	2
852	Rigor Motor, purple w/metal base and gold motor, yellow canopy, all medium g5sp	2
852	Rigor Motor, purple w/metal base and gold motor, yellow canopy, large rear/g5sp	2
853	Camaro Z28, neon yellow plastic body w/black metal base, black window, 5dot	2
853	Camaro Z28, neon yellow plastic body w/black metal base, black window, 5sp	2
853	Camaro Z28, neon yellow plastic body w/metal base, black window, 5dot	2

No.	Name	MIP
854	Porsche 959, white w/metal base and orange tampo, black interior, smoked window, 3sp	1
854	Porsche 959, white w/metal China base and pink tampo, black interior, smoked window, bbs	1
854	Porsche 959, white w/metal base and pink tampo, black interior, smoked window, t/b	1
854	Porsche 959, white w/metal base and orange tampo, black interior, smoked window, t/b	1
855	Ferrari F50, purple w/black base black interior, smoked window, t/b	1

No. 850 Rail Rodder, gray with gold chrome and metal Malaysia base, b5sp.

No. 854 Porsche 959, white with metal base and pink tampo, black interior, smoked window, t/b.

No.	Name	MIP
856	Porsche 930, metallic red w/metal Thailand base, black interior, smoked window, 3sp	1
857	T-Bird Stocker, orange plastic body w/black metal base, black window, 5dot	1
858	Hummer, white w/black stripes and orange Hummer Racer, red-tinted window, ct/b	2
858	Hummer, white w/black stripes and red Hummer Racer, red-tinted window, ct/b	2
859	Bronco, red w/blue tint, metal base black interior, smoked window, ct/b	2
860	Road Rocket, white and dark blue and metal base, white seat, 3sp	1

No.	Name	MIP
861	Twinn Mill II, gold w/black base, black window, bbs	1
862	Pontiac Salsa, dark metallic red, chrome base, black interior, black window, 5dot	1
863	Oshkosh Cement Mixer, neon yellow w/silver fenders, black base, silver interior, 3sp	2
864	Tank Truck, metallic black w/chrome tank, black base, chrome window, 5dot	1
864	Tank Truck, dark metallic burgundy w/chrome tank, black Malaysia base, chrome window, 5dot	1

No. 858 Hummer, white with black stripes and red Hummer Racer, red-tinted window, ct/b.

No. 864 Tank Truck, metallic black with chrome tank, black base, chrome window, 5dot.

No. 866 Ferrari 250, gold metallic with black base and chrome pipes black interior, smoked window, bbs.

No. 867 '97 Corvette, dark metallic blue with red base, white interior, smoked window, 5sp.

No.	Name	MIP
865	Ford F150, white w/black base and orange tampo, chrome interior, smoked window, 3sp	2
866	Ferrari 250, gold metallic w/black base and chrome pipes black interior, smoked window, bbs	1
867	'97 Corvette, metallic blue w/red base, white interior, smoked window, 5sp	2
867	'97 Corvette, dark metallic blue w/red base, white interior, smoked window, 5sp	2
868	Range Rover, green metallic w/chrome base, tan interior, smoked window, ct/b	1

No.	Name	MIP
868	Range Rover, dark green metallic w/chrome base, tan interior, smoked window, ct/b	1
869	Power Pipes, black w/orange painted base, chrome interior, orange canopy, ot/b	1
870	Chevy Stocker, purple enamel w/black metal base, black window, gt/b	1
871	Olds 442 Race Team, colors w/chrome base white interior, smoked window, 5sp	4
872	Rig Wrecker, white w/black base and red boom, chrome interior, tinted window, 5dot	2

No.	Name	MIP
873	Hydroplane, white w/red Harbor Patrol, black base, smoked canopy	2
874	Pit Crew Truck, silver w/red plastic base, red interior, blue-tinted window, 5dot	1
876	Bywayman, red w/metal base, white interior, tinted window, ct/b	2
877	Chevy 1500, silver w/black metal base, black interior, clear window, small t/b	2
881	'95 Camaro, black enamel w/black base, red interior, smoked window, t/b	2
884	Gulch Stepper, pearl yellow and purple, blue-tinted base, black window, large ct/b	2

No.	Name	MIP
889	Mercedes 380SEL, black enamel w/gold base and trim, tan interior, tinted window, gbbs	2
890	BMW Roadster, white w/metal base, red interior, smoked window, 3sp	1
894	Toyota MR2, white w/black base, white interior, smoked window, bbs	1
899	'56 Flashsider, metallic silver w/chrome base, black window, 5sp	2
908	Ford F Series CNG, P/U metallic purple w/black base, chrome interior, smoked window, 5sp	5

No. 873 Hydroplane, white with red Harbor Patrol, black base, smoked canopy.

No. 908 Ford F Series CNG, P/U metallic purple with black base, chrome interior, smoked window, 5sp.

No.	Name	MIP
991	Rodzilla, chrome w/metal base, gbbs	2
992	Ferrari F512M, red enamel w/black metal base, tan interior, smoked window, 5sp	2
993	Ferrari 348, yellow w/black Malaysia base, black and yellow interior, smoked window, 5sp	2
994	Way 2 Fast, black w/gold metal base, chrome interior, g5sp	2
995	Porsche 911, yellow w/metal base, silver interior, black tint, 5sp	1

No.	Name	MIP
995	Porsche 911, yellow w/metal base, black interior, black tint, 5sp	1
996	'32 Ford Delivery, pearl blue w/black fenders and metal base, black interior, clear window, bbs	2
997	Jaguar D-Type, red enamel, gray interior, smoked window, bbs	2
998	Firebird Funny Car, metallic red w/metal base, metal interior, tinted window, g5sp	2
999	Hot Seat, chrome w/metal base, red seat and plunger, 5sp	2

No. 996 '32 Ford Delivery, pearl blue with black fenders and metal base, black interior, clear window, bbs.

No. 997 Jaguar D-Type, red enamel, gray interior, smoked window, bbs.

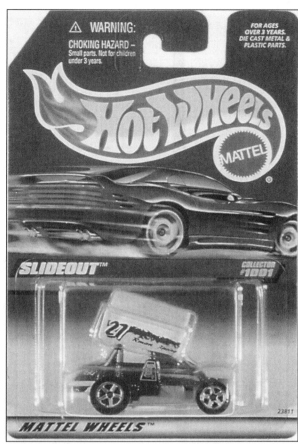

No. 1001 Slideout, metallic blue with yellow, white Malaysia base, 5sp.

No.	Name	MIP
1000	'59 Impala, white w/chrome base, black interior, black tint, gbbs	4
1001	Slideout, metallic blue w/yellow, white Malaysia base, 5sp	2
1003	Ferrari F40, black w/metal base red interior, smoked window, 5sp	2
1009	Peterbilt Dump Truck, blue w/white box and metal base, blue-tinted window, 5sp	2
1010	Ford Stake Bed Truck, teal w/gray stake bed chrome interior, blue-tinted window, 5dot	2
1012	Flame Stopper, white w/black base, black window, ct/b	2

No.	Name	MIP
1015	Mercedes C-Class, yellow w/black base, red interior, clear window, bbs	2
1018	'32 Ford Coupe, white w/black base, black interior, black interior, 5sp	2
1022	'63 T-Bird, gold and black w/metal base, white interior, black tint, bbs	2
1024	Classic Cobra, white w/metal base, black interior, black tint, 5sp	2
1025	Mercedes SLK, metallic blue w/metal base, white interior, black tint, t/b	2
1026	Dodge Carvan, metallic orange w/black base, white interior, black tint, 5sp	2
1027	Custom C3500, magenta w/black base, black interior, blue tint, 5sp	2
1028	'56 Flashsider, yellow w/chrome base, black tint, 3sp	2
1029	'40 Ford, red w/chrome base, white interior, clear window, 5sp	2
1030	Porsche 959, silver w/metal base, black interior, blue tint, 5dot	2
1031	Aeroflash, green w/black metal base, black interior, clear window, 3sp	2
1032	Ford GT90, yellow w/metal base, black interior, clear window, 3sp	2
1035	'70 Cuda, purple w/chrome base, black interior, black tint, 3sp	2
1038	Dodge Viper, silver w/black base, black interior, clear window, 3sp	2
1040	Panoz GTR-1, metallic green w/black base, black interior, black tint, 3sp	2

No.	Name	MIP
1041	Supercomp, silver w/chrome base, black interior, 5sp	2
1043	Rail Rodder, white w/metal base, blue chrome interior, bk5sp	2
1044	Whatta Drag, black w/metal base, gold chrome interior, red tint, 5dot	2
1045	Dodge Ram, black and white w/white base, white interior, clear window, 5sp	2
1046	Police Cruiser, white w/black base, black interior, blue tint, 3sp	2
1047	Olds Aurora, black and white w/black base, tan interior, clear window, 5dot	2

No.	Name	MIP
1048	Rescue Ranger, white w/chrome base, blue tint interior, blue tint, 5sp	2
1049	Treadator, black w/blue base, chrome window	2
1051	'65 Mustang, black w/metal base, tan interior, black tint, g5sp	2
1052	Rigormotor, red w/metal base, chrome interior, black tint, 5sp	2
1053	Hydroplane, black w/black base, chrome interior, yellow tint	2
1054	Porsche 959, black w/metal tan interior, clear window, bbs	2

No. 1051 '65 Mustang, black with metal base, tan interior, black tint, g5sp.

No. 1058 '96 Mustang, metallic red with metal base, black interior, black tint, gbbs.

No.	Name	MIP
1055	School Bus, black w/black base, black interior, red tint, 5dot	2
1056	Corvette Stingray, mustard yellow w/metal base, clear window, gbbs	2
1057	Thunder Streak, metallic red and blue w/metal base, blue interior, bk7sp	2
1058	'96 Mustang, metallic red w/metal base, black interior, black tint, gbbs	2
1059	Dodge Ram 1500, metallic green w/gray base, chrome interior, clear window, 5dot	2
1060	Ramp Truck, black and yellow w/metal base, black window, 5dot	2

No.	Name	MIP
1061	Rescue Ranger, white w/red base, red interior, red tint, 5dot	2
1062	Rail Rodder, dark blue w/metal base, gold interior	2
1063	'70 Cuda, orange w/chrome base, black interior, black tint, 3sp	2
1064	Lakester, metallic silver w/silver base, chrome interior, blue tint, 5sp	2
1065	Firebird, white w/gray base, black interior, black tint, gy-bk7sp	2
1066	Mustang Cobra, metallic gold w/black base, black interior clear window, 5sp	2

No. 1064 Lakester, metallic silver with silver base, chrome interior, blue tint, 5sp.

No. 1065 Firebird, white with gray base, black interior, black tint, gy-bk7sp.

No. 1067 Express Lane, orange with metal base, red interior, 5sp.

No. 1069 '40 Ford Trailer Edition, white and orange with chrome base, orange interior, clear window, chrr.

No.	Name	MIP
1067	Express Lane, orange w/metal base, red interior, 5sp	2
1068	Dodge Concept, metallic silver w/metal base, black interior, clear window, gbbs	2
1069	'40 Ford, yellow w/black base, black interior, black tint, 5dot	2
1069	'40 Ford Trailer Edition, white and orange w/chrome base, orange interior, clear window, chrr	20
1070	'32 Ford Coupe, metallic red w/gray base, black interior, clear window, 5 dot	3
1071	Panoz GTR-1, black w/black base, red interior, clear window, 3sp	2

No.	Name	MIP
1073	Ford GT90, red w/metal base, black interior, black tint, t/b	2
1074	Blimp, black and red w/red canopy	2
1075	Scorchin Scooter, red w/metal base, black seat	3
1076	'59 Caddy, metallic blue w/chrome base, white interior, blbbs	2
1077	'57 Chevy, red w/chrome base, black interior, black tint, gbbs	2
1078	Camaro Z28, metallic blue w/metal base, black windows, 3sp	2
1079	'63 Split-Window, metallic gray w/black base, black interior, clear, 5dot	2

No. 1074 Blimp, black and red with red canopy.

No. 1075 Scorchin Scooter, red with metal base, black seat.

No.	Name	MIP
1080	Hummer, metallic green w/metal base, silver windows, ct/b	2
1081	Power Plower, metallic green w/metal base, lime interior, yellow tint, ct/b	2
1082	Jaguar XJ220, metallic gold w/black base, tan interior, black tint, g3sp	2
1083	Blown Camaro, metallic aqua w/metal base, black interior, black tint, bbs	2
1085	Porsche 928, metallic gold w/metal base, black window, 5dot	2
1086	Toyota MR2, metallic purple w/black base, gray interior, clear window, 3sp	2

No.	Name	MIP
1087	Rig Wrecker, yellow w/chrome base, blue interior, clear window, 5 dot	2
1088	Speed Machine, black w/metal base, white interior, yellow tint, g5dot	2
1089	25th Ann. Countach, metallic silver w/black base, black interior, clear window, 5dot	2
1090	'97 Corvette, black w/black base, white interior, blue tint, 3sp	2
1091	Power Rocket renamed X-ploder, black w/metal base, chrome interior, red tint, t/b	2
1092	58 Corvette, black w/black base, chrome interior, black tint, bbs	2

No.	Name	MIP
1093	BMW 850i, metallic gold w/gold base, black interior, black tint, gbbs	2
1094	Ferrari Berlinetta, red w/metal base, black interior, clear window, 5sp	2
1095	Mercedes SLK, metallic silver w/black metal base, black interior, black tint, t/b	2
1096	Avis Quattro, chrome w/black base, black interior, black tint, 5sp	2
1097	'31 Doozie, metallic red w/metal base, black interior, clear window, bbs	2
1098	'37 Bugatti, black and yellow w/metal base, chrome interior, clear window, bbs	2

No. 1105 Mustang Mach 1, metallic blue with black base, black interior, clear window, bbs.

No.	Name	MIP
1099	Road Rocket, red and black w/metal base, red interior, bbs	2
1100	Power Pipes, white w/metal orange base, gold chrome interior, red tint, 5dot	2
1101	Randa Range, metallic aqua w/metal base white interior, clear window, ct/b	2
1102	Mini Truck, black w/black base, red interior, black tint, gbbs	2
1103	80's Corvette, gold w/metal base, black interior, black tint, bbs	2
1104	Twang Thang, metallic orange w/purple base, gold chrome interior, black tint, g5sp	2
1105	Mustang Mach 1, metallic blue w/black base, black interior, clear window, bbs	2
1106	Go Cart, orange w/orange metal base, black interior, 5dot	3
1107	Chrysler Thunderbolt, metallic blue w/black base, white interior, black tint, 3sp	2
1115	Ferrari F355, Challenge silver w/metal base, black interior, black tint, 5sp	2
1118	Ferrari 456M, red w/metal base, tan interior, clear window, 5sp	2
1119	Ferrari Spider, red w/metal base, tan interior, clear window, 5sp	2
1120	Ferrari F50, red w/black metal, black interior, clear window, 5sp	2
1121	Chevy 1500, orange w/silver base, black interior, clear window, 5dot	2

1995 Model Series

No.	Name	MIP
341	#3-'58 Corvette, pearl purple, no chrome, gray interior, 7sp	4
341	#3-'58 Corvette, pink, chrome interior, bw	6
341	#3-'58 Corvette, pink, chrome interior, 7sp	4
341	#3-'58 Corvette, light pearl purple, chrome interior, 7sp	4
341	#3-'58 Corvette, pearl purple, chrome interior, 5sp	4
341	'58 Corvette, pearl purple, chrome interior, 5dot; not on Model Series pack	2
341	'58 Corvette, pearl purple, chrome interior, 5sp; not on Model Series pack	2
341	#3-'58 Corvette, pearl purple, chrome interior, 7sp	20
342	#2-Mercedes SL, red w/dark red plastic base, tan interior, uh	3
342	Mercedes SL, black and gray, red interior, bbs; not on Model Series pack	2
342	#2-Mercedes SL, red w/matching base, tan interior, uh	3
342	#2-Mercedes SL, red w/dark red plastic base, tan interior, 5sp	3
342	#2-Mercedes SL, black and gray, tan interior, 5sp	30
342	#2-Mercedes SL, black and gray, red interior, bbs	2
342	#2-Mercedes SL, red w/matching base, tan interior, 5sp	3
342	#2 Mercedes SL, black and gray, red interior, 5sp	3
342	#2-Mercedes SL, black and gray, red interior, 7sp	3
343	#1-Speed Blaster, blue, pink chrome, uh	4
343	#1-Speed Blaster, blue, chrome window, uh	4
343	Speed Blaster, green, chrome window, 5dot; not on Model Series pack	2
343	#1-Speed Blaster, green, chrome window, t/b	5
343	#1-Speed Blaster, green, chrome window, 3sp	3
343	#1-Speed Blaster, green w/gray base, gray window, 5dot	3
343	#1-Speed Blaster, green, chrome window, 5dot	2
343	#1-Speed Blaster, green, chrome window, 5sp	3
343	#1-Speed Blaster, blue, pink chrome, 5sp	3
343	#1-Speed Blaster, blue, long gas tank, pink chrome, uh	50
344	#8-Camaro Convertible, red black interior, clear window, 5sp	3
344	Camaro Convertible, red, black interior, 5sp; not on Model Series pack	2
344	Camaro Convertible, red w/India base, '98 black interior, clear window, 5sp; not on Model Series pack	2
344	#8-Camaro Convertible, red black interior, clear window, 3sp	5
344	#8-Camaro Convertible, red w/black Malaysia base, black interior, clear window, g7sp	5
344	#8-Camaro Convertible, red w/China base, black interior, clear window, 5sp	3
344	#8-Camaro Convertible, red, black interior, t/b	3
344	#8-Camaro Convertible, green, gray interior, uh	5

No.	Name	MIP
344	#8-Camaro Convertible, green, gray interior, 5sp	3
344	#8-Camaro Convertible, green, gray interior, 3sp	3
345	#4-Speed-a-Saurus, purple, chrome engine, 5sp	2
345	#4-Speed-a-Saurus, green, chrome engine, 5sp	2
345	#4-Speed-a-Saurus, green, chrome engine, bw	3
345	Speed-a-Saurus, purple, chrome engine, 5sp; not on Model Series pack	2
346	#6-Hydroplane, blue and white race team colors, chrome interior	3
347	#5-Power Pistons, burgundy, gray interior, 7sp	18

No. 346 #6-Hydroplane (1995 Model Series), blue and white race team colors, chrome interior.

No.	Name	MIP
347	#5-Power Pistons, burgundy, gray interior, 5sp	4
347	Power Pistons, burgundy, w/painted base, gray interior, t/b; not on Model Series pack	2
347	#5-Power Pistons, bronze, gray interior, 7sp/rear-5sp/fr	3
347	#5-Power Pistons, bronze, gray interior, uh	3
347	#5-Power Pistons, bronze, gray interior, 5sp	3
347	Power Pistons, burgundy, w/painted base, gray interior, 3sp; not on Model Series pack	2
347	#5-Power Pistons, burgundy, gray interior, 3sp	4
348	#7-Dodge Ram, green, chrome interior, w5dot	3
348	#7-Dodge Ram, green, chrome interior, 5sp	2
348	#7-Dodge Ram, green, chrome interior, 5dot	3
348	Dodge Ram, green, chrome interior, 5dot; not on Model Series pack	2
349	#9-Power Pipes, dark blue w/silver base, chrome interior, 7sp	7
349	Power Pipes, dark blue w/silver base, chrome interior, purple window 5dot; not on Model Series pack	2
349	#9-Power Pipes, dark blue w/silver base, chrome interior, 3sp	3
349	#9-Power Pipes, dark blue w/silver base, chrome interior, 5sp	2
349	Power Pipes, dark blue w/silver base, chrome interior, purple window 5sp; not on Model Series pack	2

No.	Name	MIP
350	#10-Ferrari 355, yellow w/black stripe, black window, 5sp	5
350	#10-Ferrari 355, yellow, black interior, 3sp	2
350	#10-Ferrari 355, yellow, black interior, t/b	2
350	#10-Ferrari 355, yellow, black interior, 5sp	2
350	#10-Ferrari 355, yellow, black interior, 7sp	3
350	#10-Ferrari 355, yellow, black interior, c5dot	2
350	#10-Ferrari 355, yellow, black interior, w5dot	3
351	#11-Power Rocket, purple w/silver base, black interior, 3sp	4
351	#11-Power Rocket, purple w/silver base, black interior, t/b	4
351	#11-Power Rocket, purple w/silver base, black interior, c5dot	5
351	#11-Power Rocket, purple w/silver base, black interior, w5dot	5
351	Power Rocket, purple w/silver painted base, chrome interior, 5dot; not on Model Series pack	2
351	#11-Power Rocket, purple w/metal base, black interior, 5sp	4
352	#12-Big Chill, white, chrome canopy, pink ski	2
352	#12-Big Chill, white, chrome canopy, orange ski	4
352	#12-Big Chill, white, w/blue and orange tampo, chrome canopy, orange ski	3
352	#12-Big Chill, white, w/black tampo, chrome canopy, orange ski	3

No.	Name	MIP
352	Big Chill, white w/black tampo, chrome canopy, orange ski; not on Model Series pack	2

1995 Treasure Hunt Series

No.	Name	MIP
353	#1-Olds 442, metallic blue w/white scoops, white interior, clear window, rl/rr	50
354	Passion, gold, gold and black rr-gd w/white lines	100
355	'67 Camaro, white, rr-gy-gr	200
355	'67 Camaro, white, rr-gy-gr front, rr-gy-ch in rear	600
356	'57 T-Bird, rr-gr w/white lines	45
357	VW Bug, lime, t5 purple	100
358	'63 Split Window, blue, rr-gr	80
359	#7-Stutz Blackhawk, black red interior, clear window, rl/rr	120
360	#8-Rolls-Royce, dark metallic red w/tan top red interior, clear window, r6sp	65
361	#9-Classic Caddy, metallic green w/green fenders, tan interior, g6sp	70
363	Classic Cobra, green, g6s	120
364	#12-'31 Doozie, yellow w/black fenders, black interior, clear window, y6sp	60

1996 First Editions

No.	Name	MIP
367	#2-Chevy 1500 Pick Up, silver w/metal base, silver interior, smoked window, large b7sp	6
367	#2-Chevy 1500 Pick Up, silver w/metal base, silver interior, smoked window, small b7sp	2
367	#2-Chevy 1500 Pick Up, silver w/silver painted base, silver interior, smoked window, small b7sp	2
367	#2-Chevy 1500 Pick Up, silver w/metal base (China), silver interior, clear window, 5sp	2

No.	Name	MIP
368	'70 Dodge Daytona, red, t/b; not on First Edition pack	2
369	#8-Sizzlers (Turbo Flame), red and white w/gray motor and metal base, 5sp	3
369	#8-Sizzlers (Turbo Flame), red and white w/painted silver base, 5sp	2
369	#8-Sizzlers (Turbo Flame), red and white, 5dot	3
369	#7-Road Rocket, transparent green, gbbs	2
369	#8-Turbo Flame, red and white, 5sp	3
370	#5-Rail Rodder, (China) black, chrome engine and wheels, large rear 5sp	3
370	#5-Rail Rodder, black, chrome engine and wheels, small rear 5sp	3
370	#5-Rail Rodder, black, chrome engine and wheels, large rear 5sp	3
370	#5-Rail Rodder, black, no chrome engine or wheels, large rear 5sp	3
370	Rail Rodder, black w/chrome engine and wheels, small rear 5sp; not on First Edition pack	3

No. 370 #5-Rail Rodder (1996 First Editions), black, chrome engine and wheels, small rear 5sp.

No.	Name	MIP
372	#6-VW Bus Funny Car, blue, front 5sp	60
373	#4-Street Cleaver, yellow flame tampo, 5sp	2
373	#4-Street Cleaver, yellow, no tampo, w5dot	2
373	#4-Street Cleaver, yellow, no tampo, all large 5dot	2
373	#4-Street Cleaver, yellow, no tampo, 5dot	2
373	#4-Street Cleaver, yellow, no tampo, t/b	2
373	#4-Street Cleaver, yellow, no tampo, all large 5sp	2
373	#4-Street Cleaver, yellow, no tampo, 5sp	3
373	#4-Street Cleaver, yellow/no tampo, gray engine, all large 5dot	3
373	#4-Street Cleaver, yellow flame tampo, 3sp	2
374	#9-Radio Flyer Wagon, red w/painted silver base, 5sp	8
374	#9-Radio Flyer Wagon, red, 5sp	2
374	#9-Radio Flyer Wagon, red w/metal China base, bw	3
374	#9-Radio Flyer Wagon, red w/metal China base, bw rear/5sp front	2
375	#10-Dog Fighter, dark red, t/b	2
375	#10-Dog Fighter, dark red, unchromed engine and suspension, 5sp	2
375	#10-Dog Fighter, dark red, 5sp	2
375	#10-Dog Fighter, dark red, 5dot	5
376	#11-Twang-Thang (Guitar Car), silver, 5sp	3
377	#12-Ferrari F50, red, bbs	2
377	#12-Ferrari F50, (new casting) red w/gray plastic base (China), black interior, bbs	2

No.	Name	MIP
377	Ferrari F50, red w/gray plastic India base, '98 black interior, clear window bbs; not on First Edition pack	2
378	#1-'96 Mustang, dark red silver, lights, tan interior, t/b	6
378	#1-'96 Mustang, dark red silver, lights, tan interior, 7sp	7
378	#1-'96 Mustang, dark red silver, lights, tan interior, 3sp	12
378	#1-'96 Mustang, dark red silver, lights, tan interior, c5dot	15
378	#1-'96 Mustang, dark red silver, lights, tan interior, 5sp	6
382	#3-'70 Dodge Daytona, red, tan interior, gbbs	2
382	#3-'70 Dodge Daytona, red, tan interior, g7sp	2
382	#3-'70 Dodge Daytona, red, tan interior, t/b	2

1996 Treasure Hunt Series

No.	Name	MIP
428	#1-'40's Woodie, yellow, yrr w/yellow lines	30
428	#1-'40s Woodie, yellow, rr-y w/gold lines	65
428	#1-'40s Woodie, yellow, rr-y w/white lines	70
428	'40s Woodie, rr-y w/white lines	75
428	'40s Woodie, yellow, rr-y w/gold lines	70
429	#10-Lamborghini Countach, fluorescent orange, c6sp	20
430	#3-Ferrari 250, gray, rr	20
431	#4-Jaguar XJ 220, green, g6sp	20
432	#5-'59 Caddy, red, rr	25
433	#6-Dodge Viper RT/10, red, bbs	10
433	#6-Dodge Viper RT/10, white, w6sp	40
434	#7-'57 Chevy, purple, rr	35
435	#8-Ferrari 355, white, gold star	18

No.	Name	MIP
436	#9-'58 Corvette, silver, rr	30
437	#2-Auburn 852, olive, grr	20
438	#11-Dodge Ram 1500, maroon, rr	25
439	#12-'37 Bugatti, blue, c6sp	25

1997 First Editions

No.	Name	MIP
509	#1-Firebird, funny car, dark blue, metal interior, 5sp	3
510	#12-25th. Countach, pearl yellow, clear window, black interior, 5dot	2
512	#3-Excavator, white w/blue tampo, black treads	18
513	#2-Ford 150, red smoked window, 5sp	2
514	#7-Way 2 Fast, orange enamel, w/Malaysia base, chrome interior, 5sp	2
514	#7-Way 2 Fast, orange enamel, w/Thailand base, ('98) chrome interior, 5sp	2
514	#7-Way 2 Fast, orange enamel, w/Malaysia base, no chrome interior, 5sp	2
514	#7-Way 2 Fast, orange enamel w/painted Thailand base chrome interior, 5sp	2
515	#11-'97 Corvette, metallic dark green smoked window, tan interior, bbs	3

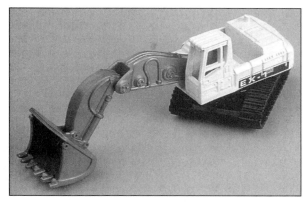

No. 512 #3-Excavator (1997 First Editions), white with blue tampo, black treads.

No.	Name	MIP
515	#11-'97 Corvette, metallic light green smoked window, tan interior, bbs	3
516	#10-Mercedes C-Class, black w/gray plastic base, gray interior, gbbs	2
517	#5-'59 Chevy Impala, light pearl purple, white interior, g7sp	6
517	#5-'59 Chevy Impala, light pearl purple, white interior, gbbs	6
518	#6 BMW M Roadster, metallic silver, metal base, red interior, 3sp	2
518	#6-BMW M Roadster, metallic silver, black painted base, red interior, 5sp	2
518	#6-BMW M Roadster, metallic silver, metal base, red interior, 5sp	2
518	#6-BMW Z3 Roadster, metallic silver, metal base, red interior, 5sp	2
519	#9-Scorchin' Scooter (A), purple w/silver, orange and blue flames, black seat	4
519	#9-Scorchin' Scooter (A), purple w/blue chrome engine, silver, orange and blue flames, black seat	4
519	#9-Scorchin' Scooter, purple w/silver and blue flames, black seat	4
520	#4-Saltflat Racer, light red w/silver painted Malaysia base ('97), 5sp	2
520	#4-Saltflat Racer, dark red w/silver painted Thailand base ('98), 5sp	2
523	1970 Plymouth Barracuda, w/chrome base black interior, tinted window, 5sp	6

1997 Treasure Hunt Series

No.	Name	MIP
578	#1-'56 Flashsider, metallic green, chrome window, 5sp	26
579	#2-Silhouette II, white, blue tint window, white interior, w3sp	15
580	#3-Mercedes 500SL, black, clear window, white interior, 5sp	15
581	#4-Street Cleaver, black w/red and gold tampo, gold base, all large 5sp	22
582	#5-GM Lean Machine, chrome and metallic dark red, chrome window, 5sp	25
583	#6-Hot Rod Wagon, yellow, gold-tinted engine y5sp	36
584	#7-Olds Aurora, purple, gray interior, 5sp	15
585	#8-Dogfighter, metallic green, yellow base, orange prop, 5sp	15
586	#9-Buick Wildcat, metalflake silver, black window, 3sp	15
587	#10-Blimp, blue, white Gondola	15
588	#11-Avus Quattro, gold, white interior, t/b	15
589	#12-Rail Rodder, white	20

1998 First Editions

No.	Name	MIP
633	#4-Dodge Caravan, dark red, metallic w/gray base, white interior, smoked window, t/b	3
633	#4-Dodge Caravan, brown, metallic w/gray base, white interior, smoked window, t/b	3
633	#4-Dodge Caravan, dark red, metallic w/gray base, white interior, smoked window, 5sp	3

No.	Name	MIP
634	#3-Dodge Sidewinder, neon orange w/gray base, purple interior, smoked window, 5sp	3
635	#8-'65 Impala, purple w/yellow and orange tampo, tan interior, clear window, gbbs	5
636	#7-'32 Ford, black w/mostly yellow flames (w/post), red interior, clear window, 5sp	15
636	#7-'32 Ford, black w/yellow and red flames (no post), red interior, clear window, t/b	2
636	#7-'32 Ford, black w/mostly yellow flames (no post), red interior, clear window, 5sp	10

No.	Name	MIP
637	#1-Escort Rally, pearl white w/pearl blue trim, red interior, smoked window, bbs	3
637	#1-Escort Rally (Ford), pearl white w/pearl blue trim, red interior, smoked window, bbs	3
638	#6-Jaguar D-type, metallic blue, gray interior, clear window, bbs	3
638	#6-Jaguar D-type, metallic blue, gray interior, clear window, 5sp	3
638	#6-Jaguar D-type, metallic blue, gray interior, clear window, small front 5sp	3

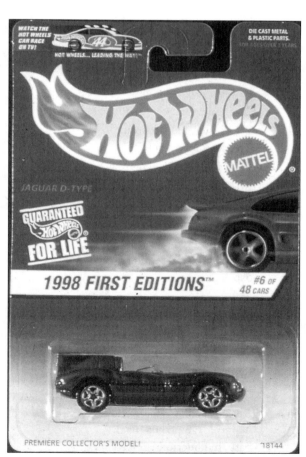

No. 638 #6-Jaguar D-type (1998 First Editions), metallic blue, gray interior, clear window, 5sp.

No. 639 #5-Jaguar XK8 (1998 First Editions), pearl green, black interior, clear window, bbs.

No. 640 #2-Slideout (1998 First Editions), purple and orange with gray base, 5sp.

No.	Name	MIP
638	#6-Jaguar D-type, metallic blue, gray interior, clear window, t/b	3
639	#5-Jaguar XK8, pearl green, white interior, clear window, bbs	75
639	#5-Jaguar XK8, pearl green, black interior, clear window, bbs	3
640	#2-Slideout, purple and orange w/gray base, 5sp	4
644	#9-'63 T-Bird, teal w/metal base, white interior, clear window, 5dot	4
644	#9-'63 T-Bird, teal w/metal base, white interior, clear window, new 5dot	4

No.	Name	MIP
645	#10-Dairy Delivery, white w/bright pink tampo and straight top stripe aqua interior/clear window, 5sp	2
645	#10-Dairy Delivery, white w/dark pink tampo and curved top stripe, aqua interior, clear window, 5sp	2
645	#10-Dairy Delivery, white w/bright pink tampo and curved top stripe, aqua interior/clear window, 5sp	2
646	#11-Mercedes SLK, yellow pearl w/silver side paint, tan interior, smoked window, 5dot	2
646	#11-Mercedes SLK, yellow w/white side paint, black interior, smoked window, 5dot	10
646	#11-Mercedes SLK, yellow pearl w/silver side paint, tan interior, smoked window, 5sp	2
647	#12-Lakester, red w/chrome headers, chrome interior, clear window, 5sp	2
648	#13-Hot Seat, white w/black seat, blue metal engine and base, 5sp	2
648	#13-Hot Seat, white w/black seat, metal engine and base, 5sp	2
650	#23-Solar Eagle III, yellow w/blue cells and black base, black window	2
651	#21-Go Kart, neon green w/black and orange tampo, black seat, 5sp	5
652	#15-Pikes Peak Celica, yellow w/purple tampo and black base, red interior, smoked window, gbbs	3

No. 652 #15-Pikes Peak Celica (1998 First Editions), yellow with purple tampo and black base, red interior, smoked window, gbbs.

No. 657 #19-Panoz GTR-1 (1998 First Editions), white with black Malaysia base, black interior, clear window, bbs.

No.	Name	MIP
652	#15-Pikes Peak Celica, yellow w/lavender tampo and black base, red interior, smoked window, gbbs	6
653	#16-IROC Firebird, gold w/gray base, light gray interior, tinted window, b5sp	2
654	#20-'40 Ford Pick-up, dark blue w/chrome base, gray interior, blue window, 5sp	2
654	#20-'40 Ford Pick-up, pearl blue w/chrome base, gray interior, blue window, 5sp	15
655	#22-Super Comp Dragster, black w/five decals and chrome base, gray cage, 5sp	2

No.	Name	MIP
655	#22-Super Comp Dragster, black w/three decals and chrome base, gray cage, 5sp	10
657	#19-Panoz GTR-1, white w/black base, bright red stripes, and small logo, blue interior, clear window, bbs	2
657	#19-Panoz GTR-1, white w/black base, dark red stripes and large logo, blue interior, clear window, bbs	2
657	#19-Panoz GTR-1, white w/black Malaysia base, black interior, clear window, bbs	3
658	#25-Tow Jam, red w/chrome base, black window, small logo, 3sp	2

No. 661 #17-'70 Roadrunner (1998 First Editions), Hemi Orange with chrome base, black interior, clear window, 5sp.

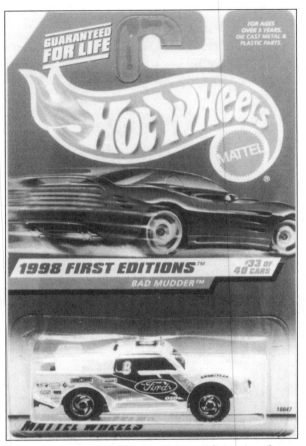

No. 662 #33-Bad Mudder (1998 First Editions), ct/b.

No.	Name	MIP
659	#24-Tail Dragger, metallic purple w/no logo or side tampo, white interior, clear window, bbs	2
659	#24-Tail Dragger, metallic purple w/metal base, white interior, clear window, bbs	2
661	#17-'70 Roadrunner, Hemi Orange w/chrome base, black interior, clear window, 5sp	2
661	#17-'70 Roadrunner, light Hemi Orange w/chrome base, black interior, clear window, 5sp	2

No.	Name	MIP
662	#33-Bad Mudder, white w/dark blue V, black wedge, light red stripe w/logo and no roof tampo, ct/b	2
662	#33-Bad Mudder, white w/light blue V, dark blue wedge, light red stripe, no roof tampo or logo, ct/b	50
662	#33-Bad Mudder, white w/dark blue V, black wedge, dark red stripe w/logo and roof tampo, ct/b	2
662	#33-Bad Mudder, white w/dark blue V, black wedge, light red stripe w/logo and roof tampo, ct/b	2
663	#26-Customised C3500, teal w/long white, blue and purple stripe, gray interior smoked window, 5dot	20

No.	Name	MIP
663	#26-Customised C3500, teal w/short blue and white stripe, gray interior, smoked window, 5dot	2
664	#27-Super Modified, black w/metal base, chrome wing, pink seat, bbs	2
665	#18-Mustang Cobra, black w/brown Mustang and gray base, gray interior, clear window, gbbs	2
665	#18-Mustang Cobra, black w/no Cosen and gray base, gray interior, clear window, gbbs	2

No.	Name	MIP
665	#18-Mustang Cobra, black w/orange Mustang and gray base, gray interior, clear window, gbbs	2
667	#34-At-A-Tude, metallic blue w/black base, chrome interior, orange window, all small/bbs	2
667	#34-At-A-Tude, metallic blue w/black base, chrome interior, orange window, large rear/bbs	2
667	#34-At-A-Tude, metallic blue w/black base, chrome interior, orange window, all large/bbs	2

No. 663 #26-Customized C3500 (1998 First Editions), teal with short blue and white stripe, gray interior, smoked window, 5dot.

No. 664 #27-Super Modified (1998 First Editions), black with metal base, chrome wing, pink seat, bbs.

No.	Name	MIP
668	#14-Ford GT-90, white w/metal base, white interior, dark blue window, 3sp	2
669	#28-Chaparral 2, white w/black metal base, black interior, clear window, bbs/2	2
670	#29-Mustang Mach 1, mustard yellow w/black base, black interior, tinted window, 5sp	2
670	#29-Mustang Mach 1, neon orange w/black base black interior, blue-tinted window, 5sp	25
671	#32-Chrysler Thunderbolt, silver w/black base, white interior, purple window, 5dot	2

No.	Name	MIP
672	#35-Dodge Concept Car, pearl orange w/metal base, smoked window, black interior, 5sp	2
672	#35-Dodge Concept Car, pearl orange w/metal base, smoked window, purple interior, 5sp	350
673	#36-Whatta Drag, metallic red and chrome w/metal base, chrome interior, orange window, 3sp	2
674	#30-Sweet 16 II, dark purple w/dark purple base, purple window, 5sp	2

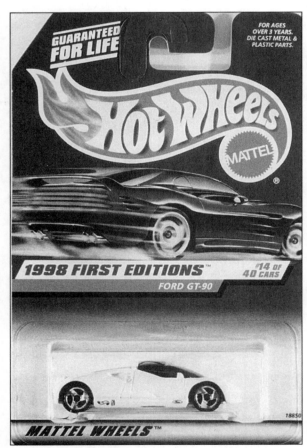

No. 668 #14-Ford GT-90 (1998 First Editions), white with metal base, white interior, dark blue window, 3sp.

No. 670 #29-Mustang Mach 1 (1998 First Editions), mustard yellow with black base, black interior, tinted window, 5sp.

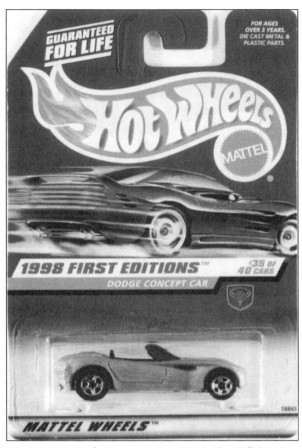

No. 672 #35-Dodge Concept Car (1998 First Editions), *pearl orange with metal base, smoked window, black interior, 5sp.*

No. 681 #38-Cat-A-Pult (1998 First Editions), *red enamel with red logo and metal base, black interior, orange window, 5sp.*

No.	Name	MIP
677	#31-Callaway C-7, silver w/black base, black interior, clear window, 5sp	2
678	#37-Express Lane, red w/metal base, black seat, 5sp	2
681	#38-Cat-A-Pult, red enamel w/black logo and metal base, black interior orange window, 5sp	2
681	#38-Cat-A-Pult, red enamel w/red logo and metal base, black interior, orange window, 5sp	20
682	#39-Fathom This, white w/black and white props, orange window	2

No.	Name	MIP
684	#40-Double Vision, metallic red w/gray base, gray seat clear canopy, gbbs	2

1998 Treasure Hunt Series

No.	Name	MIP
749	#1-Twang Thang, black w/blue chrome guitars, chrome interior, 5sp	15
750	#2-Scorchin' Scooter, red w/yellow and black tampo, black forks, black spokes	30
751	#3-Kenworth T600A, dark purple w/chrome base, black window, 3sp	17
752	#4-3 Window '34, orange w/yellow and red flames, chrome interior, 5dot	19

No. 749 #1-Twang Thang (1998 Treasure Hunt Series), black with blue chrome guitars, chrome interior, 5sp.

No. 649 #1-1936 Cord (1999 First Editions), metallic dark red with chrome base, purple interior, clear window, bbs.

No.	Name	MIP
753	#5-Turbo Flame, chrome w/black base chrome interior, green window, 5sp	15
754	#6-Saltflat Racer, black w/gold base and chrome, red window, 5sp	15
755	#7-Streat Beast, red and white w/metal base, white interior, red-tinted window, gbbs	15
756	#8-Road Rocket, chrome w/clear top and metal base, black roll bar and engine, 3sp	15
757	#9-Sol-Aire CX4, white w/flag tampo and blue base, blue interior, clear window, wbbs	15

No.	Name	MIP
758	#10-'57 Chevy, light metallic green w/gold tint base, yellow interior, yellow window, 3sp	20
760	#12-Way 2 Fast, metallic olive w/metal base, chrome interior, 5sp	15

1999 First Editions

No.	Name	MIP
1113	#21 Ferrari 360 Modena, red w/black base black interior, clear window, 5sp	2
1113	#21 Ferrari 360 Modena, red no HW tampo w/black base, black interior, clear window, 5sp	5

No.	Name	MIP
649	#1-1936 Cord, metallic dark red w/chrome base, purple interior, clear window, bbs	2
656	#3-'38 Phantom Corsair, black w/metal base gray interior, clear window, ww5sp	2
656	#3-'38 Phantom Corsair, black w/metal base, gray interior, clear window, 5sp	25
656	#3-'38 Phantom Corsair, blue w/metal base, gray interior, clear window, ww5sp	20
675	#7-Pontiac Rageous, metallic red w/black base, gray interior, smoked top, 3sp	4
675	#7-Pontiac Rageous, metallic red w/black base, gray interior, smoked top, black roof, 3sp	4

No.	Name	MIP
676	#25 Porsche 911 GT1-98, white w/black base, black interior, clear window, bbs	2
680	#24 Baby Boomer, blue w/metal base, blue interior, 5sp	2
683	#9-Tee'd Off, blue w/metal base, gray interior, 5sp	2
683	#9-Tee'd Off, pearl white w/metal base, gray interior, 5sp	10
683	#9-Tee'd Off, pearl white w/metal base, maroon interior, 5sp	3
909	#2-'99 Mustang, blue w/black base tan interior, clear window, 5sp	20

No. 656 #3-'38 Phantom Corsair (1999 First Editions), blue with metal base, gray interior, clear window, ww5sp.

No. 683 #9-Tee'd Off (1999 First Editions), pearl white with metal base, maroon interior, 5sp.

No. 909 #2-'99 Mustang (1999 First Editions), blue with black base tan interior, clear window, 5sp.

No.	Name	MIP
909	#2-'99 Mustang, dark purple w/black base, tan interior, clear window, 3sp	2
909	#2-'99 Mustang, dark purple w/black base, red interior, clear window, 5sp	25
909	#2-'99 Mustang, purple w/black base, tan interior, clear window, 5sp	2
909	#2-'99 Mustang, dark purple w/black base, tan interior, clear window, 5sp	2
910	#6-Monte Carlo Concept Car, metallic red w/silver painted base, gray interior, smoked window, 5sp	4

No.	Name	MIP
910	#6-Monte Carlo Concept Car, red w/silver painted base, gray interior, smoked window, 5sp	2
911	#5-Olds Aurora GTS-1, metalflake silver w/black base, black interior, clear window, gbbs	3
911	#5-Olds Aurora GT3, white and blue w/black base, black interior, clear window, gbbs	5
911	#5-Olds Aurora GTS-1, red w/black base, black interior, clear window, gbbs	5
911	#5-Olds Aurora GTS-1, white and blue w/black base, black interior, clear window, gbbs	3
912	#10 Porsche 911 GT3, purple w/black base, orange interior, blue tint, bbs	2
912	#10 Porsche 911 GT3, metallic silver w/white HW logo, w/black base, orange interior, blue tinted window, yellow spoiler, bbs	5
912	#10 Porsche 911 GT3, metallic silver w/red HW logo w/black base, orange interior, blue tint, bbs	5
912	#10 Porsche 911 GT3, silver w/black base, orange interior, blue black spoiler	2
913	#13 Popcycle, metallic red w/metal base, chrome interior, orange window, 3sp	20
913	#13 Popcycle, purple w/metal base, chrome interior, orange window, 3sp	2
914	#8-Semi Fast, red w/metal base and both chrome grilles, smoked window, 5sp	2
914	#8-Semi Fast, red w/metal base and one chrome grille, smoked window, 5sp	4

No.	Name	MIP
914	#8-Semi Fast, black and red w/metal base, both chrome grilles, smoked window, 5sp	2
915	#4-1970 Chevelle SS, dark blue pin stripe hood and metal base, white interior, blue-tinted window, 5sp	2
915	#4-1970 Chevelle SS, gold metal base white interior, blue-tinted window	12
915	#4-1970 Chevelle SS, dark blue no pin stripe and metal base, white interior, blue-tinted window, 5sp	2
916	#14 Phaeton, aqua w/metal base, tan interior, black tint, 5sp	2

No.	Name	MIP
917	#12 Track T, black w/metal base, metal interior, 5sp	2
918	#15 Screamin Hauler, w/metal base, metal interior, blue tint, 5 sp	2
919	#11 Fiat 500C, metallic purple w/metal base gray interior, chrome window, 5sp	2
921	#16 Ford GT-40, metallic blue w/gray plastic base, gray interior, blue tint, 5sp	2
921	#16 Ford GT-40, metallic blue w/gray plastic base, gray interior, blue tint, wide 5sp	2
922	#17 Jeepster, red w/metal base, black interior, black tint, 5sp	2

No. 916 #14 Phaeton (1999 First Editions), aqua with metal base, tan interior, black tint, 5sp.

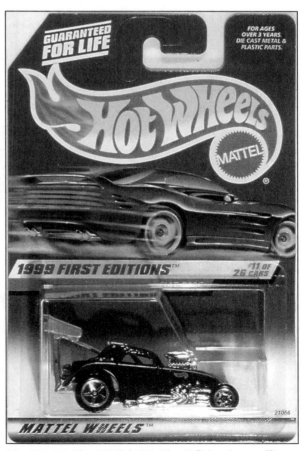

No. 919 #11 Fiat 500C (1999 First Editions), metallic purple with metal base gray interior, chrome window, 5sp.

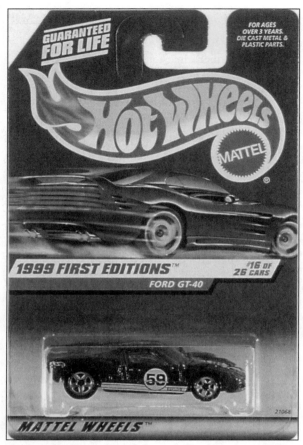

No. 921 #16 Ford GT-40 (1999 First Editions), metallic blue with gray plastic base, gray interior, blue tint, 5sp.

No. 923 #18 Turbolence (1999 First Editions), black with metal base gold chrome interior, gold chrome window, g5d.

No.	Name	MIP
923	#18 Turbolence, black w/metal base gold chrome interior, gold chrome window, g5d	2
924	#19 Pikes Peaks Tacoma, yellow w/black base black interior, clear window, gbbs	2
925	#20 Shadow MKIIA, black w/gray plastic base, gray interior, 5sp	2
925	#20 Shadow MKIIA, black w/gray plastic base, gray interior, wide 5sp	2
926	#26 Mercedes CLK-LM, silver w/black base, black interior, clear window, gbbs	2

No.	Name	MIP
927	#22 '56 Ford Truck, light blue w/gray base, chrome interior, blue tint, wide 5sp	3
928	#23 Chrysler Pronto, yellow w/black base gray interior black tint, 5sp	2

1999 Treasure Hunt Series

No.	Name	MIP
929	Mercedes 540K, red, 5sp	13
930	T-Bird Stocker, purple, 5sp	12
931	'97 Corvette, purple, 5sp	14
932	Rigor Mortor, yellow, g5sp	14
933	Ferrari F512M, black base, 5sp	50
933	Ferrari F512M, 5sp	16
934	'59 Impala, purple, gbbs	18
935	Hot Wheel 500, black, bk5sp	16

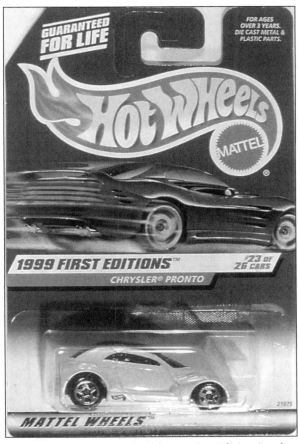

No. 928 #23 Chrysler Pronto (1999 First Editions), yellow with black base gray interior black tint, 5sp.

No. 934 '59 Impala (1999 Treasure Hunt Series), purple, gbbs.

No.	Name	MIP
936	Jaguar D-Type, black, 5sp	16
937	'32 Ford Delivery, gold, g5sp	30
938	Hot Seat, clear, 5sp	15
939	'70 Mustang, green, 5sp	30
940	Express Lane, purple, g5sp	20

Artistic License Series

No.	Name	MIP
729	Alien, white pearl w/metal base, large Alien, white interior, tinted window, 3sp	2
729	Alien, white enamel w/metal base, small Alien white interior, tinted window, 3sp	2
730	'57 Chevy, (plastic) silver w/metal base, smoked window, t/b	2

No.	Name	MIP
731	VW Bug, pearl white w/roof tampo only and metal base, black interior, blue tint, window, 5dot	2
731	VW Bug, pearl white w/metal base, black interior, blue-tinted, window, all small 5dot	2
731	VW Bug, pearl white w/metal base, black interior, blue-tinted window, 5dot	2
732	1970 Barracuda, black w/chrome China base, orange logo, light orange interior, clear window, 5sp	2
732	1970 Barracuda, black w/chrome China base, blue logo, light orange interior, clear window, 5sp	2

No. 936 Jaguar D-Type (1999 Treasure Hunt Series), black, 5sp.

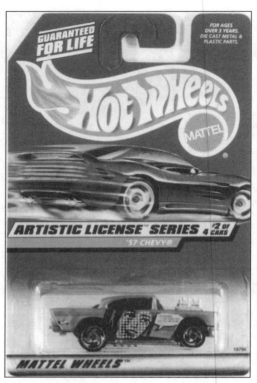

No. 730 '57 Chevy (Artistic License Series), (plastic) silver with metal base, smoked window, t/b.

No. 731 VW Bug (Artistic License Series), pearl white, 5dot.

No. 717 Hydroplane (Biohazard Series), dark neon green with black Thailand base, black interior, clear canopy.

No.	Name	MIP
732	1970 Barracuda, black w/chrome Malaysia base, orange logo, dark orange interior, smoked window, 3sp	2
732	1970 Barracuda, black w/chrome Malaysia base blue logo, dark orange interior, smoked window, 3sp	2

Biff! Bam! Boom! Series

No.	Name	MIP
541	Mini Truck, red, black interior, smoked window, t/b	6
541	Mini Truck, red, black interior, smoked window, 5dot rear/3sp front	3
541	Mini Truck, red, black interior, smoked window, 5sp	3
541	Mini Truck, red, black interior, smoked window, 3sp	3
542	Limozeen, blue, white interior, smoked window, 5sp	2
542	Limozeen, light blue w/no bullet holes in front fender, white interior, smoked window, 5sp	2
543	VW Bug, green w/logo, black interior, 5sp	4
543	VW Bug, green w/o logo, black interior, 5sp	4
543	VW Bug, green w/o logo, black interior, 7sp	18
544	Range Rover, pearl purple, gray interior, t/b	2

Biohazard Series

No.	Name	MIP
717	Hydroplane, bright neon green w/black Malaysia base, black interior, smoked canopy	2
717	Hydroplane, dark neon green w/black Thailand base, black interior, clear canopy	2
717	Hydroplane, neon green w/black Thailand base, black interior, smoked canopy	2
718	Flame Stopper, neon pink w/black base, black window and boom, yt/b	2
719	Recycling Truck, neon yellow w/orange tampo, black window, t/b	2
719	Recycling Truck, neon yellow w/black tampo, black base, black window, t/b	2
720	Rescue Ranger, black w/chrome base, yellow tint window and interior, 5dot	2
720	Rescue Ranger, black w/chrome base yellow tint window and interior, 5sp	2

Blue Streak Series

No.	Name	MIP
573	Olds 442, candy blue, black interior, 3sp	3
574	Nissan Truck, candy blue, black interior, t/b	14
575	'55 Chevy, candy blue, black window, 3sp	3
576	Speed Blaster, candy blue, w/black base, chrome window, 3sp	2
576	Speed Blaster, candy blue, w/chrome base, chrome window, 3sp	15

Buggin' Out Series

No.	Name	MIP
941	Treadator, red w/black chrome and yellow scoops, chrome window, black treads	2
941	Treadator, red w/dull chrome and yellow scoops, chrome window, black treads	2
941	Treadator, red w/chrome fenders and yellow scoops, chrome window, black treads	2
942	Shadow Jet II, gray w/green and yellow tampo and metal base, yellow interior, green window, 5sp	2

No. 941 Treadator (Buggin' Out Series), red with chrome fenders and yellow scoops, chrome window, black treads.

No. 942 Shadow Jet II (Buggin' Out Series), gray with green and yellow tampo and metal base, yellow interior, green window, 5sp.

No.	Name	MIP
943	Radar Ranger, metallic purple w/black dish and metal base, blue tint window, blue interior, ct/b	2
944	Baja Bug, blue w/metal base, orange interior, 5sp	2

Car-toon Friends

No.	Name	MIP
985	Salt Flat Racer, purple w/silver metal base, chrome interior, clear window, 5sp	2
986	XT3, orange w/black metal, black tint window, g5sp	2
987	Double Vision, black w/black base, gray interior, clear window, gbbs	2
988	Lakester, white w/black metal base, chrome interior, red tint, 5sp	2

Classic Games Series

No.	Name	MIP
981	Super Modified, blue w/metal base, black interior, gbbs	2
982	Silhouette II, light blue w/black base, white interior, blue tint window, 5dot	2
983	Sol-aire, white w/black base, black interior, clear window, 3sp	2
984	Escort Rally, red w/gray base, black interior, clear, window, bbs	2

Dark Rider Series

No.	Name	MIP
297	Splittin Image, black, dark chrome interior, 6sp	3
297	Splittin Image, black, dark chrome interior, 7sp	3

No. 987 Double Vision (Car-toon Friends), black with black base, gray interior, clear window, gbbs.

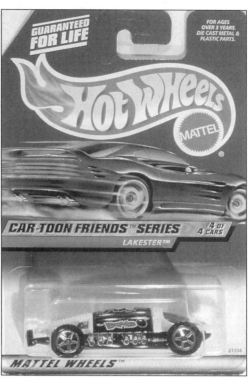

No. 988 Lakester (Car-toon Friends), white with black metal base, chrome interior, red tint, 5sp.

No. 982 Silhouette II (Classic Games Series), light blue with black base, white interior, blue tint window, 5dot.

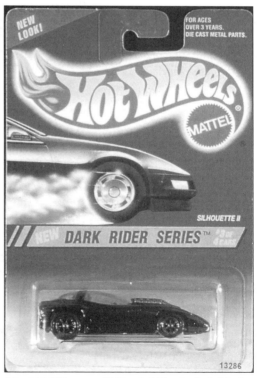

No. 299 Silhouette II (Dark Rider Series), black, with black plastic base, black interior, clear window, 6sp.

No.	Name	MIP
298	Twin Mill II, black, black interior, 6sp	3
298	Twin Mill II, black, black interior, 7sp	3
299	Silhouette II, black, w/black plastic base, black interior, clear window, 6sp	3
299	Silhouette II, black, w/dark chrome base, black interior, 6sp	3
299	Silhouette II, black, w/black plastic base, black interior, 7sp	3
300	Rigor Motor, black, chrome interior, 5sp	3
300	Rigor Motor, black, w/metal base (China), red chrome engine, bbs	2
300	Rigor Motor, black, chrome interior, 7sp	3
300	Rigor Motor, black, chrome interior, 6sp	3

Dark Rider Series II

No.	Name	MIP
400	Big Chill, black, dark chrome canopy, black ski	2
400	Big Chill, (China) metalflake silver, chrome canopy, orange ski	2
401	Street Beast, dark chrome, black interior, 7sp	2
402	Thunderstreak, dark chrome, black, dark chrome, 7sp	2
402	Thunderstreak, dark chrome, black, dark chrome, 5sp/rear-7sp/front	2
403	Power Pistons, dark chrome, black interior, 7sp	2

Dash 4 Cash Series

No.	Name	MIP
721	Jaguar XJ220, silver w/only side tampo and Malaysia base, light purple interior, clear window, t/b	2

No.	Name	MIP
721	Jaguar XJ220, silver w/black tampo and Malaysia base, light purple interior, clear window, t/b	2
721	Jaguar XJ220, silver w/black tampo and Malaysia base, dark purple interior, clear window, 3sp	2
721	Jaguar XJ220, silver w/black tampo and Malaysia base, light purple interior, clear window, 3sp	2
721	Jaguar XJ220, silver w/black tampo and Malaysia base, dark purple interior, clear window, bbs	2
721	Jaguar XJ220, silver w/black tampo and Malaysia base, light purple interior, clear window, bbs	2
722	Ferrari F40, gold w/metal Malaysia base, tan interior, tinted window, gbbs	2
723	Audi Avus, black w/black Thailand base, white interior, smoke and gold window, gbbs	2
724	Dodge Viper, white w/black Thailand base, red interior, smoked window, t/b	2

Dealer's Choice Series

No.	Name	MIP
565	Silhoutte II, pearl blue w/black Malaysia base, gold interior, clear window, 5dot	2
565	Silhoutte II, pearl blue w/black Malaysia base, gold interior, clear window, rear 5sp/front 5dot	2
566	Street Beast, white and gold, gold interior, 7sp	3
566	Street Beast, white and gold, gold interior, 5dot	3
567	Baja Bug, metallic red w/metal base, white interior, 5sp	3

No.	Name	MIP
567	Baja Bug, metallic red w/silver base, white interior, 5sp	3
567	Baja Bug, metallic red w/metal base, white interior, all small 5sp	2
568	'63 Corvette, black w/red '63 Corvette base, red interior, clear window, 5dot	3
568	'63 Corvette, black w/red base red interior, clear window, 5dot	3

Extreme Speed

No.	Name	MIP
965	Dodge Sidewinder, white w/black base, purple interior, black tint, 5sp	2
966	Callaway C7, green w/black base black interior, clear window, 5sp	2
967	Porsche Carrera, silver w/metal base white interior, black tint, g5sp	2
968	Mazda MX-5 Miata, blue w/blue metal base, green interior, clear window, bbs	2

Fast Food Series

No.	Name	MIP
416	Pizza Vette, black window, 3sp	3
416	Pizza Vette, black window, 5sp	10
417	Pasta Pipes, chrome interior, 3sp	3
418	Sweet Stocker, yellow interior, 3sp	18
419	Crunch Chief, yellow interior, 7sp	15
419	Crunch Chief, yellow interior, 3sp	4

Fire Rescue Series

No.	Name	MIP
424	Ambulance, bright green, ribbed rear step, white interior, 7sp	4
424	Ambulance, red w/black logo, ribbed rear step, white interior, 7sp	2
424	Ambulance, red w/white logo, ribbed rear step, white interior, 7sp	2
424	Ambulance, red w/black logo, ribbed rear step, white interior, 5sp	2
424	Ambulance, bright green, smooth rear step, white interior, 5sp	3
424	Ambulance, bright green, smooth rear step, white interior, 7sp	4
425	Rescue Ranger, yellow, black interior, 5sp	2
426	Flame Stopper, yellow, black window, yt/b	2
426	Flame Stopper, (China) yellow, black window, cts	2
427	Fire Eater, red, blue interior, 7sp	3
427	Fire Eater, red, blue interior, 5sp	3

Flamethrower Series

No.	Name	MIP
384	'57 T-Bird, white w/light pink flame, quarter logo, window logo, four-flame trunk, 7sp	2
384	'57 T-Bird, white w/fade pink flame, logo in window, five-flame trunk w/two on quarter panel, 7sp	2
384	'57 T-Bird, white w/copper flame, two-flames on quarter panel, five-flame trunk, window logo, 7sp	3
384	'57 T-Bird, white w/full bright pink flame, logo on quarter panel, five-flame trunk, 7sp	2
384	'57 T-Bird, white w/fade pink flame, logo on quarter panel, four-flame trunk, 7sp	2
384	'57 T-Bird, white w/light pink flame, two flame quarter, four-flame trunk, window logo, 7sp	2

No.	Name	MIP
385	Hydroplane, yellow w/gold and green flames, chrome, n/a	2
385	Hydroplane, yellow w/gold and green flames backwards on spoiler, n/a	2
386	Range Rover, red w/gold flames, tampo on quarter panel, tan interior, ct	2
386	Range Rover, red w/gold flames, window tampo, tan interior, ct	2
387	Oshkosh Snowplow, black w/yellow and blue flames, black interior, bct	14
387	Oshkosh Snowplow, black w/yellow and blue flames, black interior, ct	4

Flyn' Aces Series

No.	Name	MIP
737	'70 Dodge Daytona, metallic green w/tan base, black interior, clear window, 5sp	2
737	'70 Dodge Daytona, metallic green w/tan base, black interior, clear window, 5dot	2
738	Dogfighter, black w/yellow base, chrome seat and suspension, 5dot	2
739	Sol-air CX4, yellow, black base, black interior, clear window, 5sp	2
740	XT-3, metallic silver w/orange base, black window, 5sp	2

No. 386 Range Rover (Flamethrower Series), red with gold flames, tampo on quarter panel, tan interior, ct.

No. 738 Dogfighter (Flyn' Aces Series), black with yellow base, chrome seat and suspension, 5dot.

Game Over Series

No.	Name	MIP
957	#1-Lean Machine, purple, black tint window, 5sp	2
958	#2-Shadow Jet, yellow w/metal base, yellow interior, smoked canopy, 5sp	2
959	#3-Speed Blaster, green, lime base, gt/b	2
960	#4-Twin Mill, red w/black base black interior, black tint, bbs	2

Heet Fleet Series

No.	Name	MIP
537	Police Cruiser, green w/flames, clear window, purple interior, 3sp	4
537	Police Cruiser, green w/flames, clear window, purple interior, 5sp	2
537	Police Cruiser, green w/flames, clear window, purple interior, 5dot	4
537	Police Cruiser, green w/flames, clear window, purple interior, 7sp	14
537	Police Cruiser, green w/flames, clear window, purple interior, 7sp rear/5sp front	4
538	School Bus, green w/flames, clear window, white interior, 7sp	2
538	School Bus, (China) green w/flames, clear window, white interior, 5sp	2
538	Peterbilt Tank Truck, metallic maroon w/flames, chrome window, 5sp	14
538	School Bus, green w/flames, clear window, white interior, 5sp	2
538	School Bus, green w/flames, clear window, white interior, 3sp	14
539	Peterbilt Tank Truck, metallic maroon w/flames, no HW logo, chrome window, 7sp	2
539	Peterbilt Tank Truck, metallic maroon w/flames, chrome window, 7sp	2
540	Ramblin' Wrecker, black w/flames, smoked window, chrome 7sp	2
540	Ramblin' Wrecker, black w/flames, smoked window, chrome, t/b	2

Hot Hubs Series

No.	Name	MIP
307	Cyber Cruiser, burgundy, purple chrome, blue and orange, hh	6
308	Vampyra, purple, gold interior, green and blue 6 sp	5
308	Vampyra, purple w/black metal base (China), gold interior, bbs	2
310	Shadow Jet, green, green interior, yellow and purple, yhh	6
311	Suzuki Quadracer, (China) yellow, purple seat, cts	4
311	Suzuki Quadracer, neon yellow, purple seat, Tiger Paw	40
311	Suzuki Quadracer, yellow, purple seat, yellow and black	6
311	Suzuki Quadracer, neon yellow, purple seat, yellow and black	30

Krackle Car Series

No.	Name	MIP
280	Sharkruiser, lime and blue w/metal base, lime interior, 7sp	3
280	Sharkruiser, lime and blue w/painted base, lime interior, uh	3
280	Sharkruiser, lime and blue w/metal base, lime interior, uh	3

No.	Name	MIP
281	Turboa, purple and red w/painted base, red interior, uh	4
281	Turboa, purple and red w/metal base, red interior, 7sp	10
282	'63 Split, aqua and orange w/chrome base, two rivet, white interior, orange window, 5sp	4
282	'63 Split, aqua and orange w/gray base, two rivet, white interior, orange window 5sp	4
282	'63 Split, aqua and orange w/chrome base, two rivet, white interior, orange window, bw	3
282	'63 Split, aqua and orange w/gray base, two rivet, white interior, orange window, bw	3
282	'63 Split, aqua and orange w/chrome base, one rivet, white interior, orange window, bw	3
284	Flashfire, purple and orange, orange interior, 5sp	9
284	Flashfire, purple and yellow, yellow interior, 7sp	3
284	Flashfire, purple and yellow, yellow interior, 5sp	3
284	Flashfire, purple and yellow, yellow interior, uh	4

Low 'N Cool Series

No.	Name	MIP
697	Mini Truck, neon yellow w/black base, gray, pink and black tampo, black interior, g3sp	2
698	'59 Impala, pearl green w/light pearl purple tampo, white interior, smoked window, gbbs	2
698	'59 Impala, pearl green w/dark purple tampo, white interior, smoked window, gbbs	2

No.	Name	MIP
699	'59 Caddy, red w/yellow and blue tampo, white interior, smoked window, gbbs	2
716	Limozeen, black metalflake w/gold base white interior, smoked window, gbbs	2

Mega Graphics Series

No.	Name	MIP
973	Funny Car, fluorescent yellow w/metal base metal interior, yellow tint, 5sp	3
974	Mustang Cobra, white w/black base black interior, clear window t/b	2
975	Turbo Flame, black w/metallic red base, black interior, yellow tint, g5sp	2

No. 973 Funny Car (Mega Graphics Series), fluorescent yellow with metal base metal interior, yellow tint, 5sp.

No.	Name	MIP
976	Firebird Funny Car, metallic purple w/metal base metal interior, clear window, bk5sp	3

Mixed Signals Series

No.	Name	MIP
733	Street Roader, white and yellow w/metal base, yellow interior, smoked window, t/b	2
734	'80's Corvette, green w/metal base, black interior, smoked window, bbs	2
735	Nissan Truck, light pearl orange w/black base, black interior, clear window, large ct/b	2
736	School Bus, yellow w/black Thailand base, logo on side, black interior, clear window, 5dot	2

No.	Name	MIP
736	School Bus, yellow w/black Thailand base, logo on door, black interior, clear window, 5dot	2
736	School Bus, yellow w/black Malaysia base, logo on side, black interior, clear window, 5dot	2
736	School Bus, yellow w/black Malaysia base, logo on door, black interior, clear window, 5dot	2

Mod Bod Series

No.	Name	MIP
396	Hummer, pink, green window, ct	5

No. 735 Nissan Truck (Mixed Signals Series), light pearl orange with black base, black interior, clear window, large ct/b.

No. 736 School Bus (Mixed Signals Series), yellow with black Thailand base, logo on door, black interior, clear window, 5dot.

No.	Name	MIP
396	Hummer, pink, green window, t/b	8
397	School Bus, purple, yellow interior, 7sp	5
398	VW Bug, blue, yellow interior, 7sp	5
399	'67 Camaro, bright green, red interior, clear window, all small 5sp	40
399	'67 Camaro, bright green, red interior, clear window, 7sp	50
399	'67 Camaro, bright green, red interior, tinted window, 5sp	35
399	'67 Camaro, bright, green, red interior, clear window, 5sp	5

Pearl Driver Series

No.	Name	MIP
292	Pearl Passion, lavender, yellow interior, ww	4
292	Pearl Passion, lavender, yellow interior, 7sp	4
293	VW Bug, pink, gray interior, 5sp	10
293	VW Bug, pink, gray interior, bw	6
293	VW Bug, pink, gray interior, 7sp	6
295	Talbot Lago, blue, blue interior, 7sp	3
295	Talbot Lago, blue, blue interior, ww	3
296	Jaguar XJ220, white, tan interior, 3sp	3
296	Jaguar XJ220, white, tan interior, uh	3
296	Jaguar XJ220, white, tan interior, 5sp	3
296	Jaguar XJ220, white, tan interior, 7sp	5

Phantom Racers Series

No.	Name	MIP
529	Power Rocket, transparent green w/pink canopy, chrome interior, 3sp	2
529	Power Rocket, transparent green w/orange canopy, chrome interior, 3sp	2
530	Power Pistons, transparent red, gray interior, 3sp	2
530	Power Pistons, transparent red, gray interior, 5sp	3
531	Power Pipes, transparent blue w/purple canopy, chrome interior, 3sp	2
531	Power Pipes, transparent blue w/purple canopy, chrome interior, rear 5sp/front 3sp	2
532	Road Rocket, transparent orange and lime, orange interior, t/b	4
532	Road Rocket, transparent orange and lime, orange interior, 3sp	2

Photo Finish Series

No.	Name	MIP
331	Aerostar, white, silver window, 7sp	3
332	Flying Aces Blimp, gray, black, n/a	3
333	Tank Truck, blue, chrome window, 7sp	3
335	Hiway Hauler, green, black window, 7sp	4

Pinstripe Series

No.	Name	MIP
953	'34 3 Window, purple w/metal base, black interior, blue tint window, 5sp	2
954	Tail Dragger, black w/metal base, tan interior, clear window, bbs	2

Corgi

Corgi, Bedford Corgi Toys Van, No. 422-A. Photo courtesy Dr. Doug Sadecky.

Corgi, Bedford Milk Tanker, No. 1129-A. Photo courtesy Dr. Doug Sadecky.

Corgi, BMC Mini-Cooper S Rally Car, No. 321-A. Photo courtesy Dr. Doug Sadecky.

Corgi, Chevrolet Impala Yellow Cab, No. 480-A. Photo courtesy Dr. Doug Sadecky.

Corgi, Commer Mobile Camera Van, No. 479-A.
Photo courtesy Dr. Doug Sadecky.

Corgi, Euclid TC-12 Bulldozer, No. 1102-A. Photo courtesy Dr. Doug Sadecky.

Corgi, Ghia-Fiat 600 Jolly, No. 242. Photo courtesy Dr. Doug Sadecky.

Corgi, Jaguar E Type, No. 307-A. Photo courtesy Dr. Doug Sadecky.

Corgi, London Transport Routemaster Bus, No. 468. Photo courtesy Dr. Doug Sadecky.

Corgi, Massey Ferguson 165 Tractor with Saw, No. 73. Photo courtesy Dr. Doug Sadecky.

Corgi, Milk Truck and Trailer, No. 21-A. Photo courtesy Dr. Doug Sadecky.

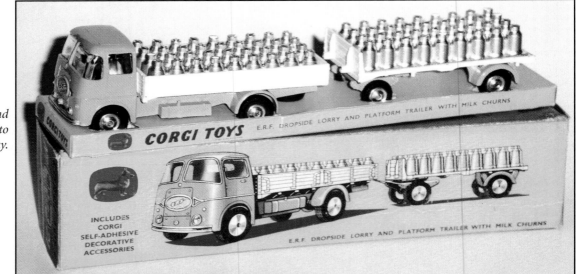

Corgi, Priestman Cub Power Shovel, No. 1128. Photo courtesy Dr. Doug Sadecky.

*Corgi, Rover 2000 Rally, No. 322.
Photo courtesy Dr. Doug Sadecky.*

*Corgi, Trojan Heinkel, No. 233-A.
Photo courtesy Dr. Doug Sadecky.*

*Corgi, Volkswagen Military Personnel Carrier,
No. 356. Photo courtesy Dr. Doug Sadecky.*

Hot Wheels, Captain America, No. 2879.

Hot Wheels, Classic '31 Ford Woody, No. 6251.

Hot Wheels, Classic Nomad, No. 6404.

Hot Wheels, Custom AMX, No. 6267.

Hot Wheels, Custom Mustang, in pack, No. 6206.

Hot Wheels, Custom Mustang, No. 6206.

Hot Wheels, Custom Police
Cruiser, No. 6269.

Hot Wheels, Evil
Weevil, No. 6471.

Hot Wheels, Flat
Out 442, No. 2506.

Hot Wheels, Gremlin
Grinder, No. 7652.

Hot Wheels, Heavy Chevy, No. 6408.

Hot Wheels, Hot Heap, No. 6219.

Hot Wheels, Human Torch, No. 2881.

Hot Wheels, Incredible Hulk Van, No. 2850.

Hot Wheels, King Kuda, No. 6411.

Hot Wheels, Mongoose Rail Dragster, No. 5952.

*Hot Wheels, Monte Carlo
Stocker, No. 7660.*

*Hot Wheels, Motocross I,
No. 7668.*

*Hot Wheels, Mustang
Stocker, No. 7664.*

*Hot Wheels, Noodle
Head, No. 6000.*

Hot Wheels, Open Fire, No. 5881.

Hot Wheels, Rolls-Royce Silver Shadow, No. 6276.

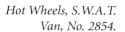

Hot Wheels, S'Cool Bus, No. 6468.

Hot Wheels, S.W.A.T. Van, No. 2854.

*Hot Wheels, Sidekick,
open, No. 6022.*

*Hot Wheels, Snake
Funny Car, No. 6409.*

*Hot Wheels, Snake Funny
Car, top up, No. 6409.*

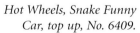

*Hot Wheels, Splittin'
Image, No. 6261.*

*Hot Wheels, Swingin'
Wing, No. 6422.*

*Hot Wheels, Torero,
No. 6260.*

Hot Wheels,
Turbofire, No. 6259.

Hot Wheels, Limited Editions,
Toy Shop – '32 Ford.

Hot Wheels, Numbered Packs, No. 1 Old No. 5.

Hot Wheels, Numbered Packs, No.
22 Talbot Lago, white, chrome
interior, smoked window, ww.

Hot Wheels, Numbered Packs, No. 29 Tail Gunner, green camo, black window, bct.

Hot Wheels, Numbered Packs, No. 53 Zombot, gold, chrome pink gun, hoc.

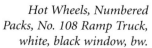

Hot Wheels, Numbered Packs, No. 102 Surf Patrol, yellow, red interior, ct.

Hot Wheels, Numbered Packs, No. 108 Ramp Truck, white, black window, bw.

Hot Wheels, Numbered Packs, No. 110 Trailbuster, turquoise, pink interior, w/blue in tampo, ct.

Hot Wheels, Numbered Packs, No. 111 Street Beast, teal and white, teal interior, ww.

Hot Wheels, Numbered Packs, No. 113 Speed Shark, purple, pink interior, bw.

Hot Wheels, Numbered Packs, No. 128
Baja Breaker, metallic purple and yellow,
w/blue tint base, red interior, bw.

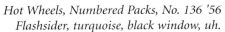

Hot Wheels, Numbered Packs, No. 136 '56
Flashsider, turquoise, black window, uh.

Hot Wheels, Numbered Packs, No.
145 Tractor, yellow, yellow seat, ytt.

Hot Wheels, Numbered Packs, No. 147
Tank Truck, red, chrome window, 7sp.

Hot Wheels, Numbered Packs, No. 148
Porsche 930, red, black interior, bw.

Hot Wheels, Numbered Packs,
No. 153 Thunderstreak, yellow
w/Pennzoil, yellow interior, bw.

Hot Wheels, Numbered Packs, No.
156 Rodzilla, light purple w/light
purple plastic base, uh.

Hot Wheels, Numbered Packs, No. 191 Aeroflash, dark pink chrome texture, black window, guh.

Hot Wheels, Numbered Packs, No. 231 Mini Truck, orange, blue interior, clear window, c5dot.

Hot Wheels, Numbered Packs, No. 242 '93 Camaro, blue, white interior, bw.

Hot Wheels, Numbered Packs, No. 259 Lumina Minivan/taxi, yellow, black interior, 5sp.

Hot Wheels, Numbered Packs, No. 274 Super Cannon, green cammo, black window, w5sp.

Hot Wheels, Numbered Packs, No. 478 Dragon Wagon, neon yellow with green base, 5sp.

Hot Wheels, Numbered Packs, No. 493 Porsche 911 Targa, neon yellow, black China base, black interior, clear window, all small 5sp.

Hot Wheels, Numbered Packs, No. 507 Peugot 205, black, blue, purple w/gray interior, red painted base, 5s.

Hot Wheels, Numbered Packs, No. 577 Police Cruiser, black and white, tan interior, b7sp.

Hot Wheels, Numbered Packs, No. 595 Corvette Sting Ray III, metallic purple, gray interior, clear window, 7sp.

Hot Wheels, Numbered Packs, No. 600 Nissan Custom Z, light blue enamel, metal China base black interior, clear window, bbs.

Hot Wheels, Numbered Packs, No. 625 Classic Packard, black, black interior, 5sp.

Hot Wheels, Numbered Packs, No. 761 Flame Stopper, red with gray boom, black window, t/b.

Hot Wheels, Numbered Packs, No. 1000 '59 Impala, white with chrome base, black interior, black tint, gbbs.

Hot Wheels, Numbered Packs (1995 Model Series), No. 345 #4-Speed-a-Saurus, green, chrome engine, 5sp.

Hot Wheels, Numbered Packs (1996 First Editions), No. 374 #9-Radio Flyer Wagon, red with painted silver base, 5sp.

Hot Wheels, Numbered Packs (1997 Treasure Hunt Series), No. 586 #9-Buick Wildcat, metalflake silver, black window, 3sp.

Hot Wheels, Numbered Packs, (Fast Food Series), No. 416 Pizza Vette, black window, 3sp.

Hot Wheels, Numbered Packs, (Fast Food Series), No. 417 Pasta Pipes, chrome interior, 3sp.

Hot Wheels, Numbered Packs, (Fast Food Series), No. 419 Crunch Chief, yellow interior, 7sp.

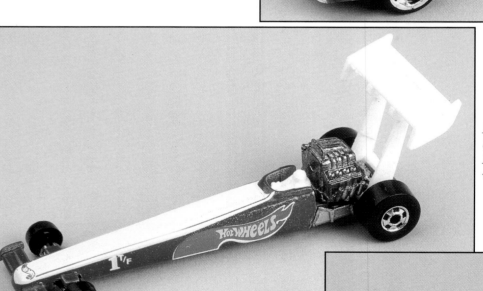

Hot Wheels, Numbered Packs (Race Team Series), No. 278 Dragster, dark metallic blue, white interior, bw.

Hot Wheels, Numbered Packs (Splatter Paint Series), No. 409 Side Splitter Funny Car, white, metal interior, 5sp.

Johnny Lightning

Johnny Lightning / Topper, Big Rig.

Johnny Lightning / Topper, Nucleon.

*Johnny Lightning /
Topper, Vicious Vette.*

*Johnny Lightning / Playing
Mantis, Cartoon Network Cars.
Photo courtesy Playing Mantis.*

*Johnny Lightning / Playing Mantis,
Cover Cars—Super Chevy, Round 3.
Photo courtesy Playing Mantis.*

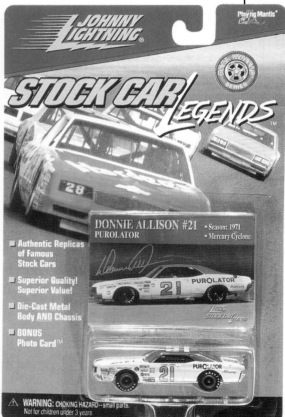

*Johnny Lightning / Playing
Mantis, Stock Car Legends,
Round 1, '71 Mercury Cyclone.*

*Johnny Lightning / Playing Mantis, Truckin'
America. Photo courtesy Playing Mantis.*

Matchbox

Matchbox, No. 4
1957 Chevy.

Matchbox, No. 17
Hoveringham Tipper.

Matchbox, No. 21
Foden Concrete Truck.

Matchbox, No. 27
Mercedes-Benz 230 SL.

Matchbox, No. 26 Foden Ready Mix Concrete Truck.

Matchbox, No. 30 8-Wheel Crane Truck.

Matchbox, No. 35
Snowtrac Tractor.

*Matchbox, No. 42 Bedford
Evening News Van.*

*Matchbox, No. 44 GMC
Refrigerator Truck.*

*Matchbox, No. 7
Ford Refuse Truck.*

Tootsietoy, Prewar, Lincoln Series, No. 6015. Zephyr. Photo courtesy John Gibson.

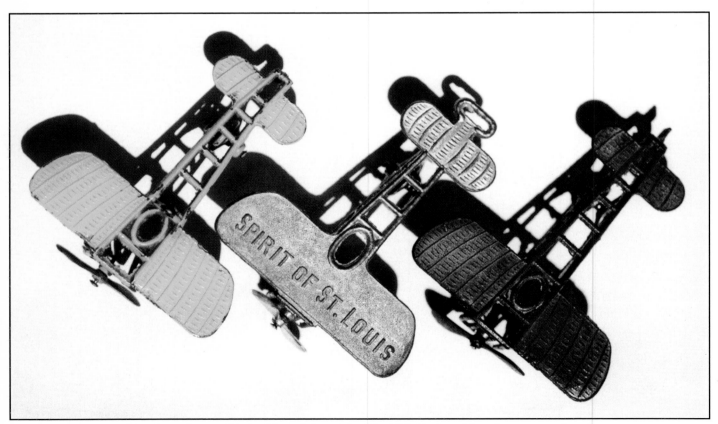

Tootsietoy, Prewar, Bleriot Plane, left to right: No. 4482 Bleriot without loop; unnumbered "Spirit of St. Louis"; No. 4482 Bleriot with loop, No. 4482. Photo courtesy John Gibson.

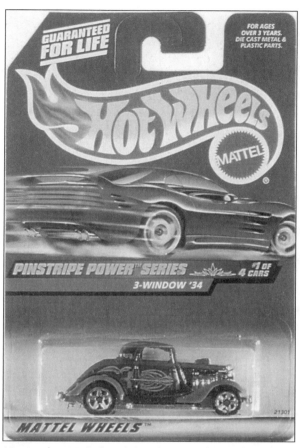

No. 953 '34 3 Window (Pinstripe Series), purple with metal base, black interior, blue tint window, 5sp.

No.	Name	MIP
955	'65 Impala, green w/chrome plastic base, tan interior, black tint window, gbbs	2
956	Auburn 852, black and silver w/metal base, white interior, clear window, bbs	2

Quicksilver Series

No.	Name	MIP
545	Chevy Stocker, red w/silver painted base, black window, four small 3sp	3
545	Chevy Stocker, red w/metal base, black window, four small 3sp	3
546	Aeroflash, purple w/white base, white window, four small 3sp	2

No.	Name	MIP
546	Aeroflash, purple w/white base, white window, 3sp	2
547	Ferrari 308, pearl white w/black metal base, black window, 5dot	2
548	T-Bird Stock Car, blue enamel w/silver painted base, black window, 5sp	2
548	T-Bird Stock Car, blue enamel w/metal base, black window, 5sp	2

Race Team Series

No.	Name	MIP
275	Lumina Stocker, dark metallic blue, white interior, uh	6
275	Lumina Stocker, light metallic blue, white interior, uh	4
275	Lumina Stocker, dark metallic blue, white interior, 7sp	4
276	Hot Wheels 500, dark metallic blue, gray interior, uh	25
276	Hot Wheels 500, dark metallic blue, gray interior, bw	5
276	Hot Wheels 500, light metallic blue, gray interior, bw	3
276	Hot Wheels 500, dark metallic blue, gray interior, 7sp	10
277	Side Splitter, dark metallic blue, metal interior, 5sp	4
277	Side Splitter, light metallic blue, metal interior, bw	4
277	Side Splitter, dark metallic blue, metal interior, bw	4
278	Dragster, dark metallic blue, white interior, bw	3
278	Dragster, dark metallic blue, white interior, 5sp	3
278	Dragster, light metallic blue, white interior, bw	3
392	Ramp Truck, (China) blue and white, smoked front window w/HW Logo, 5sp	3

No.	Name	MIP
392	Ramp Truck, blue and white, clear window, 7sp	3
392	Ramp Truck, blue and white, clear window, 5sp	2
393	Baja Bug, blue and white, white interior, 5sp	5
394	'57 Chevy, blue and white, blue interior, 5sp	5
394	'57 Chevy, blue and white, blue interior, large 3sp rear/5sp front	5
395	Bywayman, blue and white, white interior, ct	3
395	Bywayman, blue and white, white interior, t/b	3

Race Team Series III

No.	Name	MIP
533	Hummer, blue w/silver base and big antenna, gray windows, t/b	3
533	Hummer, blue w/metal base and small antenna, gray windows, t/b	3
533	Hummer, blue w/metal base and big antenna, gray windows, t/b	3
534	Chevy 1500 Pickup, blue race team colors, white interior, smoked window, 5sp	2
534	Chevy 1500 Pickup, blue race team colors, white interior, smoked window, 3sp	4
534	Chevy 1500 Pickup, team colors/silver base, white interior, smoked window, 5sp	2
534	Chevy 1500 Pickup, blue/race team colors, white interior, smoked window, 5dot	4
534	Chevy 1500 Pickup, blue/race team colors, white interior, smoked window, 7sp	12
535	3-Window '34, blue/race team colors, blue interior, 5sp	3

No.	Name	MIP
536	'80's Corvette, blue/race team colors, transparent blue roof, white interior, 5sp	2
536	'80's Corvette, blue race team colors, dark blue roof, white interior, 5sp	4
536	'80's Corvette, blue/race team colors, transparent blue roof, white interior, 5dot	4

Race Team Series IV

No.	Name	MIP
725	'67 Camaro, race team colors w/metal base, white interior, tinted window, 5sp	2
726	Mercedes C-Class, race team colors w/black base, white interior, clear window, 5sp	2

No. 725 '67 Camaro (Race Team Series IV), race team colors with metal base, white interior, tinted window, 5sp.

No.	Name	MIP
727	Shelby Cobra 427 S/C, race team colors, metal base, white interior, smoked window, 5sp	2
728	'63 Corvette, race team colors, chrome base, white interior, tinted window, 5sp	2

Race Truck Series

No.	Name	MIP
380	Dodge Ram 1500, (China) gray red interior, smoked window, 5sp	2
380	Dodge Ram 1500, red w/no hood or roof tampo, red interior, b7sp	4
380	Dodge Ram 1500, red, red interior, b7sp	8
380	Dodge Ram 1500, red, red interior, no letter, b7sp	3
381	Kenworth T600, silver, blue interior, b7sp	4
381	Kenworth T600 (Ford LTL pack), silver, blue interior, b7sp	8
382	'56 Flashsider, black side logo, chrome window, b7sp	3
382	'56 Flashsider, black side logo, chrome window, no letter, b7sp	3
382	'56 Flashsider, black rear logo, chrome window, b7sp	3
383	Nissan Truck, dark blue, gray interior, bct	7
383	Nissan Truck, dark blue, gray interior, ct	3

Racing Metals Series

No.	Name	MIP
336	Race Truck, chrome, smoked window, red interior, cct	3
337	Ramp Truck, pink chrome, black window, 7sp	6
337	Ramp Truck, purple chrome, black window, 7sp	4

No.	Name	MIP
337	Ramp Truck, blue chrome, black window, 7sp	4
338	Camaro Racer, light blue chrome, no Baldwin, white interior, 5sp	3
338	Camaro Racer, light blue chrome w/Baldwin, white interior, 5sp	7
340	Dragster, light blue chrome, white interior, 5sp	4

Real Rider Series

No.	Name	MIP
317	Dump Truck, neon yellow, black interior, yrr	20
318	Mercedes Unimog, orange and gray, orange interior, orr	20
320	'59 Caddy convertible, red, white interior, crr	35
321	Corvette Stingray, green, gray interior, grr	45

Roarin Rods Series

No.	Name	MIP
302	Mini Truck, tan, tan interior, smoked window, 7sp	5
302	Mini Truck, tan, tan interior, smoked window, 5sp	3
302	Mini Truck, tan w/orange base, tan interior, smoked window, 5sp	20
302	Mini Truck, tan, tan interior, smoked window, uh	3
303	Street Roader, orange and black, black interior, oct	10
304	Roll Patroll, white and black, black interior, yct	4
304	Roll Patroll, white and black, black interior, cct	8
305	Cobra, neon yellow, black plastic base, olive interior, 7sp	4
305	Cobra, yellow, 5s	90

No.	Name	MIP
305	Cobra, neon yellow, black metal base, olive interior, 7sp	4

Rockin' Rods Series

No.	Name	MIP
569	Twang Thang, metallic red chrome interior, 5sp	3
570	Ferrari 355, black, purple interior, 5sp	2
570	Ferrari 355, black, purple interior, 3sp	4
571	Turbo Flame, purple w/black base, yellow window, 5sp	2
572	Porsche 930, metallic green w/metal base, black interior, smoked window, 5dot	4
572	Porsche 930, metallic green w/metal base, black interior, smoked window, 5sp	2

Silver Series

No.	Name	MIP
322	Fire Eater, chrome, blue interior, 7sp	4
322	Fire Eater, chrome, blue interior, bw	5
323	Rodzilla, chrome, gold engine, 7sp	3
323	Rodzilla, chrome, gold engine, uh	3
325	Propper Chopper, chrome black interior, blue window, n/a	4
328	School Bus, chrome, white interior, bw	6
328	School Bus, chrome, white interior, 3sp	4
328	School Bus, chrome, white interior, 5sp	4
328	School Bus, chrome, tinted windows, bw	15
328	School Bus, chrome, white interior, 7sp	5

Silver Series II

No.	Name	MIP
420	Dump Truck, chrome, black box, ct/b	12
420	Dump Truck, chrome, chrome box, ct/b	2
421	'40's Woodie, logo in side window, chrome black interior, 7sp	3
421	'40's Woodie, logo in side window, chrome black interior, 5sp	3
421	'40's Woodie, logo in rear window, chrome black interior, 5sp	3
422	'57 Chevy, chrome, orange window, 5sp	3
423	Oscar Mayer Wienermobile, chrome, b5sp	3

Space Series

No.	Name	MIP
388	Radar Ranger, white and orange, orange interior, cct	3
389	GM Lean Machine, blue and white, no taillights, orange HWSA, b5sp	3
389	GM Lean Machine, blue and white w/metal base, orange HWSA, b5sp	3
390	Alien, blue and white, black, 5sp	3
391	Treadator, white pearl and orange, blue chrome	10
391	Treadator, light blue pearl and orange, blue chrome	3

Speed Gleamer Series

No.	Name	MIP
312	3 Window '34, green, chrome aqua interior, 7sp	6
313	T-Bucket, purple, white interior, purple window, 5sp	4
313	T-Bucket, purple white interior, purple window, 7sp	7

No.	Name	MIP
313	T-Bucket, purple white interior, clear window, 5sp	25
315	Ratmobile, black, chrome interior, uh	4
315	Ratmobile, black, chrome interior, 7sp	6
316	Limozeen, gold, white interior, ww	10
316	Limozeen, gold, white interior, 7sp	8

Speed Spray Series

No.	Name	MIP
549	Hydroplane, white w/aqua blue tampo, blue base, chrome interior	2
550	Street Roader, white, brown tampo, red interior, ct/b	2
551	XT-3, blue, white base, orange canopy, 5sp	2
552	Funny Car, pearl magenta, metal interior, 5sp	3

Splatter Paint Series

No.	Name	MIP
408	Rescue Ranger, orange, blue interior, t/b	2
408	Rescue Ranger, orange, blue interior, 5sp	2
408	Rescue Ranger, orange, black interior, 5sp	2
409	Side Splitter Funny Car, white, metal interior, 5sp	3
410	'55 Chevy, yellow, red interior, t/b	4
410	'55 Chevy, yellow, red interior, 5sp	3
411	'80's Camaro, white, white interior, 5sp	3

Sports Car Series

No.	Name	MIP
404	Porsche 930, silver, black interior, 7sp	3
405	Custom Corvette, purple w/logo on windshield and fender, gray interior, 7sp	35
405	Custom Corvette, purple w/logo on front fender, gray interior, 7sp	3
405	Custom Corvette, purple w/logo on windshield, gray interior, 5sp	3
405	Custom Corvette, purple w/logo on windshield, gray interior, 7sp	3
405	Custom Corvette, purple w/logo on windshield, red interior, 7sp	35
406	Cobra 427 S/C, pearl white w/metal base black interior, clear window, 7sp	3
406	Cobra 427 S/C, pearl white w/metal base black interior, clear window, 5sp	55
407	'59 Caddy, black, white interior, ww7sp rear/7sp front	75
407	'59 Caddy, black, white interior, 7sp	3

Spy Print Series

No.	Name	MIP
553	Stealth, purple w/metal base, purple window, t/b	2
553	Stealth, purple w/silver painted base, purple window, t/b	2
553	Stealth, purple w/silver painted base, purple window, 3sp	2
553	Stealth, purple w/metal base, purple window, 3sp	2
554	Alien, blue and white w/smoked window, white and blue, interior t/b	2
554	Alien, blue and white w/smoked window, white and blue interior, 3sp	2

No.	Name	MIP
555	Sol-Aire CX4, metallic maroon w/white sides, black window, t/b	2
555	Sol-Aire CX4, metallic maroon w/white sides, black window, 3sp	2
556	Custom Corvette, black w/yellow, red and white tampo, gray interior, 3sp	2

Steel Stamp Series

No.	Name	MIP
285	Steel Passion, black and rose, red interior, ww	4
285	Steel Passion, black and rose, red interior, clear window, ww	4
285	Steel Passion, black and rose, red interior, 7sp	4
287	Zender Fact 4, black, white interior, clear window, 5sp	8
287	Zender Fact 4, black, white interior, 3sp	4
287	Zender Fact 4, black, white interior, uh	4
287	Zender Fact 4, black, white interior, 5sp	4
289	'56 Flashsider, burgundy, chrome window, 5sp	4
289	'56 Flashsider, burgundy, chrome window, 7sp	4
289	56 Flashsider, burgundy, chrome window, uh	4
290	'57 Chevy, blue, blue interior, blue window, uh	4
290	'57 Chevy, blue, black interior, smoked window, 5sp	8
290	'57 Chevy, blue, blue interior, blue window, 5sp	15
290	'57 Chevy, blue, blue interior, blue window, 7sp	4

Street Art Series

No.	Name	MIP
850	Propper Chopper, pearl green w/black base, black interior, yellow window	2
949	Mini Truck, black w/black base, black interior, clear window, t/b	2
951	Ambulance, purple w/chrome base, purple interior, orange tint window, 5sp	2
951	Ambulance, purple w/chrome base, purple interior, orange tint window, 3sp	2
952	School Bus, silver w/black base, yellow interior, red tint, 5dot	3
952	School Bus, yellow w/black base, yellow interior, red tint window, 5dot	2

Street Beast Series

No.	Name	MIP
557	Mercedes-Benz Unimog, red and black, w/tan top, red interior, ct/b	3
558	Jaguar XJ220, orange w/black side tampo, black interior, yt/b	3
558	Jaguar XJ220, orange w/no side tampo, black interior, yt/b	3
559	Blown Camaro, yellow w/metal Malaysia base, black interior, ot/b	3
559	Blown Camaro, yellow w/metal black base, black interior, ot/b	3
560	Corvette Stingray, white, blue interior, yt/b	3

Street Eaters Series

No.	Name	MIP
412	Speed Machine, light green, red interior, 7sp	5

No. 689 Shadow Jet II (Techno Bits Series), black with brown tampo and metal base, chrome interior, green window, b5sp.

No.	Name	MIP
690	Power Pistons, purple w/yellow tampo, yellow interior and window, 3sp	2
691	Shadow Jet, metallic black w/gold trim and metal base, black interior, smoked window, 5sp	10
691	Shadow Jet, blue w/metal base, black interior, smoked window, 5sp	2
691	Shadow Jet, purple w/metal base, black interior, smoked window, 5sp	2
692	Radar Ranger, neon green w/black base, purple window, t/b	2

No. 980 Splittin' Image II (Terrorific Series), gold with black base, pink chrome window, 3sp.

Terrorific Series

No.	Name	MIP
977	At-a-tude, green w/black base, chrome interior, green tint, bk5sp	3
978	Cat-a-pult, orange w/metal base, black interior black tint window, 5sp	2
979	Sweet 16 II, black w/metal base gold chrome interior, yellow tint window, 5sp	2
980	Splittin' Image II, gold w/black base, pink chrome window, 3sp	2

Tropicool Series

No.	Name	MIP
693	Ice Cream Truck, white w/black base, white logo, green interior, 5sp	2

No.	Name	MIP
693	Ice cream Truck, white w/black base, black logo, green interior, 5sp	2
693	Ice cream Truck, white w/black base, w/o Fruits and Veggies, black logo, green interior, 5sp	2
694	Baja Bug, white w/metal base, flat red in tampo, red interior, large rear, 5sp	2
694	Baja Bug, white w/metal base, red enamel in tampo, red interior, all small 5sp	2
695	Classic Caddy, red w/black fenders red, yellow, gray, white and black stripes, gray interior, 3sp	2

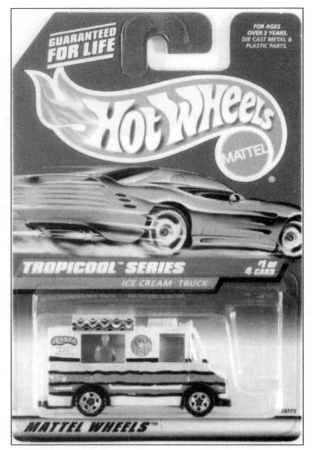

No. 693 Ice cream Truck (Tropicool Series), white with black base, black logo, green interior, 5sp.

No.	Name	MIP
695	Classic Caddy, red w/black fenders red, yellow, gray, white and black stripes, gray interior 5sp	2
695	Classic Caddy, red w/black fenders red, yellow, gray, white and black stripes, gray interior, bbs	2
696	Corvette Convertible, neon green, black Custom Corvette base, blue interior, smoke window, 3sp	2
696	Corvette Convertible, neon green, black base w/o CC, blue interior, smoke window, 3sp	2
696	Corvette Convertible, neon green, black Custom Corvette base, blue interior, smoke window, bbs	2

White Ice Series

No.	Name	MIP
561	Speed Machine, pearl white, red window, 3sp	2
562	Shadow Jet, pearl white, yellow window, 5sp	2
563	Splittn' Image II, pearl white, chrome windows, 3sp	2

X-Ray Cruiser Series

No.	Name	MIP
1114	63 Split Window, black w/chrome base white interior, black tint, g5sp	3
945	Mercedes C-Class, black w/light tampo and black base, white interior, yellow window, gbbs	4
945	Mercedes C-Class, black w/dark tampo and black base, white interior, yellow window, gbbs	4

Name	MIP
946 Lamborghini Diablo, teal w/black painted base, gray interior, smoked window, 5sp	2
947 '67 Camaro, blue enamel w/metal Malaysia base, white interior, tinted window, 5sp	2
947 '67 Camaro, blue enamel w/metal Malaysia base, white interior, tinted window, 3sp	2
948 Jaguar XJ220, yellow w/black base blue interior, clear window, 3sp	2

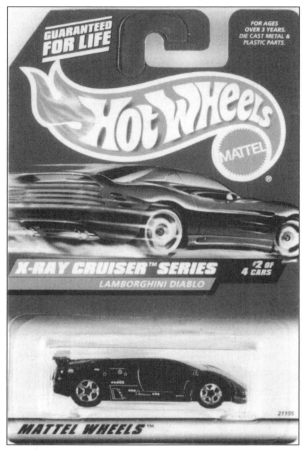

No. 946 Lamborghini Diablo (X-Ray Cruiser Series), teal with black painted base, gray interior, smoked window, 5sp.

LIMITED EDITION

No. Name	MIP
1995 ASA Chevy Lumina, white, 7,000 made	16
1999 National Balloon Rally – Dairy Delivery, blue, white	18
55 Candy Apple Chevy, red, white, 5,000 made	42
55 Chevy – Tim Flock, black	12
56 Flashsider, black	20
99 Mustang, Hot Wheels colors, Mexico exclusive, 10,000 made	14
Airwalk – '57 Chevy (Nordstroms), black	32
Auburn-Cord – Duesenberg Museum, 1936 Cord 810, black, 25,000 made	12
Barbie – '93 Camaro, dark pink, 2nd ed., 8,000 made	50
Barbie – '93 Camaro, light pink, 1st ed., 7,000 made	70
Barbie – Highway Hauler, pink, white	65
Blue Angels – Fat Fendered, 40, blue, 20,000 made	20
Blue Angels – VW Bus, blue, 20,000 made	55
Bobs Toy Show – Delivery Van, red, No. 13, on collector number card, 8,000 made	22
Boise Roadster Show – '33 Ford Roadster, black, 12,000 made	20
Carefree Gum – '70 Funny Car, Mongoose, blue, 10,000 made	16
Carefree Gum – '70 Funny Car, Snake, yellow, 10,000 made	16
Carroll Shelby – '65 Shelby Cobra 427 SC, gray	35
Chicago Cubs – white '65 Camaro/gray '69 Mustang, 10,000 made, on one card	80
Colorado Rockies – Hot Wheels 500, 10,000 made	42
Corvette Central – '58 Corvette, blue	20

Name	MIP
Corvette Central – '63 Corvette, gray, 10,000 made	16
Corvette Central – '75 Corvette, yellow, 10,000 made	16
Corvette Central – '88 Corvette, white, 10,000 made	18
Davis Printing – Highway Hauler, black, white, 7,000 made	13
Don Garlits – Custom Dodge Ram Truck, black, 10,000 made	22
Early Times – '32 Ford Delivery, white, purple fen, on collector number card, No. 135	80
Early Times – '32 Ford Vicky, 10,000 made	15
Early Times – 3-Window '34, yellow, 7,000 made	37
Early Times – Fat Fendered '40, black, yellow, 7,000 made	35
Early Times – Tail Dragger, orange, red, 10,000 made	18
Early Times – Way 2 Fast, 10,000 made	18
Edelbrock – '63 Corvette Sting Ray, blue	18
Edelbrock – '68 Trans Am Camaro, black, brown	22
Firebird Raceway – '32 Ford Hot Rod Coupe, red, 15,000 made	14
Firebird Raceway – Ignitor Sedan, 10,000 made	12
Fisher-Price – '65 Mustang Conv, white, 8,000 made	18
Full Grid – TE – Dairy Delivery, blue, silver, No. 1004, on collector number card, 15,000 made	20
Full Grid – TE – Dodge Ram 1500, blue, No. 1059, on collector number card, 15,000 made	18
Full Grid – TE – SCTA '40 Ford Pickup, orange, white, on collector number card, 15,000 made	20

Name	MIP
Full Grid – TE – Way 2 Fast, red, No. 994, on collector number card, 15,000 made	18
Funny Car – Mongoose, red, 10,000 made	18
Funny Car – Snake, white, 10,000 made	22
Golden Knights, VW Bus, black	15
Grand National Roadster Show, '33 Ford Roadster, red, 15,000 made	16
Grand National Roadster Show, '33 Ford Roadster, maroon, 1,000 made	28
Hills – '58 Corvette Conv, 5,000 made	70
Hills – '67 Camaro – blue/white, 7,500 made	60
Hills – '67 GTO	24
Hills – '70 Mustang Mach I, red	24
Hills – '70 Plymouth Barracuda	22
Hot Rod Magazine – '70 Plymouth Barracuda, purple, 2,000 made	180
Hot Rod Power Tour – '70 Mustang, Hot Wheels colors, 10,000 made	24
Hot Rod Tour Edition – '70 Mustang, Hot Wheels colors, 5,000 made	30
Hot Wheels Championship Auto Shows – Way 2 Fast, white, 10,000 made	24
Houston Astros – '65 Mustang Conv, white, Coca-Cola	42
HW Newsletter – '57 Chevy, turquoise, in bag, No. 2	50
HW Newsletter – '59 Cadillac Conv, white, in bag, No. 3	16
HW Newsletter – '65 Mustang, turquoise, black interior, in bag, No. 1	90
HW Newsletter – '65 Mustang, turquoise, tan interior, in bag, 500 made, No. 1	45
HW Newsletter – Delivery Van, white	22
HW Newsletter – Delivery Van, black	20
HW Newsletter – Highway Hauler, red, white, No. 9, on collector number card, 7,000 made	22

Name	MIP
HW Newsletter – Passion, black, 1999 Hot Wheels Convention, in bag, 1,200 made	100
JC Whitney – '32 Ford Delivery, turquoise, white, in bag	90
JC Whitney – '40s Ford Truck, black	18
JC Whitney – '40s Woodie, red	25
JC Whitney – '55 Chevy, teal, white	30
JC Whitney – '56 Flashsider, white	13
JC Whitney – Baja Bug, yellow	25
JC Whitney – Chevy Nomad, green	15
JC Whitney – Chevy Nomad, yellow	15
JC Whitney – Custom Camper Van, green	15
JC Whitney – Dairy Delivery, red, white	14
JC Whitney – Ford F-150 Truck, green	12
JC Whitney – Jeep, white	15
JC Whitney – Roadrunner, purple	18
JC Whitney – Scorchin Scooter, black, silver	30
JC Whitney – Scorchin Scooter, red, white, blue	30
JC Whitney – VW Bug, red	22
JC Whitney – VW Bus, white	135
Jiffy Lube – '65 Impala, white	15
Jiffy Lube – '67 Pontiac GTO, black	15
Jiffy Lube – Dairy Delivery, red	14
Jiffy Lube – Scorchin Scooter, black	18
Jiffy Lube – Tail Dragger, white, red, 25,000 made	15
Jiffy Lube – Viper RT/10, black	12
Jiffy Lube – VW Bus, yellow	28
Jurassic Park – Helicopter, red	100
Jurassic Park – Helicopter, aqua	42
LAPD – Police 'B' Wagon, black w/white top, 1,000 made	46
LAPD – Police 'B' Wagon, black, 10,000 made	32
LAPD – Police Cruiser, 10,000 made	32

Name	MIP
LAPD – Police Helicopter	26
Lexmark – '67 Mustang Fastback, white	25
Lexmark – 3-Window '34, black	22
Lexmark – 3-Window '34, white	22
Lexmark – AMX, red, white, blue	25
Lexmark – Fat Fendered '40, red	20
Lexmark – Passion, white	20
Lexmark – Tail Dragger, black	25
Los Angeles Dodgers – Dodge Viper, blue, white, 10,000 made	14
M&D Toys – '32 Ford Delivery, black, 10,000 made	22
M&D Toys – '55 Chevy, Fireball Roberts, white, 12,000 made	15
M&D Toys – '55 Chevy, Smokey Yunick, black, 12,000 made	15
M&D Toys – '55 Chevy, Smokey Yunick, blue, 12,000 made	15
M&D Toys – '58 Corvette Conv, red, No. 14, on collector number card, 7,000 made	30
M&D Toys – Deep Purple Nomad, purple, rr, 6,000 made	20
M&D Toys – Deep Purple Nomad, purple, ww, 6,000 made	20
M&D Toys – Golden '59 Caddy, gold, red interior, 5,000 made	16
M&D Toys – Golden '59 Caddy, gold, white interior, 5,000 made	16
M&D Toys – Old No. 5, yellow, 7,000 made	20
M&D Toys – Pearl Passion, white, No. 48, on collector number card, 8,000 made	30
M&D Toys – Pink Passion, pink, 8,000 made	48
M&D Toys – Rail Dragster, Mongoose, blue, No. 90, on collector number card, 8,000 made	16
M&D Toys – Rail Dragster, Snake, yellow No. 90, on collector number card, 8,000 made	16

Name	MIP
M&D Toys – Red Passion, red, 7,000 made	36
Malleco Tower Cranes – VW Bus, red	30
Mervyns California – Custom '50 Buick, blue	16
Mervyns California – Scorchin Scooter, black	20
Minnesota Street Rod Ass. – '40s Woodie, black, beige, 10,000 made	18
Museum of Heritage – '35 Caddy, blue fen, 5,000 made	12
Museum of Heritage – '35 Caddy, red fen, 5,000 made	12
Navy Seals – VW Bus, blue	20
New York Mets – Dodge Viper, blue, same as pack No. 1006 but has commemorative sticker, on collector number card, 10,000 made	18
Norwalk Raceway Park – '57 Chevy, red, 12,000 made	20
Oakland As – Ford Taurus, green, yellow	25
Penske Auto Center – '70 Mustang Mach 1, red	16
Racing Through the Years – Highway Hauler, gold, black, 8,000 made	25
Randy's Stuff – VW Bug, pink, 3,000 made	100
Randy's Stuff – VW Bug, purple, 7,000 made	33
Rebel Run – Passion, black, 7,000 made	40
Redline – SCool Bus, white, 10,000 made	20
Rod & Custom – Passion, red, 7,000 made	26
Rod & Custom – T-Bucket, black, 7,000 made	30
Seattle Toy Show – '65 Mustang Conv, black	20
Seattle Toy Show – '67 Camaro Z-28, black, 8,000 made	28

Name	MIP
Seattle Toy Show – '70 Olds 442, black, 7,000 made	30
Seattle Toy Show – '70 Olds 442, black, 7,000 made	33
Seattle Toy Show – Custom Mustang, blue, 10,000 made	20
Seattle Toy Show – Nomad, blue, 7,000 made	20
Steadly Tudor (Fat Fendered '40), white, 7,000 made	36
Thunderbirds – VW Bus, blue, 30,000 made	28
Tomart – '53 Corvette, red	14
Toy Cars & Vehicles – '65 Mustang, red, 10,000 made	15
Toy Cars & Vehicles – '70 Plymouth Barracuda, purple, 10,000 made	18
Toy Shop – '32 Ford, red, 10,000 made	15
Toy Shop – '63 T-Bird, black, 10,000 made	15
Toys for Tots – Scorchin Scooter, white	25
U.S. Camaro Club – '67 RS/SS Camaro, red	20
U.S. Charities Racing Team – Hummer, black, U.S. flag	24
Viper Club – Dodge Viper, black, 9,999 made	22
White's Guide – '56 Flashsider, gold	16
White's Guide – '56 Flashsider, yellow	16
White's Guide – Scorchin Scooter, black	16
White's Guide – Scorchin Scooter, gold	16
YamaHauler – Go Kart, blue, silver chrome, 10,000 made	18
YamaHauler – Golden Go-Cart, blue, gold chrome, 10,000 made	28
YamaHauler – Highway Hauler, white	14
YamaHauler – Highway Hauler, blue	18

Johnny Lightning

Johnny Lightnings, 1:64-scale die-cast cars, were originally made by Topper Toys of Elizabeth, New Jersey from 1969-1971. Like other companies, Johnny Lightnings were made to compete with Mattel's new line of toy, Hot Wheels.

Henry Orenstein, owner of Topper Toys, felt the only way to compete with Hot Wheels was speed. Johnny Lightnings were made with Celcon wheels mounted on plastic bushings and then lubricated. It was claimed that Johnny Lightnings could achieve a speed of 400 mph when raced down a track. This, along with their unique open-door style set the first eight designs—Custom Eldorado, Custom GTO, Custom El Camino, Custom Thunderbird, Custom Toronado, Custom Ferrari, Custom Mako Shark and Custom XKE—apart from the competition.

Topper's decision to sponsor a rookie named Al Unser for the 1970 Indy 500 changed the public perception towards Johnny Lightnings. The subsequent media attention after Unser's miraculous win lifted sales to the point where Johnny Lightnings were regarded as the only legitimate threat to Hot Wheels. *Sport's Illustrated* even chronicled their competition in a December 1970 article sighting the intense rivalry between the two camps. Topper capitalized on its new-found fame in many ways, including a very successful promotion with the national cereal manufacturer General Mills.

Forty-seven models were manufactured in two years before financial mismanagement halted production in 1971. Orenstein was indicted of misleading business practices, claiming there were more Johnny Lightnings made than were actually produced.

Johnny Lightnings by Playing Mantis

South Bend, Indiana-based toymaker Playing Mantis, began producing die-cast cars under the Johnny Lightning name in 1994. Tom Lowe, president, an avid die-cast collector, had a closet full of die-cast, including Toppers Johnny Lightnings. Lowe decided it was time to revive the toy line.

After conducting a trademark search, it was discovered that Topper had abandoned the Johnny Lightning name. Playing Mantis applied for a trademark and it was granted to them shortly after. Collectors should note that any time they see "Johnny Lightning®" that it is a registered trademark of Playing Mantis and that it refers to modern Johnny Lightnings.

Since 1994, Playing Mantis has produced over 1,000 die-cast cars and has been able to

Closed or Open Doors, that is the Question

The process of manufacturing the original Johnny Lightning "great eight"—Eldorado, GTO, El Camino, Thunderbird, Toronado, Ferrari, Mako Shark, and XKE—included a step in which workers applied a thin strip of metal to the inside of the chassis, forming a hinge for the doors. This extra step was eliminated midway through 1969. The molds were changed to a unibody style thus creating a closed door appearance. The key to understanding the rarity of these cars in their dual forms is twofold. It must be determined when production began for each car before the body style change, and then estimate how long these molds were in use.

It's easy to distinguish three separate production runs among the eight cars. First, the El Dorado stands alone in uniqueness. It is generally regarded as the first car built out of the starting gates for Topper. For this reason, we know that it is the most abundant of the five rare Detroits. It seems that the mold for this piece was retired shortly after opening doors were eliminated. This makes the El Dorado, in the closed door form, one of the rarest of all castings.

The four remaining Detroits had a short production run that started after the El Dorado and intersected about midway through this transition period. This means that the GTO, El Camino, Thunderbird and Toronado are fairly evenly split between open- and closed-door style with a few more of the open-door models available (sixty percent open and forty percent closed).

The remaining three cars, the Ferrari, Mako and XKE, all had a long career in the Johnny Lightning lineup. They were introduced right before the mold change, so these cars were very valuable in the open-door style and very common with closed doors.

Any high quality Detroit car in either an open or closed version will be a highlight in any collection. Likewise, an open-door Ferrari, Mako or XKE are variations that should not be passed over by new collectors.

secure licensing for toys based on Speed racer, Monopoly and The Munsters. Although, some of their most popular models are those based on actual cars—Camaros, Corvettes and Mustangs.

In order to honor the Johnny Lightning beginnings, Playing Mantis issued a line of Commemoratives. These are replicas of the original Topper cars, not reproductions. The packaging is similar to Topper's, but it is easy to see that they are new—"Playing Mantis" and "Commemorative Limited Edition" are marked directly on the package. The Playing Mantis name can also be found on the base of each model. As with many modern Johnny Lightnings, the Commemorative series cars are accompanied by a collector coin.

Playing Mantis has been able to corner part of a market that was previously dominated by Mattel's Hot Wheels. Gaining popularity with collectors, Playing Mantis' Partridge Family Bus was voted as the best 1:64-scale die-cast by *Toy Shop* magazine readers in 1999.

Market Update

Topper Johnny Lightnings are an often-overlooked segment in the vintage die-cast marketplace. There is currently a buyer's market for Johnny Lightnings. This is a tremendous window of opportunity for collectors, common yet high-quality pieces are extremely affordable in today's secondary market.

While the value of many of Playing Mantis' Johnny Lightnings are in the $5-$15 range, some examples can go for as much as five times that amount. The White Lightning series are highly desired by collectors.

Contributors to Johnny Lightning/Topper: Tom Brown, tmbrown@edgenet.net; Ray Falcoa, johnnylray@aol.com.

Johnny Lightning/Topper

Name	Good	EX	MNP	MIP
'32 Roadster, 1969	20	25	60	125
A.J. Foyt Indy Special, black wall tires, 1970	20	40	60	250
Al Unser Indy Special, black wall tires, 1970	50	100	200	500
Baja, 1970	20	45	125	200
Big Rig, came w/add on extras called Customs; prices reflect fully accessorized cars, 1971	35	65	150	275
Bubble, Jet Powered, 1970	25	45	75	150
Bug Bomb, black wall tires, 1970	25	40	90	225
Condor, black wall tires, 1970	75	150	200	1200
Custom Camaro, prototype, only one known to exist, 1968-69	n/a	n/a	6000	n/a
Custom Charger, prototype, only one known to exist, 1968-69	n/a	n/a	6000	n/a

Name	Good	EX	MNP	MIP
Custom Continental, prototype, only six known to exist, 1968-69	n/a	n/a	4000	n/a
Custom Dragster, mirror finish, 1969	100	150	250	1000
Custom Dragster, w/plastic canopy, 1969	35	60	150	200
Custom Dragster, without canopy, 1969	10	35	75	125
Custom El Camino, w/sealed doors, 1969	70	100	300	500
Custom El Camino, mirror finish, 1969	100	200	350	1125
Custom El Camino, w/opening doors, 1969	100	150	275	475
Custom Eldorado, w/sealed doors, 1969	75	150	300	1000
Custom Eldorado, w/opening doors, 1969	100	150	275	275
Custom Ferrari, w/opening doors, mirror finish, 1969	150	300	450	1000

'32 Roadster (Topper Toys). Photo Courtesy Dennis Seleman.

Custom Eldorado, with opening doors (Topper Toys). Photo Courtesy Dennis Seleman.

Name	Good	EX	MNP	MIP
Custom Ferrari, w/sealed doors, 1969	15	35	80	125
Custom Ferrari, w/opening doors, 1969	45	150	275	500
Custom GTO, w/opening doors, 1969	100	200	350	1500
Custom GTO, mirror finish, 1969	100	200	475	1000
Custom GTO, w/sealed doors, 1969	125	200	350	1700
Custom Mako Shark, w/opening doors, 1969	50	125	350	500
Custom Mako Shark, w/sealed doors, 1969	15	40	75	225
Custom Mako Shark, w/opening doors, mirror finish, 1969	100	200	500	2000
Custom Mustang, prototype, only one known to exist, 1968-69	n/a	n/a	6000	n/a
Custom Spoiler, black wall tires, 1970	20	35	65	150
Custom T-Bird, w/opening doors, 1969	40	100	250	475
Custom T-Bird, mirror finish, 1969	100	200	400	5000
Custom T-Bird, w/sealed doors, 1969	65	150	300	700
Custom Toronado, mirror finish, 1969	300	450	600	2000
Custom Toronado, w/sealed doors, 1969	200	300	500	1500

Name	Good	EX	MNP	MIP
Custom Toronado, w/opening doors, 1969	175	225	400	1000
Custom Turbine, w/unpainted interior, 1969	15	25	45	125
Custom Turbine, mirror finish, 1969	100	150	225	500
Custom Turbine, red, black, white painted interior, 1969	25	50	150	200
Custom XKE, w/opening doors, 1969	45	150	275	400
Custom XKE, w/sealed doors, 1969	15	35	80	100
Custom XKE, w/opening doors, mirror finish, 1969	150	300	450	800
Double Trouble, black wall tires, 1970	40	75	100	1500
Flame Out, black wall tires, 1970	30	60	125	350
Flying Needle, Jet Powered, 1970	25	45	100	225
Frantic Ferrari	15	35	45	90
Glasser, Jet Powered, 1970	20	40	75	150

Custom T-Bird, with opening doors (Topper Toys). Photo Courtesy Dennis Seleman.

Leapin' Limo (Topper Toys).

Name				MIP
Hairy Hauler, came w/add on extras called Customs; prices reflect fully accessorized cars, 1971	35	65	150	275
Jumpin' Jag, black wall tires, 1970	15	35	80	175
Leapin' Limo, black wall tires, 1970	25	50	125	400
Mad Maverick, black wall tires, 1970	40	75	150	450
Monster, jet powered, 1970	20	40	74	150
Movin' Van, black wall tires, 1970	20	35	65	90
Nucleon, black wall tires, 1970	15	35	80	225
Parnelli Jones Indy Special, black wall tires, 1970	20	40	60	250
Pipe Dream, came w/add on extras called Customs; prices reflect fully accessorized cars, 1971	35	65	150	275
Sand Stormer, black wall tires, 1970	10	20	35	90
Sand Stormer, black roof, black wall tires, 1970	25	50	100	200

Name				MIP
Screamer, jet powered, 1970	25	45	75	200
Sling Shot, black wall tires, 1970	25	50	95	250
Smuggler, black wall tires, 1970	20	35	75	150
Stiletto, black wall tires, 1970	40	60	85	300
TNT, black wall tires, 1970	20	40	75	175
Triple Threat, black wall tires, 1970	20	40	90	200
Twin Blaster, came w/add on extras called Customs; prices reflect fully accessorized cars, 1971	35	65	150	275
Vicious Vette, black wall tires, 1970	15	35	80	225
Vulture w/wing, black wall tires, 1970	45	75	130	500
Wasp, black wall tires, 1970	45	80	100	400
Wedge, Jet Powered, 1970	25	45	75	200
Whistler, black wall tires, 1970	45	75	125	300
Wild Winner, came w/add on extras called Customs; prices reflect fully accessorized cars, 1971	35	60	125	250

Smuggler (Topper Toys). Photo Courtesy Mark Rich.

Sand Stormer (Topper Toys).

Johnny Lightning/Playing Mantis

.COM CARS (INTERNET PROGRAM)

Name	MIP
Bikini.com, Mustang Trans-Am	5
CBS Sports, Monte Carlo	5
Ebay, Viper GTS-R	6
Millenium VW Bus	6
Playing Mantis Internet Car, Firebird	5
Yahoo!, IRL Car	5

AMERICA'S FINEST

Name	MIP

Round 1

Name	MIP
'95 Caprice, Honolulu Police	6
'97 Camaro, Contra Costa County, CA	6
'97 Crown Victoria, North Carolina State Police	6
'97 Crown Victoria, Indiana State Police, exclusive car	12
'97 Tahoe, Mesquite Texas Police	6

Round 2

Name	MIP
'95 Caprice, St. Louis Metropolitan Police, White Lightning	15
'97 Camaro, Texas Highway Patrol, White Lightning	20
'97 Crown Victoria, Niles Township Police, White Lightning	20
'97 Tahoe, Michigan State Police, White Lightning	20

AMERICAN BLUE

Name	MIP

Round 1

Name	MIP
'95 Caprice, New Hampshire	5
'97 Camaro, South Carolina	5

Name	MIP
'97 Crown Victoria, New Orleans	5
'97 Tahoe, Chevrolet	5
1977 Dodge Royal Monaco, Chicago	5
Dodge Royal Monaco, New York	5
Ford Galaxy 300, Cook County	5

Round 2

Name	MIP
'66 Ford Galaxy 300, Kissimmee Police	5
'77 Dodge Royal Monaco, Mount Prospect	5
'95 Caprice, Key West Police	5
'97 Camaro, Nevada Hwy. Police	5
'97 Crown Victoria, New Orleans Harbor, bonus car	5
'98 Hummer, S.P.O.C.	5
Chevy Tahoe, Wisconsin State PD	5

Round 3

Name	MIP
'66 Ford Galaxy 300, Missouri State Highway Patrol	5
'95 Caprice, California Hwy Patrol	5
'95 Corvette ZR-1, Baltimore Police, bonus car	5
'97 Camaro, Oregon State Police	5
'97 Chevy Tahoe, Spring Grove Police	5
'97 Crown Victoria, Detroit Police	5
'97 Crown Victoria, Georgia State Police	5

AMERICAN CHROME

Name	MIP
'53 Buick Super	5

Name	MIP
'55 Chrysler C-300	5
'55 Ford Crown Victoria	5
'57 Lincoln Premier	5
'58 Chevy Impalla	5

ANNIVERSARY CARS

Name	MIP

Round 1

'70 Challenger R/T	5
'70 Cobra 429	5
'70 Superbird	5

Round 2

'70 AMC Rebel Machine	5
'70 Camaro RS	5
'70 Mustang Boss 302	5

Round 3

'70 Buick GSX	5
'70 Camaro Z28	5
'70 Olds 4-4-2	5

Round 4

'70 Chevelle	5
'70 Corvette	5
'70 Superbee	5

BRITISH INVASION

Name	MIP

Round 1

'58-'60 MGA TWIN CAM	5
'58-'61 Austin-Healey Srite	5
'58-'61 Triumph TR3A	5
'62-'71 MGB	5

Round 2

'58-'60 MGA Twin Cam	5
'58-'61 Austin-Healey Sprite	5
'58-'61 Triumph TR3A	5
'61 Jaguar Convertible	5
'62 Sunbeam	5
'62-'71 MGB	5

CAMAROS

Name	MIP

First Shots

'67 Camaro Z28	15
'68 Camaro	11
'69 Camaro SS	11
'72 Camaro RS	12
'76 Camaro LT	10
'82 Camaro Z28	10

Round 1

'67 Camaro, bonus car	7
'67 Camaro RS/SS	6
'68 Camaro RS/SS	6
'69 Camaro RS	6
'70 Camaro RS/SS	5
'77 Camaro Z28	5
'82 Camaro Z28	4

Round 2

'67 Camaro RS/SS	6
'68 Camaro RS/SS	6
'69 Camaro RS	5
'70 Camaro RS/SS	4
'77 Camaro Z28	4
'82 Camaro Z28	4

Camaros, (Playing Mantis).

Name	MIP

Round 3

'67 Camaro RS/SS	5
'67 Coupe Camaro	5
'68 RS/SS Camaro	5
'69 COPO Camaro	5
'73 RS Camaro	4
'76 Coupe Camaro	4
'87 IROC-Z Camaro	4

Round 4

'67 Camaro RS/SS	5
'68 Camaro Z-28	6
'69 Camaro RS/SS 396	5
'72 Camaro RS	4
'76 Camaro LT	4
'89 Camaro IROC-Z	3

CARTOON NETWORK CARS

Name	MIP
Flintstone's Sports Car	5
Speed Buggy	5
Wacky Racers Compact Pussy Cat	5
Wacky Racers Mean Machine	5

CLASSICS GOLD

Name	MIP

Round 1

'33 Willys	5
'56 Chevy	5
'63 Impala	5
'66 Mustang	5
'69 Camaro	5
'69 Rambler	5
'70 Cougar	5
'70 Olds 442	5
'74 Olds	5
Grand National	5

Round 2

'69 AMX	5

Wacky Racers Mean Machine (Playing Mantis).

Name	MIP
'70 Buick GS	5
'78 Corvette	5
'84 Monte Carlo SS	5

Round 3

1941 Willy's Pro Street	5
1969 Mercury Cougar	5
1971 Challenger Convertible	5
1974 Ford Torino	5
1997 Chevy Tahoe	5
Midnight Express	5

Round 4

1941 Willy's Pro Street	5
1965 Mustang	5
1969 AMX Javelin, bonus car	5
1972 Olds Cutlass	5
1978 Mustang Cobra	5
1996 Dodge Viper GTS	5
1997 Chevy Tahoe	5

Round 5

1959 El Camino	5
1967 Pontiac GTO	5
1972 Boss Mustang	5
1996 Dodge Viper	5

Classics Gold, Round 2 (Playing Mantis). Photo Courtesy Playing Mantis.

Name	MIP
1996 Impala SS	5
Yellow Cab	5

Round 6
Name	MIP
1941 Willy	5
1969 AMX	5
1970 Olds 4-4-2	5
1978 King Cobra	5
1995 Impala SS	5
Boothill Express	5

COMMEMORATIVE

Name	MIP

Round 1
Name	MIP
Bug Bomb	5
Custom '32 Roadster	5
Custom El Camino	5
Custom GTO	6
Custom XKE	5
Movin' Van	5
The Wasp	5
Vicious Vette	6

Round 2
Name	MIP
Custom Continental	4
Custom Mako Shark	6
Custom Mustang	4
Custom Spoiler	4
Custom T-Bird	4
Custom Toronado	4

Name	MIP
Custom Turbine	4
Nucleon	4
T.N.T.	4
Triple Threat	4

Round 3
Name	MIP
Custom Camaro	4
Custom Charger	4

Round 4
Name	MIP
Custom Dragster	4
Custom Eldorado	4
Custom Stiletto	4
Flame Out	4
Mad Maverick	4
Sand Stormer	4

Round 5
Name	MIP
Custom El Camino	4
Custom GTO	4
Custom Mako Shark	6
Custom T-Bird	4
Custom Toronado	4

Round 6
Name	MIP
Beep Jeep	4
Commuter	4
Skinni Mini	4
Tow'd	4

Name	MIP
White Lightnings	
Bug Bomb	10
Custom '32 Roadster	10
Custom Continental	12
Custom El Camino	12
Custom GTO	12
Custom Mako Shark	15
Custom Mustang	15
Custom Spoiler	10
Custom T-Bird	15
Custom Toronado	10
Custom Turbine	10
Custom XKE	10
Nucleon	10
T.N.T.	10
The Wasp	10
Triple Threat	10
Vicious Vette	15

CORVETTE COLLECTION

Name	MIP
First Shots	
'53 Corvette	10
'63 Corvette Sting Ray	10
'63 Grand Sport	10
'65 Corvette Sting Ray Coupe	10
'70 Corvette Sting Ray Coupe	10
'98 Corvette Convertible	10
Round 1	
'54 Corvette Nomad	8
'57 Corvette Roadster	4
'62 Corvette Convertible	4
'65 Mako Shark II	5
'67 Corvette 427 Sting Ray	4
'80 Aerovette	5
'82 Corvette	5
'95 Corvette ZR-1	5
Corvette Indy	4
Corvette Sting Ray III	4

Name	MIP
Round 2	
'53 Corvette	4
'63 Corvette Sting Ray	4
'63 Grand Sport	4
'65 Corvette Sting Ray Coupe	4
'70 Corvette Sting Ray Coupe	4
'98 Corvette Convertible	4
White Lightnings	
'54 Corvette Nomad	120
'57 Corvette Roadster	65
'62 Corvette Convertible	65
'65 Mako Shark II	60
'67 Corvette 427 Sting Ray	65
'80 Aerovette	45
'82 Corvette	75
'95 Corvette ZR-1	95

COVER CARS—MUSTANG ILLUSTRATED

Name	MIP
Round 1	
'68 Mustang GT	5
'69 Mach 1	5
'73 Mach 1	5
'77 Cobra II	5
'94 Boss	5
Ford Mustang Convertible	5
Round 2	
'65 Mustang Convertible	5
'67 GTA	5
'68 Shelby GT 350	5
'69 Mach 1	5
'72 Mustang	5
'88 GT	5

COVER CARS—SUPER CHEVY

Name	MIP
Round 3	
'54 Corvette	5

Name	MIP
'57 Chevelle	5
'63 Nova SS	5
'66 Malibu	5
'68 Chevelle	5
'69 Z-28	5

Round 4

Name	MIP
'57 Chevy	5
'61 Convertible Corvette	5
'63 Corvette Grand Sport	5
'63 Impala Z-11	5
'68 Camaro SS	5
'72 Camaro RS	5

Round 5

Name	MIP
'57 Chevy	5
'61 Corvette	5
'63 Impala Z-11	5
'67 Camaro RS/SS	5
'69 Camaro RS/SS 396	5
'98 Corvette (Pace car)	5

DRAGSTERS USA

Round 1

Name	MIP
Blue Max, '71 Mustang	4
Chi-Town Hustler, '72 Charger	4
Color Me Gone, '72 Challenger	4
Drag-On Lady, '69 AMX	4
Motown Shaker, '71 Vega	4
Hawaiian, 71 Charger	4
Revellution, '71 Demon	4
L.A.P.D., '92 Camaro	4
Sox 'N Martin, '71 Cuda	4

Round 2

Name	MIP
Fast Orange—Whit Bazemore, '94 Daytona	3
Kendall GT-1—Chuck Etchells, '96 Avenger	3
King of the Burnouts—Spurlock, '95 Avenger	3

Name	MIP
Mantis, '97 Firebird	3
Mooneyes—Kenji Okazaki, '95 Avenger	3
Otter Pops—Ed McCulloch, '91 Olds	3
Pioneer—Tom Hoover, '95 Daytona	3
Rug Doctor—Jim Epler, '94 Olds	3
Sentry Gauges—Bruce Larson, '90 Olds	3
Western Auto—Al Hofmann, '95 Firebird	3

DRAGSTERS USA, VINTAGE CARS

Round 3

Name	MIP
Barry Setzer, '71 Vega	5
Bob Banning, '72 Challenger	5
Don Garlits, '71 Charger	5
Gene Snow, '72 Charger	5
Jungle Jim, '71 Vega	5
Mantis, '71 Vega	5
Mr. Norm's, '72 Charger	5
Ramchargers, '71 Duster	5
Trojan Horse, '71 Mustang	5
Wildman, '72 Charger	5
Wonder Wagon, '71 Vega	5

Gene Snow, '72 Charger (Playing Mantis).

EMERGENCY VEHICLES

Name	MIP

Round 1

2000 Chevy Silverado, extended cab w/seats in back	4
2000 Chevy Silverado, pick up w/oil dry bin	4
2000 Ford F-250 HD, extended cab w/oil dry bin	4
2000 Ford F-350 Tow Truck	4

Round 2

2000 Chevy Silverado, IRL	4
2000 Chevy Silverado, Indy 500	4
2000 Chevy Silverado Fire Equip., IRL	4
2000 Chevy Silverado Fire Equip., Indy 500	4
2000 Chevy Silverado Oil Dri, IRL	4
2000 Chevy Silverado Oil Dri, Indy 500	4

Round 3

2000 Chevy Silverado, pick up w/oil dry bin, Brickyard 400	4
2000 Chevy Silverado, extended cab w/seats in back, Brickyard 400	4
2000 Chevy Silverado pick up, Brickyard 400	4

Evel Kneivel, (Playing Mantis). Photo Courtesy Playing Mantis.

Name	MIP
2000 Ford F-250 HD, extended cab, NASCAR	4
2000 Ford F-350 Tow Truck, NASCAR	4
Chevy Tahoe, Brickyard 400	4

EVEL KNIEVEL

Name	MIP
Harley Davidson 750 XR	5
Triumph T-120 Bonneville 650	5
X-2 Sky Cycle	5

FRIGHTNING LIGHTNING

Name	MIP

First Shots

Drag-U-La	18
Heavenly Hearse	15
Meat Wagon	15
Munster's Coach	18
Surf Hearse	15
Undertaker	15

Round 1

Boothill Express	5
Christine	5
Elvira	5
Ghostbusters	5
Haulin' Hearse	5
Mysterion	5
Vampire Van	5

Round 2

Drag-U-La	5
Heavenly Hearse	5
Meat Wagon	5
Munster's Coach	5
Surf Hearse	5
Undertaker	5

Frightning Lightning, Round 2 (Playing Mantis). Photo Courtesy Playing Mantis.

Funny Car Legends, Round 1 (Playing Mantis). Photo Courtesy Playing Mantis.

FUNNY CAR LEGENDS

Name	MIP

Round 1

Al Vandewoude's Flying Dutchman, '68 Charger	5
Bruce Larson's USA-1, '70 Camaro	5
Don Schumacher's "Stardust", '70 Cuda	5
Jim Green's "Green Elephant", '74 Vega	5
Jungle Jim, '75 Monza	5
Shirl Greer's "Chain Lightning", '74 Mustang	5

Round 2

Dicky Harrell, '71 Vega	4
Gene Snow's Rambunctious, '70 Challenger	4

Name	MIP
Jim Murphy's "Holy Smokes", '73 Satellite	4
Lew Arrington's "Brutus", '73 Mustang	4
Tom Hoover's "Showtime", '78 Corvette	4
Tom Hoover's "White Bear Dodge", '72 Charger	4

Round 3

Blue Max, '74 Mustang	4
Connie Kalitta, '73 Mustang	4
Dunn and Reath Satellite, '73 Satellite	4
Larry Arnold's "Kingfish", '70 Cuda	4
Radice Wise, '74 Vega	4
Ramchargers, '70 Challenger	4

Name	MIP

Round 4

Bunny Burkett, '94 Daytona 4

Cruz Pedregon "McDonald's", '91 Olds 4

Gordon Mineo, Flash Gordon, '75 Monza 4

Kosty Ivanof, '78 Corvette 4

Malcom Durham, '70 Camaro 4

Mr. Norms Charger, '68 Charger 4

FUTURE PRO STOCKS

Name	MIP

Dynagear—Steve Schmidt, '96 Olds 5

Mama Rosa's Pizza—Osborne, '96 Olds 5

Six Flags—Tom Martino, '96 Firebird 5

Splitfire—Jim Yates, '96 Firebird 5

Summit—Mark Pawuk, '96 Firebird 5

Super Clean—Larry Morgan, '96 Olds 5

HOLLYWOOD ON WHEELS

Name	MIP

Round 1

Andy Griffith Police Cruiser 5

Back to the Future 6

Blue Brothers 2000 4

Blues Brothers 4

Dragnet 4

Monkee Mobile 5

Partridge Family 5

Starsky & Hutch 5

Round 2

'71 Hemi Cuda, Nash Bridges 4

Dodge Ram, Walker Texas Ranger 4

Jaguar XKE, Austin Powers 4

Round 3

Austin Powers (Felicity) '65 Corvette Convertible 4

Barrismobile 4

Black Beauty 5

Mod Squad Woody 5

Mystery Machine 6

Robocop, four-door hard top pickup 4

Supercar, Supercar 4

Hollywood on Wheels, Round 1 (Playing Mantis). Photo Courtesy Playing Mantis.

Name	MIP
'64 Aston Martin, Thunderball	6
'87 Aston Martin, The Living Daylights	6
Ford Mustang Convertible, Goldfinger	7
Ford Mustang Mach 1, Diamonds are Forever	6
Lotus Espirit, For Your Eyes Only	5
Lotus Espirit, The Spy Who Loved Me	6
Mercury Cougar Convertible, On Her Majesty's	6
Sunbeam, Dr. No	10
Toyota 2000GT Convertible, You Only Live Twice	6

Round 2

Name	MIP
'57 Chevy Convertible	6
'64 Aston Martin	6
'65 Ford Mustang Convertible	6
'95 Corvette	6
BMW Z-3, Goldeneye	7
BMW Z-8, The World Is Never Enough	5

JOHNNY LIGHTNING RED CARD SERIES

Name	MIP

Round 1

Name	MIP
'41 Willy's Coupe	5
'57 Chevy.	8
'72 GtO.	5
'73 Trans Am.	5
Bad Man.	5
Bad News.	5
Shelby 427 Cobra.	5
Speedwagon.	5

Round 2

Name	MIP
'57 Vette Gasser	6
'69 SuperBee	5

Name	MIP
Cheetah	5
Li'l Van	5

JURASSIC PARK

Name	MIP
Hum-Vee Hunter Vehicle	4

KISS RACING DREAMS

Name	MIP
Ace Frehley, '97 Firebird	5
Gene Simmons, '94 Daytona	5
Paul Stanley, '91 Olds	5
Peter Criss, '96 Avenger	5

LOST IN SPACE

Name	MIP
Jupiter II	5
Robot B-9	5
Space Chariot	5
Space Pod	5

MAGMAS

Name	MIP

Round 1

Name	MIP
'70 A. Unser Indy, 1:43-scale	7
Drag-u-la, 1:43-scale	8
T'rantula, 1:43-scale	7

Round 2

Name	MIP
'68 Camaro, 1:43-scale	7
'70 A. Unser Indy, 1:43-scale	7
'70 Challenger Trans Am, 1:43-scale	7
'71 Mustang Boss 351, 1:43-scale	7
'71 Mustang Mach 1, 1:43-scale	7
'71 Plymouth Roadrunner, 1:43-scale	7
Drag-u-la, 1:43-scale	7
T'rantula, 1:43-scale	8

Name	MIP

Round 3

Donkey Kong, Grand Prix, 1:43-scale	6
Smash Brothers, Taurus, 1:43-scale	6
Yoshi, Taurus, 1:43-scale	6
Zelda, Grand Prix, 1:43-scale	6

MILITARY VEHICLES

Name	MIP
'90's Humvee	4
'90's M1 Tank	4
WW II 6x6 Truck	4
WW II Half Track	4
WW II Jeep	4
WW II WC54 Ambulance	4

MODERN MUSCLE

Name	MIP
Chevy Monte Carlo	4
Dodge Viper	4
Ford Mustang	4
Jaguar XK8	4
Miata	4
Pontiac Firebird Trans-Am	4

MONOPOLY

Name	MIP
'33 Willys, Monopoly	5
'40 Ford, Reading Railroad	5
'57 Chevy, Illinois Ave.	5
'67 Mustang, Community Chest	5
'98 Corvette, Monopoly	5
Cameo, Water Works	5
Crown Victoria, Go To Jail	5
LA Dart, Chance	5
Tahoe, B&O Railroad	5
Tameless Tiger, Park Place	5
Utility Van, Electric Company	5
Viper, Luxury Tax	5

Mopar Box Set (Playing Mantis). Photo Courtesy Playing Mantis.

MOPAR BOX SET

Name	MIP
'70 Superbird, '71 440 Cuda, '59 Hemi Roadrunner, '70 Challenger, '68 Hemi Charger, '70 Dodge Super , set of ten	12

MOPAR MUSCLE

Name	MIP
'69 Charger	5
'69 Daytona	5
'70 Cuda	5
'70 Roadrunner GTX	5
'71 Duster	5
'71 Satellite/RR/GTX	5

MUSCLE CARS

Name	MIP

Round 1

'65 Pontiac GTO Convertible	7
'69 Mercury Cougar Eliminator	5
'69 Olds 442	4
'69 Pontiac GTO Judge	7

Muscle Cars, Round 3 (Playing Mantis). Photo Courtesy Playing Mantis.

Name	MIP
'70 Chevy Chevelle SS	5
'70 Dodge Super Bee	5
'70 Ford Boss 302 Mustang	7
'70 Plymouth Superbird	5
'71 Plymouth Hemi Cuda	5
'72 Chevy Nova SS	4

Round 2

Name	MIP
'66 Chevy Malibu	4
'68 Dodge Charger	4
'68 Ford Shelby GT-500	5
'69 Plymouth Roadrunner	4
'69 Pontiac Firebird	4
'70 Buick GSX	4
'70 Dodge Challenger	5
'72 AMC Javelin AMX	4

Round 3

Name	MIP
'65 Chevy II Nova	5
'67 GTO	6
'68 Chevelle	5
'70 AAR Cuda	5
'70 AMC Rebel Machine	5
'70 Challenger T/A	5
'70 Torino	5
'71 Demon	5
'71 GTO Judge	5
'73 Charger	5

Round 4

Name	MIP
'64 Pontiac GTO	4
'67 Cougar	4

Name	MIP
'67 Cutlass	4
'67 Pontiac Firebird	4
'69 Chevy Nova	4
'70 Mercury Cyclone	4

White Lightnings

Name	MIP
'65 Chevy II Nova	25
'67 GTO	30
'68 Chevelle	25
'70 AAR Cuda	30
'70 AMC Rebel Machine	25
'70 Challenger T/A	25
'70 Torino	25
'71 Demon	25
'73 Charger	25

PEWTER CARS

Round 1

Name	MIP
'57 Chevy, pewter	4
'68 Camaro, pewter	4
Corvette Lamans, pewter	4
Dodge Viper, pewter	4
Hummer, pewter	4
Jungle Jim, pewter	4
Mustang, pewter	4
Six Pack, pewter	4
Space Shuttle, pewter	4
Stealth, pewter	4
Topper El Camino, pewter	4

RACING DREAMS

Name	MIP
Army, '71 Charger	5
DQ-Dilly Bar, '71 Demon	6
Hawaiin Punch, '72 Challenger	6
Hershey's, '94 Olds	6
James Bond - Goldfinger, '71 Vega	6
Jurrassic Park the Ride, '94 Daytona	6
Mooneyes, '71 Mustang	5
Nintendo-Star Fox, '96 Avenger	6
Popsicle, '72 Charger	7
Trix, '97 Firebird	6

Round 2

Name	MIP
Coast Guard, Monte Carlo	6
Lucky Charms, Grand Prix	7
Nintendo-Mario 64, Grand Prix	7
Pez, Monte Carlo	8
Planters-Mr. Peanut, Thunderbird	7
TGI Friday's, Thunderbird	6

Round 3

Name	MIP
Frosted Flakes	6
Fudgsicle	7
McDonald's Big Mac	6
Pennzoil	6
Reese's-Hershey	5

Round 4

Name	MIP
Blizzard	6
Cocoa Puffs	6
Grimace	6
Hawaiin Punch, orange	6
Monkees (Direct Mail car)	9
Mug Rootbeer	6
Nintendo-Zelda	6
Pez	9
Yohsi	6

RACING MACHINES

Round 1

Name	MIP
Current Camaro Trans Am, PLC Direct	4
Current Mustang Trans-Am, Preformed, Ruhlman	4
IRL Race Car, Powerteam	4
Viper GTS-R, Bobby Archer	4

Round 2

Name	MIP
'94 Daytona, Bunny Car	4

Racing Dreams, Round 1 (Playing Mantis). Photo Courtesy Playing Mantis.

Name	MIP
'98 Avenger, Tom Hoover Pioneer	4
Current Camaro Trans Am, Glacier Tek	4
Current Mustang Trans-Am, Homelink	5
Viper GTS-R, Team Oreca	4

Round 3

Name	MIP
'69 AMX, AMX Petes Patriot	5
'72 Charger, Gene Snow Funny Car	4
'98 Avenger, Red Line Oil Funny Car	4
94 Olds, McDonalds Funny Car	4
Firebird, Splitfire	4
Tameless Tiger, Tameless Tiger	4

Round 4

Name	MIP
'69 Pontiac GTO Judge, The Judge, Arnie Beswick	5
'71 Vega, Wonder Wagon	4
'94 Daytona, Roland Leong's Hawaiian Punch	4
'96 Saleen Racer, Saleen Mustang	4
'97 Firebird, NAPA Dragster	4
'98 Avenger, PM Bug Car, Jim Dunn	4
'98 Avenger, JL Car, Jim Dunn, bonus car, No. 1	4

RACING MACHINES IRL CARS—1999

Name	MIP
IRL Race Car, Scott Goodyear	5
IRL Race Car, Kenny Brack.	5
IRL Race Car, Greg Ray.	5
IRL Race Car, Indy Event Car, 1999.	5
IRL Race Car, Luyendyk '98 winner car, twin w/1990.	7
IRL Race Car, Eliseo Salazar.	5
IRL Race Car, Arie Luyendyk '99 car.	5
IRL Race Car, Scott Sharp	5

Name	MIP
IRL Race Car, Mark Dismore	5
IRL Race Car, Billy Boat	5

RACING MACHINES IRL CARS—2000

Name	MIP
IRL Race Car, Robby McGhee, Mall.com #5	5
IRL Race Car, Greg Ray, Menards #2 1999 and #3 2000 twin	5
IRL Race Car, Indy Event Car, 2000	5
IRL Race Car, Robby McGhee, Energizer #55	5
IRL Race Car, Robbie Buhl, Purex #24	5
IRL Race Car, Buddy Lazier, Tae Bo #91	5
IRL Race Car, Mark Dismore, Bryant #28	5
IRL Race Car, Scott Goodyear, Pennzoil #4	5
IRL Race Car, Greg Ray, Menards #3	5
IRL Race Car, Scott Sharp, Delphi #8	5

ROCK N ROLLERS

Name	MIP
'64 Mustang	6
'67 GTO	6
Bad Bird	6
Cobra	6
Fink Speedwagon	6
Flathead Flyer	6

SHOW RODS—GEORGE BARRIS

Name	MIP
'41 "Tribute" Ford Phaeton	4
'51 Burgundy Mercury Converible	4
Emperer	4

Name	MIP
Fireball 500	6
Kopper Kart	6
Sam Barris—'49 Merc	4
Speed Coupe	4
Wildkat	4

White Lightnings

Name	MIP
'41 "Tribute" Ford Phaeton	20
'51 Burgundy Mercury Converible	20
Emperer	20
Fireball 500	25
Kopper Kart	20
Sam Barris—'49 Merc	20
Speed Coupe	20
Wildkat	20

Show Rods—Tom Daniel Show Rods

Name	MIP
Baja Bandito	3
Desert Fox, Rommel's Rod	3
Dog Catcher	3
Fast Buck	3
LA Kid or Daddy's Deuce	3

Name	MIP
Rat Vega or Poison Pinto	3
Smug Bug	3
TD's Ride, CA Street Vette	4
Triple T	3
Wild Bull Surfer	3

Showstoppers

Name	MIP
Round 1	
Chuck Wagon	3
Dodge Rebellion	3
Hemi Xpress	3
Little Red Wagon	5
Round 2	
Hemi Under Glass	3
Hurst Hairy Olds	3
LA Dart	3
Tameless Tiger	3
Round 3	
Dodge Material	3
Frank Monaghan	3
Little Red Wagon	3
Thunder Wagon	3

Showstoppers, Round 3 (Playing Mantis).
Photo Courtesy Playing Mantis.

SPECIAL EDITION

Name	MIP

Round 1
'54 Chevy Panel 15
'56 Chevy 15
'60's VW Van 15
Dodge A-100 15

Round 2
'33 Willys 15
'66 Mustang 350H. 15
Bugaboo. 15
Buick Grand National. 15
NSX. 15
Plymouth Prowler. 15
The VW Thing 15
VW Concept One 15

Round 3
'63 Chevy Impala 15
'69 AMC Hurst SC/Rambler 15
'70 Cougar Convertible 15

SPEED RACER

Name	MIP

Round 1
Assassin..5
GRX: Fastest Car 5
Racer X Shooting Star............................5
Speed Racer Mach 5 15

Round 2
Captain Terror 5
Mach 5..11
Shooting Star..5
Snake Oiler...5

STOCK CAR LEGENDS

Name	MIP

Round 1
'67 Ford Fairlane, Mario Andretti..........4
'69 Daytona, Bobby Isaac......................4

Name	MIP

'71 Mercury Cyclone, Donny Allison.....4
'73 Dodge Charger, Marty Robbins........4
'81 Grand Prix, Rusty Wallace 4
'85 Ford Thunderbird, Buddy Baker.......4

Round 2
'69 Torino Talladega, David Pearson......4
'70 Superbird, Pete Hamilton.................4
'71 Plymouth Satellite, Pete Hamilton...4
'77 Olds Cutlass, Cale Yarborough........4
'79 Chevy Monte Carlo, Darrell Waltrip.4
'83 Chevy Monte Carlo, Cale Yarborough.4

Round 3
'67 Ford Fairlane, David Pearson...........4
'69 Daytona, Buddy Baker......................4
'69 Torino Talladega, LeeRoy Yarbrough.4
'71 Mercury Cyclone, Donny Allison, Purolator....4

Stock Car Legends, Round 1 (Playing Mantis). Photo Courtesy Playing Mantis.

Speed Racer, Round 1 (Playing Mantis). Photo Courtesy Playing Mantis.

Name	MIP
'83 Chevy Monte Carlo, Darrell Waltrip	4
'85 Ford Thunderbird, Buddy Baker	4

Round 4

Name	MIP
'70 Superbird, Richard Brooks	4
'71 Plymouth Satellite, Fred Lorenzen	4
'73 Dodge Charger, Neil Bonnett	4
'77 Olds Cutlass, AJ Foyt	4
'79 Chevy Monte Carlo, Benny Parsons	4
'81 Grand Prix, Geoff Bodine	4

STREET FREAKS

Round 1

Name	MIP
'67 Mustang	6
'67 Shelby	5
'69 Mach 1	4
'70 AMC Rebel Machine	4
'71 GTO Judge	6
'73 Mach 1	4

Round 2

Name	MIP
1963 Mustang	5
1967 GTO	5
1968 Chevelle	5
1976 Cobra	4
1987 Mustang	4
1994 Mustang	4

Round 3

Name	MIP
'65 Nova	4
'69 Camaro	5
'70 AAR	4
'70 Torino	4
'71 Demon	5
'73 Charger	7

White Lightning 1

Name	MIP
'67 Mustang	20
'67 Shelby	20
'69 Mach 1	20
'70 AMC Rebel Machine	20
'71 GTO Judge	20
'73 Mach 1	20

White Lightning 2

Name	MIP
1963 Mustang	20
1967 GTO	20
1968 Chevelle	20
1976 Cobra	15
1987 Mustang	15
1994 Mustang	15

SURF RODS

Round 1

Name	MIP
'29 Crew Cab, Laguna Longboards	4
'59 El Camino, Redondo Gonzos	4
'60's VW Van, Huntington Hunnies	4
Dan Fink Speedwagon, Woody	4
Rumblur, The Hang 10 Men	4
Surfbusters, Surf Daddies	4

Round 2

Name	MIP
'29 Ford, Torrance Terrors	4
'50 Ford F-1, Hermosa Beach Bums 3	4

Name	MIP
'54 Chevy Panel Truck, Waimea Mamas	4
Emperor, Malibu Babes	4
Haulin' Hearse, Santa Monica Maniacs	4
Meat Wagon, Cowabunga Boyz	3

TEAM LIGHTNING

Name	MIP

Round 1

Name	MIP
Black Beauty, Frankenstude	3
Crash Bandicoot Viper.	3
Munsters '29 Crew Cab.	3
Three Stooges Flathead Fly.	3

Round 2

Name	MIP
Bad Medicine, Bela Lugosi's Dracula	3
Bugaboo, Bozo the Clown	3
Count Chocula Pro Street	3
Dodge Ram, Blow Pops	3
Meatwagon, Alfred Hitchcock Vertigo	3
Willys, 3 Stooges Moe	3

TOP FUEL

Name	MIP

Round 1

Name	MIP
'60's Front Engine Top Fuel, Ramchargers	3
'60's Front Engine Top Fuel, Tommy Ivo	3
'70's Rear Engine Car, Don Garlits "Swamp Rat 19"	3
'70's Rear Engine Car, Jeb Allen "Praying Mantis"	3
'70's Rear Engine Car, Warren Coburn and Miller "Rain For Rent"	5

Round 2

Name	MIP
'60's Front Engine Top Fuel, Hawaiian	3

Name	MIP
'60's Front Engine Top Fuel, Tony Nancy	5
'60's Front Engine Top Fuel, Soapy Sales	3
'70's Rear Engine Car, Tommy Ivo Rod Shop	3
'70's Rear Engine Car, Walton Cerny & Moody	3
'70's Rear Engine Car, Don Garlits	3

Round 3

Name	MIP
'60's Front Engine Top Fuel, John Wiebe	3
'60's Front Engine Top Fuel, BB & Mulligan.	3
'60's Front Engine Top Fuel, Steve Carbone '71 Dragster.	3
'70's Rear Engine Car, Jungle Jim.	3
'70's Rear Engine Car, Don Garlits Swamp Rat 24.	3
'70's Rear Engine Car, Diamond Jim Annin.	3

Round 4

Name	MIP
'60's Front Engine Top Fuel, Creitz and Donovan	3
'60's Front Engine Top Fuel, Garlits Swamp Rat X	3
'60's Front Engine Top Fuel, Jerry Ruth Dragster	3
'70's Rear Engine Car, Benny Osborne	3
'70's Rear Engine Car, Jade Grenade	3
'70's Rear Engine Car, Keeling and Clayton California Charger	3

TRUCKIN' AMERICA

Name	MIP
'29 Ford	6
'40 Ford.	4
'50 Ford F-1.	4
'55 Chevy Cameo.	4

Name	MIP
'59 El Camino	4
'60's Studebaker Champ	6
'71 El Camino	4
'78 Li'l Red Express	6
'91 GMC Syclone	7
'96 Dodge Ram	4

White Lightnings

Name	MIP
'29 Ford	20
'40 Ford	20
'50 Ford F-1	20
'55 Chevy Cameo	20
'59 El Camino	20
'60's Studebaker Champ	20
'71 El Camino	20
'78 Li'l Red Express	20
'91 GMC Syclone	20
'96 Dodge Ram	20

TRUCKS—KISS ALBUM

Name	MIP
'29 Ford, KISS The Original Album	5
'40 Ford, KISS Destroyer	5
'59 El Camino, KISS Love Gun	5
'71 El Camino, KISS Unmasked	5
'78 Li'l Red Express, KISS Dressed to Kill	5
'91 GMC Syclone, KISS Dynasty	5

VIP

Name	MIP
Ford Mustang	4
Jaguar XK8	4
Miata	4

VOLKSWAGENS

Name	MIP
'60's VW Bug	5
2000 New Beetle	5
Karman Ghia	5
Smug Bug	5

WACKY WINNERS

Name	MIP
Bad Medicine	4
Bad News	7
Badman	7
Cherry Bomb	5
Draggin' Dragon	4
Garbage Truck	4
Root Beer Wagon	4
T'rantula	5
Tijuana Taxi	4
Trouble Maker	4

WORKHORSES/TRUE GRIT

Name	MIP

Round 1

Basic Step Van, Tootsie Roll	3
Basic Step Van, Froot Loops	3
Utility Van, PEZ	3

Wacky Winners (Playing Mantis).

Matchbox

Matchbox Toys grew out of a company started in 1947 by two Navy friends, Leslie Smith and Rodney Smith (no relation). On June 19, 1947, the two partners combined portions of their first names, and the name Lesney was born. John (Jack) Odell, who had been the die maker at Die Casting Machine Tools, Ltd., soon joined them (Odell went on to start Lledo in the 1980s).

Toy legend has it that Odell designed Lesney's first toy—an Aveling Barford Road Roller—in 1947 for his daughter to take with her to school. An instant hit with the kids, the 4-1/2-inch Road Roller easily fit into a match box. A Toy was born.

The Road Roller was a success. Encouraged by the brisk sales, three other toys were produced that year—a 4-1/2-inch Caterpillar Bulldozer, a 3-1/8-inch Caterpillar Tractor, and a 3-3/4-inch Cement Mixer.

Several different Matchbox series were introduced over the years—King Size, Super Kings and Sky Busters. Since 1953, the most collectible is the original 1-75 series. Each model was given a number between one and seventy-five. New cars were introduced year after year, often given the same number as a previous model. No. 1 belongs to several different models each released in different years—Dodge Challenger, Mercedes-Benz Lorry, Mod Rod, Revin Rebel and Road Roller.

Models of Yesteryear, the brainchild of Odell, were introduced in 1956. Marketed to adults, the line featured miniature replicas of antique cars and enjoyed strong sales in England.

When Mattel introduced Hot Wheels, Matchbox began losing shelf space to the wildly popular models. In order to compete, Matchbox's Superfast line was rushed to stores. The original sixty Superfast models had regular wheels, brighter color schemes and Mag-style hubs. But in their haste to rush the toys to the market, mistakes were made. Some rare variations include Superfast cars with regular paint or incorrect wheels. Die-cast models from 1969-1971 are oftentimes called Transitional Superfast.

Although the production of Matchbox continued, the England factory was closed in 1982 when Universal Group purchased Lesney. Since then, the Matchbox line has been bought and sold many times, with it finally ending up with their rival, Mattel.

Market

Matchbox models continue to be collectible, especially the early 1-75 series and the Transitional Superfast models. As with many collectors, the box is of the utmost importance to collectors. While the value of a loose model can be high, that value will rise substantially if it is with the original packaging.

Clubs

Matchbox International
Collectors Club
P.O. Box 28072
Waterloo, Ontario N2L 6J8 Canada

Matchbox, U.S.A.
62 Mills Rd.
Durham, CT 06422-2602

Matchbox Collectors Club
P.O. Box 977
Newfield, NJ 08344

No.	Name	Good	Ex	Mint
	London E Class Tramcar, red, cream roof; News of the World decals	25	60	90
	"B" Type London Bus, red w/black driver; black wheels; eight over four side windows; Dewar's labels	45	60	85
1	Aveling Barford Road Roller, green body, canopy, tow hook, 1962, 2-5/8"	7	10	15
1	Diesel Road Roller, dark green body, flat canopy, tow hook, driver, 1953, 1-7/8"	15	25	35
1	Dodge Challenger, red body, white plastic top, silver interior, wide five spoke wheels, 1976, 2-15/16"	3	5	8
1	Mercedes-Benz Lorry, metallic gold, removable orange or yellow canopy, 1970, 3"	4	6	8
1	Mercedes-Benz Lorry, pale green body, removable orange plastic canopy, 1967, 3"	5	7	15
1	Mod Rod, yellow body, tinted windows, red or black wheels, 1971, 2-7/8"	10	15	20
1	Revin' Rebel, orange body, blue top, black interior, large five-spoke rear wheels, 1982	2	3	5
1	Road Roller, light green or dark green body, canopy, metal rollers, tow bar, driver, 1958, 2-3/8"	20	25	35
1	Road Roller, pale green body, canopy, tow hook, dark tan or light tan driver, 1953, 2-1/4"	25	45	65
2	Dumper, green body, red dumper, gold trim, thin driver, green painted wheels, 1953, 1-5/8"	35	50	70
2	Dumper, green body, red dumper, no trim color, fat driver, 1957, 1-7/8"	20	30	40
2	Hovercraft, metallic green top, tan base, silver engine, yellow windows, 1976, 3-1/8"	4	8	12
2	Jeep Hot Rod, cream seats and tow hook, wide four-spoke wheels, 1971, 2-5/16"	7	10	15

No.	Name	Good	Ex	Mint
2	Mercedes-Benz Trailer, pale green body, removable orange canopy, tow hook, black plastic wheels, 1968, 3-1/2"	5	7	15
2	Mercedes-Benz Trailer, metallic gold body, removable canopy, rotating tow bar, 1970, 3-1/4"	3	5	15
2	Muirhill Dumper, red cab, green dumper, black plastic wheels, 1961, 2-1/6"	10	20	25
3	Bedford Ton Tipper, gray cab, gray wheels, dual rear wheels, 1961, 2-1/2"	10	15	20
3	Cement Mixer, blue body and rotating barrel, orange metal wheels, 1953, 1-5/8"	25	35	45
3	Mercedes-Benz Ambulance, ivory interior, Red Cross label on side doors, 1970, 2-7/8"	5	10	15
3	Monteverdi Hai, dark orange body, blue tinted windows, ivory interior, 1973, 2-7/8"	3	6	8
3	Porsche Turbo, metallic brown body, black base, yellow interior, wide five-arch wheels, 1978, 3"	4	7	10
4	1957 Chevy, metallic rose body, chrome interior, large five-arch rear wheels, 1979, 2-15/16"	2	8	12

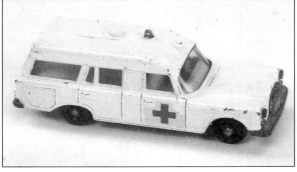

No. 3 Mercedes-Benz Ambulance.

No.	Name	Good	Ex	Mint
4	Gruesome Twosome, metallic gold body, wide five-spoke wheels, 1971, 2-7/8"	5	7	10
4	Massey Harris Tractor, red body w/rear fenders, tan driver, four spoke metal front wheels, 1954	30	40	55
4	Massey Harris Tractor, red body, no fenders, tan driver, solid metal front wheels, hollow inside rear wheels, 1957, 1-5/8"	25	40	50
4	Pontiac Firebird, metallic blue body, silver interior, slick tires, 1975, 2-7/8"	2	7	12
4	Stake Truck, yellow cab, green tinted windows, 1967, 2-7/8"	5	10	30
4	Stake Truck, cab colors vary, 1970, 2-7/8"	5	7	15
4	Triumph Motorcycle and Sidecar, silver/blue body, wire wheels, 1960, 2-1/8"	25	40	60
5	Jeep 4x4 Golden Eagle, brown body, wide four-spoke wheels, eagle decal on hood, 1982	2	5	8
5	London Bus, red body, 1957, 2-1/4"	20	45	65
5	London Bus, red body, white plastic seats, black plastic wheels, 1965, 2-3/4"	5	10	30
5	London Bus, red body, gold grille, metal wheels, 1954, 2"	20	45	65
5	London Bus, red body, silver grille and headlights, 1961, 2-9/16"	10	20	25
5	Lotus Europa, metallic blue body, clear windows, ivory interior and tow hook, 1969, 2-7/8"	5	7	10
5	Seafire Boat, white deck, blue hull, silver engine, red pipes, 1975, 2-15/16"	6	8	10

No.	Name	Good	Ex	Mint
5	U.S. Mail Jeep, blue body, white base and bumpers, black plastic seat, white canopy, wide five-arch rear wheel, 1978, 2-3/8"..................5		10	15
6	Euclid Quarry Truck, yellow body, three round axles, two front black plastic wheels, two solid rear dual wheels, 1964, 2-5/8" 15		25	30
6	Euclid Quarry Truck, yellow body, four ribs on dumper sides, plastic wheels, 1957, 2-1/2" 10		20	25
6	Ford Pick-up, red body, white removable canopy, five spoke wheels, 1970, 2-3/4".......5		7	15
6	Ford Pick-up, red body, white removable plastic canopy, four black plastic wheels, 1968, 2-3/4" 10		15	20
6	Mercedes-Benz 350 SL, orange body, black plastic convertible top, light yellow interior, 1973, 3".......................5		10	20
6	Quarry Truck, orange cab, gray dumper w/six vertical ribs, metal wheels, 1954, 2-1/8" 15		30	50
7	Ford Anglia, blue body, green tinted windows, 1961, 2-5/8"..10		15	30
7	Ford Refuse Truck, orange cab, gray plastic dumper, silver metal loader, 1966, 3"..............7		10	15
7	Ford Refuse Truck, gray plastic body, silver metal dumper, 1970, 3"..........................6		8	15
7	Hairy Hustler, metallic bronze, silver interior, five-spoke front wheels, cloverleaf rear wheels, 1971, 2-7/8" 5		7	10
7	Horse Drawn Milk Float, orange body, white driver and bottle load, brown horse w/white mane and hoofs, 1954, 2-1/4" 25		55	90

No.	Name	Good	Ex	Mint
7	Rompin' Rabbit, white body, red windows, yellow lettered "Rompin Rabbit" on side, 1982....................................2		3	5
7	Volkswagen Golf, green body, black base and grille, 1976, 2-7/8".....................................4		8	12
8	Caterpillar Tractor, yellow body, no driver, plastic rollers, rubber treads, rounded axles, 1964, 2".......... 10		15	20
8	Caterpillar Tractor, yellow body and driver, large smoke stack, metal rollers, rubber treads, crimped axles, 1959, 1-5/8"....................................20		35	45
8	Caterpillar Tractor, driver has same color hat as body, metal rollers, rubber treads, crimped axles, 1955, 1-1/2" ...40		60	80
8	Ford Mustang, wide five spoke wheels, interior and tow hook are the same color, 1970, 2-7/8"............................ 10		25	50
8	Ford Mustang Fastback, white body, red interior, clear windows, 1966, 2-7/8" 7		10	30
8	Pantera, white body, blue base, red/brown interior, five-spoke rear slicks, 1975, 3" 35		45	60
8	Caterpillar Tractor, yellow body and driver, large smoke stack, metal rollers, rubber treads, rounded axles, 1961, 1-7/8"......................................10		15	25

No. 8 Ford Mustang Fastback.

No. 9 Merryweather Marquis Fire Engine. Photo Courtesy Gary Linden.

No.	Name	Good	Ex	Mint
9	Boat and Trailer, white hull, blue deck, clear windows, five-spoke wheels on trailer, 1970, 3-1/4"	3	5	20
9	Boat and Trailer, white hull, blue deck, clear windows, five-spoke wheels on trailer, 1966, 3-1/4"	4	6	15
9	Dennis Fire Escape Engine, red body, metal wheels, no front bumper, 1955, 2-1/4"	10	20	30
9	Fiat Abarth, white body, red interior, 1982	2	3	5
9	Ford Escort RS2000, white body, black base and grille, tan interior, wide multispoke wheels, 1978, 3"	3	5	7
9	Merryweather Marquis Fire Engine, 1959	15	25	40
10	Mechanical Horse and Trailer, red cab w/three metal wheels, gray trailer w/two metal wheels, 1955, 2-3/8"	15	25	35
10	Mechanical Horse and Trailer, red cab, ribbed bed in trailer, metal front wheels on cab, 1958, 2-15/16"	25	35	45

No.	Name	Good	Ex	Mint
10	Pipe Truck, red body, gray pipes, "Leyland" or "Ergomatic" on front base, eight black plastic wheels, 1966, 2-7/8"	7	10	15
10	Pipe Truck, black pipe racks, eight thin five-spoke wheels, 1970, 2-7/8"	4	6	15
10	Piston Popper, metallic blue body, white interior, 1973, 2-7/8"	4	6	8
10	Plymouth Gran Fury Police Car, white body w/black detailing, "Police" on doors, white interior, 1979, 3"	3	4	5
10	Sugar Container Truck, blue body, eight gray plastic wheels, "Tate & Lyle" decals on sides and rear, 1961, 2-5/8"	30	55	75
11	Cobra Mustang, orange body, "The Boss" on doors, 1982	2	3	5
11	Flying Bug, metallic red, gray windows, small five-spoke front wheels, large five-spoke rear wheels, 1972, 2-7/8"	5	7	10
11	Jumbo Crane, yellow body, black plastic wheels, 1965, 3"	5	10	15
11	Scaffolding Truck, silver body, green tinted windows, black plastic wheels, 1969, 2-1/2"	4	7	25
11	Road Tanker, red body, gas tanks, "11" on baseplate, black plastic wheels, 1958, 2-1/2"	20	55	80
11	Scaffolding Truck, silver/gray body, green tinted windows, yellow pipes, 1969, 2-7/8"	5	10	25
11	Road Tanker, green body, flat base between cab and body, gold trim on front grille, gas tanks, metal wheels, no number cast, 1955, 2"	60	265	360

Matchbox boxes, top row, left to right: No. 48 Dumper Truck; No. 13 Dodge Wreck Truck; Middle row, left to right: No. 19 Lotus Racing Ca; No. 49 Mercedes-Benz Unimog. Bottom: No. 11 Scaffolding Truck.

No.	Name	Good	Ex	Mint
12	Safari Land Rover, metallic gold, clear windows, tan luggage, thin five-spoke wheels, 1970, 2-13/16"	10	20	30
12	Big Bull, orange body, green plow blade, base and sides, chrome seat and engine, orange rollers, 1975, 2-1/2"	4	6	8
12	Setra Coach, clear windows, ivory interior, thin five-spoke thin wheels, 1970, 3"	5	7	10
12	Safari Land Rover, clear windows, white plastic interior and tow hook, black plastic wheels, 1965, 2-1/3"	7	10	20
12	Citroen CX, metallic body, silver base and lights, blue plastic hatch door, 1979, 3"	4	8	12

No.	Name	Good	Ex	Mint
12	Land Rover, olive green body, no driver, tow hook, 1959, 2-1/4"	35	55	75
12	Land Rover, olive green body, tan driver, metal wheels, 1955, 1-3/4"	20	25	35
13	Dodge Wreck Truck, green and yellow body, 1970	10	15	25
13	Baja Dune Buggy, metallic green, orange interior, silver motor, 1971, 2-5/8"	3	4	6
13	Snorkel Fire Engine, red body, yellow plastic snorkel and fireman, 1977, 3"	3	5	7
13	Dodge Wreck Truck, yellow cab, rear body, red plastic hook, green windows, 1970, 3"	10	15	40

No. 12 Land Rover. Photo Courtesy Gary Linden.

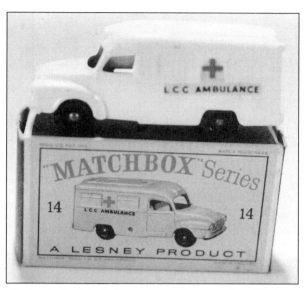

No. 14 Bedford Ambulance. Photo Courtesy Gary Linden.

No.	Name	Good	Ex	Mint
13	Thames Wreck Truck, red body, bumper and parking lights, 1961, 2-1/2"	15	25	30
13	Bedford Wreck Truck, tan body, red metal crane and hook, 1955, 2"	30	40	55
13	Bedford Wreck Truck, tan body, red metal crane and hook, crane attached to rear axle, 1958, 2-1/8"	30	45	60
13	Dodge Wreck Truck, green cab and crane, yellow body, green windows, 1965, 3"	300	500	700
14	Iso Grifo, blue body, light blue interior and tow hook, clear windows, 1968, 3"	5	7	15
14	Rallye Royal, metallic pearl gray body, black plastic interior, wide five-spoke wheels, 1973, 2-7/8"	3	4	5
14	Daimler Ambulance, silver trim, "AMBULANCE" cast on sides, red cross on roof, 1958, 2-5/8"	40	65	85
14	Bedford Ambulance, white body, silver trim, two opening rear doors, 1962, 2-5/8"	15	60	80

No.	Name	Good	Ex	Mint
14	Mini Haha, red body, pink driver, silver engine, large spoke rear slicks, 1975, 2-3/8"	5	9	12
14	Daimler Ambulance, cream body, silver trim, no number cast on body, "AMBULANCE" cast on sides, 1956, 1-7/8"	20	35	45
14	Iso Grifo, five-spoke wheels, clear windows, 1969, 3"	5	10	15
15	Atlantic Tractor Super, orange body, tow hook, spare wheel behind cab on body, 1959, 2-5/8"	15	30	40
15	Hi Ho Silver, metallic pearl gray body, 1971, 2-1/2"	7	10	15
15	Refuse Truck, blue body, gray dumper w/opening door, 1963, 2-1/2"	10	15	20
15	Volkswagen 1500 Saloon, off white body and interior, clear windows, "137" on doors, 1968, 2-7/8"	10	20	30
15	Fork Lift Truck, red body, yellow hoist, 1972, 2-1/2"	3	4	6

No. 15 Refuse Truck.

No.	Name	Good	Ex	Mint
15	Volkswagen 1500 Saloon, clear windows, "137" on doors, red decal on front, 1968, 2-7/8"	7	15	20
15	Prime Mover, silver trim on grille and tank, tow hook same color as body, 1956, 2-1/8"	20	35	50
16	Atlantic Trailer, orange body, eight gray plastic wheels w/knobby treads, 1957, 3-1/4"	15	50	80
16	Badger Exploration Truck, metallic red body, silver grille, 1974, 2-1/4"	3	4	6
16	Scammel Mountaineer Dump Truck/Snow Plow, gray cab, orange dumper body, six plastic wheels, 1964, 3"	10	20	25
16	Atlantic Trailer, tan body, six metal wheels, tan tow bar, 1956, 3-1/8"	15	25	35
16	Case Tractor Bulldozer, red body, yellow base, motor and blade, black plastic rollers, 1969, 2-1/2"	5	9	12
16	Pontiac Trans Am, white body, red interior, clear windows, blue eagle decal, 1982	2	3	4
17	Austin Taxi Cab, maroon body, 1960, 2-1/4"	35	50	70

No.	Name	Good	Ex	Mint
17	Hoveringham Tipper, red body, orange dumper, 1963, 2-7/8"	7	10	25
17	Bedford Removals Van, maroon body, peaked roof, gold grille, 1956, 2-1/8"	35	115	150
17	Horse Box, Ergomatic Cab, red cab, green plastic box, gray side door, 1969	10	15	20
17	Horse Box, blue tinted windows, thin five-spoke wheels, white plastic horses inside box, 1970, 2-3/4"	5	10	15
17	Londoner Bus, red body, white interior, wide five-spoke wheels, 1972, 3"	10	15	20
18	Hondarora Motorcycle, red frame and fenders chrome bars, fork, engine, black seat, 1975, 2-3/8"	5	15	25
18	Caterpillar Bulldozer, yellow body w/driver, green rubber treads, 1961, 2-1/4"	10	15	25
18	Field Car, yellow body, tan roof, red wheels, ivory interior and tow hook, 1970, 2-5/8"	5	7	20
18	Field Car, yellow body, tan plastic roof, ivory interior and tow hook, green plastic tires, 1969, 2-5/8"	50	145	200
18	Caterpillar D8 Bulldozer, yellow body and driver, red blade and side supports, 1956, 1-7/8"	25	35	45
18	Caterpillar Bulldozer, yellow body and driver, yellow blade, No. 18 cast on back of blade, metal rollers, 1958, 2"	30	45	65
18	Caterpillar Crawler Bulldozer, yellow body, no driver, green rubber treads, 1964, 2-3/8"	30	45	60

No.	Name	Good	Ex	Mint
19	Lotus Racing Car, white driver, large rear wheels, 1966, 2-3/4".....................10		15	20
19	Lotus Racing Car, metallic purple, white driver, wide five-spoke wide wheels w/cloverleaf design, 1970, 2-3/4".......................5		10	15
19	Aston Martin Racing Car, metallic green, metal steering wheel and wire wheels, black plastic tires, 1961, 2-1/2".....................10		30	45
19	MG Midget, silver or gold grilles, tan driver, 1958, 2-1/4"...................20		45	75
19	Road Dragster, ivory interior, silver plastic motor, 1970, 2-7/8".......................3		4	6
19	MG Midget, white body, tan driver, red seats, spare tire on trunk, 1956, 2".....................30		60	75
19	MGA Sports Car, white body variation, silver wheels, tan driver, silver or gold grilles, 1958, 2-1/4"...................50		95	125
19	Cement Truck, red body, yellow plastic barrel w/red stripes, large wide arch wheels, 1976, 3".......................4		5	7

No.	Name	Good	Ex	Mint
19	Peterbilt Cement Truck, green body, orange barrel, "Big Pete" decal on hood, 1982........2		3	5
20	Chevrolet Impala Taxi Cab, orange/yellow or bright yellow body, ivory or red interior and driver, 1965, 3"...10		15	20
20	Desert Dawg Jeep 4x4, white body, red top and stripes, white "Jeep" and yellow, red and green, "Desert Dawg" decal, 1982 2		3	5
20	ERF 686 Truck, dark blue body, silver radiator, eight plastic silver wheels, No. 20 cast on black base, 1959, 2-5/8"......................25		45	60
20	Lamborghini Marzel, amber windows, ivory interior, 1969, 2-3/4"............15		20	35
20	Police Patrol, white body, "Police" on orange side stripe, orange interior, 1975, 2-7/8"........................6		8	12
20	Stake Truck, gold trim on front grille and side gas tanks, ribbed bed, metal wheels, 1956, 2-3/8"...........50		75	100
21	Commer Milk Truck, pale green body, clear or green tinted windows, ivory or cream bottle load, 1961, 2-1/4".......................20		30	40

No. 19 MG Midget. Photo Courtesy Gary Linden.

No. 21 Commer Milk Truck.

No. 25 Bedford Dunlop Truck.

No. 25 BP Petrol Tanker.

No.	Name	Good	Ex	Mint
21	Foden Concrete Truck, orange/yellow body and rotating barrel, green tinted windows, eight plastic wheels, 1968, 3".........3		5	15
21	Foden Concrete Truck, red body, orange barrel, green base and windows, five-spoke wheels, 1970, 2-7/8".......2		10	20
21	Long Distance Coach, green body, black base, "No. 21" cast on baseplate, "London to Glasgow" orange decal on sides, 1958, 2-5/8" 20		60	45

No.	Name	Good	Ex	Mint
21	Long Distance Coach, light green body, black base, "London to Glasgow" orange decal on sides, 1956, 2-1/4" ... 10		20	25
21	Renault 5TL, yellow body and removable rear hatch, tan interior, silver base and grille, 1978, 2-11/16" 4		9	15
21	Road Roller, yellow body, red seat, black plastic rollers, 1973, 2-5/8"............................ 7		10	15
22	Blaze Buster, red body, silver interior, yellow label, five-spoke slicks, 1975, 3"............... 4		6	8
22	Freeman Inter-City Commuter, clear windows, ivory interior, wide five-spoke wheels, 1970, 3" 5		7	10
22	Pontiac Grand Prix Sports Coupe, light gray interior and tow hook, clear windows, four black plastic wheels, 1964, 3" 6		9	12
22	Pontiac Grand Prix Sports Coupe, light gray interior, clear windows, thin five-spoke wheels, 1970, 3"............. 2		4	6
22	Vauxhall Cresta, w/or without silver grille, tow hook, plastic wheels, 1958, 2-5/8" ... 20		40	60
22	Vauxhall Sedan, dark red body, cream or off-white roof, tow hook, 1956, 2-1/2"................. 15		30	45
23	Atlas Truck, metallic blue cab, silver interior, orange dumper, red and yellow labels on doors, 1975, 3".......... 6		8	10
23	Audi Quattro, white body, red and black print sides, clear windows, "Audi Sport" on doors, 1982.....................2		3	5
23	Berkeley Cavalier Trailer, decal on lower right rear of trailer, metal wheels, flat tow hook, 1956, 2-1/2"................. 10		30	40

No.	Name	Good	Ex	Mint
23	Bluebird Dauphine Trailer, green w/gray plastic wheels, decal on lower right rear of traler, opening door on left rear side, 1960, 2-1/2"	45	135	200
23	GT 350, white body, blue stripes on hood, roof and rear deck, 1970, 2-7/8"	3	4	5
23	Trailer Caravan, yellow or pink body w/white roof, blue removable interior, 1965, 2-7/8"	4	7	15
23	Volkswagen Camper, orange top, clear windows, five-spoke wheels, 1970, 2-1/8"	5	7	10
24	Datsun 280ZX, black body and base, clear windows, five-spoke wheels, 1979, 2-7/8"	2	3	5
24	Rolls-Royce Silver Shadow, metallic red body, ivory interior, clear windows, silver hub caps or solid silver wheels, 1967, 3"	10	15	20
24	Rolls-Royce Silver Shadow, ivory interior, clear windows, five-spoke wheels, 1970, 3"	5	7	20
24	Shunter, metallic green body, red base, tan instruments, no window, 1978, 3"	3	5	7
24	Team Matchbox, white driver, silver motor, wide cloverleaf wheels, 1973, 2-7/8"	15	20	25
24	Weatherhill Hydraulic Excavator, metal wheels, "Weatherhill Hydraulic" decal on rear, 1956, 2-3/8"	20	25	35
24	Weatherhill Hydraulic Excavator, yellow body, small and medium front wheels, large rear wheels, 1959, 2-5/8"	10	15	20
25	Bedford Dunlop Truck, dark blue body, silver grille, 1956, 2-1/8"	10	25	50
25	BP Petrol Tanker, yellow hinged cab, white tanker body, six black plastic wheels, 1964, 3"	8	15	20
25	Celica GT, blue body, black base, white racing stripes and "78" on roof and doors, 1978, 2-15/16"	3	7	12
25	Celica GT, yellow body, blue interior, red "Yellow Fever" on hood, side racing stripes, clear windows, large rear wheels, 1982	2	4	6
25	Ford Cortina, clear windows, ivory interior and tow hook, thin five-spoke wheels, 1970, 2-3/4"	3	6	10
25	Ford Cortina G.T., light brown body in various shade, ivory interior and tow hook, 1968, 2-7/8"	4	7	10
25	Mod Tractor, metallic purple, orange/yellow seat and tow hook, 1972, 2-1/8"	10	15	20
25	Volkswagen 1200 Sedan, silver-blue body, clear or tinted windows, 1960, 2-1/2"	20	40	55
26	Big Banger, red body, blue windows, small front wheels, large rear wheels, 1972, 3"	4	6	8
26	Cosmic Blues, white body, blue "COSMIC BLUES" and stars on sides, 1970, 2-7/8"	2	3	4
26	Foden Ready Mix Concrete Truck, orange body, gray plastic rotating barrel, w/or without silver grille, six gray wheels, 1961, 2-1/4"	60	130	180
26	Foden Ready Mix Concrete Truck, orange body and rotating barrel, silver or gold grille, four silver plastic wheels, 1956, 1-3/4",	50	100	140

No.	Name	Good	Ex	Mint
26	GMC Tipper Truck, red cab, silver/gray tipper body, wide four-spoke wheels, 1970, 2-1/2"	10	15	20
26	GMC Tipper Truck, red tipping cab, silver tipper body w/swinging door, four wheels, 1968, 2-5/8"	5	7	20
26	Site Dumper, yellow body and dumper, black base, 1976, 2-5/8"	2	3	5
27	Bedford Low Loader, light blue cab, dark blue trailer, silver grille and side gas tanks, four metal wheels on cab, two metal wheels on trailer, 1956, 3-1/8"	100	350	450
27	Bedford Low Loader, green cab, tan trailer, silver grille, four gray wheels on cab, two wheels on trailer, 1959, 3-3/4"	20	55	75
27	Cadillac Sedan, w/or without silver grille, clear windows, white roof, silver wheels, 1960, 2-3/4"	15	30	40
27	Lamborghini Countach, yellow body, silver interior and motor, five-spoke wheels, 1973, 2-7/8"	5	7	10
27	Mercedes-Benz 230 SL, unpainted metal grille, red plastic interior and tow hook, black plastic wheels, 1966, 3"	5	10	20
27	Mercedes-Benz 230 SL, metal grille, blue tinted windshield, five-spoke wheels, 1970, 2-7/8"	5	10	20
27	Swing Wing Jet, red top and fins, white belly and retractable wings, 1981, 3"	2	3	5
28	Bedford Compressor Truck, silver front and rear grilles, metal wheels, 1956, 1-3/4"	15	35	45

No.	Name	Good	Ex	Mint
28	Formula Racing Car, gold body, silver engine and pipes, white driver and "Champion," black "8" on front and sides, large cloverleaf rear wheels, 1982	2	3	5
28	Jaguar Mark 10, light brown body, off-white interior, working hood, gray motor and wheels, 1964, 2-3/4"	35	65	90
28	Lincoln Continental MK-V, red body, tan interior, 1979, 3"	10	15	20
28	Mack Dump Truck, pea green body, green windows, large balloon wheels w/cloverleaf design, 1970, 2-5/8"	2	5	15
28	Mack Dump Truck, orange body, green windows, four large plastic wheels, 1968, 2-5/8"	4	7	15
28	Stroat Armored Truck, metallic gold body, brown plastic observer coming out of turret, wide five-spoke wheels, 1974, 2-5/8"	8	15	25

No. 28 Bedford Compressor Truck. Photo Courtesy Gary Linden.

Hollywood on Wheels, Round 2 (Playing Mantis). Photo Courtesy Playing Mantis.

HOT RODS

Name	MIP

Round 1

Name	MIP
'29 Crew Cab	5
'62 Bad Bird.	5
'66 Pro Street.	5
'69 Pro Street.	5
'72 Goin Goat.	5
'86 Beastmobile.	5
Bumongous.	5
Flathead Flyer.	5
Frankenstude.	5
Rumblur.	5

Round 2

Name	MIP
'23 T-Bucket	4
'27 T-Roadster	4
'32 Ford HiBoy	4
'33 Ford Delivery	4
'34 Ford Coupe	4
'37 Ford Coupe	4

HUMMERS

Name	MIP

Round 1

Name	MIP
Atlantic Beach Rescue Hummer	5
Civilian Hummer, four-door wagon, black	5
M1025A2 Tow Missile Carrier	5
Rod Hall's Off-Road Racing Hummer	5

Round 2

Name	MIP
ATR Rescue Hummer	4
Civilian - 2dr pickup	4
Civilian Hummer, four-door wagon, silver, bonus car	4
St. Joe Sheriff Hummer	4
US Marines Humvee	4

Round 3

Name	MIP
Army National Guard	3
Army Reserve Hummer	3
Civilian Hummer, four-door wagon (Red bonus car)	3
Gatorade Hummer	3
Tom Wamberg Race Hummer	3

HURST MUSCLE

Name	MIP
'69 Hurst Olds	5
'69 SC/Rambler	5
'74 Hurst Olds	5
Hurst Hairy Olds	5
Hurst Hemi Under Glass	5

INDY PACE CARS

Name	MIP
Round 1	
'69 Camaro	6
'70 Olds 442	4
'74 Hurst Olds	4
'75 Buick Century	4
'77 Olds Delta 88	4
'78 Corvette	4
'79 Mustang	4
'92 Allante	4
Round 2	
'68 Torino	6
'69 Camaro	6
'70 Olds 442	6
'71 Challenger	6
'72 Olds	6
'73 Cadillac Eldorado	6
'74 Hurst Olds	6
'77 Olds Delta 88	6
'78 Corvette	6
'79 Mustang	6
'98 Corvette Convertible	6

Name	MIP
Round 3	
'64-1/2 Mustang	6
'67 Camaro	6
'68 Torino	6
'82 Camaro	6
'96 Viper GTS	6
'98 Corvette	6

INDY RACE CARS

Name	MIP
Round 1	
'69 Andretti	6
'70 A. Unser	6
'74 Rutherford	6
'75 B. Unser	6
'77 A.J. Foyt	6
'78 A. Unser	6
'79 Mears	6
'92 A. Unser Jr.	6

JAMES BOND

Name	MIP
'64 Aston Martin, Goldeneye	7

James Bond, Round 1 (Playing Mantis). Photo Courtesy Playing Mantis.

No.	Name	MIP
412	Speed Machine, light green, red interior, 5sp	2
413	Silhoutte II, tampo on rear, purple, orange interior, 5sp	2
413	Silhoutte II, tampo on front, purple, orange interior, 5sp	2
414	Propper Chopper, (China) blue w/orange base, orange interior, blue window	2
414	Propper Chopper, blue w/orange base, orange interior, clear window	2
414	Propper Chopper, blue w/orange base, orange interior, blue window	2
415	Roll Patrol, brown w/orange base, dark orange, interior, yct	5
415	Roll Patrol, brown w/orange base, dark orange, interior, yt/b	3
415	Roll Patrol, brown w/orange base, light orange interior, yt/b	3
415	Roll Patrol, brown w/orange base, light orange, interior, yct	5

Sugar Rush Series 98

No.	Name	MIP
741	Mazda MX-5 Miata, orange w/orange base, Reese's, black interior, smoked window, 5sp	2
742	Funny Car, white w/metal base, Hershey's, black window, 5sp	2
743	'95 Camaro, dark metallic blue w/black base, Crunch, black interior, clear window, 5sp	2
744	'96 Mustang Convertible, yellow w/metal base Butterfinger, black interior, clear window, 5sp	2

Sugar Rush Series 99

No.	Name	MIP
969	'70 Road Runner, yellow w/chrome plastic base, black interior, clear window, 5dot	2
970	Jaguar XK8, red w/black base, tan interior, black tint, gbbs	2
971	Pikes Peak Celica, white w/black base, black interior, clear window, bbs	2
972	Dodge Concept, white w/metal base, blue interior, clear window, 5dot	2

Surf N Fun Series

No.	Name	MIP
961	'40's Woodie, purple, visible JcWhitney tampo on sides of hood, w/metal base, black interior, blue tint, 5sp	10

No. 972 Dodge Concept (Sugar Rush Series 99), white with metal base, blue interior, clear window, 5dot.

No.	Name	MIP
961	'40's Woodie, purple w/metal base black interior, blue tint, 5sp	2
962	VW Bug, metallic blue w/metal base, white interior, black tint, 5sp	2
963	'55 Chevy, metallic red w/chrome base, black tint windows, 3sp	2
964	'55 Nomad, white w/metal base, white interior, black tint, g5sp	2

Tattoo Machines

No.	Name	MIP
685	'57 T-Bird, metallic blue/chrome base, blue interior, blue tint window, 3sp	2

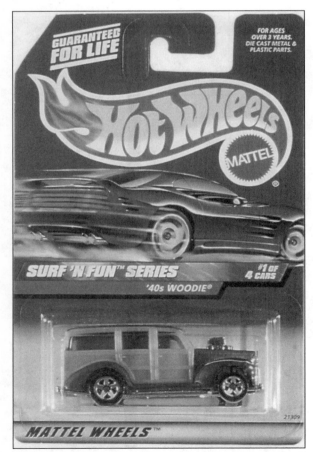

No. 961 '40's Woodie (Surf N Fun Series), purple with metal base black interior, blue tint, 5sp.

No.	Name	MIP
686	'93 Camaro, neon green/black base, white interior, smoked window, 3sp	2
686	'93 Camaro, neon green/black base, white interior, smoked window, t/b	2
687	Stutz Blackhawk, metallic red w/white cove, white interior, tinted window, 3sp	2
687	Stutz Blackhawk, brown w/white cove, white interior, tinted window, 3sp	2
687	Stutz Blackhawk, rootbeer w/white cove white interior, tinted window, 3sp	2
688	Corvette Stingray, orange, metal base black interior, smoked window, 3sp	2
688	Corvette Stingray, orange w/metal base black interior, smoked window, t/b	2

Techno Bits Series

No.	Name	MIP
689	Shadow Jet II, black w/red tampo and metal base, chrome interior, green window, b5sp	2
689	Shadow Jet II, black w/brown and red tampo, metal base, chrome interior, green window, b5sp	2
689	Shadow Jet II, black w/brown tampo and metal base, chrome interior, green window, b5sp	2
690	Power Pistons, purple w/yellow tampo, yellow interior and window, t/b	2
690	Power Pistons, dark purple w/yellow tampo, yellow interior and window, t/b	2
690	Power Pistons, purple w/yellow tampo, yellow interior and window, bbs	2

No. 28 Mack Dump Truck.

No.	Name	Good	Ex	Mint
28	Thames Trader Compressor Truck, yellow body, black wheels, 1959, 2-3/4"	20	25	35
29	Austin A55 Cambridge Sedan, two-tone green, light green roof and rear top half of body, dark metallic green hood and lower body, 1961, 2-3/4"	10	20	25
29	Bedford Milk Delivery Van, tan body, white bottle load, 1956, 2-1/4"	15	25	30
29	Fire Pumper Truck, red body, metal grille, white plastic hose and ladders, 1966, 3"	3	7	20
29	Fire Pumper Truck, red body, metal grille, white plastic hose and ladders, 1970, 3"	2	5	20
29	Racing Mini, clear windows, wide five-spoke wheels, 1970, 2-1/4"	5	7	10
29	Shovel Nose Tractor, yellow body and base, red plastic shovel, silver engine, 1976, 2-7/8"	8	15	20
30	6-Wheel Crane Truck, silver body, orange crane, metal or plastic hook, gray wheels, 1961, 2-5/8"	20	30	40

No.	Name	Good	Ex	Mint
30	8-Wheel Crane Truck, green body, orange crane, red or yellow hook, eight black wheels on four axles, 1965, 3"	15	20	25
30	8-Wheel Crane Truck, red body, yellow plastic hook, thin five-spoke wheels, 1970, 3"	5	7	10
30	Articulated Truck, blue cab, white grille, silver/gray dumper, five-spoke accent wheels, 1981, 3"	3	5	6
30	Beach Buggy, pink, yellow paint splatters, clear windows, 1970, 2-1/2"	3	4	6
30	Ford Prefect, blue body, metal wheels, silver grille, black tow hook, 1956, 2-1/4"	20	60	90
30	Peterbilt Quarry Truck, yellow body, gray dumper, silver tanks, "Dirty Dumper" on sides, six wheels, 1982	2	4	6
30	Swamp Rat, green deck, yellow plastic hull, tan soldier, black engine and prop, 1976, 3"	2	4	6
31	Ford Customline Station Wagon, yellow body, no windows, w/or without red painted taillights, 1957, 2-5/8"	20	30	40
31	Ford Fairlane Station Wagon, green or clear windows, w/or without red painted tail lights, 1960, 2-3/4"	10	30	35
31	Lincoln Continental, clear windows, ivory interior, five-spoke wheels, 1970, 2-3/4"	5	10	30
31	Lincoln Continental, clear windows, ivory interior, black plastic wheels, 1964, 2-7/8"	10	15	20

No.	Name	Good	Ex	Mint
31	Mazda RX-7, gray body w/sunroof, black interior, 1982	15	25	35
31	Mazda RX-7, white body, black base, burgundy stripe, black "RX-7", 1979, 3"	3	4	5
31	Volks Dragon, red body, purple tinted windows, 1971, 2-1/2"	3	4	5
32	Atlas Extractor, red/orange body, gray platform, turret and treads, black wheels, 1981, 3"	2	4	6
32	Jaguar XK 140 Coupe, w/or without silver grille, w/or without red painted taillights, 1957, 2-3/8"	20	30	40
32	Jaguar XKE, metallic red body, ivory interior, clear or tinted windows, 1962, 2-5/8"	15	20	35
32	Leyland Petrol Tanker, green cab, white tank body, blue tinted windows, eight plastic wheels, 1968, 3"	25	40	50
32	Leyland Petrol Tanker, green cab, white tank body, blue tinted windows, thin five-spoke wheels, 1970, 3"	10	20	50
32	Maserati Bora, metallic burgundy, clear windows, bright yellow interior, wide five-spoke wheels, 1972, 3"	5	7	10
33	Datsun or 126X, yellow body, amber windows, silver interior, 1973, 3"	5	8	10
33	Ford Zephyr 6MKIII, blue/green body shades, clear windows, ivory interior, 1963, 2-5/8"	15	20	30
33	Ford Zodiac MKII Sedan, w/or without silver grille, w/or without red painted taillights, 1957, 2-5/8"	20	30	45
33	Lamborghini Miura, clear windows, frosted rear window, five-spoke wheels, 1970, 2-3/4"	25	40	50
33	Lamborghini Miura, metal grille, silver plastic wheels, red or white interior, clear or frosted back window, 1969, 2-3/4"	10	15	20
33	Police Motorcyclist, white frame, seat and bags, silver engine and pipes, wire wheels, 1977, 2-1/2"	5	7	10
34	Chevy Pro Stocker, white body, red interior, clear front and side windows, frosted rear window, 1981, 3"	2	3	5
34	Formula 1 Racing Car, metallic pink, white driver, clear glass, wide four-spoke wheels, 1971, 2-7/8"	7	10	15
34	Vantastic, orange body, white base and interior, silver engine, large rear slicks, 1975, 2-7/8"	4	7	9
34	Volkswagen Camper Car, silver body, orange interior, black plastic wheels, raised roof, six windows, 1967, 2-5/8"	15	20	30
34	Volkswagen Camper Car, silver body, orange interior, black plastic wheels, short raised sun roof, 1968, 2-5/8"	10	20	25
34	Volkswagen Microvan, blue body, gray wheels, "Matchbox International Express" on sides, 1957, 2-1/4"	30	40	50

No. 32 Jaguar XKE.

No.	Name	Good	Ex	Mint
34	Volkswagen Microvan, light green body, dark green interior, flat roof, green tinted green window, 1962, 2-3/5"..................20	20	30	40
35	Fandango, white body, red interior, chrome rear engine, large five-spoke rear wheels, 1975, 3"......................3	3	5	8
35	Marshall Horse Box, red cab, brown horse box, silver grille, three rear windows in box, 1957, 2"..........................20	20	25	35
35	Merryweather Fire Engine, metallic red body, blue windows, white removable ladder on roof, thin five-spoke wheels, 1969, 3".............5	5	7	10
35	Pontiac Trans Am T Roof, black body, red interior, yellow "Turbo" on doors, yellow eagle on hood, 1982......2	2	3	5
35	Snowtrac Tractor, red body, silver painted grille, green windows, white rubber treads, 1964, 2-3/8".................10	10	15	20
35	Zoo Truck, 1981 4	4	7	10
36	Austin A50, silver grille, w/or without silver rear bumper, no windows, 1957, 2-3/8".......15	15	20	30
36	Formula 5000, orange body, silver rear engine, large cloverleaf rear slicks, 1975, 3"................................5	5	7	10

No.	Name	Good	Ex	Mint
36	Hot Rod Draguar, metallic red body, clear canopy, wide five-spoke wheels, 1970, 2-13/16"...................................4	4	6	8
36	Lambretta TV 175 Motor Scooter and Sidecar, metallic green, three wheels, 1961, 2"...25	25	35	45
36	Opel Diplomat, ivory interior and tow hook, clear windows, thin five-spoke wheels, 1970, 2-7/8".................5	5	7	15
36	Opel Diplomat, metallic light gold body, white interior and tow hook, clear windows, black plastic wheels, 1966, 2-3/5"......................................10	10	15	20
36	Refuse Truck, red metallic body, silver/gray base, orange plastic container, 1980, 3"......................................2	2	3	4
37	Cattle Truck, gray plastic box, white plastic cattle inside, five-spoke thin wheels, green tinted windows, 1970, 2-1/2"...5	5	7	20
37	Cattle Truck, yellow body, gray plastic box w/fold down rear door, black plastic wheels, green tinted windows, 1966, 2-1/4".............7	7	10	15

No. 36 Opel Diplomat.

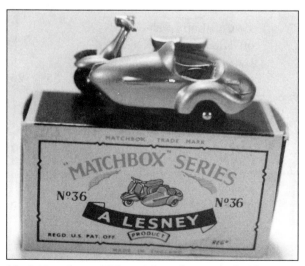

No. 36 Lambretta TV 175 Motor Scooter and Sidecar.
Photo Courtesy Gary Linden.

No. 37 Cattle Truck.

No. 37 Coca-Cola Lorry.

No.	Name	Good	Ex	Mint
37	Coca-Cola Lorry, orange/yellow body, uneven case load, open base, metal rear fenders, 1957, 2-1/4"	25	75	140
37	Coca-Cola Lorry, yellow body of various shades, even case load, silver wheels, black base, 1960, 2-1/4"	25	55	125
37	Skip Truck, red body, yellow plastic bucket, light amber windows, silver interior, 1976, 2-11/16"	3	5	7
37	Soopa Coopa, metallic blue, amber windows, yellow interior, 1972, 2-7/8"	3	4	5
37	Sun Burner, black body, red and yellow flames on hood and sides, 1972, 3"	2	3	4

No.	Name	Good	Ex	Mint
38	Camper, red body, off-white camper, unpainted base, 1980, 3"	3	5	7
38	Honda Motorcycle and Trailer, metallic blue-green cycle w/wire wheels, black plastic tires, orange trailer, 1967, 2-7/8"	10	15	20
38	Honda Motorcycle and Trailer, yellow trailer, thin five-spoke wheels, 1970, 2-7/8"	5	7	20
38	Jeep, olive green body, black base and interior, wide five-spoke reverse-accent wheels, no hubs, 1976, 2-3/8"	5	8	12
38	Karrier Refuse Collector, silver grille headlights and bumper, 1957, 2-3/8"	15	25	30
38	Stingeroo Cycle, metallic purple body, ivory horse head at rear of seat, wide five-spoke rear wheels, 1973, 3"	4	6	8
38	Vauxhall Victor Estate Car, yellow body, red or green interior, clear windows, 1963, 2-5/8"	10	18	25
39	Clipper, metallic dark pink, amber windows, bright yellow interior, 1973, 3"	3	4	5
39	Ford Tractor, blue body, black plastic steering wheel and tires, w/or without yellow hood, 1967, 2-1/8"	5	10	20
39	Ford Zodiac Convertible, peach/pink body shades, tan driver, metal wheels, silver grille, 1957, 2-5/8"	35	65	90
39	Pontiac Convertible, purple body, w/or without silver grille, cream or ivory interior, silver wheels, 1962, 2-3/4"	30	50	75

No.	Name	Good	Ex	Mint
39	Rolls-Royce Silver Shadow II, metallic silver gray body, red interior, clear windshield, 1979, 3-1/16"	3	5	7
40	Bedford Tipper Truck, red cab, silver grille, two front wheels, four dual rear wheels, 1957, 2-1/8"	25	40	50
40	Corvette T Roof, white body and interior, black "09" on door, red and black racing stripes, 1982	2	3	5
40	Hay Trailer, blue body w/tow bar, yellow plastic racks, yellow plastic wheels, 1967, 3-3/4"	5	10	15
40	Horse Box, orange cab, off-white van w/tan plastic door, small wheels, 1977, 2-13/16"	4	5	7
40	Leyland Royal Tiger Coach, silver-gray body, green tinted windows, four plastic wheels, 1961, 3"	10	15	20
40	Vauxhall Guildsman, pink body, light green windows, light cream interior and tow hook, wide five-spoke wheels, 1971, 3"	3	4	5
41	Chevrolet Ambulance, white body, blue windows and dome light, gray interior, 1978, 2-15/16"	4	7	10
41	D-Type Jaguar, dark green body, tan driver, open air scoop, 1957, 2-13/16"	15	30	55
41	D-Type Jaguar, dark green body, tan driver, silver wheels, open and closed air scoop, 1960, 2-7/16"	50	100	150
41	Ford GT, white or yellow body, red interior, clear windows, yellow or red plastic wheels, 1965, 2-5/8"	20	30	40
41	Ford GT, white body, red interior, clear windows, five spoke wheels, 1970, 2-5/8"	5	7	20
41	Kenworth Conventional Aerodyne, red cab and chassis, silver tanks and pipes, black and white stripes on cab, 1982	2	3	5
41	Siva Spider, metallic red body, cream interior, clear windows, wide five-spoke wheels, 1972, 3"	5	7	10
42	1957 Ford T-Bird, red convertible, white interior, silver grille and trunk mounted spare, 1982	3	5	6
42	Bedford Evening News Van, yellow/orange body, silver grille, 1957, 2-1/4"	15	35	45
42	Iron Fairy Crane, four-spoke wheels, yellow plastic hook, 1970, 3"	25	35	50
42	Iron Fairy Crane, red body, yellow-orange crane, black plastic wheels, yellow plastic single-cable hook, 1969, 3"	7	10	30
42	Mercedes-Benz Container Truck, red body, black base and grille, removable ivory container w/red top and back door, six wheels, 1977, 3"	4	5	7
42	Studebaker Lark Wagonaire, blue body, sliding rear roof panel, white plastic interior and tow hook, 1965, 3"	10	15	20
42	Tyre Fryer, metallic red body, cream interior, clear windows, wide five-spoke wheels, 1972, 3"	3	4	6
43	0-4-0 Steam Loco, red cab, bin and tanks, black boiler, coal, and base, 1978, 3"	4	5	7
43	Aveling Barford Tractor Shovel, yellow body, yellow or red driver, four large plastic wheels, 1962, 2-5/8"	10	15	25

No.	Name	Good	Ex	Mint
43	Dragon Wheels Volkswagen, light green body, amber windows, silver interior, orange on black "Dragon Wheels" on sides, large rear wheels, 1972, 2-13/16"	5	7	9
43	Hillman Minx, w/or without silver grille, w/or without red painted taillights, 1958, 2-5/8"	15	20	30
43	Perterbilt Conventional, black cab and chassis, silver grille, fenders and tanks, red and white side stripes, six wheels, 1982, 3"	2	3	5
43	Pony Trailer, yellow body, clear windows, gray plastic rear fold-down door, four plastic wheels, 1968, 2-5/8"	7	10	15
43	Pony Trailer, yellow body, clear windows, gray rear door, thin five-spoke wheels, 1970, 2-5/8"	3	5	15
44	Boss Mustang, yellow body, amber windows, silver interior, wide cloverleaf wheels, 1972, 2-7/8"	3	4	6
44	Chevy 4x4 Van, green body and windows, white "Ridin High" w/horse and fence on sides, 1982	2	3	5

No. 44 Rolls-Royce Silver Cloud.

No.	Name	Good	Ex	Mint
44	GMC Refrigerator Truck, red ribbed roof cab, turquoise box w/gray plastic rear door that opens, green windows, 1967	7	10	20
44	GMC Refrigerator Truck, green windows, four-spoke wheels, gray plastic rear door, 1970, 2-13/16"	5	7	15
44	Railway Passenger Car, cream plastic upper and roof, red metal lower, black base, 1978, 3-1/16"	3	5	7
44	Rolls-Royce Phantom V, clear windows, ivory interior, black plastic wheels, 1964, 2-7/8"	15	20	30
44	Rolls-Royce Silver Cloud, metallic blue body, no windows, w/or without silver grille, 1958, 2-5/8"	15	20	25
45	BMW 3.0 CSL, orange body, yellow interior, 1976, 2-7/8"	3	5	7
45	Ford Corsair with Boat, pale yellow body, red interior and tow hook, green roof rack w/green plastic boat, 1965, 2-3/8"	10	15	20
45	Ford Group 6, metallic green body, ivory interior, clear windows, wide five-spoke wheels, 1970, 3"	5	7	10
45	Kenworth Caboner Aerodyne, white body w/blue and brown side stripes, silver grille, tanks and pipes, 1982	2	3	5
45	Vauxhall Victor Saloon, yellow body, w/or without green tinted windows, w/or without silver grille, 1958, 2-3/8"	10	15	25
46	Ford Tractor, blue body, black base, lage black plastic rear wheels, 1987, 2-3/16"	3	5	8

No.	Name	Good	Ex	Mint
46	Hot Chocolate, metallic brown front lid and sides, black roof, 1972, 2-13/16"	3	4	5
46	Mercedes-Benz 300 SE, clear windows, ivory interior, black plastic wheels, 1968, 2-7/8"	5	10	20
46	Mercedes-Benz 300 SE, clear windows, ivory interior, thin five-spoke wheels, 1970, 2-7/8"	5	10	20
46	Morris Minor 1000, dark green body, metal wheels, no windows, 1958, 2"	20	30	45
46	Pickford Removal Van, green body, w/or without silver grilles, 1960, 2-5/8"	15	30	50
46	Stretcha Fetcha, white body, blue windows, pale yellow interior, 1972, 2"	6	8	12
47	1 Ton Trojan Van, red body, no windows, 1958, 2-1/4"	25	35	45
47	Beach Hopper, dark metallic blue body, hot pink splattered over body, bright orange interior, tan driver, 1974, 2-5/8"	3	4	5

No.	Name	Good	Ex	Mint
47	Commer Ice Cream Canteen, metallic blue body, cream or white plastic interior w/man holding ice cream cone, black plastic wheels, 1963	60	95	100
47	DAF Tipper Container Truck, silver cab, yellow tipper box, thin five-spoke wheels, 1970, 3"	4	6	20
47	DAF Tipper Container Truck, aqua or silver cab, yellow tipper box w/light gray or dark gray plastic roof, 1968, 3"	6	8	12
47	Pannier Tank Loco, green body, black base and insert, six large plastic wheels, 1979, 3"	3	5	7
48	Dumper Truck, red body, green tinted windows, 1966, 3"	10	20	25
48	Dumper Truck, bright blue cab, yellow body, green windows, 1970, 3"	5	7	25
48	Pi-Eyed Piper, metallic blue body, amber windows, small front wheels, large rear wheels, 1972, 2-7/8"	5	7	10
48	Meteor Sports Boat and Trailer, metal boat w/tan deck and blue hull, black metal trailer w/tow bar, 1958, 2-3/8"	30	45	60

No. 46 Morris Minor 1000. Photo Courtesy Gary Linden.

No. 47 1Ton Trojan Van. Photo Courtesy Gary Linden.

No.	Name	Good	Ex	Mint
48	Red Rider, red body, white "Red Rider" and flames on sides, 1972, 2-7/8"...................2		3	4
48	Sambron Jacklift, yellow body, black base and insert, no window, orange and yellow fork and boom combinations, 1977, 3-1/16".....4		7	10
48	Sports Boat and Trailer, plastic boat, red or white deck, hulls in red, white or cream, gold or silver motors, blue metal two-wheel trailer, 1961, boat 2-3/8", trailer 2-5/8"................35		65	80
49	Chop Suey Motorcycle, metallic dark red body, yellow bull's head on front handle bars, 1973, 2-3/4"..........5		7	10
49	M3 Army Personnel Carrier, olive green body, gray rubber treads, 1958, 2-1/2" 15		25	30
49	Mercedes-Benz Unimog, silver grille, four black plastic tires, 1967, 2-1/2" 10		15	20
50	Articulated Truck, purple tinted windows, small wide wheels, wide five-spoke wheels, 1973, 2-3/4" 6		8	12

No.	Name	Good	Ex	Mint
50	Commer Pickup Truck, w/or without silver grille and bumpers, four wheels, 1958, 2-1/2"......................................35	35	55	75
50	Harley-Davidson Motorcycle, silver and brown metallic frame and tank, chrome engine and pipes, brown rider, 1980, 2-11/16" 2		3	7
50	John Deere Tractor, green body and tow hook, yellow plastic wheels, 1964, 2-1/8"............... 10		20	30
50	Kennel Truck, metallic green body, clear or blue tinted canopy, four plastic dogs, 1969, 2-3/4"..............................5		15	40
50	Kennel Truck, green windows, light blue tinted canopy, four plastic dogs, 1970, 2-3/4".........5		15	45
51	8-Wheel Tipper, blue tinted windows, eight black plastic wheels, 1969, 3".......................7		10	15
51	8-Wheel Tipper, yellow cab, silver/gray tipper, blue windows, thin five-spoke wheels, 1970, 3".......................4		6	8
51	Albion Chieftan, yellow body, tan and light tan bags, small round decal on doors, 1958, 2-1/2"...................................... 10		20	25
51	Citroen SM, clear windows, frosted rear windows, five-spoke wheels, 1972, 3"............3		4	6
51	Combine Harvester, red body, black painted base, yellow plastic grain chute, 1978, 2-3/4"......................................3		5	8
51	John Deere Trailer, green tipping body w/tow bar, two small yellow wheels, three plastic barrels, 1964, 2-5/8" ... 20		35	50
51	Midnight Magic, black body, silver stripes on hood, five-spoke front wheels, cloverleaf rear windows, 1972...2		3	4

No. 49 M3 Army Personnel Carrier. Photo Courtesy Gary Linden.

No.	Name	Good	Ex	Mint
52	BRM Racing Car, blue or red body, white plasti driver, yellow wheels, 1965, 2-5/8"	10	20	25
52	Dodge Charger, clear windows, black interior, five spoke wide wheels, 1970, 2-7/8"	4	6	8
52	Maserati 4 Cl. T/1948, red or yellow body, cream or white driver w/or without circle on left shoulder, 1958, 2-3/8"	10	17	25
52	Police Launch, white deck, blue hull and men, 1976, 3"	2	4	6
53	Aston Martin DB2 Saloon, metallic light green, 1958, 2-1/2"	20	30	40
53	BMW M1, silver gray metallic body w/plastic hood, red interior, black stripes and "52" on sides, 1981, 2-15/16"	2	4	5
53	Flareside Pick-up, blue body, white interior, grille and pipes, clear windshield, lettered w/"326," "Baja Bouncer" and "B.F. Goodrich", 1982	2	4	5
53	Ford Zodiac, clear windows, ivory interior, five-spoke wheels, 1970, 2-3/4"	5	7	15
53	Ford Zodiac MK IV, metallic silver blue body, clear windows, ivory interior, four black plastic wheels, 1968, 2-3/4"	7	10	15

No.	Name	Good	Ex	Mint
53	Jeep CJ6, red body, unpainted base, bumper and winch, five-spoke rear-accent wheels, 1977, 2-15/16"	2	3	5
53	Mercedes-Benz 220 SE, silver grille, clear windows, ivory interior, four wheels, 1963, 2-3/4"	15	25	30
53	Tanzara, orange body, silver interior, small front wheels, larger rear wheels, 1972, 3"	3	4	5
54	Cadillac Ambulance, white body, blue tinted windows, white interior, red cross labels on sides, 1970, 2-3/8"	5	7	20
54	Ford Capri, ivory interior and tow hook, clear windows, wide five-spoke wheels, 1971, 3"	3	4	6
54	NASA Tracking Vehicle, white body, silver radar screen, red windows, blue "Space Shuttle Command Center," red "NASA" on roof, 1982	2	3	5
54	Personnel Carrier, olive green body, green windows, black base and grille, tan men and benches, 1976, 3"	4	5	7
54	S & S Cadillac Ambulance, white body, blue tinted windows, white interior, red cross decal on front doors, 1965, 2-7/8"	10	15	30
54	Saracen Personnel Carrier, olive green body, six black plastic wheels, 1958, 2-1/4"	10	17	25
55	Ford Cortina, metallic gold/green body, unpainted base and grille, wide multispoke wheels, 1979, 3-1/16"	3	4	5
55	Ford Cortina, metallic tan body, yellow interior, blue racing stripes, 1982	2	4	6

No. 53 Ford Zodiac MK IV.

No. 54 Saracen Personnel Carrier.

No. 55 Ford Fairlane Police Car.

No. 56 Fiat 1500. Photo Courtesy Gary Linden.

No.	Name	Good	Ex	Mint
55	Ford Fairlane Police Car, silver grille, ivory interior, clear windows, four plastic wheels, 1963, 2-5/8"	20	55	100
55	Ford Galaxie Police Car, white body, ivory interior, driver and tow hook, clear windows, 1966, 2-7/8"	10	15	30
55	Hellraiser, white body, unpainted base and grille, silver rear engine, 1975, 3"	3	5	7
55	Mercury Police Car, white body, ivory interior w/two figures, clear windows, four silver wheels w/black plastic tires, 1968, 3"	10	15	40
55	Mercury Police Car, white body, ivory interior, two occupants, thin five-spoke wheels, 1970, 3"	5	7	15
55	Mercury Police Station Wagon, white body, ivory interior, no occupants, wide five-spoke wheels, 1971, 3"	5	7	10
56	BMC 1800 Pininfarina, clear windows, ivory interior, five-spoke wheels, 1970, 2-3/4"	7	10	15

No.	Name	Good	Ex	Mint
56	Fiat 1500, silver grille, red interior and tow hook, brown or tan luggage on roof, 1965, 2-1/2"	10	15	20
56	Hi-Tailer, white body, silver engine and windshield, wide five-spoke front wheels, wide cloverleaf rear wheels, 1974, 3"	4	6	8
56	London Trolley Bus, red body, two trolley poles on top of roof, six wheels, 1958, 2-5/8"	45	70	90

No.	Name	Good	Ex	Mint
56	Mercedes-Benz 450 SEL, metallic blue body, unpainted base and grille, 1979, 3".....................3		4	5
56	Mercedes-Benz Taxi, tan plastic interior, unpainted base, clear plastic windows, red "Taxi" sign on roof, 1980, 3".....................3		4	5
56	Peterbilt Tanker, blue cab, white tank w/red "Milk's the One", silver tanks, grille, and pipes, 1982..........................15		25	40
57	Chevrolet Impala, pale blue roof, metallic blue body, green tinted windows, 1961, 2-3/4"...................20		25	35
57	Eccles Trailer Caravan, orange roof, green plastic interior, thin five-spoke wheels, 1970, 3".....................5		7	10
57	Land Rover Fire Truck, red body, blue tinted windows, white plastic removable ladder, 1970, 2-1/2"..........5		7	20
57	Land Rover Fire Truck, red body, blue tinted windows, white plastic ladder on roof, 1966, 2-1/2"............10		15	25
57	Wild Life Truck, yellow body, red windows, light blue tinted canopy, 1973, 2-3/4"......3		4	6

No. 58 D.A.F. Girder Truck.

No.	Name	Good	Ex	Mint
57	Wolseley 1500, w/or without grilles, four wheels, 2-1/8" long, 1958.............20		30	35
58	BEA Coach, blue body, four wheels w/small knobby treads, 1958, 2-1/2"........20		25	35
58	D.A.F. Girder Truck, green windows, thin five-spoke wheels, red plastic girders, 1970, 2-7/8"...............5		7	20
58	D.A.F. Girder Truck, cream body shades, green tinted windows, six black wheels, red plastic girders, 1968, 3"......7		10	15
58	Drott Excavator, red or orange body, movable front shovel, green rubber treads, 1962, 2-5/8"..........35		50	70
58	Faun Dump Truck, yellow cab and dumper, black base, 1976, 2-7/8"...............5		10	15
58	Woosh-n-Push, yellow body, red interior, large rear wheels, 1972, 2-7/8"........3		4	5
59	Ford Fairlane Fire Chief's Car, red body, ivory interior, clear windows, four plastic wheels, 1963, 2-5/8".......35		75	125
59	Ford Galaxie Fire Chief's Car, red body, ivory interior, driver and tow hook, clear windows, four black plastic wheels, 1966, 2-7/8"........5		10	40
59	Ford Galaxie Fire Chief's Car, red body, ivory interior and tow hook, clear windows, thin four-spoke wheels, 1970, 2-7/8"............3		7	30
59	Ford Thames Van, silver grille, reads "Singer" on the side, four plastic knobby wheels, 1958, 2-1/8"..........35		75	110

No. 59 Ford Thames Van.

No.	Name	Good	Ex	Mint
59	Mercury Fire Chief's Car, red body, ivory interior, two occupants, clear windows, wide five-spoke wheels, 1971, 3"	5	7	20
59	Planet Scout, metallic green top, green bottom and base, silver interior, grille and roof panels, large multispoke rear wheels, 1975, 2-3/4"	4	5	7
59	Porsche 928, metallic brown body, black base, wide five-spoke wheels, 1980, 3"	3	5	6
60	Lotus Super Seven, butterscotch, clear windshield, black interior and trunk, wide four-spoke wheels, 1971, 2-7/8"	5	7	10
60	Morris J2 Pickup, blue body, open windshield and side door windows, four plastic wheels, 1958, 2-1/4"	15	25	30
60	Piston Popper, yellow body, red windows, silver engine, labels top and sides, large rear wheels, 1982	2	3	5

No.	Name	Good	Ex	Mint
60	Site Hut Truck, blue body, blue windows, four black plastic wheels, 1966, 2-1/2"	7	10	15
60	Site Hut Truck, blue cab, blue windows, thin five-spoke wheels, 1970, 2-1/2"	5	7	15
61	Alvis Stalwart, white body, yellow plastic removable canopy, green windows, six plastic wheels, 1966, 2-5/8"	20	30	50
61	Blue Shark, metallic dark blue, white driver, clear glass, wide four-spoke wheels, 1971, 3"	3	4	6
61	Ferret Scout Car, olive green, tan driver faces front or back, four black plastic wheels, 1959, 2-1/4"	10	20	25
61	Ford Wreck Truck, red body, black base and grille, frosted amber windows, 1978, 3"	3	5	7
62	Corvette, metallic red body, unpainted base, gray interior, 1979	2	4	6
62	General Service Lorry, olive green body, six black wheels, 1959, 2-5/8"	15	25	30
62	Mercury Cougar, red interior and tow hook, thin five-spoke wheels, 1970, 3"	3	5	15
62	Mercury Cougar, metallic lime green body shades, red plastic interior and tow hook, silver wheels, 1968, 3"	7	10	15
62	Mercury Cougar "Rat Rod", red interior and tow hook, small five-spoke front wheels, larger five-spoke rear windows, 1970, 3"	4	6	8
62	Renault 17TL, white interior, green tinted windows, green "9" in yellow and black circle, 1974, 3"	5	7	10

No.	Name	Good	Ex	Mint
62	Television Service Van, cream body, green tinted windows w/roof window, four plastic wheels, 1963, 2-1/2" 25		40	50
63	Dodge Challenger, green body, black base, bumpers and grille, clear windows, 1980, 2-7/8" 3		5	7
63	Dodge Crane Truck, yellow body, green windows, six black plastic wheels, rotating crane cab, 1968, 3"long 7		10	15
63	Dodge Crane Truck, yellow body, green windows, four spoke wide wheels, yellow plastic hook, 1970, 2-3/4"........5		7	20
63	Foamite Fire Fighting Crash Tender, red body, six black plastic wheels, white plastic hose and ladder on roof, 1964, 2-1/4" 10		15	40
63	Ford Service Ambulance, olive green body, four plastic wheels, round white circle on sides w/red cross, 1959, 2-1/2" 15		20	45
63	Freeway Gas Truck, red cab, purple tinted windows, small wide wheels on front, cloverleaf design, 1973, 3" 10		15	20

No. 64 Scammel Breakdown Truck. Photo Courtesy Gary Linden.

No.	Name	Good	Ex	Mint
64	MG-1100, ivory interior and tow hook, one occupant and dog, clear windows, 1970, 2-5/8"........................7		10	15
64	MG-1100, green body, ivory interior, driver, dog and tow hook, clear windows, four black plastic wheels, 1966, 2-5/8"........................5		7	15
64	Scammel Breakdown Truck, olive green, double cable hook, six black plastic wheels, 1959, 2-1/2"...............15		25	30
64	Slingshot Dragster, pink body, white driver, five spoke thin front wheels, wide eight-spoke rear wheels, 1971, 3" 7		10	15
65	Airport Coach, white top and roof, metallic blue bottom, amber windows, yellow interior, comes w/varying airline logo decals, 1977, 3".....5		10	15
65	Claas Combine Harvester, red body, yellow plastic rotating blades and front wheels, black plastic front tires, solid rear wheels, 1967, 3"...............7		10	15
65	Jaguar 3.4 Litre Saloon, silver grille, silver or black bumpers, four gray plastic wheels, 1959, 2-1/2"................7		10	15
65	Jaguar 3.8 Litre Sedan, red body shades, green tinted windows, four plastic wheels, 1962, 2-5/8"................5		7	30
65	Saab Sonnet, metallic blue body, amber windows, light orange interior and hood, wide five-spoke wheels, 1973, 2-3/4"...........5		7	10
66	Citroen DS 19, light or dark yellow body, w/or without silver grille, four plastic wheels, 1959, 2-1/2"..............10		30	40

Matchbox boxes, top row, left to right: No. 68 Mercedes-Benz Coach; No. 29 Fire Pumper Truck. Bottom row, left to right: No. 66 Greyhound Bus; No. 61 Alvis Stalwart.

No.	Name	Good	Ex	Mint
66	Ford Transit, orange body, unpainted base, yellow interior, green windows, 1977, 2-3/4".............................2		3	4
66	Greyhound Bus, silver body, white interior, amber windows, thin five-spoke wheels, 1970, 3".....................5		10	20
66	Greyhound Bus, silver body, white plastic interior, clear or dark amber windows, six black plastic wheels, 1967, 3"..............................25		35	45
66	Harley-Davidson Motorcycle/Sidecar, metallic bronze body, three wire wheels, 1962, 2-5/8"...............20		45	75
66	Mazda RX 500, orange body, purple windows, silver rear engine, wide five-spoke wheels, 1971, 3".........................3		4	5
67	Datsun 260Z 2+2, metallic burgundy body, black base and grille, yellow interior, 1978, 3".................3		4	6

No. 67 Volkswagen 1600 TL.

No.	Name	Good	Ex	Mint
67	Hot Rocker, metallic lime/green body, white interior and tow hook, wide five-spoke wheels, 1973, 3".....3		5	7
67	Saladin Armoured Car, olive green body, rotating gun turret, six black plastic wheels, 1959, 2-1/2"...............15		20	25
67	Volkswagen 1600 TL, ivory interior, clear windows, five-spoke wheels, 1970, 2-5/8".......5		10	20
67	Volkswagen 1600 TL, ivory interior, four black plastic tires, 1967, 2-3/4"...................10		15	20

No. 68 Austin MK II Radio Truck. Photo Courtesy Gary Linden.

No.	Name	Good	Ex	Mint
68	Austin MK II Radio Truck, olive green body, four black plastic wheels, 1959, 2-3/8"	20	25	30
68	Chevy Van, orange body, unpainted base and grille, large rear wheels, 1979, 3"	3	5	7
68	Mercedes-Benz Coach, white plastic top half, white plastic interior, clear windows, four black plastic wheels, 1965, 2-7/8"	30	40	55
68	Porsche 910, amber windows, ivory interior, five-spoke wheels, 1970, 2-7/8"	7	10	15
69	Armored Truck, red body, white plastic roof, silver/gray base and grille, "Wells Fargo" on sides, 1978, 2-13/16"	3	5	8
69	Commer 30 CWT Van, silver grille, sliding left side door, four plastic wheels, yellow "Nestle's" decal on upper rear panel, 1959, 2-1/4"	10	30	40
69	Hatra Tractor Shovel, orange or yellow movable shovel arms, four plastic tires, 1965, 3"	20	30	40

No. 69 Commer 30 CWT Van. Photo Courtesy Gary Linden.

No. 70 Dodge Dragster.

No.	Name	Good	Ex	Mint
69	Rolls-Royce Silver Shadow Coupe, amber windshield, five-spoke wheels, 1969, 3"	5	7	10
70	Dodge Dragster, pink body, clear windows, silver interior, wide five-spoke front wheels, 1971, 3"	7	10	15
70	Ferrari 308 GTB, red body and base, black plastic interior, side stripe, 1981, 2-15/16"	2	3	5
70	Ford Thames Estate Car, yellow upper, bluish-green lower, four plastic wheels, 1959, 2-1/8"	10	15	30
70	Grit Spreader Truck, dark red cab, four black plastic wheels, 1966, 2-5/8"	5	7	15

No.	Name	Good	Ex	Mint
70	Grit Spreader Truck, red cab, yellow body, green windows, gray plastic rear pull, 1970, 2-5/8"	6	8	15
71	Austin 200 Gallon Water Truck, olive green body, four black plastic wheels, 1959, 2-3/8"	10	25	30
71	Cattle Truck, metallic brown body, yellow/orange cattle carrier, 1976, 3"	4	6	7
71	Ford Heavy Wreck Truck, red cab, white body, green windows and dome light, wide four-spoke wheels, 1970, 3"	15	25	30
71	Ford Heavy Wreck Truck, red cab, white bumper, amber or green windows, 1968, 3"	25	75	100
71	Jeep Gladiator Pickup Truck, red body, clear windows, green or white interior, four black plastic wheels, fine treads, 1964, 2-5/8"	18	25	30
71	Jumbo Jet Motorcycle, dark metallic blue body, red elephant head on handle bars, wide wheels, 1973, 2-3/4"	4	6	8
72	Bomag Road Roller, yellow body, base and wheel hubs, black plastic roller, 1979, 2-15/16"	2	4	6
72	Fordson Tractor, blue body w/tow hook, 1959, 2"	10	20	25
72	Hovercraft, white body, black bottom and base, red props, 1972, 3"	4	7	10
72	Jeep CJ5, red interior and tow hook, eight-spoke wheels, 1970, 2-3/8"	5	7	10
72	Jeep CJ5, yellow body, red plastic interior and tow hook, four yellow wheels, black plastic tires, 1966, 2-3/8"	10	15	20
72	Maxi Taxi, yellow body, black "MAXI TAXI" on roof, five-spoke wheels, 1973, 3"	2	3	4
73	10 Ton Pressure Refueller, bluish gray body, six gray plastic wheels, 1959, 2-5/8"	20	25	35
73	Ferrari F1 Racing Car, light and dark red body, plastic driver, white and yellow "73" decal on sides, 1962, 2-5/8"	15	25	40
73	Mercury Station Wagon, red body, ribbed rear roof, ivory interior w/two dogs, 1972, 3"	3	5	7
73	Mercury Station Wagon, red body, ribbed rear roof, ivory interior w/two dogs, 1970, 3"	3	5	10
73	Mercury Station Wagon, metallic lime green body shades, ivory interior w/dogs in rear, 1968, 3-1/8"	7	10	15
73	Model A Ford, off white body, black base, green fenders and running boards, 1979	2	3	5
73	Weasel, metallic green body, large five-spoke slicks, 1974, 2-7/8"	3	4	6

No. 73 10 Ton Pressure Refueller. Photo Courtesy Gary Linden.

No.	Name	Good	Ex	Mint
74	Cougar Village, metallic green body, yellow interior, unpainted base, 1978, 3-1/16"	3	4	6
74	Daimler Bus, double deck, white plastic interior, thin five-spoke wheels, 1970, 3"	7	10	20
74	Daimler Bus, double deck, white plastic interior, four black plastic wheels, 1966, 3"	10	15	20
74	Mobile Refreshment Canteen, cream, white, or silver body, upper side door opens w/interior utensils, "Refreshment" on front side, 1959, 2-5/8"	15	40	65
74	Orange Peel, white body, wide orange and black stripe and black "Orange Peel" on each side, 1971, 3"	3	4	5
74	Toe Joe, metallic lime green body, yellow interior, wide five-spoke wheels, 1972, 2-3/4"	3	4	6
75	Alfa Carabo, pink body, ivory interior, black trunk, wide five-spoke wheels, 1971, 3"	3	4	5
75	Ferrari Berlinetta, metallic green body of various shades, ivory interior and tow hook, wire or silver plastic wheels, 1965, 3"	10	20	25
75	Ferrari Berlinetta, ivory interior, thin five-spoke wheels, 1970, 2-3/4"	5	7	25
75	Ford Thunderbird, cream top half, pink bottom half, green tinted windows, 1960, 2-5/8"	25	35	45
75	Seasprite Helicopter, white body, red base, black blades, 1977	3	5	7
Y-1	1936 Jaguar SS 100, 1977	8	10	17
Y-2	1911 'B' Type London Bus, 1955	25	50	90

No. Y-2 1911 Renault 2-Seater.

No.	Name	Good	Ex	Mint
Y-2	1911 Renault 2-Seater, 1963	12	20	36
Y-2	Prince Henry Vauxhall, 1970	8	10	21
Y-3	1907 London 'E' Class Tramcar, 1955	30	75	120
Y-3	1910 Benz Limousine, 1965	10	20	50
Y-3	1934 Riley MPH, 1972	6	10	20
Y-4	Sentinel Steam Wagon, 1955	30	75	120
Y-4	1909 Opel Coupe, 1966	10	15	30
Y-4	1930 Duesenberg Model J, 1976	5	8	10
Y-5	1907 Peugeot, 1968	10	20	35
Y-5	1927 Talbot Van, 1978	5	8	12
Y-5	1929 LeMans Bentley, 1955	20	40	80
Y-5	1929 Supercharged 4-1/2 Litre Bentley, 1960	8	15	30
Y-6	1916 A.E.C. "Y" type Lorry Truck, 1955	25	50	75
Y-6	1913 Cadillac, 1967	12	20	35
Y-6	1926 Type "35" Bugatti, 1961	30	65	90
Y-6	Rolls-Royce Fire Engine, 1978	6	10	15
Y-7	1913 Mercer Raceabout Sportcar, 1961	4	8	15
Y-7	1912 Rolls-Royce, 1967	10	25	50
Y-7	1914 4-Ton Leyland, 1955	50	75	130
Y-8	1914 Sunbeam Motorcycle with Sidecar, 1962	45	80	115

No.	Name	Good	Ex	Mint
Y-8	1914 Stutz Roadster, 1968	10	20	35
Y-8	1926 Morris Cowley "Bullnose", 1955	15	35	65
Y-8	1945 MGTC Sports Car, 1978	5	10	15
Y-9	1924 Fowler "Big Lion" Showman Engine, 1967	10	20	55
Y-9	1912 Simplex, 1967	10	20	55
Y-10	1906 Rolls-Royce Silver Cloud, 1968	8	10	20
Y-10	1908 Grand Prix Mercedes Racing Car, 1957	8	15	30
Y-10	1928 Mercedes-Benz 36/220, 1963	10	20	55
Y-11	1912 Packard Landaulet, 1963	12	25	45
Y-11	1920 Aveling & Porter Steam Roller, 1957	20	45	95
Y-11	1938 Lagonda Drophead Coupe, 1972	5	10	20
Y-12	1899 Horse-Bus (London), 1957	30	60	100
Y-12	1909 Thomas Flyabout, 1967	10	20	45
Y-12	1912 Model "T" Ford, 1979	5	10	15
Y-13	1911 Daimler, 1965	15	30	60
Y-13	1918 Crossley Truck, 1972	5	10	25

No. Y-11 1912 Packard Landaulet.

No.	Name	Good	Ex	Mint
Y-14	1911 Maxwell Roadster, 1965	8	15	30
Y-14	1931 Stutz Bearcat, 1972	4	8	15
Y-15	1907 Rolls-Royce "Silver Ghost", 1960	10	20	50
Y-15	1930 Packard Victoria, 1969	5	10	20
Y-16	1904 Spyker Veteran Automobile, 1961	10	25	50
Y-16	1928 Mercedes SS, 1971	5	10	20
Y-17	1938 Hispano Suiza, 1972	5	10	20
Y-18	1937 Cord 812, 1979	5	10	20
Y-19	1935 Auburn 851, 1980	5	10	20
Y-20	1938 Mercedes 540K, 1981	5	10	20
Y-21	1929 Woody Wagon, 1981	4	8	15
Y-22	Model A Van	4	6	10

Racing Champions

In 1989, Bob Dods, Boyd Meyer and Peter Chung combined their toy sales experience and the growing popularity of NASCAR to form Racing Champions with a single line of 1:64-scale die-cast stock cars. The company went on to become one of the leading manufacturers of NASCAR collectibles, from trading cards to die-cast banks.

The Glen Ellyn, Ill.-based company sells more than 1,500 different styles of racing vehicles in four different scales—1:64, 1:43, 1:24 and 1:18—ranging in retail price from $2 to $60.

By acquiring The Ertl Company, Inc. in April 1999, Racing Champions branched out into the world of agricultural, custom die-cast collectibles and model kits. The combination of the two makes Racing Champions one of the largest die-cast companies in the world.

Market Update

This area of collecting is different from the others represented in this book. Collectors collect Hot Wheels Numbered Packs because they are Hot Wheels, and the same can be said for Corgi, Tootsietoy and Matchbox. Those who collect Racing Champions items do so because of the name associated with the car—Jeff Gordon, Mark Martin, Terry Labonte. And while the popularity of NASCAR the sport remains strong, the value of NASCAR die-cast has been slowing lately. Early Racing Champions lines, like the original line of 1:64-scale stock cars, will hold their value. Other areas will depend on a myriad of factors—sustained popularity of the driver, Winston Cup standing, sponsor and regional fluctuations.

Car	MIP
Allen, Jr., Glenn	
#99 Luxaire, stock car, 1:64-scale, 1997	5
#99-Luxaire, team transporter, 1:64-scale, 1996	20
#99-Luxaire, team transporter, 1:87-scale, 1996	8
#99-Luxaire, stock car, 1:24-scale, 1997	15
Allen, Loy	
#19-Healthsource, stock car, 1:24-scale, 1996	25
#19-Healthsource, stock car, 1:64-scale, 1996	15
Andretti, John	
#37-Kmart, stock car, 1:64-scale, 1996	7
#37-Kmart, stock car, 1:24-scale, 1996	20
#37-Kmart/Little Caesars, team transporter, 1:64-scale, 1996	25
#37-Kmart/Little Caesars, premier stock car, 1:64-scale, 1996	7
#37-Kmart/Little Caesars, stock car, 1:64-scale, 1996	7
Barfield, Ron	
#94-New Holland, stock car, 1:24-scale, 1997	15
#94-New Holland, stock car, 1:64-scale, 1997	5
Bender, Tim	
#17-Kraft, stock car, 1:64-scale, 1997	5
Benson, Jr., Johnny	
#30 Pennzoil, stock car, Pinnacle Series, 1:64-scale, 1997	6
#30-Pennzoil, premier stock car w/opening hood, 1:64-scale, 1996	12
#30-Pennzoil, stock car, 1:64-scale, 1997	5
#30-Pennzoil, stock car, 1:24-scale, 1997	15
#30-Pennzoil, team transporter w/mini stock car, 1:144-scale, 1997	2

Car	MIP
#30-Pennzoil, team transporter w/mini stock car, 1:87-scale, 1997	10
#30-Pennzoil, team transporter, 1:64-scale, 1997	22
#30-Pennzoil, team transporter w/two stock cars, 1:64-scale, 1997	25
#30-Pennzoil, stock car, 1:24-scale, 1996	20
#30-Pennzoil, stock car w/opening hood, 1:24-scale, 1996	50
#30-Pennzoil, premier stock car w/opening hood, 1:18-scale, 1996	30
#30-Pennzoil, team transporter w/mini stock car, 1:87-scale, 1996	8
#30-Pennzoil, team transporter, 1:64-scale, 1996	15
#30-Pennzoil, team transporter w/stock car, 1:64-scale, 1996	25
#30-Pennzoil, team transporter w/two stock cars, 1:64-scale, 1996	25
#30-Pennzoil, team transporter w/stock car, 1:64-scale, 1997	25
#30-Pennzoil/Preview Edition, stock car, 1:64-scale, 1997	5
#30-Pennzoil/Preview Edition, stock car, 1:24-scale, 1997	20
Bessey, Joe	
#9-Delco Remy, premier stock car w/opening hood, 1:18-scale, 1996	30
#9-Delco Remy, stock car w/opening hood, 1:24-scale, 1996	25
#9-Delco Remy, stock car, 1:24-scale, 1996	20
#9-Delco Remy, stock car, 1:64-scale, 1996	5
#9-Delco Remy/Preview Edition, stock car, 1:24-scale, 1996	20
#9-Delco Remy/Preview Edition, stock car, 1:64-scale, 1996	5
#9-Power Team, stock car, 1:24-scale, 1997	15
#9-Power Team, stock car, 1:64-scale, 1997	5
Bodine, Brett	
#11-Frontier, stock car, 1:24-scale, 1997	15

Car	MIP
#11-Frontier, team transporter, 1:64-scale, 1997	22
#11-Frontier, team transporter w/stock car, 1:64-scale, 1997	25
#11-Frontier, team transporter w/two stock cars, 1:64-scale, 1997	25
#11-Frontier, stock car, 1:64-scale, 1997	5
#11-Frontier, team transporter w/mini stock car, 1:144-scale, 1997	3
#11-Frontier, team transporter w/mini stock car, 1:87-scale, 1997	10
#11-Lowe's, stock car, 1:64-scale, 1996	4
#11-Lowe's, premier stock car w/opening hood, 1:64-scale, 1996	8
#11-Lowe's, stock car, 1:24-scale, 1996	20
#11-Lowe's, stock car w/opening hood, 1:24-scale, 1996	25
#11-Lowe's, team transporter w/mini stock car, 1:87-scale, 1996	8
#11-Lowe's, team transporter, 1:64-scale, 1996	15
#11-Lowe's, team transporter w/stock car, 1:64-scale, 1996	25
#11-Lowe's, team transporter w/two stock cars, 1:64-scale, 1996	25
#11-Lowe's, premier team transporter w/stock car, 1:64-scale, 1996	20
#11-Lowe's 50th Anniversary, stock car, 1:64-scale, 1996	15
#11-Lowe's Gold, stock car, 1:24-scale, 1996	40
#11-Lowe's/Preview Edition, team transporter, 1:64-scale, 1996	15
#11-Lowe's/Preview Edition, team transporter w/mini stock car, 1:87-scale, 1996	8
#11-Lowe's/Preview Edition, team transporter w/stock car, 1:64-scale, 1996	25
#11-Lowe's/Preview Edition, stock car, 1:24-scale, 1996	20

Bodine, Geoff

Car	MIP
#7 QVC, stock car, Pinnacle Series, 1:64-scale, 1997	6

Car	MIP
#7-QVC, team transporter w/stock car, 1:64-scale, 1997	25
#7-QVC, stock car, 1:64-scale, 1997	5
#7-QVC, premier stock car w/opening hood, 1:64-scale, 1997	8
#7-QVC, roaring racer stock car w/real engine sounds, 1:64-scale, 1997	25
#7-QVC, stock car, 1:24-scale, 1997	15
#7-QVC, team transporter w/mini stock car, 1:144-scale, 1997	5
#7-QVC, team transporter, 1:64-scale, 1997	20
#7-QVC, stock car, 1:64-scale, 1996	5
#7-QVC, premier stock car w/opening hood, 1:64-scale, 1996	10
#7-QVC, stock car, 1:24-scale, 1996	20
#7-QVC, premier stock car w/opening hood, 1:18-scale, 1996	30
#7-QVC, team transporter w/mini stock car, 1:87-scale, 1996	8
#7-QVC, team transporter, 1:64-scale, 1996	15
#7-QVC, team transporter w/mini stock car, 1:87-scale, 1997	10
#7-QVC/Chrome, premier stock car w/opening hood, 1:64-scale, 1997	8
#7-QVC/Preview Edition, team transporter w/mini stock car, 1:144-scale, 1997	2
#7-QVC/Preview Edition, team transporter, 1:64-scale, 1997	20
#7-QVC/Preview Edition, team transporter w/mini stock car, 1:87-scale, 1997	10

Bodine, Todd

Car	MIP
#36-Stanley Tools, team transporter, 1:64-scale, 1997	20
#36-Stanley Tools, team transporter w/mini stock car, 1:87-scale, 1997	11
#36-Stanley Tools, team transporter w/mini stock car, 1:144-scale, 1997	3
#36-Stanley Tools, stock car, 1:64-scale, 1997	5

Car	MIP

Bown, Jim

#51-Lucks, premier stock car w/opening hood, 1:18-scale, 1996 30

#51-Lucks, stock car w/opening hood, 1:24-scale, 1996..........................25

#51-Lucks, stock car, 1:64-scale, 1996 4

#57-Matco Tools, premier stock car w/opening hood, 1:18-scale, 1996 40

#57-Matco Tools, premier stock car w/opening hood, 1:64-scale, 1996 12

Bradberry, Gary

#19-Child Support Recovery, stock car, 1:24-scale, 1997 15

Burton, Jeff

#9-Track Gear, team transporter w/mini stock car, 1:87-scale, 1998 10

#9-Track Gear, stock car, 1:64-scale, 1998 4

#99 Exide, stock car, Pinnacle Series, 1:64-scale, 1997.............................6

#99-Exide, team transporter, 1:64-scale, 1996 20

#99-Exide, stock car, 1:24-scale, 1996.....................20

#99-Exide, stock car, 1:64-scale, 1996.....................5

#99-Exide, team transporter, 1:64-scale, 1998 8

#99-Exide, team transporter w/mini stock car, 1:87-scale, 1998...........................10

#99-Exide, stock car, 1:24-scale, 1998........................

#99-Exide, premier stock car, 1:64-scale, 1998 6

#99-Exide, premier stock car w/opening hood, 1:64-scale, 1998 8

#99-Exide, stock car, 1:64-scale, 1998.....................4

#99-Exide Chrome, stock car, 1:64-scale, 1998.............................4

#99-Exide/Preview Edition, stock car, 1:64-scale, 1998.............................4

Burton, Ward

#22-MBNA, team transporter w/stock car, 1:64-scale, 1996...................25

#22-MBNA, team transporter, 1:64-scale, 1996 20

#22-MBNA, team transporter w/mini stock car, 1:87-scale, 1996..........................8

#22-MBNA, premier stock car w/opening hood, 1:18-scale, 1996...30

#22-MBNA, stock car, 1:24-scale, 1996...20

#22-MBNA, premier stock car w/opening hood, 1:64-scale, 1996...12

#22-MBNA, stock car, 1:64-scale, 1996...15

#22-MBNA/Preview Edition, stock car, 1:24-scale, 1996 20

#22-MBNA/Preview Edition, stock car, 1:64-scale, 1996 15

Combs, Rodney

#43-Lance Snacks, team transporter, 1:64-scale, 1996 20

#43-Lance Snacks, team transporter w/mini stock car, 1:87-scale, 1996...8

#43-Lance Snacks, stock car, 1:64-scale, 1996 5

#43-Lance Snacks, team transporter, 1:64-scale, 1997 20

#43-Lance Snacks, team transporter w/mini stock car, 1:87-scale, 1997...10

#43-Lance Snacks, team transporter w/mini stock car, 1:144-scale, 1997 3

#43-Lance Snacks, stock car, 1:64-scale, 1997 5

Cope, Derrike

#12-Badcock, stock car, 1:64-scale, 1996...12

#12-Mane 'N Tail/Preview Edition, team transporter w/stock car, 1:64-scale, 1996 25

#12-Mane 'N Tail/Preview Edition, team transporter, 1:64-scale, 1996...15

#12-Mane 'N Tail/Preview Edition, team transporter w/mini stock car, 1:87-scale, 1996 8

#12-Mane 'N Tail/Preview Edition, stock car, 1:24-scale, 1996 20

Car	MIP
#12-Mane 'N Tail/Preview Edition, team transporter w/two stock cars, 1:64-scale, 1996	25
#36 Skittles, stock car, Pinnacle Series, 1:64-scale, 1997	6
#36-Skittles, team transporter w/two stock cars, 1:64-scale, 1997	25
#36-Skittles, premier stock car w/opening hood, 1:64-scale, 1997	8
#36-Skittles, stock car, 1:24-scale, 1997	15
#36-Skittles, stock car w/opening hood, 1:24-scale, 1997	25
#36-Skittles, team transporter w/mini stock car, 1:144-scale, 1997	3
#36-Skittles, team transporter w/mini stock car, 1:87-scale, 1997	10
#36-Skittles, team transporter, 1:64-scale, 1997	20
#36-Skittles, stock car, 1:64-scale, 1997	5
#36-Skittles, team transporter w/stock car, 1:64-scale, 1997	30
#36-Skittles/Premier Gold, premier stock car w/opening hood, 1:18-scale, 1997	400
#36-Skittles/Premier Gold, premier stock car w/opening hood, 1:24-scale, 1997	85

Cope, Mike

Car	MIP
#58-Penrose, stock car, 1:64-scale, 1996	5

Craven, Ricky

Car	MIP
#2-DuPont, stock car, 1:64-scale, 1996	5
#2-DuPont, premier stock car w/opening hood, 1:18-scale, 1996	30
#2-DuPont, stock car w/opening hood, 1:24-scale, 1996	25
#2-DuPont, stock car, 1:24-scale, 1996	20
#2-DuPont, premier stock car w/opening hood, 1:64-scale, 1996	12
#2-DuPont Teflon/Preview Edition, premier stock car w/opening hood, 1:18-scale, 1996	30

Car	MIP
#2-DuPont Teflon/Preview Edition, stock car, 1:64-scale, 1996	5
#2-DuPont Teflon/Preview Edition, stock car w/opening hood, 1:24-scale, 1996	25
#2-DuPont Teflon/Preview Edition, stock car, 1:24-scale, 1996	20
#2-Raybestos, team transporter, 1:64-scale, 1997	20
#2-Raybestos, team transporter w/mini stock car, 1:87-scale, 1997	12
#2-Raybestos, team transporter w/mini stock car, 1:144-scale, 1997	5
#2-Raybestos, stock car, 1:24-scale, 1997	15
#2-Raybestos, stock car, 1:64-scale, 1997	5
#25-Hendrick Motorsports, stock car, 1:64-scale, 1997	5
#25-Hendrick Motorsports, stock car, 1:24-scale, 1997	15
#41-Hendrick, stock car, 1:64-scale, 1996	5
#41-Hendrick, premier stock car w/opening hood, 1:64-scale, 1996	12
#41-Hendrick, stock car, 1:24-scale, 1996	18
#41-Kodak, stock car, 1:64-scale, 1996	5

Dallenbach, Wally

Car	MIP
#15-Hayes Modems, team transporter, 1:64-scale, 1996	25
#15-Hayes Modems, team transporter w/mini stock car, 1:87-scale, 1996	8
#15-Hayes Modems, premier stock car w/opening hood, 1:18-scale, 1996	40
#15-Hayes Modems, stock car, 1:24-scale, 1996	50
#15-Hayes Modems, premier stock car w/opening hood, 1:64-scale, 1996	18
#46-First Union, premier stock car w/opening hood, 1:64-scale, 1997	8
#46-First Union, stock car, 1:64-scale, 1997	5

Car	MIP
#46-First Union, team transporter w/two stock cars, 1:64-scale, 1997	25
#46-First Union, team transporter w/stock car, 1:64-scale, 1997	25
#46-First Union, team transporter, 1:64-scale, 1997	20
#46-First Union, team transporter w/mini stock car, 1:87-scale, 1997	10
#46-First Union, team transporter w/mini stock car, 1:144-scale, 1997	2
#46-First Union, stock car, 1:24-scale, 1997	15
#46-First Union, roaring racer stock car w/real engine sounds, 1:64-scale, 1997	23

Dillon, Mike

Car	MIP
#72-Detroit Gasket, team transporter w/mini stock car, 1:144-scale, 1997	5
#72-Detroit Gasket, stock car, 1:24-scale, 1997	15
#72-Detroit Gasket, stock car, 1:64-scale, 1997	5

Elliott, Bill

Car	MIP
#94 McDonald's, stock car, Pinnacle Series, 1:64-scale, 1997	6
#94-Mac Tonight, team transporter, 1:64-scale, 1997	25
#94-Mac Tonight, stock car, 1:64-scale, 1997	5
#94-Mac Tonight, premier stock car w/opening hood, 1:64-scale, 1997	8
#94-Mac Tonight, roaring racer stock car w/real engine sounds, 1:64-scale, 1997	30
#94-Mac Tonight, stock car, 1:24-scale, 1997	20
#94-Mac Tonight, team transporter w/mini stock car, 1:87-scale, 1997	15
#94-Mac Tonight, team transporter w/mini stock car, 1:144-scale, 1997	4
#94-McDonalds, premier team transporter w/premier stock car, 1:64-scale, 1996	25

Car	MIP
#94-McDonalds, team transporter w/mini stock car, 1:87-scale, 1997	15
#94-McDonalds, team transporter, 1:64-scale, 1997	20
#94-McDonalds, team transporter w/stock car, 1:64-scale, 1997	32
#94-McDonalds, team transporter w/two stock cars, 1:64-scale, 1997	25
#94-McDonalds, premier team transporter w/premier stock car, 1:64-scale, 1997	25
#94-McDonalds, stock car w/opening hood and display stand, 1:24-scale, 1997	30
#94-McDonalds, stock car, 1:24-scale, 1997	20
#94-McDonalds, team transporter w/mini stock car, 1:144-scale, 1997	4
#94-McDonalds, roaring racer stock car w/real engine sounds, 1:64-scale, 1997	25
#94-McDonalds, team transporter w/two stock cars, 1:64-scale, 1996	25
#94-McDonalds, premier stock car w/Pinnacle collector card, opening hood, display stand and serial numbers, 1:64-scale, 1997	12
#94-McDonalds, stock car, 1:64-scale, 1997	5
#94-McDonalds, stock car, 1:64-scale, 1996	5
#94-McDonalds, premier stock car w/opening hood, 1:64-scale, 1996	12
#94-McDonalds, stock car, 1:24-scale, 1996	20
#94-McDonalds, stock car w/opening hood and display stand, 1:24-scale, 1996	30
#94-McDonalds, premier stock car w/opening hood, 1:18-scale, 1996	30
#94-McDonalds, team transporter w/mini stock car, 1:87-scale, 1996	8
#94-McDonalds, team transporter, 1:64-scale, 1996	20

Car	MIP
#94-McDonalds, team transporter w/stock car, 1:64-scale, 1996	25
#94-McDonalds/Hurry Back, stock car, 1:24-scale, 1996	20
#94-McDonalds/Hurry Back, stock car, 1:64-scale, 1996	5
#94-McDonalds/Premier Gold, premier stock car w/opening hood, painted interior and serial number on chassis, 1:18-scale, 1997	400
#94-McDonalds/Premier Gold, premier stock car w/opening hood, painted interior and serial number on chassis, 1:24-scale, 1997	90
#94-McDonalds/Preview Edition, stock car, 1:64-scale, 1997	5
#94-McDonalds/Preview Edition, premier stock car w/opening hood, 1:64-scale, 1997	8
#94-McDonalds/Preview Edition, stock car, 1:64-scale, 1996	4
#94-McDonalds/Preview Edition, stock car, 1:24-scale, 1996	20
#94-McDonalds/Preview Edition, stock car, 1:24-scale, 1997	15
#94-Monopoly, stock car w/opening hood and display stand, 1:24-scale, 1996	30
#94-Monopoly, premier stock car w/opening hood, 1:18-scale, 1996	30
#94-Monopoly, stock car, 1:24-scale, 1996	25
#94-Monopoly, premier stock car w/opening hood, 1:64-scale, 1996	12
#94-Monopoly, team transporter w/stock car, 1:64-scale, 1996	25

Fedewa, Tim

Car	MIP
#40-Kleenex, stock car, 1:64-scale, 1996	5
#40-Kleenex, stock car, 1:64-scale, 1997	5
#40-Kleenex/Preview Edition, team transporter, 1:64-scale, 1996	20
#40-Kleenex/Preview Edition, stock car, 1:24-scale, 1996	20
#40-Kleenex/Preview Edition, stock car, 1:64-scale, 1996	5

Foster, Jimmy

Car	MIP
#11-Speedvision, team transporter w/two stock cars, 1:64-scale, 1997	30
#11-Speedvision, team transporter w/stock car, 1:64-scale, 1997	30
#11-Speedvision, team transporter, 1:64-scale, 1997	22
#11-Speedvision, team transporter w/mini stock car, 1:87-scale, 1997	10
#11-Speedvision, team transporter w/mini stock car, 1:144-scale, 1997	3
#11-Speedvision, stock car, 1:64-scale, 1997	5

Fuller, Jeff

Car	MIP
#47-Sunoco, team transporter, 1:64-scale, 1996	25
#47-Sunoco, premier stock car w/opening hood, 1:18-scale, 1996	30
#47-Sunoco, stock car w/opening hood and display stand, 1:24-scale, 1996	40
#47-Sunoco, stock car, 1:64-scale, 1996	10
#47-Sunoco, stock car, 1:24-scale, 1997	15
#47-Sunoco, roaring racer stock car w/real engine sounds, 1:64-scale, 1997	22
#47-Sunoco, stock car, 1:64-scale, 1997	5
#47-Sunoco/Preview Edition, team transporter w/two stock cars, 1:64-scale, 1996	30
#47-Sunoco/Preview Edition, team transporter w/stock car, 1:64-scale, 1996	30
#47-Sunoco/Preview Edition, team transporter, 1:64-scale, 1996	25
#47-Sunoco/Preview Edition, team transporter w/mini stock car, 1:87-scale, 1996	10
#47-Sunoco/Preview Edition, stock car w/opening hood and display stand, 1:24-scale, 1996	20

Car	MIP
#47-Sunoco/Preview Edition, stock car, 1:24-scale, 1996	20
#47-Sunoco/Preview Edition, stock car, 1:64-scale, 1996	5

Gannon, Kevin

Car	MIP
#32 Chevy, stock car, 1:24-scale, 1996	20
#32 Ford, stock car, 1:24-scale, 1996	20

Glenn, Jr., Allen

Car	MIP
#24-DuPont, premier stock car w/opening hood, 1:64-scale, 1996	15
#24-DuPont, stock car, 1:64-scale, 1997	10
#24-DuPont, stock car, 1:24-scale, 1997	25
#24-DuPont, team transporter w/mini stock car, 1:144-scale, 1997	15
#24-DuPont, stock car, 1:64-scale, 1996	30
#24-DuPont, stock car, 1:24-scale, 1996	40
#24-DuPont, stock car w/opening hood and display stand, 1:24-scale, 1996	40
#24-DuPont, premier stock car w/opening hood, 1:18-scale, 1996	40
#24-DuPont, team transporter w/mini stock car, 1:87-scale, 1996	20
#24-DuPont, team transporter, 1:64-scale, 1996	25
#24-DuPont, team transporter w/stock car, 1:64-scale, 1996	25
#24-DuPont, premier team transporter w/premier stock car, 1:64-scale, 1996	30
#24-DuPont Chrome, stock car bank w/opening hood, 1:24-scale, 1996	40
#24-DuPont/Preview Edition, team transporter w/mini stock car, 1:144-scale, 1997	15
#24-DuPont/Preview Edition, stock car, 1:24-scale, 1997	25
#24-DuPont/Preview Edition, premier stock car w/opening hood, 1:64-scale, 1997	8
#24-DuPont/Preview Edition, stock car, 1:64-scale, 1997	5

Car	MIP
#24-DuPont/Preview Edition, stock car, 1:24-scale, 1996	20
#99-Luxaire, stock car, 1:24-scale, 1996	20

Gordon, Robby

Car	MIP
#40-Coors, premier team transporter w/premier stock car, 1:64-scale, 1997	25
#40-Coors, tam transporter w/stock car, 1:64-scale, 1997	25
#40-Coors, stock car, 1:64-scale, 1997	5
#40-Coors/Premier Gold, premier stock car w/opening hood, painted interior and serial number on chassis, 1:18-scale, 1997	410
#40-Coors/Premier Gold, premier stock car w/opening hood, painted interior and serial number on chassis, 1:24-scale, 1997	45
#40-Sabco, team transporter w/two stock cars, 1:64-scale, 1997	25
#40-Sabco, team transporter w/stock car, 1:64-scale, 1997	25
#40-Sabco, team transporter, 1:64-scale, 1997	20
#40-Sabco, team transporter w/mini stock car, 1:87-scale, 1997	10
#40-Sabco, team transporter w/mini stock car, 1:144-scale, 1997	3
#40-Sabco, stock car, 1:24-scale, 1997	15
#40-Sabco, roaring racer stock car w/real engine sounds, 1:64-scale, 1997	25
#40-Sabco, premier stock car w/opening hood, 1:64-scale, 1997	8
#40-Sabco, stock car, 1:64-scale, 1997	5

Green, David

Car	MIP
#96 Caterpillar, stock car, Pinnacle Series, 1:64-scale, 1997	6
#96-Busch, stock car, 1:24-scale, 1996	35
#96-Busch, premier stock car w/opening hood, 1:64-scale, 1996	12

Car	MIP
#96-Busch, stock car, 1:64-scale, 1996	12
#96-Busch Chrome, stock car bank w/opening hood, 1:24-scale, 1996	200
#96-Caterpillar, team transporter, 1:64-scale, 1997	20
#96-Caterpillar, premier stock car w/opening hood, 1:64-scale, 1997	14
#96-Caterpillar, premier stock car w/Pinnacle collector card, opening hood, display stand and serial numbers, 1:64-scale, 1997	12
#96-Caterpillar, roaring racer stock car w/real engine sounds, 1:64-scale, 1997	20
#96-Caterpillar, stock car, 1:24-scale, 1997	15
#96-Caterpillar, stock car w/opening hood and display stand, 1:24-scale, 1997	20
#96-Caterpillar, premier stock car w/opening hood, 1:18-scale, 1997	40
#96-Caterpillar, stock car bank w/opening hood and display stand, 1:24-scale, 1997	35
#96-Caterpillar, stock car, 1:64-scale, 1997	5
#96-Caterpillar, team transporter w/mini stock car, 1:87-scale, 1997	13
#96-Caterpillar, team transporter w/stock car, 1:64-scale, 1997	25
#96-Caterpillar, team transporter w/two stock cars, 1:64-scale, 1997	25
#96-Caterpillar, premier team transporter w/premier stock car, 1:64-scale, 1997	25
#96-Caterpillar, team transporter w/mini stock car, 1:144-scale, 1997	2

Green, Jeff

Car	MIP
#29-Cartoon Network, team transporter, 1:64-scale, 1997	20
#29-Cartoon Network, team transporter w/mini stock car, 1:87-scale, 1997	11

Car	MIP
#29-Cartoon Network, team transporter w/mini stock car, 1:144-scale, 1997	3
#29-Cartoon Network, stock car, 1:24-scale, 1997	15
#29-Cartoon Network, stock car, 1:64-scale, 1997	5

Grissom, Steve

Car	MIP
#29-Hanna Barbera Flintstones, premier team transporter w/premir stock car, 1:64-scale, 1996	20
#29-Hanna Barbera Flintstones, stock car, 1:24-scale, 1996	20
#29-Hanna Barbera Flintstones, stock car w/opening hood and display stand, 1:24-scale, 1996	25
#29-Hanna Barbera Flintstones, premier stock car w/opening hood, 1:18-scale, 1996	30
#29-Hanna Barbera Flintstones, team transporter w/mini stock car, 1:87-scale, 1996	8
#29-Hanna Barbera Flintstones, team transporter, 1:64-scale, 1996	25
#29-Hanna Barbera Flintstones, team transporter w/stock car, 1:64-scale, 1996	25
#29-Hanna Barbera Flintstones, stock car, 1:64-scale, 1996	10
#29-WCW, premier stock car w/opening hood, 1:64-scale, 1996	12
#29-WCW, premier team transporter w/premier stock car, 1:64-scale, 1996	25
#29-WCW, stock car, 1:24-scale, 1996	20
#29-WCW, stock car w/opening hood and display stand, 1:24-scale, 1996	25
#29-WCW, premier stock car w/opening hood, 1:18-scale, 1996	30
#29-WCW, team transporter w/mini stock car, 1:87-scale, 1996	8
#29-WCW, team transporter, 1:64-scale, 1996	20
#29-WCW, team transporter w/stock car, 1:64-scale, 1996	25

Car	MIP
#29-WCW, team transporter w/two stock cars, 1:64-scale, 1996	25
#29-WCW, stock car, 1:64-scale, 1996	10

Hamilton, Bobby

Car	MIP
#43-STP 1972 Blue Pontiac on 1996 Pontiac body, stock car, 1:64-scale, 1996	10
#43-STP 1979 Blue/Red Pontiac on 1996 Pontiac body, stock car, 1:64-scale, 1996	10
#43-STP 1984 Blue/Red Pontiac on 1996 Pontiac body, stock car, 1:64-scale, 1996	10
#43-STP 1996 Silver Pontiac, premier team transporter w/premier stock car, 1:64-scale, 1996	25
#43-STP 1996 Silver Pontiac, team transporter, 1:64-scale, 1996	20
#43-STP 1996 Silver Pontiac, team transporter w/mini stock car, 1:87-scale, 1996	8
#43-STP 1996 Silver Pontiac, premier stock car w/opening hood, 1:18-scale, 1996	40
#43-STP 1996 Silver Pontiac, stock car, 1:24-scale, 1996	25
#43-STP 1996 Silver Pontiac, premier stock car w/opening hood, 1:64-scale, 1996	15
#43-STP 1996 Silver Pontiac, stock car, 1:64-scale, 1996	20

Houston, Tommy

Car	MIP
#6-Suburban Propane, stock car, 1:24-scale, 1996	20
#6-Suburban Propane, stock car, 1:64-scale, 1996	5

Irvan, Ernie

Car	MIP
#28 Havoline, stock car, Pinnacle Series, 1:64-scale, 1997	6
#28-Texaco, team transporter w/stock car, 1:64-scale, 1997	28
#28-Texaco, stock car, 1:64-scale, 1997	5
#28-Texaco, premier stock car w/opening hood, 1:64-scale, 1997	10

Car	MIP
#28-Texaco, premier stock car w/Pinnacle collector card, opening hood, display stand and serial numbers, 1:64-scale, 1997	15
#28-Texaco, roaring racer stock car w/real engine sounds, 1:64-scale, 1997	30
#28-Texaco, stock car, 1:24-scale, 1997	15
#28-Texaco, team transporter w/mini stock car, 1:144-scale, 1997	15
#28-Texaco, team transporter, 1:64-scale, 1997	22
#28-Texaco, stock car, 1:64-scale, 1996	4
#28-Texaco, premier stock car w/opening hood, 1:64-scale, 1996	12
#28-Texaco, stock car, 1:24-scale, 1996	20
#28-Texaco, stock car w/opening hood and display stand, 1:24-scale, 1996	30
#28-Texaco, team transporter w/mini stock car, 1:87-scale, 1996	8
#28-Texaco, team transporter, 1:64-scale, 1996	20
#28-Texaco, team transporter w/stock car, 1:64-scale, 1996	25
#28-Texaco, team transporter w/two stock cars, 1:64-scale, 1996	25
#28-Texaco, team transporter w/mini stock car, 1:87-scale, 1997	13
#28-Texaco Anneversary, stock car, 1:24-scale, 1997	30
#28-Texaco/Preview Edition, stock car, 1:64-scale, 1997	5
#28-Texaco/Preview Edition, stock car, 1:24-scale, 1997	15

Jarrett, Dale

Car	MIP
#32-Gillette, roaring racer stock car w/real engine sounds, 1:64-scale, 1997	22
#32-Gillette, stock car, 1:24-scale, 1997	15
#32-Gillette, team transporter w/mini stock car, 1:144-scale, 1997	5
#32-Gillette, team transporter w/mini stock car, 1:87-scale, 1997	11

Car	MIP
#32-Gillette, team transporter, 1:64-scale, 1997	20
#32-Gillette, team transporter w/stock car, 1:64-scale, 1997	25
#32-Gillette, stock car, 1:64-scale, 1997	5
#32-White Rain, team transporter w/two stock cars, 1:64-scale, 1997	25
#88-Ford Quality Care, premier stock car w/opening hood, 1:64-scale, 1996	12
#88-Ford Quality Care, premier team transporter w/premier stock car, 1:64-scale, 1996	25
#88-Ford Quality Care, stock car, 1:24-scale, 1996	20
#88-Ford Quality Care, stock car w/opening hood and display stand, 1:24-scale, 1996	30
#88-Ford Quality Care, premier stock car w/opening hood, 1:18-scale, 1996	30
#88-Ford Quality Care, team transporter w/mini stock car, 1:87-scale, 1996	8
#88-Ford Quality Care, team transporter, 1:64-scale, 1996	20
#88-Ford Quality Care, team transporter w/stock car, 1:64-scale, 1996	25
#88-Ford Quality Care, team transporter w/two stock cars, 1:64-scale, 1996	25
#88-Ford Quality Care, stock car, 1:64-scale, 1996	12

Jones, Buckshot

Car	MIP
#00-Aquafresh, stock car, 1:64-scale, 1997	5

Keller, Jason

Car	MIP
#57-Halloween Havoc, stock car, 1:24-scale, 1996	20
#57-Halloween Havoc, stock car, 1:64-scale, 1996	5
#57-Slim Jim, stock car, 1:64-scale, 1996	5
#57-Slim Jim, premier stock car w/opening hood, 1:18-scale, 1996	30
#57-Slim Jim, team transporter w/stock car, 1:64-scale, 1997	25

Car	MIP
#57-Slim Jim, team transporter, 1:64-scale, 1997	20
#57-Slim Jim, team transporter w/mini stock car, 1:87-scale, 1997	10
#57-Slim Jim, team transporter w/mini stock car, 1:144-scale, 1997	5
#57-Slim Jim, stock car, 1:24-scale, 1997	15
#57-Slim Jim, stock car, 1:64-scale, 1997	5
#57-Slim Jim/Preview Edition, stock car w/opening hood and display stand, 1:24-scale, 1996	25
#57-Slim Jim/Preview Edition, stock car, 1:24-scale, 1996	20
#57-Slim Jim/Preview Edition, stock car, 1:64-scale, 1996	5

Labonte, Bobby

Car	MIP
#18 Interstate Battery, stock car, Pinnacle Series, 1:64-scale, 1997	6
#18-Interstate, stock car, 1:24-scale, 1996	25
#18-Interstate, team transporter w/mini stock car, 1:87-scale, 1997	10
#18-Interstate, team transporter, 1:64-scale, 1997	30
#18-Interstate, team transporter w/stock car, 1:64-scale, 1997	25
#18-Interstate, team transporter w/two stock cars, 1:64-scale, 1997	25
#18-Interstate, premier stock car w/opening hood, 1:18-scale, 1997	45
#18-Interstate, stock car w/opening hood and display stand, 1:24-scale, 1997	20
#18-Interstate, stock car, 1:24-scale, 1997	15
#18-Interstate, roaring racer stock car w/real engine sounds, 1:64-scale, 1997	25
#18-Interstate, team transporter w/mini stock car, 1:144-scale, 1997	5

Car	MIP
#18-Interstate, premier stock car w/opening hood, 1:64-scale, 1996	12
#18-Interstate, premier stock car w/opening hood, 1:18-scale, 1996	30
#18-Interstate, team transporter w/mini stock car, 1:87-scale, 1996	8
#18-Interstate, team transporter, 1:64-scale, 1996	20
#18-Interstate, team transporter w/stock car, 1:64-scale, 1996	30
#18-Interstate, team transporter w/two stock cars, 1:64-scale, 1996	30
#18-Interstate, premier stock car w/Pinnacle collector card, opening hood, display stand and serial numbers, 1:64-scale, 1997	12
#18-Interstate, premier stock car w/opening hood, 1:64-scale, 1997	8
#18-Interstate, stock car, 1:64-scale, 1997	5
#18-Interstate, stock car, 1:64-scale, 1996	4
#18-Interstate/Premier Gold, premier stock car w/opening hood, painted interior and serial number on chassis, 1:18-scale, 1997	340
#18-Interstate/Preview Edition, team transporter, 1:64-scale, 1996	20
#18-Interstate/Preview Edition, stock car, 1:24-scale, 1997	20
#18-Interstate/Preview Edition, premier stock car w/opening hood, 1:64-scale, 1997	8
#18-Interstate/Preview Edition, stock car, 1:64-scale, 1997	5
#18-Interstate/Preview Edition, team transporter w/mini stock car, 1:87-scale, 1996	8
#18-Interstate/Preview Edition, team transporter w/stock car, 1:64-scale, 1996	30
#18-Interstate/Preview Edition, team transporter w/two stock cars, 1:64-scale, 1996	30
#18-Interstate/Preview Edition, stock car, 1:24-scale, 1996	25

Car	MIP
#44-Shell, stock car, 1:64-scale, 1996	10
#44-Shell, premier stock car w/opening hood, 1:64-scale, 1996	25
#44-Shell, stock car, 1:24-scale, 1996	30
#44-Shell, team transporter w/mini stock car, 1:87-scale, 1996	8
#44-Shell, team transporter, 1:64-scale, 1996	25

Labonte, Terry

Car	MIP
#5 Kellogg's, stock car, Pinnacle Series, 1:64-scale, 1997	8
#5-Bayer, stock car, 1:24-scale, 1996	30
#5-Bayer, stock car, 1:64-scale, 1997	5
#5-Bayer, premier stock car w/opening hood, 1:64-scale, 1996	12
#5-Bayer, stock car w/opening hood and display stand, 1:24-scale, 1996	35
#5-Bayer, premier stock car w/opening hood, 1:18-scale, 1996	30
#5-Bayer, team transporter, 1:64-scale, 1996	30
#5-Bayer, team transporter, 1:64-scale, 1997	20
#5-Bayer, team transporter w/mini stock car, 1:87-scale, 1997	13
#5-Bayer, stock car, 1:24-scale, 1997	25
#5-Bayer, team transporter w/mini stock car, 1:144-scale, 1997	6
#5-Bayer, stock car, 1:64-scale, 1996	4
#5-Bayer/Preview Edition, stock car, 1:64-scale, 1996	5

1997 Pinnacle Series, 1:64-scale, left to right: David Green, #96 Caterpillar; Terry Labonte, #5 Kellogg's; Sterling Marlin, #4 Kodak; Hut Stricklin, #8 Circuit City. Photo Courtesy Racing Champions.

Car	MIP
#5-Bayer/Preview Edition, stock car, 1:24-scale, 1996	20
#5-Kellogg's, team transporter w/mini stock car, 1:87-scale, 1997	13
#5-Kellogg's, team transporter, 1:64-scale, 1997	25
#5-Kellogg's, team transporter w/stock car, 1:64-scale, 1997	25
#5-Kellogg's, team transporter w/two stock cars, 1:64-scale, 1997	30
#5-Kellogg's, premier team transporter w/premier stock car, 1:64-scale, 1997	25
#5-Kellogg's, stock car w/opening hood and display stand, 1:24-scale, 1997	35
#5-Kellogg's, stock car, 1:24-scale, 1997	20
#5-Kellogg's, team transporter w/two stock cars, 1:64-scale, 1996	35
#5-Kellogg's, roaring racer stock car w/real engine sounds, 1:64-scale, 1997	25
#5-Kellogg's, team transporter w/stock car, 1:64-scale, 1996	35
#5-Kellogg's, premier stock car w/Pinnacle collector card, opening hood, display stand and serial numbers, 1:64-scale, 1997	15
#5-Kellogg's, stock car, 1:64-scale, 1997	5
#5-Kellogg's, team transporter w/mini stock car, 1:144-scale, 1997	5
#5-Kellogg's, team transporter, 1:64-scale, 1996	30
#5-Kellogg's, team transporter w/mini stock car, 1:87-scale, 1996	8

Terry Labonte, #5-Kellogg's.

Car	MIP
#5-Kellogg's, stock car w/opening hood and display stand, 1:24-scale, 1996	35
#5-Kellogg's, stock car, 1:24-scale, 1996	20
#5-Kellogg's, stock car, 1:64-scale, 1996	5
#5-Kellogg's, premier stock car w/opening hood, 1:64-scale, 1997	12
#5-Kellogg's Ironman, stock car, 1:64-scale, 1996	15
#5-Kellogg's Ironman, premier stock car w/opening hood, 1:64-scale, 1996	12
#5-Kellogg's Tony the Tiger, team transporter w/mini stock car, 1:87-scale, 1997	13
#5-Kellogg's Tony the Tiger, stock car, 1:64-scale, 1997	8
#5-Kellogg's Tony the Tiger, team transporter w/mini stock car, 1:144-scale, 1997	5
#5-Kellogg's Tony the Tiger, team transporter, 1:64-scale, 1997	25
#5-Kellogg's Tony the Tiger, team transporter w/stock car, 1:64-scale, 1997	25
#5-Kellogg's Tony the Tiger, team transporter w/two stock cars, 1:64-scale, 1997	25
#5-Kellogg's Tony the Tiger, stock car, 1:24-scale, 1997	30
#5-Kellogg's/Premier Gold, premier stock car w/opening hood, painted interior and serial number on chassis, 1:24-scale, 1997	125
#5-Kellogg's/Preview Edition, team transporter w/mini stock car, 1:87-scale, 1997	13
#5-Kellogg's/Preview Edition, team transporter, 1:64-scale, 1996	25
#5-Kellogg's/Preview Edition, stock car w/opening hood and display stand, 1:24-scale, 1996	20
#5-Kellogg's/Preview Edition, stock car, 1:24-scale, 1996	20
#5-Kellogg's/Preview Edition, stock car, 1:64-scale, 1996	5

Car	MIP
#5-Kellogg's/Preview Edition, stock car, 1:64-scale, 1997	5
#5-Kellogg's/Preview Edition, premier stock car w/opening hood, 1:64-scale, 1997	10
#5-Kellogg's/Preview Edition, team transporter w/mini stock car, 1:144-scale, 1997	5
#5-Kellogg's/Preview Edition, team transporter, 1:64-scale, 1997	25
#5-Kellogg's/Preview Edition, stock car, 1:24-scale, 1997	15

Lajoie, Randy

Car	MIP
#74-Fina, team transporter, 1:64-scale, 1996	2
#74-Fina, team transporter w/mini stock car, 1:87-scale, 1996	8
#74-Fina, stock car, 1:64-scale, 1996	5
#74-Fina, stock car, 1:24-scale, 1997	25
#74-Fina, roaring racer stock car w/real engine sounds, 1:64-scale, 1997	25
#74-Fina, stock car, 1:64-scale, 1997	5

LePage, Kevin

Car	MIP
#88-Hype, team transporter w/two stock cars, 1:64-scale, 1997	25
#88-Hype, team transporter w/stock car, 1:64-scale, 1997	25
#88-Hype, team transporter, 1:64-scale, 1997	20
#88-Hype, team transporter w/mini stock car, 1:87-scale, 1997	10
#88-Hype, team transporter w/mini stock car, 1:144-scale, 1997	3
#88-Hype, stock car, 1:24-scale, 1997	15
#88-Hype, stock car, 1:64-scale, 1997	5

Little, Chad

Car	MIP
#23-John Deere, stock car bank w/opening hood and display stand, 1:24-scale, 1996	40
#23-John Deere, stock car, 1:64-scale, 1996	5
#23-John Deere, premier stock car w/opening hood, 1:64-scale, 1996	12
#23-John Deere, stock car w/opening hood and display stand, 1:24-scale, 1996	40

Car	MIP
#23-John Deere, team transporter w/mini stock car, 1:87-scale, 1996	12
#23-John Deere, team transporter, 1:64-scale, 1996	20
#23-John Deere, team transporter w/stock car, 1:64-scale, 1996	25
#23-John Deere, team transporter w/two stock cars, 1:64-scale, 1996	25
#23-John Deere, stock car, 1:24-scale, 1996	30
#23-John Deere Dealer Special, stock car, 1:64-scale, 1996	12
#23-John Deere Dealer Special, team transporter, 1:64-scale, 1996	25
#23-John Deere Dealer Special, team transporter w/stock car, 1:64-scale, 1996	30
#23-John Deere Dealer Special, premier stock car w/opening hood, 1:64-scale, 1996	18
#97 John Deere, stock car, Pinnacle Series, 1:64-scale, 1997	6
#97-John Deere, team transporter w/two stock cars, 1:64-scale, 1997	25
#97-John Deere, premier stock car w/opening hood, 1:64-scale, 1997	10
#97-John Deere, premier stock car w/Pinnacle collector card, opening hood, display stand and serial numbers, 1:64-scale, 1997	12
#97-John Deere, roaring racer stock car w/real engine sounds, 1:64-scale, 1997	25
#97-John Deere, stock car, 1:24-scale, 1997	20
#97-John Deere, stock car w/opening hood and display stand, 1:24-scale, 1997	25
#97-John Deere, team transporter w/mini stock car, 1:144-scale, 1997	5
#97-John Deere, team transporter w/mini stock car, 1:87-scale, 1997	12
#97-John Deere, team transporter, 1:64-scale, 1997	25

Car	MIP
#97-John Deere, team transporter w/stock car, 1:64-scale, 1997	25
#97-John Deere, stock car, 1:64-scale, 1997	8
#97-Sterling Cowboy, stock car w/opening hood and display stand, 1:24-scale, 1996	25
#97-Sterling Cowboy, stock car, 1:24-scale, 1996	20
#97-Sterling Cowboy, premier stock car w/opening hood, 1:64-scale, 1996	10
#97-Sterling Cowboy, stock car, 1:64-scale, 1996	15
#97-Sterling Cowboy, premier stock car w/opening hood, 1:18-scale, 1996	30

Marcis, Dave

Car	MIP
#71-Prodigy, premier stock car w/opening hood, 1:64-scale, 1996	20

Markham, Curtis

Car	MIP
#63-Lysol, team transporter, 1:64-scale, 1996	20
#63-Lysol, team transporter w/mini stock car, 1:87-scale, 1996	8
#63-Lysol, stock car, 1:24-scale, 1996	20
#63-Lysol, stock car, 1:64-scale, 1996	5
#63-Lysol/Preview Edition, team transporter, 1:64-scale, 1996	25
#63-Lysol/Preview Edition, team transporter w/mini stock car, 1:87-scale, 1996	8
#63-Lysol/Preview Edition, stock car, 1:24-scale, 1996	20

Marlin, Sterling

Car	MIP
#4 Kodak, stock car, Pinnacle Series, 1:64-scale, 1997	6
#4-Kodak, premier stock car w/opening hood, 1:64-scale, 1996	12
#4-Kodak, team transporter, 1:64-scale, 1997	20
#4-Kodak, team transporter w/stock car, 1:64-scale, 1997	25
#4-Kodak, team transporter w/two stock cars, 1:64-scale, 1997	25

Car	MIP
#4-Kodak, roaring racer stock car w/real engine sounds, 1:64-scale, 1997	22
#4-Kodak, premier stock car w/Pinnacle collector card, opening hood, display stand and serial numbers, 1:64-scale, 1997	11
#4-Kodak, stock car, 1:24-scale, 1997	15
#4-Kodak, team transporter w/mini stock car, 1:144-scale, 1997	3
#4-Kodak, team transporter w/mini stock car, 1:87-scale, 1997	13
#4-Kodak, stock car, 1:64-scale, 1996	4
#4-Kodak, stock car, 1:64-scale, 1997	5
#4-Kodak, premier stock car w/opening hood, 1:18-scale, 1996	30
#4-Kodak, team transporter w/mini stock car, 1:87-scale, 1996	8
#4-Kodak, team transporter, 1:64-scale, 1996	15
#4-Kodak, team transporter w/stock car, 1:64-scale, 1996	25
#4-Kodak, team transporter w/two stock cars, 1:64-scale, 1996	20
#4-Kodak, stock car w/opening hood and display stand, 1:24-scale, 1997	25
#4-Kodak Back to Back, stock car, 1:24-scale, 1996	25
#4-Kodak Back to Back, premier stock car w/opening hood, 1:18-scale, 1996	30
#4-Kodak Back to Back, stock car bank w/opening hood and display stand, 1:24-scale, 1996	25
#4-Kodak Back to Back, team transporter w/stock car, 1:64-scale, 1996	25
#4-Kodak-Gold, roaring racer stock car w/real engine sounds, 1:64-scale, 1997	30
#4-Kodak/Preview Edition, premier stock car w/opening hood, 1:64-scale, 1997	8
#4-Kodak/Preview Edition, team transporter w/mini stock car, 1:87-scale, 1996	8

Car	MIP
#4-Kodak/Preview Edition, stock car, 1:24-scale, 1997	20
#4-Kodak/Preview Edition, stock car, 1:64-scale, 1997	5
#4-Kodak/Preview Edition, stock car, 1:24-scale, 1996	20
#4-Kodak/Preview Edition, team transporter, 1:64-scale, 1996	25
#4-Kodak/Preview Edition, team transporter w/stock car, 1:64-scale, 1996	25
#4-Kodak/Preview Edition, team transporter w/two stock cars, 1:64-scale, 1996	25
#4-Kodak/Preview Edition, stock car, 1:64-scale, 1996	4

Martin, Mark

Car	MIP
#6 Valvoline, stock car, Pinnacle Series, 1:64-scale, 1997	6
#6-Valvoline, premier team transporter w/premier stock car, 1:64-scale, 1997	30
#6-Valvoline, stock car, 1:64-scale, 1997	8
#6-Valvoline, premier stock car w/Pinnacle collector card, opening hood, display stand and serial numbers, 1:64-scale, 1997	20
#6-Valvoline, roaring racer stock car w/real engine sounds, 1:64-scale, 1997	35
#6-Valvoline, stock car, 1:24-scale, 1997	20
#6-Valvoline, stock car w/opening hood and display stand, 1:24-scale, 1997	30
#6-Valvoline, team transporter w/mini stock car, 1:144-scale, 1997	8
#6-Valvoline, team transporter w/mini stock car, 1:87-scale, 1997	15
#6-Valvoline, team transporter, 1:64-scale, 1997	25
#6-Valvoline, team transporter w/stock car, 1:64-scale, 1997	25
#6-Valvoline, team transporter w/two stock cars, 1:64-scale, 1997	30
#6-Valvoline, team transporter, 1:64-scale, 1996	20

Car	MIP
#6-Valvoline, premier team transporter w/premier stock car, 1:64-scale, 1996	25
#6-Valvoline, team transporter w/stock car, 1:64-scale, 1996	25
#6-Valvoline, team transporter w/mini stock car, 1:87-scale, 1996	10
#6-Valvoline, stock car w/opening hood and display stand, 1:24-scale, 1996	35
#6-Valvoline, stock car, 1:24-scale, 1996	20
#6-Valvoline, stock car, 1:64-scale, 1996	18
#6-Valvoline, premier stock car w/opening hood, 1:64-scale, 1996	10
#6-Valvoline, team transporter w/two stock cars, 1:64-scale, 1996	25
#6-Valvoline/Premier Gold, premier stock car w/opening hood, painted interior and serial number on chassis, 1:18-scale, 1997	425
#6-Valvoline/Premier Gold, premier stock car w/opening hood, painted interior and serial number on chassis, 1:24-scale, 1997	120
#6-Valvoline/Preview Edition, stock car, 1:64-scale, 1996	5
#6-Valvoline/Preview Edition, stock car, 1:64-scale, 1997	8
#6-Valvoline/Preview Edition, premier stock car w/opening hood, 1:64-scale, 1997	10
#6-Valvoline/Preview Edition, stock car, 1:24-scale, 1997	18
#6-Valvoline/Preview Edition, stock car, 1:24-scale, 1996	20
#6-Valvoline/Preview Edition, team transporter w/mini stock car, 1:144-scale, 1997	8
#6-Valvoline/Preview Edition, team transporter w/mini stock car, 1:87-scale, 1997	15
#6-Valvoline/Preview Edition, team transporter, 1:64-scale, 1997	25
#60-Winn Dixie, stock car, 1:64-scale, 1996	10

Car	MIP
#60-Winn Dixie, stock car, 1:64-scale, 1997	8
#60-Winn Dixie, team transporter w/mini stock car, 1:87-scale, 1997	15
#60-Winn Dixie, team transporter w/mini stock car, 1:144-scale, 1997	8
#60-Winn Dixie, roaring racer stock car w/real engine sounds, 1:64-scale, 1997	35
#60-Winn Dixie, premier stock car w/opening hood, 1:18-scale, 1996	30

Mast, Rick

Car	MIP
#1-Hooters, tem transporter w/stock car, 1:64-scale, 1997	25
#75 Remington, stock car, Pinnacle Series, 1:64-scale, 1997	6
#75-Remington, team transporter w/mini stock car, 1:144-scale, 1997	5
#75-Remington, stock car, 1:64-scale, 1997	5
#75-Remington, premier stock car w/opening hood, 1:64-scale, 1997	8
#75-Remington, premier stock car w/Pinnacle collector card, opening hood, display stand and serial numbers, 1:64-scale, 1997	13
#75-Remington, stock car, 1:24-scale, 1997	15
#75-Remington, team transporter w/mini stock car, 1:87-scale, 1997	10
#75-Remington, team transporter, 1:64-scale, 1997	20
#75-Remington, team transporter w/stock car, 1:64-scale, 1997	25
#75-Remington, team transporter w/two stock cars, 1:64-scale, 1997	25
#75-Remington, premier team transporter w/premier stock car, 1:64-scale, 1997	25
#75-Remington, roaring racer stock car w/real engine sounds, 1:64-scale, 1997	25

Car	MIP
#75-Remington/Premier Gold, premier stock car w/opening hood, painted interior and serial number on chassis, 1:18-scale, 1997	300
#75-Remington/Preview Edition, stock car, 1:64-scale, 1997	5
#75-Remington/Preview Edition, stock car w/opening hood and display stand, 1:24-scale, 1997	20
#75-Remington/Preview Edition, stock car, 1:24-scale, 1997	15
#75-Remington/Preview Edition, premier stock car w/opening hood, 1:64-scale, 1997	8

Mayfield, Jeremy

Car	MIP
#37-Kmart, team transporter, 1:64-scale, 1997	20
#37-Kmart, team transporter w/mini stock car, 1:87-scale, 1997	10
#37-Kmart, team transporter w/mini stock car, 1:144-scale, 1997	3
#37-Kmart, stock car, 1:24-scale, 1997	15
#37-Kmart, roaring racer stock car w/real engine sounds, 1:64-scale, 1997	22
#37-Kmart, premier stock car w/Pinnacle collector card, opening hood, display stand and serial numbers, 1:64-scale, 1997	12
#37-Kmart, premier stock car w/opening hood, 1:64-scale, 1997	8
#37-Kmart, stock car, 1:64-scale, 1997	5
#Kmart, stock car, Pinnacle Series, 1:64-scale, 1997	6

McLaughlin, Mike

Car	MIP
#34-Royal Oak, team transporter w/mini stock car, 1:87-scale, 1996	8
#34-Royal Oak, premier stock car w/opening hood, 1:18-scale, 1996	30
#34-Royal Oak, stock car, 1:24-scale, 1996	20

Car	MIP
#34-Royal Oak, premier stock car w/opening hood, 1:64-scale, 1996	12
#34-Royal Oak, stock car, 1:64-scale, 1996	10
#34-Royal Oak, team transporter w/two stock cars, 1:64-scale, 1997	30
#34-Royal Oak, team transporter w/stock car, 1:64-scale, 1997	30
#34-Royal Oak, team transporter, 1:64-scale, 1997	20
#34-Royal Oak, team transporter w/mini stock car, 1:87-scale, 1997	11
#34-Royal Oak, team transporter w/mini stock car, 1:144-scale, 1997	5
#34-Royal Oak, stock car, 1:64-scale, 1997	5

Moise, Patty

Car	MIP
#14-Purex/Dial, team transporter w/two stock cars, 1:64-scale, 1996	25
#14-Purex/Dial, team transporter w/stock car, 1:64-scale, 1996	25
#14-Purex/Dial, team transporter, 1:64-scale, 1996	15
#14-Purex/Dial, team transporter w/mini stock car, 1:87-scale, 1996	8
#14-Purex/Dial, stock car, 1:64-scale, 1996	5
#14-Purex/Dial/Preview Edition, stock car, 1:24-scale, 1996	20
#14-Purex/Dial/Preview Edition, stock car, 1:64-scale, 1996	5

Musgrave, Ted

Car	MIP
#16 Primestar, stock car, Pinnacle Series, 1:64-scale, 1997	6
#16-Family Channel, team transporter w/two stock cars, 1:64-scale, 1996	25
#16-Family Channel, team transporter w/stock car, 1:64-scale, 1996	25
#16-Family Channel, team transporter, 1:64-scale, 1996	15
#16-Family Channel, team transporter w/mini stock car, 1:87-scale, 1996	8

Car	MIP
#16-Family Channel, premier stock car w/opening hood, 1:18-scale, 1996	30
#16-Family Channel, stock car, 1:24-scale, 1996	20
#16-Family Channel, premier stock car w/opening hood, 1:64-scale, 1996	12
#16-Family Channel, stock car, 1:64-scale, 1996	5
#16-Family Channel/Preview Edition, stock car, 1:24-scale, 1996	20
#16-Family Channel/Preview Edition, stock car, 1:64-scale, 1996	5
#16-Family Channel/Preview Edition, team transporter w/mini stock car, 1:87-scale, 1996	8
#16-Family Channel/Preview Edition, team transporter, 1:64-scale, 1996	15
#16-Primestar, stock car, 1:64-scale, 1997	5
#16-Primestar, team transporter w/two stock cars, 1:64-scale, 1997	25
#16-Primestar, team transporter w/stock car, 1:64-scale, 1997	25
#16-Primestar, team transporter, 1:64-scale, 1997	20
#16-Primestar, team transporter w/mini stock car, 1:87-scale, 1997	10
#16-Primestar, team transporter w/mini stock car, 1:144-scale, 1997	2
#16-Primestar, stock car, 1:24-scale, 1997	15
#16-Primestar, roaring racer stock car w/real engine sounds, 1:64-scale, 1997	25
#16-Primestar, premier stock car w/Pinnacle collector card, opening hood, display stand and serial numbers, 1:64-scale, 1997	13
#16-Primestar, premier stock car w/opening hood, 1:64-scale, 1997	8
#16-Primestar, premier team transporter w/premier stock car, 1:64-scale, 1997	25

Car	MIP

Nemechek, Joe

#42-Bell South, team transporter
w/two stock cars, 1:64-scale,
1997 25

#42-Bell South, premier stock car
w/opening hood, 1:64-scale,
1997 8

#42-Bell South, premier stock car
w/Pinnacle collector card,
opening hood, display stand
and serial numbers,
1:64-scale, 1997 12

#42-Bell South, roaring racer stock
car w/real engine sounds,
1:64-scale, 1997 22

#42-Bell South, stock car, 1:24-scale,
1997 15

#42-Bell South, team transporter
w/mini stock car,
1:144-scale, 1997 5

#42-Bell South, team transporter
w/mini stock car, 1:87-scale,
1997 10

#42-Bell South, team transporter,
1:64-scale, 1997 20

#42-Bell South, stock car, 1:64-scale,
1997 5

#42-Bell South, team transporter
w/stock car, 1:64-scale, 1997 25

#87 Bell South, stock car, Pinnacle
Series, 1:64-scale, 1997 6

#87-Bell South, roaring racer stock
car w/real engine sounds,
1:64-scale, 1997 22

#87-Bell South, stock car, 1:24-scale,
1997 15

#87-Bell South, stock car, 1:64-scale,
1997 5

#87-Burger King, stock car, 1:64-
scale, 1997 5

#87-Burger King, premier stock car
w/opening hood, 1:64-scale,
1997 8

#87-Burger King, stock car, 1:24-
scale, 1997 15

#87-Burger King, team transporter
w/mini stock car, 1:87-scale,
1997 11

#87-Burger King, team transporter,
1:64-scale, 1997 20

Olsen, Mike

#61-Little Trees, stock car, 1:64-
scale, 1996 6

Parsons, Phil

#10-Channellock, team transporter,
1:64-scale, 1996 15

#10-Channellock, stock car,
1:64-scale, 1996 4

#10-Channellock, team transporter
w/two stock cars, 1:64-scale,
1997 25

#10-Channellock, team transporter
w/stock car, 1:64-scale, 1997 25

#10-Channellock, team transporter,
1:64-scale, 1997 22

#10-Channellock, team transporter
w/mini stock car, 1:87-scale,
1997 10

#10-Channellock, team transporter
w/mini stock car,
1:144-scale, 1997 2

#10-Channellock, stock car,
1:24-scale, 1997 15

#10-Channellock, stock car,
1:64-scale, 1997 5

Pearson, Larry

#92-Stanley Tools, premier stock car
w/opening hood, 1:18-scale,
1996 30

#92-Stanley Tools, premier stock car
w/opening hood, 1:64-scale,
1996 10

Petty, Kyle

#49-NWO, team transporter w/stock
car, 1:64-scale, 1997 25

#49-NWO, team transporter,
1:64-scale, 1997 22

#49-NWO, team transporter w/mini
stock car, 1:87-scale, 1997 10

#49-NWO, team transporter w/mini
stock car, 1:144-scale, 1997 6

#49-NWO, stock car, 1:24-scale,
1997 35

#49-NWO, stock car, 1:64-scale,
1997 10

Car	MIP

Pressley, Robert

#29 Cartoon Network, stock car, Pinnacle Series, 1:64-scale, 1997 6

#29-Cartoon Network, roaring racer stock car w/real engine sounds, 1:64-scale, 1997 25

#29-Cartoon Network, stock car, 1:64-scale, 1997 5

#29-Cartoon Network, premier stock car w/Pinnacle collector card, opening hood, display stand and serial numbers, 1:64-scale, 1997 15

#29-Cartoon Network, stock car, 1:24-scale, 1997 15

#29-Cartoon Network, team transporter w/mini stock car, 1:144-scale, 1997 3

#29-Cartoon Network, team transporter w/mini stock car, 1:87-scale, 1997 11

#29-Cartoon Network, team transporter, 1:64-scale, 1997 24

#29-Cartoon Network, team transporter w/stock car, 1:64-scale, 1997 25

#29-Cartoon Network, team transporter w/two stock cars, 1:64-scale, 1997 25

#29-Cartoon Network, premier team transporter w/premier stock car, 1:64-scale, 1997 30

#29-Cartoon Network, premier stock car w/opening hood, 1:64-scale, 1997 8

#29-Cartoon Network/Preview Edition, stock car, 1:64-scale, 1997 5

#29-Cartoon Network/Preview Edition, team transporter, 1:64-scale, 1997 24

#29-Cartoon Network/Preview Edition, team transporter w/mini stock car, 1:87-scale, 1997 11

#29-Cartoon Network/Preview Edition, team transporter w/mini stock car, 1:144-scale, 1997 3

#29-Cartoon Network/Preview Edition, stock car w/opening hood and display stand, 1:24-scale, 1997 20

#29-Cartoon Network/Preview Edition, stock car, 1:24-scale, 1997 20

#29-Cartoon Network/Preview Edition, premier stock car w/opening hood, 1:64-scale, 1997 8

Reeves, Stevie

#7-Clabber Girl/Preview Edition, stock car, 1:24-scale, 1996 20

#7-Clabber Girl/Preview Edition, stock car, 1:64-scale, 1996 5

#96-Clabber Girl, team transporter, 1:64-scale, 1996 20

#96-Clabber Girl, stock car, 1:64-scale, 1996 5

Rudd, Ricky

#1-DeWalt, team transporter w/two stock cars, 1:64-scale, 1997 25

#1-DeWalt, team transporter w/stock car, 1:64-scale, 1997 25

#10 Tide, stock car, Pinnacle Series, 1:64-scale, 1997 6

#10-Tide, stock car, 1:64-scale, 1996 4

#10-Tide, stock car, 1:64-scale, 1997 5

#10-Tide, premier stock car w/opening hood, 1:64-scale, 1997 8

#10-Tide, premier stock car w/Pinnacle collector card, opening hood, display stand and serial numbers, 1:64-scale, 1997 12

#10-Tide, roaring racer stock car w/real engine sounds, 1:64-scale, 1997 22

#10-Tide, stock car, 1:24-scale, 1997 15

#10-Tide, stock car w/opening hood and display stand, 1:24-scale, 1997 20

#10-Tide/Mountain Spring, stock car, 1:64-scale, 1997 5

#10-Tide/Mountain Spring, stock car, 1:24-scale, 1997 18

Car	MIP
#10-Tide/Mountain Spring, roaring racer stock car w/real engine sounds, 1:64-scale, 1997	22
#10-Tide/Premier Gold, premier stock car w/opening hood, painted interior and serial number on chassis, 1:18-scale, 1997	340
#10-Tide/Premier Gold, premier stock car w/opening hood, painted interior and serial number on chassis, 1:24-scale, 1997	60
#10-Tide/Preview Edition, team transporter w/mini stock car, 1:87-scale, 1996	8
#10-Tide/Preview Edition, stock car, 1:64-scale, 1997	5
#10-Tide/Preview Edition, team transporter w/stock car, 1:64-scale, 1996	25
#10-Tide/Preview Edition, premier stock car w/opening hood, 1:64-scale, 1996	10
#10-Tide/Preview Edition, stock car, 1:24-scale, 1996	20
#10-Tide/Preview Edition, premier stock car w/opening hood, 1:18-scale, 1996	30
#10-Tide/Preview Edition, team transporter w/mini stock car, 1:87-scale, 1996	8
#10-Tide/Preview Edition, team transporter, 1:64-scale, 1996	15
#10-Tide/Preview Edition, team transporter w/two stock cars, 1:64-scale, 1996	25
#10-Tide/Preview Edition, stock car, 1:24-scale, 1997	18

Sauter, Jay

Car	MIP
#40-First Union, stock car, 1:24-scale, 1996	20
#40-First Union, stock car, 1:64-scale, 1996	7

Schrader, Ken

Car	MIP
#25-Budweiser, premier stock car w/opening hood, 1:18-scale, 1996	50
#25-Budweiser, stock car, 1:64-scale, 1996	5

Car	MIP
#25-Hendrick Motorsports, stock car, 1:24-scale, 1996	40
#25-Hendrick Motorsports, premier stock car w/opening hood, 1:64-scale, 1996	15
#33-Generic, stock car, 1:24-scale, 1997	15
#33-Generic, roaring racer stock car w/real engine sounds, 1:64-scale, 1997	22
#33-Generic, stock car, 1:64-scale, 1997	5
#52-AC Delco, stock car w/opening hood and display stand, 1:24-scale, 1996	25
#52-AC Delco, stock car, 1:24-scale, 1996	20
#52-AC Delco, premier stock car w/opening hood, 1:64-scale, 1996	12
#52-AC Delco, stock car, 1:64-scale, 1996	5
#52-AC Delco/Preview Edition, stock car, 1:24-scale, 1996	20
#52-AC Delco/Preview Edition, stock car, 1:64-scale, 1996	5

Shepard, Morgan

Car	MIP
#75-Remington, team transporter, 1:64-scale, 1996	20
#75-Remington, stock car w/opening hood and display stand, 1:24-scale, 1996	35
#75-Remington, stock car, 1:24-scale, 1996	30
#75-Remington, stock car, 1:64-scale, 1996	10

Skinner, Mike

Car	MIP
#31-Realtree, premier stock car w/opening hood, 1:18-scale, 1996	90
#31-Realtree, stock car w/opening hood and display stand, 1:24-scale, 1996	70
#31-Realtree, stock car, 1:24-scale, 1996	90
#31-Realtree, premier stock car w/opening hood, 1:64-scale, 1996	30
#31-Realtree, stock car, 1:64-scale, 1996	25

Car	MIP
Speed, Lake	
#9-Spam, stock car, 1:24-scale, 1996	22
#9-Spam, stock car, 1:64-scale, 1996	5
#9-Spam/Preview Edition, stock car, 1:24-scale, 1996	20
#9-Spam/Preview Edition, stock car, 1:64-scale, 1996	5
#9-University of Nebraska, premier stock car w/opening hood, 1:64-scale, 1997	25
Stricklin, Hut	
#8 Circuit City, stock car, Pinnacle Series, 1:64-scale, 1997	6
#8-Circuit City, team transporter w/stock car, 1:64-scale, 1997	25
#8-Circuit City, team transporter, 1:64-scale, 1997	20
#8-Circuit City, team transporter w/mini stock car, 1:87-scale, 1997	10
#8-Circuit City, team transporter w/mini stock car, 1:144-scale, 1997	5
#8-Circuit City, stock car, 1:24-scale, 1997	15
#8-Circuit City, roaring racer stock car w/real engine sounds, 1:64-scale, 1997	22
#8-Circuit City, premier stock car w/Pinnacle collector card, opening hood, display stand and serial numbers, 1:64-scale, 1997	12
#8-Circuit City, stock car, 1:64-scale, 1997	5
#8-Circuit City/Preview Edition, team transporter, 1:64-scale, 1997	20
#8-Circuit City/Preview Edition, team transporter w/mini stock car, 1:87-scale, 1997	10
#8-Circuit City/Preview Edition, team transporter w/mini stock car, 1:144-scale, 1997	5
Trickle, Dick	
#90-Heilig Meyers, stock car, 1:24-scale, 1997	15
#90-Heilig Meyers, stock car, 1:64-scale, 1997	5

Car	MIP
Wallace, Kenny	
#81-Square D, team transporter w/two stock cars, 1:64-scale, 1996	25
#81-Square D, team transporter w/stock car, 1:64-scale, 1996	25
#81-Square D, team transporter, 1:64-scale, 1996	20
#81-Square D, team transporter w/mini stock car, 1:87-scale, 1996	8
#81-Square D, stock car w/opening hood and display stand, 1:24-scale, 1996	30
#81-Square D, stock car, 1:24-scale, 1996	20
#81-Square D, stock car, 1:64-scale, 1996	5
Wallace, Mike	
#90-Duron Paint, stock car, 1:24-scale, 1996	20
#90-Duron Paint, stock car, 1:64-scale, 1996	5
#90-Helig Meyers, team transporter, 1:64-scale, 1996	20
#90-Helig Meyers, team transporter w/mini stock car, 1:87-scale, 1996	8
#90-Helig Meyers/Preview Edition, team transporter w/two stock cars, 1:64-scale, 1996	25
#90-Helig Meyers/Preview Edition, team transporter w/stock car, 1:64-scale, 1996	25
#90-Helig Meyers/Preview Edition, team transporter, 1:64-scale, 1996	20
#90-Helig Meyers/Preview Edition, team transporter w/mini stock car, 1:87-scale, 1996	8
#90-Helig Meyers/Preview Edition, stock car, 1:24-scale, 1996	20
#90-Helig Meyers/Preview Edition, stock car, 1:64-scale, 1996	5
#91-Spam, team transporter, 1:64-scale, 1997	20
#91-Spam, team transporter w/mini stock car, 1:144-scale, 1997	4
#91-Spam, stock car, 1:24-scale, 1997	15

Car	MIP
#91-Spam, roaring racer stock car w/real engine sounds, 1:64-scale, 1997	22
#91-Spam, stock car, 1:64-scale, 1997	5

Wallace, Rusty

Car	MIP
#2-Miller, premier stock car w/opening hood, 1:64-scale, 1997	8
#2-Miller, stock car, 1:64-scale, 1997	10
#2-Miller, stock car, 1:24-scale, 1997	25
#2-Miller, stock car w/opening hood and display stand, 1:24-scale, 1997	30
#2-Miller, stock car bank w/opening hood and display stand, 1:24-scale, 1997	60
#2-Miller, team transporter, 1:64-scale, 1997	22
#2-Miller/Premier Gold, premier stock car w/opening hood, painted interior and serial number on chassis, 1:24-scale, 1997	55
#2-Miller/Premier Gold, premier stock car w/opening hood, painted interior and serial number on chassis, 1:18-scale, 1997	400
#2-Penske, stock car, 1:64-scale, 1997	5
#2-Penske, premier stock car w/opening hood, 1:64-scale, 1997	8
#2-Penske, roaring racer stock car w/real engine sounds, 1:64-scale, 1997	22
#2-Penske, stock car, 1:24-scale, 1997	15
#2-Penske, team transporter w/mini stock car, 1:144-scale, 1997	6
#2-Penske, team transporter w/mini stock car, 1:87-scale, 1997	12
#2-Penske, team transporter, 1:64-scale, 1997	20
#2-Penske, team transporter w/two stock cars, 1:64-scale, 1997	30
#2-Penske, team transporter w/stock car, 1:64-scale, 1997	30
#2-Penske Racing, stock car, 1:64-scale, 1997	5
#2-Penske Racing, team transporter w/stock car, 1:64-scale, 1997	28

Car	MIP
#2-Penske Racing, premier team transporter w/premier stock car, 1:64-scale, 1997	25
#2-Penske Racing, team transporter, 1:64-scale, 1997	20
#2-Penske Racing, team transporter w/mini stock car, 1:87-scale, 1997	12
#2-Penske Racing, stock car, 1:24-scale, 1997	15
#2-Penske Racing, premier stock car w/opening hood, 1:64-scale, 1997	8
#2-Penske/Preview Edition, stock car, 1:64-scale, 1997	5

Waltrip, Darrell

Car	MIP
#17-Western Auto, stock car, 1:64-scale, 1996	4
#17-Western Auto, team transporter w/two stock cars, 1:64-scale, 1996	25
#17-Western Auto, team transporter w/stock car, 1:64-scale, 1996	25
#17-Western Auto, team transporter, 1:64-scale, 1996	15
#17-Western Auto, team transporter w/mini stock car, 1:87-scale, 1996	8
#17-Western Auto, premier stock car w/opening hood, 1:18-scale, 1996	30
#17-Western Auto, stock car, 1:24-scale, 1996	20
#17-Western Auto Anniversary/Chrome Version, stock car, 1:64-scale, 1997	10
#17-Western Auto Anniversary/Chrome Version, team transporter w/mini stock car, 1:144-scale, 1997	8
#17-Western Auto Anniversary/Chrome Version, premier stock car w/opening hood, 1:64-scale, 1997	12
#17-Western Auto Anniversary/Chrome Version, stock car, 1:24-scale, 1997	25

Car	MIP
#17-Western Auto Chrome, stock car bank w/opening hood, 1:24-scale, 1996	20
#17-Western Auto/Blue Version, premier stock car w/opening hood, 1:64-scale, 1997	8
#17-Western Auto/Blue Version, stock car, 1:64-scale, 1997	5
#17-Western Auto/Blue Version, stock car, 1:24-scale, 1997	15
#17-Western Auto/Blue Version, roaring racer stock car w/real engine sounds, 1:64-scale, 1997	25
#17-Western Auto/Preview Edition, team transporter, 1:64-scale, 1996	15
#17-Western Auto/Preview Edition, stock car, 1:64-scale, 1996	4
#17-Western Auto/Preview Edition, team transporter w/mini stock car, 1:87-scale, 1996	8
#17-Western Auto/Preview Edition, team transporter w/stock car, 1:64-scale, 1996	25
#17-Western Auto/Preview Edition, team transporter w/two stock cars, 1:64-scale, 1996	25
#17-Western Auto/Preview Edition, stock car, 1:24-scale, 1996	20

Waltrip, Michael

Car	MIP
#12-MW Windows, team transporter, 1:64-scale, 1996	25
#12-MW Windows, team transporter w/mini stock car, 1:87-scale, 1996	8
#12-MW Windows, stock car, 1:64-scale, 1996	5
#21 Citgo, stock car, Pinnacle Series, 1:64-scale, 1997	6

Car	MIP
#21-Citgo, team transporter w/two stock cars, 1:64-scale, 1996	25
#21-Citgo, stock car, 1:64-scale, 1997	5
#21-Citgo, premier stock car w/opening hood, 1:64-scale, 1997	8
#21-Citgo, premier stock car w/Pinnacle collector card, opening hood, display stand and serial numbers, 1:64-scale, 1997	12
#21-Citgo, roaring racer stock car w/real engine sounds, 1:64-scale, 1997	25
#21-Citgo, stock car, 1:24-scale, 1997	15
#21-Citgo, team transporter w/mini stock car, 1:144-scale, 1997	5
#21-Citgo, team transporter w/mini stock car, 1:87-scale, 1997	11
#21-Citgo, team transporter, 1:64-scale, 1997	20
#21-Citgo, team transporter w/stock car, 1:64-scale, 1996	25
#21-Citgo, stock car, 1:64-scale, 1996	5
#21-Citgo, stock car, 1:24-scale, 1996	20
#21-Citgo, stock car bank w/opening hood and display stand, 1:24-scale, 1996	30
#21-Citgo, team transporter w/mini stock car, 1:87-scale, 1996	8
#21-Citgo, team transporter, 1:64-scale, 1996	20
#21-Citgo/Preview Edition, stock car, 1:64-scale, 1996	5
#21-Citgo/Preview Edition, stock car, 1:24-scale, 1996	20
#21-Citgo/Preview Edition, stock car, 1:24-scale, 1997	20
#21-Citgo/Preview Edition, stock car, 1:64-scale, 1997	5

Tootsietoy

Tootsietoy is one of the best-known names in the world of toy collecting, and for good reason. The toys, products of a Chicago company that now has a century of manufacturing behind it, have long appealed to parents because of their cheap price, and to kids because of their high play value. During the company's heyday, roughly from the 1930s through 1960s, a person would have had to search long and hard to find a child with no knowledge of the trademark.

Dowst and Company started in 1876 in the publishing trade, and moved into manufacturing after the 1893 Columbian World Exposition in Chicago, where the new die-casting technology was introduced to the public. By then named Dowst Brothers, the company released its first die-cast-body, free-axle toy car in 1911, the generic Limousine. The first specific-model car, the Model T Ford touring car, followed in 1914. The name Tootsietoy was adopted in the early 1920s and was registered in 1924 as the company's trademark. Theodore Dowst, who joined the firm in 1906, is generally seen as the guiding force behind the growth of toy production at Dowst Brothers. He remained with the company even after its purchase by Nathan Shure in 1926, until 1945. For most collectors, the toys of the Ted Dowst period are the most noteworthy.

High points in the world of Tootsietoy collecting include the 1933 Graham series, notable for its use of three-piece construction, with separately die-cast bodies, chassis and radiator grilles, and the 1935 LaSalles, which used four-piece construction, adding a casting for the rear bumpers. Collectors also avidly seek the 1932-33 Funnies series cars, which featured such comic figures as Andy Gump, Uncle Walt and Moon Mullins.

Market Update

Interest seems to be growing in the various advertising toys Tootsietoy produced through the years, ranging from the 1932 Wrigley's Railroad Express truck to more recent U-Haul and Coast-to-Coast vehicles. Collector demand for post-war toys remains stable at a fairly low level; and it may not grow stronger any time soon, given the heavy contemporary interest in detailed scale models as opposed to made-for-play toys. On the other hand, interest in the post-Vietnam toys is inching upward, reflecting the maturing of the later Baby Boomers.

Contributors: Mark Rich, P.O. Box 971, Stevens Point, WI 54481-0971; John Gibson, 9713 Pleasant Gate Lane, Potomac, MD 20854.

PREWAR

No.	Name	Good	Ex	Mint
	Ford Model A Delivery Van, "US Mail," sold in sets only, 1931	38	56	75
23	Racer w/Driver, 1927	35	60	80
464	Buick Touring Car, 1925	28	42	55
4528	Limousine, 1911	24	32	40
4570	Ford Model T Tourer, 1914	35	50	65
4610	Ford Model T Pickup, 1916	35	50	70
4629	Sedan, marked "Yellow Cab", 1923	15	25	60
4636	Buick Coupe, 1924	23	34	45
4642	Army Long-Range Cannon, 1931	13	18	25
4646	Caterpillar Tractor, w/treads, 1931	27	41	55
4651	Fageol Safety Coach, 1927	30	45	65
4652	Hook & Ladder Fire Engine, 1927	39	52	75
4653	Water Tower Fire Engine, 1927	38	56	75
4654	Huber Star Farm Tractor, 1927	40	65	95
4655	Ford Model A Coupe, 1928	20	30	40
4665	Ford Model A Sedan, 1929	20	30	40

5091 Funnies Series (1932)

No.	Name	Good	Ex	Mint
5101	Andy Gump Roadster, mechanical	225	340	450
5101	Andy Gump Roadster	175	265	350
5102	Uncle Walt Roadster, mechanical	225	340	450
5102	Uncle Walt Roadster	175	265	350
5103	Smitty Motorcyle, mechanical	225	340	450

Tootsietoy Funnies Series, 1932.

No. 4570 Ford Model T Tourer. Photo Courtesy David Richter.

No.	Name	Good	Ex	Mint
5103	Smitty Motorcyle	175	265	350
5104	Moon Mullins Police Wagon	175	265	350
5104	Moon Mullins Police Wagon, mechanical	225	340	450
5105	Kayo Ice Wagon	175	265	350
5105	Kayo Ice Wagon, mechanical	225	340	450
5106	Uncle Willie rowboat	175	265	350
5106	Uncle Willie rowboat, mechanical	225	340	450

No. 5104 Moon Mullins Police Wagon. Photo Courtesy John Gibson.

No. 5105 Kayo Ice Wagon. Photo Courtesy John Gibson.

No. 4659 Autogyro.

Airplanes

No.	Name	Good	Ex	Mint
	Army DC-4 Transport, 1941	40	75	110
	Dive-Bomber Waco Biplane, 1937	50	95	140
	United DC-4 Supre Mainliner, 1941	35	65	95
119	U.S. Army Northrup Alpha Pursuit Plane, 1936	25	50	75
125	Lockheed Electra, twin-engine, 1937	25	50	75
717	TWA DC-2, 1937	30	60	90
718	U.S. Navy Waco C-Model Biplane, 1937	45	85	125
719	Crusader, twin boom, twin engine, 1937	35	70	100
721	Curtis P-40 Pursuit, silver, 1941	70	140	200
1030	USN Los Angeles Dirigible, 1937	45	85	125
4482	Bleriot Plane, 1910	40	80	120
4649	Ford Tri-Motor, 1932	45	85	125
4650	Biplane, open-spoke tires, 1926	45	85	125
4659	Autogyro, 1934	40	80	120
4660	Aerodawn, rubber tires, 1928	30	55	80
4660	Aerodawn, metal tires, 1928	30	60	85

Camelback Delivery Van Series (1937), 3" Vehicles

No.	Name	Good	Ex	Mint
123	Lewis's	135	205	275

No. 4634 Milk, most common in series.

No. 4635 Florist, rarest in series. Photo Courtesy John Gibson.

No. 113 '35 Wrecker.

No.	Name	Good	Ex	Mint
123	McLeans	145	215	285
123	Miller & Rhoads	145	215	285
123	Shepards	145	215	285
123	Special Delivery	25	38	50
123	Wieboldt's	145	215	285

Depression-Years Miniatures (1931)

No.	Name	Good	Ex	Mint
	Buick Marquette Coupe, 1931	10	15	20
	Buick Marquette Sedan, 1931	10	15	20
	Mack Insurance Patrol Fire Truck, 1931	25	35	45
102	Buick Marquette Roadster	13	19	25
105	Mack Tank Truck, 1932	25	40	55
106	Low Wing Monoplane, w/propeller, tin wings, 1932	35	55	70

No.	Name	Good	Ex	Mint
107	High Wing Monoplane, w/propeller, tin wings, 1932	35	55	70
108	Caterpillar tractor w/tread, 1932	23	34	45
109	Ford Stake Truck, 1932	20	30	40
110	Bluebird Dayton Racer, 1932	25	40	55

Federal Delivery Van Series (1924)

No.	Name	Good	Ex	Mint
4630	Grocery	35	55	85
4631	Bakery	50	80	105
4632	Market	35	60	75
4633	Laundry	45	65	95
4634	Milk, most common in series	25	40	55
4635	Florist, rarest in series	95	175	225

Ford V8 Series (1935), 3" Vehicles

No.	Name	Good	Ex	Mint
111	'34 Sedan	30	45	60
111	'35 Sedan	15	23	30
112	'34 Coupe	33	49	65
112	'35 Coupe	18	26	35
113	'34 Wrecker	38	56	75
113	'35 Wrecker	33	49	65
114	'34 Convertible Coupe	40	60	80
114	'35 Convertible Coupe	30	45	60
115	'34 Convertible Sedan	40	60	80
115	'35 Convertible Sedan	30	45	60
116	'35 Roadster	23	34	45
117	'35 Roadster Fire Chief Car	50	75	100
118	DeSoto Airflow Sedan	27	40	55

GM Series (1927)

No.	Name	Good	Ex	Mint
6001	Buick Roadster	30	45	60
6002	Buick Coupe	28	41	55
6003	Buick Brougham	28	41	55
6004	Buick Sedan	28	41	55
6005	Buick Touring Car	50	75	100
6006	Buick Screenside Delivery Truck	35	53	70
6101	Cadillac Roadster	40	60	80
6102	Cadillac coupe	40	60	80
6103	Cadillac Brougham	40	60	80
6104	Cadillac Sedan	40	60	80
6105	Cadillac Touring Car	60	90	120
6106	Cadillac Screenside Delivery Truck	48	71	95
6201	Chevrolet Roadster	33	50	65
6202	Chevrolet Coupe	33	50	65
6203	Chevrolet Brougham	33	50	65

No. 6105 Cadillac Touring Car. Photo Courtesy John Gibson.

No. 6401 No-Name Roadster. Photo Courtesy John Gibson.

No. 6406 No-Name Screenside Delivery Truck. Photo Courtesy John Gibson.

Commercial Tire & Supply Co. Van. Photo Courtesy John Gibson.

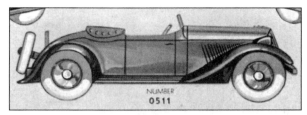

No. 511 Roadster, five wheel. Photo Courtesy 1933 Tootsietoy catalog.

No. 516 Towncar, five wheel. Photo Courtesy John Gibson.

No. 616 Towncar, six wheel. Photo Courtesy John Gibson.

No. 1017 Torpedo Coupe.

No.	Name	Good	Ex	Mint
6204	Chevrolet Sedan	33	50	65
6205	Chevrolet Touring Car	55	83	110
6206	Chevrolet Screenside Delivery Truck	35	53	70
6301	Oldsmobile Roadster	38	55	75
6302	Oldsmobile Coupe	35	53	70
6303	Oldsmobile Brougham	35	53	70
6304	Oldsmobile Sedan	35	53	70
6305	Oldsmobile Touring Car	55	83	110
6306	Oldsmobile Screenside Delivery Truck	45	68	90
6401	No-Name Roadster	55	83	110
6402	No-Name Coupe	55	83	110
6403	No-Name Brougham	55	83	110
6404	No-Name Sedan	55	83	110
6405	No-Name Touring Car	75	113	150
6406	No-Name Screenside Delivery Truck	65	95	125

Graham Series (1933), 4" Vehicles

No.	Name	Good	Ex	Mint
	Bild-A-Car Coupe, four wheel	65	95	130
	Bild-A-Car Roadster, four wheel	85	130	175
	Bild-A-Car Sedan, four wheel	65	95	130
	Commercial Tire & Supply Co. Van	75	110	150

No.	Name	Good	Ex	Mint
511	Roadster, five wheel	80	125	165
512	Coupe, five wheel	70	110	145
513	Sedan, five wheel	70	110	145
514	Convertible Coupe, five wheel	80	120	160
515	Convertible Sedan, five wheel	80	120	160
516	Towncar, five wheel	88	130	175
611	Roadster, six wheel	80	125	165
612	Coupe, six wheel	72	110	145
613	Sedan, six wheel	70	110	145
614	Convertible Coupe, six wheel	80	120	160
615	Convertible Sedan, six wheel	80	120	160
616	Towncar, six wheel	75	110	150
806	Wrecker	75	110	150
808	Tootsietoy Dairy Delivery Van	75	110	150
809	Army Ambulance	75	110	150

Jumbo Series (1936), 6" Vehicles

No.	Name	Good	Ex	Mint
	Torpedo Cross-Country Greyhound Bus	25	55	80
1016	Auburn Torpedo Roadster	23	34	45
1017	Torpedo Coupe	20	30	40
1018	Torpedo Sedan	20	30	40
1019	Torpedo Pickup Truck	20	30	40
1027	Torpedo Wrecker	23	34	45

No.	Name	Good	Ex	Mint
1045	Greyhound Bus, w/tin bottom 55		50	70
1045	Trans-America Bus, sold only in sets, 1941 90		130	175

LaSalle Series (1935), 4" Vehicles

No.	Name	Good	Ex	Mint
712	Coupe..........115		180	240
713	Sedan 115		180	240
714	Convertible Coupe..........125		205	265
715	Convertible Sedan 125		205	265

Lincoln Series (1935), 4" Vehicles

No.	Name	Good	Ex	Mint
180	Zephyr and Roamer House Trailer 555		740	925
180	Zephyr and Roamer House Trailer, wind-up 660		880	1100
716	Briggs-Lincoln prototype, "Doodlebug" 75		95	125
6015	Zephyr, wind-up 240		365	485
6015	Zephyr 165		245	325
6016	Wrecker, wind-up 350		525	700
6016	Wrecker 250		230	350

Mack Delivery Trucks and Vans (1933), 4" Vehicles

No.	Name	Good	Ex	Mint
804	City Fuel Company Coal Truck, four wheel, 1937..........60		95	130

No. 716 Briggs-Lincoln prototype, "Doodlebug". Photo Courtesy John Gibson.

No. 804 City Fuel Company Coal Truck, four wheel. Photo Courtesy John Gibson.

No.	Name	Good	Ex	Mint
804	City Fuel Company Coal Truck, ten wheel, 1933..........75		115	150
807	Delivery Motorcycle, adapted from 5103 85		125	175
810	Commercial Tire & Supply Co. Van..........112		168	225
810	Railway Express Co., Wrigley's Gum, one-piece cab, 1935 70		105	150
810	Railway Express Co., Wrigley's Gum, two-piece cab 75		115	165

Mack Fire Truck Series (1937), 4" Vehicles

No.	Name	Good	Ex	Mint
1040	Hook and Ladder 35		50	70
1041	Hose Car 35		55	75
1042	Insurance Patrol, open end..........30		45	60
1042	Insurance Patrol, w/ladder and rear fireman 35		55	75

No. 804 City Fuel Company Coal Truck, ten wheel. Photo Courtesy John Gibson.

No. 1040 Hook and Ladder. Photo Courtesy John Gibson.

No. 1041 Hose Car.

No. 1042 Insurance Patrol, open end.

No. 187 Auto Transport with three 1940s Buicks.

Mack Tractor-Trailers, 1:43-scale (1931)

No.	Name	Good	Ex	Mint
187	Auto Transport, trailer holds three 1940s Buicks in tilted position, 1941	275	415	550
190	Auto Transport four-car Hauler, w/101-103 Buicks and 109 Ford, 1933	115	170	225
190	Auto Transport three-car Hauler, w/101-103 Buicks, 1931	105	140	175
191	Contractor Set, w/Mack AC hauling three spoke-wheeled tipper trailers, 1933	75	100	150
192	Tootsietoy Dairy Tanker, two-piece cab, three trailers, 1933	120	160	200
192	Tootsietoy Dairy Tanker, one-piece cab, three trailers	75	115	150
198	Auto Transport, one-piece cab, three '35 Fords	125	200	275
198	Auto Transport, two-piece cab, three '35 Fords	150	250	350
801	Express Stake Semi-Trailer, one-piece cab, 1933	55	80	105
801	Express Stake Semi-Trailer, two-piece cab	80	105	135

No. 801 Express Stake Semi-Trailer.

No. 802 Domaco Tank Semi-Trailer. Photo Courtesy John Gibson.

No. 803 Long Distance Hauling Semi-Trailer. Photo Courtesy John Gibson.

No.	Name	Good	Ex	Mint
802	Domaco Tank Semi-Trailer, two-piece cab	90	120	150
802	Domaco Tank Semi-Trailer, one-piece cab, 1933	60	90	120
803	Long Distance Hauling Semi-Trailer, 1933	85	130	175
805	Tootsietoy Dairy Semi-Trailer, dual tires, 1933	70	105	140
805	Tootsietoy Dairy Semi-Trailer, single tires	60	90	120

No. 192 Tootsietoy Dairy Tanker. Photo Courtesy Phillips.

No. 805 Tootsietoy Dairy Semi-Trailer. Photo Courtesy John Gibson.

Mack Trucks, 1:72-scale (1925)

No.	Name	Good	Ex	Mint
170	Interchangeable Truck Set	50	65	80
4638	Stake Truck	23	34	45
4639	Coal Truck	23	34	45
4640	Tank Truck	23	34	45
4643	Anti-Aircraft Gun Army Truck, 1931	25	38	50
4644	Searchlight Army Truck, 1931	25	40	55
4645	US Mail Air Mail Service, 1931	35	55	75
4670	A&P Trailer Truck, 1929	100	150	200
4670	American Railway Express Trailer Truck, 1929	115	170	225
4680	Overland Bus Lines, 1929	45	65	95

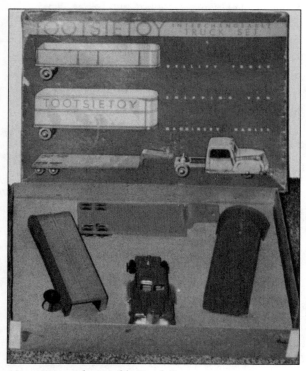

No. 170 Interchangeable Truck Set.

No. 4670 A&P Trailer Truck. Photo Courtesy John Gibson.

No. 4680 Overland Bus Lines. Photo Courtesy John Gibson.

Midget Series/Cracker Jacks (1936), 1" Vehicles

No.	Name	Good	Ex	Mint
120	Oil Tank Truck, 1936, 3"	23	34	45
121	Ford Pickup Truck, 1936, 3"	18	26	35
510	Boxed Set, eight piece	75	100	150
510	Boxed Set, ten piece	90	130	175
610	Boxed Set, twelve piece	100	150	200
1628	Bus	6	9	12
1629	Wrecker	7	10	14
1630	Racer	5	7	10
1631	DeSoto Airflow Sedan	5	7	10
1632	Zephyr Railcar	7	10	14
1634	Fire Engine	7	10	14
1635	Delivery Van	6	9	12
1666	Army Tank	4	6	8
1667	Armored Car	6	9	12

Miniature Ships

No.	Name	Good	Ex	Mint
1405	Fleet, nine-piece carded battleship assortment: USS Idaho, USS Indiana, USS Tennessee, USS Texas, USS New Mexico, USS Maryland, USS Arizona, USS New York, USS Pennsylvania, 1941	50	75	100

No.	Name	Good	Ex	Mint
1408	Naval Defense, fourteen-piece carded assortment, 1941	70	105	140
1811	Sea Champions, five-piece carded set contains two No. 1638 battleships, one No. 1618 submarine, one No. 1619 destroyer, and one No. 1620 aero carrier, 1946	30	45	60

Other Prewar Tootsietoys

No.	Name	Good	Ex	Mint
230	LaSalle Sedan, despite the release date, item was issued during postwar period, 3"	15	20	30
231	Chevy Coupe, despite the release date, item was issued during postwar period, 3"	15	20	30
232	Buick Roadmaster Touring Coupe, despite the release date, item was issued during postwar period, 3"	15	20	30
233	Boattail Roadster, despite the release date, item was issued during postwar period, 3"	15	20	30

No.	Name	Good	Ex	Mint
234	GMC Box Truck, despite the release date, item was issued during postwar period, 3"	15	20	30
235	Oil Tank Truck, despite the release date, item was issued during postwar period, 3"	13	18	25
236	Hook and Ladder Fire engine, despite the release date, item was issued during postwar period, 3"	20	30	40
237	Insurance Patrol Fire Engine, despite the release date, item was issued during postwar period, 3"	15	25	35
238	Hose Wagon Fire Engine, despite the release date, item was issued during postwar period, 3"	20	30	40
239	'38 Ford Paneled Station Wagon, despite the release date, item was issued during postwar period, 3"	20	30	40
1010	Wrigley GMC Box Truck, 4"	55	80	110
1011	Massey-Ferguson Farm Tractor, w/driver, 1941, 4"	200	300	400
1043	Small Ford Sedan or Coupe, 111 or 112, and Camping Trailer, 1937	35	53	70

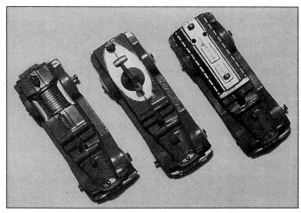

No. 1010 Wrigley GMC Box Truck. Photo Courtesy John Gibson.

No. 1011 Massey-Ferguson Farm Tractor. Photo Courtesy John Gibson.

No. 1044 Roamer House Trailer. Photo Courtesy John Gibson.

1046 Paneled Station Wagon. Photo Courtesy John Gibson.

No. 1008 Texaco.

No. 1009 Shell. Photo Courtesy John Gibson.

No.	Name	Good	Ex	Mint
1044	Roamer House Trailer w/door and tin bottom, 1937	275	415	550
1046	Paneled Station Wagon, 4"	43	64	85
4634	Army Supply Truck, 4"	33	50	65
4635	Armored Car, 1938, 4"	33	50	65
4647	Renault Tank, w/treads, 1931, 3"	23	34	45
4648	Steamroller, 1931, 3"	65	95	125
4654	Farm Tractor, Army Field Battery Set No. 5071	58	86	115
4666	Bluebird Dayton Record Car, 1932, 4"	30	45	55
7003	Farm Set, w/Ford Truck and Tractor, Huber StarBox Trailer, and Huber Star Scraper-Raker, 1928	135	205	275

Reo Oil Truck Series (1938), Distinctive 6" Trucks

No.	Name	Good	Ex	Mint
1006	Standard	35	55	80
1007	Sinclair	35	55	80
1008	Texaco	35	55	80
1009	Shell	40	60	90

POSTWAR

Name	Good	Ex	Mint
1931 Ford B Hot Rod, 1960, 3"	8	12	20
1938 Buick Y Experimental Convertible, 4"	20	30	40
1940 Ford Special Deluxe Convertible, 1960, 6"	20	30	401
1940 Ford V-8 Hot Rod, 1960, 6"	15	22	30
1941 Chrysler Windsor Convertible, 4"	20	30	40
1941 International Army Ambulance, 4"	24	34	50
1941 International K1 Panel Truck, 4".	22	32	45
1941 White Army Half Track, 4"	10	16	25
1942 Chrysler Thunderbolt Experimental Roadster, 6"	22	32	40
1946 International K11 Oil Tanker, Texaco, 6"	25	40	65
1946 International K11 Oil Tanker, Sinclair, 6"	25	35	55
1946 International K11 Oil Tanker, Shell, 6"	25	40	65
1946 International K11 Oil Tanker, Standard, 6"	25	35	55
1947 Chevrolet Fleetmaster Coupe, 4".	13	19	25
1947 Hudson Streamlined Pickup, 4"...	22	32	45
1947 Kaiser Sedan, 6"	28	37	50
1947 Mack L-Line Dump Truck, 6"	14	25	35
1947 Mack L-Line Fire Pumper, 6"	25	40	65
1947 Mack L-Line Stake Truck, 6"	22	32	45
1947 Mack L-Line Wrecker, 6"	14	25	35
1947 Offenhauser Race Car, 4"	13	19	25
1947 Offenhauser Race Car, on trailer, 4"	15	22	30
1947 Studebaker Champion Coupe, rare, 3"	25	35	55
1947 Willys Jeepster, 3"	10	15	20
1948 Buick Super Estate Wagon, 6"	27	42	65
1948 Cadillac 60 Special Four-door Sedan, 6"	18	26	35
1948 GMC 3751 Greyhound Diesel Bus, 6"	25	35	55

No. 1942 Chrysler Thunderbolt Experimental Roadster. Photo Courtesy Gerald F. Slack.

No. 1947 Hudson Streamlined Pickup. Photo Courtesy John Gibson.

No. 1948 Buick Super Estate Wagon. Photo Courtesy John Gibson.

No.	Name	Good	Ex	Mint
1949	Buick Roadmaster Four-door Sedan, 6"	20	34	45
1949	Ford Custom Convertible, 3"	10	15	25
1949	Ford Custom Four-door Sedan, 3"	10	15	25
1949	Ford F1 Pickup, 3"	10	15	25
1949	Ford F6 Oil Tanker, 4"	13	19	25
1949	Ford F6 Oil Tanker, Shell, 6"	25	35	55
1949	Ford F6 Stake Truck, 4"	15	22	30
1949	Indianapolis No. 3 Race Car, 3"	10	15	25
1949	Mercury Fire Chief Sedan, 4"	22	32	45
1949	Mercury Four-door Sedan, 4"	15	24	35
1949	Oldsmobile 88 Convertible, 4"	20	30	40
1950	Chevrolet Army Ambulance, 4"	15	24	35
1950	Chevrolet Deluxe Panel, 4"	14	21	28
1950	Chevrolet Deluxe Panel Truck, 3"	10	15	25
1950	Chevrolet Fleetline Deluxe Sedan, two door, 3"	10	15	25
1950	Chrysler Windsor Convertible, 6"	70	95	125
1950	Dodge Pickup, 4"	15	22	30
1950	Ford F6 Oil Tanker, Sinclair, 6"	25	35	55
1950	Jeep CJ3	5	7	14
1950	Jeep CJ3 Army, 4"	9	15	22
1950	Plymouth Special Deluxe Sedan, four door, 3"	10	15	25
1950	Pontiac Cheftain Deluxe Coupe Sedan, 4"	20	30	40
1950	Pontiac Fire Chief Chieftain Sedan, 4"	22	32	45
1950	Twin Coach Bus, 3"	12	21	30
1951	Buick Le Sabre Experimental Roadster, 6"	25	38	55
1951	Ford F6 Oil Tanker, Standard, 6"	25	35	55
1952	Ford F6 Oil Tanker, Texaco, 6"	25	35	55

No.	Name	Good	Ex	Mint
1952	Ford Mainline Four-door Sedan, 3"	12	21	32
1952	Lincoln Capri Two-door Hardtop, 6"	28	37	50
1952	Mercury Custom Sedan, four door, 4"	15	22	30
1953	Chrysler New Yorker Sedan, four door, 6"	18	28	45
1954	American La France Pumper, 3"	10	15	25
1954	Buick Century Estate Wagon, 6"	20	34	45
1954	Buick Special Experimental Coupe, 6"	23	38	50
1954	Cadillac 62 Sedan, four door, 6"	20	30	40
1954	Ford Ranch Wagon, 3"	8	12	20
1954	Ford Ranch Wagon, 4"	15	24	35
1954	Jaguar XK120 Roadster, 3"	8	12	20
1954	MG Roadster, 6"	10	20	30
1954	MG Roadster, 3"	8	12	20
1954	Nash Metropolitan Convertible, 3"	25	35	50
1954-55	Chevrolet Corvette Roadster, 4"	15	22	30
1955	Chevrolet Bel Air Sedan, four door, 3"	8	12	20
1955	Ford Customline V-8 Sedan, two door, 3"	8	12	20
1955	Ford Thunderbird Coupe, 3"	7	11	18
1955	Ford Thunderbird Coupe, 4"	20	30	40
1955	Mack B-Line Cement Mixer, axle-driven drum, 6"	30	40	55
1955	Mack B-Line Cement Mixer, 6"	22	32	45
1955	Mack L-Line Stake Truck, w/"Tootsietoy" tin cover, 1958, 6"	50	75	100
1955	Oldsmobile 98 Holiday Hardtop, two door, 4"	15	24	35
1956	Austin-Healey 100-5 Roadster	20	30	40
1956	Caterpillar Bulldozer, 6"	20	30	40
1956	Caterpillar Road Scraper, 6"	18	26	35

Name	Good	Ex	Mint
1956 Chevrolet Cameo Pickup, 4"........13		19	25
1956 Dodge D100 Panel Truck, 6".......23		38	50
1956 Ferrari Racer, 6"......................18		28	45
1956 Ford C600 Oil Tanker, 3".............8		12	20
1956 Jaguar XK140 Coupe, 6".............15		22	30
1956 Lancia Racer, 6"......................18		27	45
1956 Mercedes 190SL Coupe, 6".........10		20	30
1956 Packard Patrician Sedan, four door, 6"...................................28		37	50
1956 Porsche Spyder Roadster, 6"........10		20	30
1956 Triumph TR3 Roadster, 3"............7		11	18
1957 Ford F100 Styleside Pickup, 3"......5		7	14
1957 Ford Fairlane 500 Convertible, 3"..8		12	20
1957 GMC Greyhound Scenicruiser Bus, 6".................................22		32	45
1957 Jaguar Type D, 3".........................8		12	20
1957 Plymouth Belvedere, two-door hardtop, 3".................................8		12	20
1959 Ford Country Sedan Station Wagon, 6"...........................10		20	30
1959 Oldsmobile Dynamic 88 Convertible, 6"........................14		25	35
1959 Pontiac Star Chief Sedan, four door, 4"...................................10		16	25
1960 Chevrolet El Camino Pickup, w/camper and boat, 6"............17		32	50
1960 Chevrolet El Camino Pickup, 6"..12		22	30
1960 Chrysler Windsor Convertible, 4"..13		19	25
1960 Ford Country Sedan Station Wagon, 3"................................8		12	20
1960 Ford Falcon Sedan, two door, 3"....5		8	15
1960 International Metro Van, rare, 6"...100		125	150
1960 Jeep CJ5, w/snow-plow, 6"..........25		35	55
1960 Jeep CJ5, 6"................................9		18	25
1960 Rambler Super Cross-Country Wagon, 4"...............................15		24	35
1960 Studebaker Lark Custom Convertible, 3".............................9		16	22
1960 Volkswagen 113, 6"....................10		20	30
1960 Volkswagen Bug, 3"......................7		11	18
1962 Ford C600 Oil Tanker Truck, 6"..20		30	40
1962 Ford Country Sedan Station Wagon, 6"................................8		18	25
1962 Ford Econoline Pickup, 6"...........20		30	40

Name	Good	Ex	Mint
1969 Ford LTD Hardtop, two door, last of the larger-size die-cast Tootsietoys, 4"....................... 13		19	25
Army Cannon, four wheel, 4"............. 10		15	25
Army Cannon, six wheel, 4"............. 12		21	30
U-Haul Trailer, 3"................................. 4		6	8
U-Haul Trailer, 4"................................. 5		10	15

'47 International K5 Tractor-Trailers

Name	Good	Ex	Mint
Auto Transporter, scaled to match 6" vehicles................................. 30		42	55
Machinery Hauler, scaled to match 6" vehicles................................. 30		42	55
Shipping Van, "Tootsietoy Trucking," scaled to match 6" vehicles.... 27		37	50
Utility Truck, scaled to match 6" vehicles................................. 27		37	50

'47 Mack L-Line Tractor-Trailers (1954)

Name	Good	Ex	Mint
Hook and Ladder, scaled to match 6" vehicles................................. 35		55	75
Log Hauler, scaled to match 6" vehicles................................. 35		55	75
Machinery Hauler, scaled to match 6" vehicles................................. 35		55	75
Oil Tanker, Tootsietoy Line, scaled to match 6" vehicles 50		75	125
Oil Tanker, scaled to match 6" vehicles................................. 32		50	70
Pipe Truck 35		55	75
Shipping Van, Tootsietoy Line, scaled to match 6" vehicles 50		50	75
Shipping Van, Tootsietoy Coast to Coast, scaled to match 6" vehicles................................. 37		57	80
Stake Truck, closed sides, scaled to match 6" vehicles 35		55	75
Stake Truck, open sides, scaled to match 6" vehicles 50		70	115

'55 Mack B-Line Tractor-Trailers (1960)

Name	Good	Ex	Mint
Auto Transport, scaled to match 6" vehicles................................. 30		42	65
Boat Transport, scaled to match 6" vehicles................................. 28		40	60
Hook and Ladder, scaled to match 6" vehicles................................. 28		40	60
Log Hauler, scaled to match 6" vehicles................................. 28		40	60

Name	Good	Ex	Mint
Machinery Hauler, scaled to match 6" vehicles	28	40	60
Oil Tanker, "Mobil," scaled to match 6" vehicles	32	50	70
Oil Tanker, "Tootsietoy Line," scaled to match 6" vehicles	40	60	80
Pipe Truck, scaled to match 6" vehicles	28	40	60
Shipping Van, scaled to match 6" vehicles	28	40	60
Stake Truck, closed sides, scaled to match 6" vehicles	28	40	60
Utility Truck, scaled to match 6" vehicles	25	35	55

'58 International RC180 Tractor-Trailers (1962)

Name	Good	Ex	Mint
Auto Transport, metal trailer scaled to match 6" vehicles	42	65	85
Auto Transport, plastic trailer, scaled to match 6" vehicles	24	32	45
Boat Transport, plastic trailer, scaled to match 6" vehicles	24	32	45
Machinery Hauler, scaled to match 6" vehicles	25	35	55
Shipping Van, "Dean Van Lines," plastic trailer, scaled to match 6" vehicles	40	60	80

'59 Chevrolet Tractor-Trailers (1965)

Name	Good	Ex	Mint
Auto Transport, scaled to match 6" vehicles	50	75	125
Hook and Ladder, scaled to match 6" vehicles	50	75	125
Log Hauler, scaled to match 6" vehicles	45	70	100
Machinery Hauler, scaled to match 6" vehicles	45	70	100
Oil Tanker, scaled to match 6" vehicles	45	70	100

Airplanes

Name	Good	Ex	Mint
Beechcraft Bonanza, 1948	8	16	25
Boeing 707, 1958	18	35	55
Coast Guard Seaplane, 1950	50	100	150
F-86 Sabre Jet, single casting, 1956	7	13	20
F-86 Sabre Jet, two-casting body, 1950	8	16	25
Lockheed Constellation, 1951	45	90	135

Name	Good	Ex	Mint
P-38 Fighter, twin boom, twin engine, 1950	40	75	110
P-39 Fighter, 1947	50	100	150
P-80 Shooting Star, 1948	10	20	30
Twin-Engine Convair, twin engine, 1950	35	65	95

Classic Series (1960)

Name	Good	Ex	Mint
1906 Cadillac Coupe, w/plastic wheels, 4"	8	12	18
1907 Stanley Steamer Runabout, w/plastic wheels, 4"	8	12	18
1912 Ford Model T Touring Car, w/plastic wheels, 4"	8	12	18
1919 Stutz Bearcat, w/plastic wheels, 4"	8	12	18
1921 Mack Dump Truck, w/plastic wheels, 4"	10	15	25
1929 Ford Model A Coupe, w/plastic wheels, 4"	8	12	18

HO Pocket Series (1960)

Name	Good	Ex	Mint
Cadillac	8	15	20
Dump Truck	10	15	22
Ford Sunliner Convertible, w/midget racer Trailer	12	22	35
Ford Sunliner Convertible, w/boat trailer	10	18	30
Ford Wrecker Truck	10	15	22
Metro Van, various	8	15	20
Metro Van, Railway Express	10	17	25
Rambler Station Wagon, w/U-Haul trailer	10	18	30
Township School Bus	10	17	25

Little Toughs/Midget Series (1970)

Name	Good	Ex	Mint
American La France Aerial Ladder Truck	5	8	12
American La France Ladder Truck	4	6	10
Auto Transport Semi-Cab and Trailer	12	17	25
Cement Truck	6	8	12
Coast to Coast Shipping Semi-cab and Van	12	17	25
Dump Truck	6	8	12
Heavy duty Hydraulic Crane	8	12	17
Logging Semi-cab and Trailer	6	8	12
Mobil Semi-cab and Tanker	10	15	20
Shipping Semi-cab and Van	6	8	12
Shuttle Truck, 1967	2	3	4

More Great Books For Serious Collectors

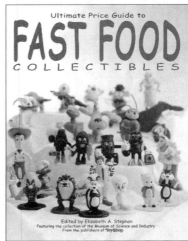

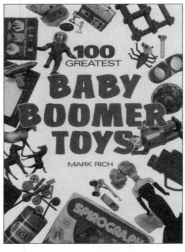

2001 Toys & Prices
8th Edition
edited by Sharon Korbeck and Elizabeth A. Stephan
One of today's hottest collecting areas - TV Toys - now has its own chapter, highlighting your favorites from the 1940s through the 1990s. Space toys fans will now have an easier-to-use section, including a spotlight on ultra-hot robots. Both the casual collector and veteran enthusiast will find over 58,000 values on more than 20,000 toys including cast-iron banks, lunch boxes, board games, Barbie, PEZ, space toys, Fisher-Price, Hot Wheels, restaurant toys and more.
Softcover • 6 x 9 • 936 pages
700 b&w photos • 8-page color section
Item# TE08 • $18.95

The Encyclopedia of Marx Action Figures
A Price & Identification Guide
by Tom Heaton
This book is a complete guide to the over 230 Marx action figures produced, with detailed photos that show the boxes and accessories, allowing you to identify and value your figures. Values are given in three grades: mint in box/carded; poor box and most accessories; loose with some accessories.
Softcover • 8-1/2 x 11
192 pages
425 color photos
Item# MARX • $24.95

Marx Toys Sampler
Playthings from an Ohio Valley Legend
by Michelle Smith
If "Marx mania" has you in its grasp, here's a new book that's sure to capture your attention and interest. In this first behind-the-scenes look at the internal operations and production output of the Marx Toys plant in Glen Dale, West Virginia, you'll learn about Marx toys and the people who produced them. And, you'll find a comprehensive listing, supported by more than 150 photographs, representing over thirty years of lithographed metal and cast plastic toy production-a valuable tool for identifying and dating items in your own collection of Marx Playsets, doll houses, figures, and other toys.
Softcover • 8-1/2 x 11 • 192 pages
150 b&w photos • 32-page color section, 100 color photos
Item# MXTS • $26.95

Saturday Morning TV Collectibles
'60s '70s '80s
by Dana Cain
Zoinks! Do you remember all of the Saturday morning kids' programs? This encyclopedia of 1960s to 1980s kids' show collectibles will certainly refresh your memory. If you're already a veteran collector, this guide is great, as it features in-depth listings, prices and photos of your favorite Saturday morning program collectibles. If you're a novice or beginning hobbyist, you'll find your favorite character collectibles and how much you should pay. More than 3,500 items priced.
Softcover • 8-1/2 x 11 • 288 pages
750 b&w photos • 16-page color section, 200 color photos
Item# TOON • $24.95

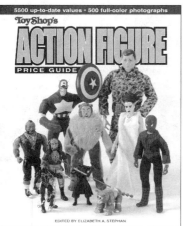

Toy Shop's Action Figure Price Guide
edited by Elizabeth A. Stephan
Does your Luke Skywalker action figure have a telescoping light saber? Have you ever wondered if it has any value? You might be surprised by the value of ol' Luke had you not played with him. What about those Transformer figures that were all the rage 15 years ago? Toy Shop's Action Figure Price Guide will help answer all of your action figure questions. This up-to-date guide will prove to be indispensable with over 2500 listings, 5000 values and 500 photos, not to mention the in-depth history and market update of the action figure hobby.
Softcover • 8-1/4 x 10-7/8 • 256 pages • 500 color photos
Item# ACFIG • $24.95

Pedal Car Restoration and Price Guide
by Andrew G. Gurka
Now, learn how to restore pedal cars, find parts and date cars by comparison to automotive styling trends. Price guide uncovers the latest values.
Softcover • 8-1/2 x 11
240 pages
316 b&w photos
16-page color section
Item# PCR01 • $24.95

Shipping and Handling: $3.25 1st book; $2 ea. add'l. Foreign orders $20.95 1st item, $5.95 ea. add'l.
Sales tax: CA, IA, IL, PA, TN, VA, WA, WI residents please add appropriate sales tax.

Satisfaction Guarantee: If for any reason you are not completely satisfied with your purchase, simply return it within 14 days and receive a full refund, less shipping.
Retailers call toll-free 888-457-2873 ext 880, M-F, 8 am - 5 pm

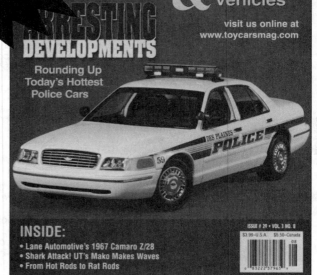